Postmodern Music/ Postmodern Thought

WITHDRAWN

Studies in Contemporary Music and Culture

Joseph Auner, *Series Editor*
Associate Professor of Music
The State University of New York at Stony Brook

Advisory Board
Philip Brett, Susan McClary, Robert P. Morgan, Robert Walser

Messiaen's Language of Mystical Love
edited by Siglind Bruhn

Expression in Pop-Rock Music
A Collection of Critical and Analytical Essays
edited by Walter Everett

Postmodern Music/Postmodern Thought
edited by Judy Lochhead and Joseph Auner

John Cage
Music, Philosophy, and Intention, 1933–1950
edited by David W. Patterson

STUDIES IN CONTEMPORARY MUSIC AND CULTURE
VOLUME 4

POSTMODERN MUSIC/ POSTMODERN THOUGHT

EDITED BY

JUDY LOCHHEAD AND JOSEPH AUNER

ROUTLEDGE
NEW YORK AND LONDON

Published in 2002 by
Routledge
270 Madison Ave,
New York NY 10016

Published in Great Britain by
Routledge
2 Park Square, Milton Park,
Abingdon, Oxon, OX14 4RN

Transferred to Digital Printing 2008

**Library of Congress Cataloging-in-Publication Data available from the Libraty of
Congress**

Publisher's Note
The publisher has gone to great lengths to ensure the quality of this
reprint but points out that some imperfections in the original
may be apparent

Contents

Acknowledgments . . . .*ix*

Series Editor's Foreword . . . .*xi*
  Joseph Auner

SECTION I: THEORETICAL FOUNDATIONS AND DEBATES

CHAPTER 1
Introduction *1*
  Judy Lochhead

CHAPTER 2
The Nature and Origins of Musical Postmodernism *13*
  Jonathan D. Kramer

CHAPTER 3
Reflections of Surrealism in Postmodern Musics *27*
  Anne LeBaron

CHAPTER 4
Postmodernism and Art Music in the German Debate *75*
  Joakim Tillman

CHAPTER 5
Music and Musical Practices in Postmodernity *93*
  Timothy D. Taylor

CHAPTER 6
Postmodern Architecture/Postmodern Music *119*
  Jane Piper Clendinning

v

CHAPTER 7
Feminine/Feminist? In Quest of Names with
No Experiences (Yet) *141*
  Martin Scherzinger

SECTION II: SCALING THE HIGH/LOW DIVIDE

CHAPTER 8
Postmodern Polyamory or Postcolonial Challenge?
Cornershop's Dialogue from West, to East, to West... ....*177*
  Renée T. Coulombe

CHAPTER 9
Production vs. Reception in Postmodernism: The Górecki Case ...*195*
  Luke Howard

CHAPTER 10
"Where's It At": Postmodern Theory and the
Contemporary Musical Field *207*
  David Brackett

SECTION III: COMPOSITIONAL VOICES

CHAPTER 11
Music, Postmodernism, and George Rochberg's
Third String Quartet *235*
  Mark Berry

CHAPTER 12
Resistant Strains of Postmodernism: The Music of
Helmut Lachenmann and Brian Ferneyhough *249*
  Ross Feller

CHAPTER 13
Imploding the System: Kagel and the Deconstruction
of Modernism *263*
  Paul Attinello

CHAPTER 14
Collage vs. Compositional Control: The Interdependency of
Modernist and Postmodernist Approaches in the
Work of Mauricio Kagel *287*
  Björn Heile

SECTION IV: LINKING THE VISUAL AND AURAL DOMAINS

CHAPTER 15
Race and Reappropriation: Spike Lee Meets Aaron Copland *303*
  Krin Gabbard

CHAPTER 16
The Politics of Feminism, Postmodernism, and Rock:
Revisited, with Reference to Parmar's *Righteous Babes* *323*
  E. Ann Kaplan

CHAPTER 17
Natural Born Killers: Music and Image in Postmodern Film *335*
  Jason Hanley

Contributors *361*
Index *365*

Acknowledgments

This collection of essays had its inception at the conference "Postmodernism and Music" held at the State University of New York at Stony Brook in March 1999. The conference was organized under the auspices of the Greater New York Chapter of the American Musicological Society, Joseph Auner, chair, and the department of music, SUNY at Stony Brook, David Lawton chair. Further funding for the conference was provided by the Stony Brook College of Arts and Sciences, under the leadership of Dean Paul Armstrong, and by the Humanities Institute at Stony Brook, E. Ann Kaplan, director. We are much indebted to these various groups and people.

Further, the editors recognize the work of all the faculty and graduate students whose untiring efforts made the conference a success. These include: Lloyd Whitesell, Mark Berry, Theodore Cateforis, Murat Eyuboglu, Jason Hanley, Brian Locke, Margaret Martin, Dean Smith, and Jennifer Veit. We also thank Edith Auner for her expert help in preparing the manuscript.

Finally, we acknowledge the support of the Publications Committee of the American Musicological Society, Walter Frisch, chair. A generous subvention grant from the Gustave Reese Publication Endowment Fund helped to defray the many publication costs associated with a volume devoted to recent musical practices.

Series Editor's Foreword

Studies in Contemporary Music and Culture
Joseph Auner

Now that we have entered a new century, many of the established historical narratives of twentieth-century music are being questioned or reconfigured. New approaches from cultural studies or feminist theory, methodologies adapted from such disciplines as literary theory, philosophy, and anthropology, and debates about the canon, postmodernism, globalization, and multiculturalism are profoundly transforming our sense of both what the repertoire of twentieth- and twenty-first-century music is and how it should be understood. "Studies in Contemporary Music and Culture" provides a forum for research into topics that have been neglected by existing scholarship, as well as for new critical approaches to well-known composers, movements, and styles.

Volumes in this series will include studies of popular and rock music; gender and sexuality; institutions; the audience and reception; performance and the media; music and technology; and cross-cultural music and the whole range of the crossover phenomenon. By presenting innovative and provocative musical scholarship concerning all aspects of culture and society, it is our aim to stimulate new ways to listen to, study, teach, and perform the music of our time.

POSTMODERN MUSIC/ POSTMODERN THOUGHT

THEORETICAL FOUNDATIONS AND DEBATES

CHAPTER 1

Introduction
Judy Lochhead

Critical writings on issues of philosophical, cultural, and aesthetic postmodernism have played a prominent if not dominant role in a wide variety of humanistic disciplines during the last twenty years. Occasionally, this "postmodern debate" has migrated into the domains of the natural and mathematical sciences, raising questions about the foundations of scientific explanation. The debate has been vital, contentious, and nearly ubiquitous in a wide variety of disciplinary discussions. Within the domain of musical studies, issues of postmodernism have trickled into the discourse with little sustained discussion about how the term might apply and to what kinds of musical phenomena it might refer. Of the writing that has occurred, three types may be discerned: English-language writing about popular music, German-language writing about concert music, and English-language writing about concert music.

Of the three types, discussion of the postmodern aspects of music within popular culture has been the most prevalent. A wide variety of authors have contributed to an understanding of the new genre of music video and about how music is used in and affected by postmodern cultural forms. Some examples include: Goodwin 1987, [1988] 1990, 1992; Kaplan 1987; Lipsitz 1990, 1994; Straw [1988] 1993. In German-language musicology there was a relatively sustained response to the issues raised by Jürgen Habermas's 1981 essay "Modernity—An Incomplete Project" with respect to the compositional work of composers within the concert tradition, addressing the music of John Cage, George Rochberg, György Ligeti, Wolfgang Rihm, and Peter Ruzicka (Habermas [1981] 1987). (See also Joakim Tillman's essay in this volume for more on the "German debate" in music.) And finally, English-language musicology has recently begun to address questions of postmodernism in the concert tradition over the last decade (see, for instance, J. Kramer 1995; Morgan 1992; McClary 1989; Hartwell 1993; Pasler 1993; Watkins 1994).

The authors within these three types of discussion all address music written after World War II, employing concepts from the wide domain of postmodern thought. Since the mid-1980s another and mostly different group of authors have developed a "postmodern" musicology, defining new paradigms of understanding music in general. The resulting "New Musicology" has indeed generated a vital debate whose ripples have been felt beyond the discipline itself (see, for instance, L. Kramer 1995; McClary 1991; Tomlinson 1993). Motivated on the one hand by Foucauldian notions of cultural power and on the other by Gadamerian hermeneutics, the New Musicology typically focuses on historical music of the concert tradition (music composed before 1945) or on music outside the concert traditions (music of the popular and jazz traditions). In the New Musicology, the focus on historical music confirms what some have described as a postmodern engagement with the past through twentieth-century technological developments—notably recording technologies for music—that bring the past palpably into the present. Further, it provides critique of the various ways that music functions in social settings as a tool either of social power or affirmation[1] and as a consequence paves the way for the scholarly study of musical traditions which had typically been excluded. The influx of ideas from the various strands of postmodern thought has enacted a flattening of traditional hierarchies, effectively broadening the canon. Ironically, however, the focus on historical music within New Musicology has a conservative—perhaps even neo-conservative—effect of reinscribing the canon. This new postmodern musi-cology entails on one hand, a methodological shift in its approach to canonic works of the Western concert tradition and on the other, an embrace of music in the popular and jazz traditions as well as music out-side of the West. In the latter case, the music may be approached with either the new methods or more traditional, "modernist" ones.[2]

A vigorous scholarly interest in recent practices in the concert tradition has not arisen as a response to postmodern methodologies in the New Musicology or to postmodern thought in humanistic studies generally. Such a seeming reluctance to study and write about recent practices does not occur in the sister arts where there is a strong tradition of writing about recent work. A quick survey of books devoted to contemporary art con-firms a serious scholarly interest (see, for instance, Foster 1996; Krauss 1985; Kuspit 1993). It may be that music scholars have been concerned to let "time be the test" of musical value or to avoid the appearance of advo-cacy. But such attitudes contradict postmodern theories of "situated knowl-edge" and "institutional power" which maintain that value, not an absolute quality, arises in a context of beliefs and that the choices writers make necessarily amount to advocacy. In fact, the newly affirmed interest in writing on popular music and jazz within academic musicology entails advocacy based on revised notions of value.

One might construe the reticence of professional music scholars to write about recent music in the concert tradition as in fact advocacy not only of a particular music but of traditions of thinking about music. The more established pathways of thought about historical music—especially music of the canon—may offer more satisfying intellectual rewards for scholars, thus confirming personal and professional goals. Furthermore, those established pathways of critical and analytical appraisal which have worked for Beethoven and Mozart apply relatively well to Coltrane and the Beatles. This applicability allows an opening up of the canonic repertoire without requiring new critical/analytical methodologies. Further, one may observe that recent composers themselves write infrequently about their own or others' music—an absence that stands in stark contrast to the practices of the prior generation.[3]

The relative silence in print about recent concert music in various sorts of specialist and non-specialist scholarly venues has complex sources. It is not, however, the goal of this volume to analyze the motivations for this silence. Rather, the intent is multi-faceted: to stimulate a sustained scholarly discussion of recent musical practices, to broaden discussion of the implications of postmodern thought for music scholarship, and further to encourage conversations about music that participate in the issues and debates confronting society *today*. In other words, we hope to overcome the tendency for music to "lag behind the other arts." Our goals build upon and extend work begun at a conference, "Postmodernism and Music," held at the State University of New York at Stony Brook in March 1999 under the auspices of the Department of Music and the Greater New York Chapter of the American Musicological Society.[4]

Several of the essays here were delivered at the conference, while the remaining were solicited for the volume. They are grouped into four categories. In Section I, "Theoretical Foundations and Debates," the essays address general issues of musical postmodernism and engage a broad range of prior thought about postmodern thought generally. In Section II, "Scaling the High/Low Divide," the essays take into consideration music from domains of music making that have been considered separate and in hierarchical terms, exploring the implicit relations between these domains in postmodern practices. The essays of Section III, "Compositional Voices," investigate in some detail particular works of specific composers with respect to questions of postmodern aesthetics. And finally, the essays in Section IV, "Linking the Visual and Aural Domains," focus on how film and music are entwined in the construal of meaning in a postmodern context.

POSTMODERNISM 2000?

The question of why in the 1980s the postmodern debate never fully captured the imaginations of musicologists in English-language scholarship might well be understood as incidental to the question of why it should be necessary or relevant to raise the question of postmodernism at all in the new millennium. Two responses are relevant to this project. First, any number of writers in musical and other domains have questioned the usefulness of the term, remarking on its conceptual slipperiness and its broadstroke and hence feeble descriptive powers. While it might be attractive to refuse the term as some have suggested in various others fields, that response continues the self-imposed exclusionary practices of music scholars with respect to issues in the rest of the humanities. If musicology and music theory hope to be more than parasitic on intellectual developments in other fields, they must take up the debates, showing how musical production is implicated in its social context—how it reflects *and* constructs that context. And while such study of music should rightly consider how music of the past is used in the context of contemporary consumer society, it should also consider the musics that are produced in all of the various traditions of music-making—popular, jazz, and concert music.

The second response is practical yet equally central: the term "postmodern" freely circulates in various types of informal and formal writings about music. Consider these examples:

> From the *New York Times,* Arts and Leisure Section, July 12, 1998, the headline of an article on George Rochberg reads: "From an Early Postmodernist, a Day of Overdue Vindication"

> From the promotional blurb about Glenn Watkins's 1994 historical study of 20th century music, *Pyramids at the Louvre: Music, Culture, and Collage from Stravinsky to the Postmodernists:* "A rich and revealing picture of twentieth-century music and the arts, Watkins' work shows us what our present Postmodern aesthetic owes to our Modernist past."

> From a review in *Spin* of Sonic Youth's covers of twentieth-century avant-garde works, *Goodbye 20th Century:* "Expressway to yr skull? More like a stairway to postmodernist heaven, the two CD *Goodbye* finds SY and pals rifling through scores by venerable odd ball composers." (Hermes 2000)

The term "postmodern" is in full use in descriptions of musical practice, and its growing prevalence suggests a responsibility to demarcate the dimensions of its meanings. Further, refusal to address the term would simply amount to a refusal of postmodern linguistic theory which claims the undecidability and fluidity of meaning.

The essays included in this volume attest to both a certain unease about the term and the various ways it has been utilized. They also demonstrate the kind of category the term "postmodernism" implies: it is not a catego-

ry defined by simple "binaries" as the prefix "post" implies, and it is a category whose defining features remain elusive. Such conceptual slipperiness
is not the exclusive domain of postmodernism, however. Contemplating the
concept of time in the fourth century St. Augustine remarked: "What, then,
is time? I know well enough what it is, provided that nobody asks me; but
if I am asked what it is and try to explain, I am baffled" (Augustine 1977,
264). Not one to be deterred by such difficulties of understanding,
Augustine proceeded to write persuasively on time, his thoughts serving as
the beginning point for several centuries of writers wishing to "pin down"
a concept of time. Like Augustine, the authors included in this text have
taken on the challenge not necessarily to "pin down" and hence make
static a meaning of musical postmodernism, but rather to demarcate the
various kinds of significances the term may have in current thinking about
musical practices.

If the scholarship on music included here is to mark an engagement
with current humanistic thought about musical practices in the present,
then it needs to be cognizant of the issues that have been the focus of
debates in literature, art, philosophy, and cultural studies generally. And
while it will not be practical nor intellectually necessary to give a thorough
overview of the postmodern debate, it is helpful to delineate for readers its
broad outlines and to articulate some important sources of information.[5]

POSTMODERNITY/POSTMODERNISM: THE ISSUES

The "postmodern debate" that so dominated thinking in humantistic disciplines in the 1980s necessarily engaged questions of basic definitions. Its prefix of "post" implies a link to the modern, another term that has taken a variety of differing meanings. If the link is understood as a temporal demarcator,
then questions arise as to how clear a break is implied and to how the postmodern responds to the modern. Hal Foster argues for two kinds of responses: a postmodernism of resistance that "seeks to deconstruct modernism and
resist the status quo" and a postmodernism of reaction that "repudiates"
modernism in order to "celebrate" the status quo (Foster [1983]1998, xii).
The general issue revolves around whether the postmodern is discontinuous
or continuous with the modern trajectory and whether the modern is figured
in negative or positive terms. Such issues of response further engage the question of whether the postmodern marks an underlying change of paradigm
with respect to social order and intellectual thought or whether it denotes stylistic changes that apply to surface mannerisms.

General questions about what the postmodern might entail have been
fueled by a wide variety of thought in the humanities. Work by scholars in
the more traditional disciplines of philosophy, English, and comparative
studies have defined new areas of thought focused on gender, sexuality, and
culture which have resulted in the transformation of existing disciplines
and the creation of new ones. Questions that had been central in the tradi-

tional disciplines have been replaced or radically transformed by such recent work and by technological developments. Here I sketch out some of the changes central to the postmodern debate that are relevant for thinking about music.

Concepts of time and temporality have been transformed in the wake of theories of indeterminacy and chaos in the sciences and mathematics, of technological developments that affect the speed of travel and communication, and of a general questioning of teleology. Time and temporal processes in general are no longer understood to imply a futurally-directed progress in which events are causally related. Lyotard makes the link to historical thinking in *The Postmodern Condition*, arguing that the postmodern attitude eschews "grand narratives" and embraces instead local stories of understanding (Lyotard [1979] 1997). Extrapolating further from teleological notions of history, postmodern theorists understand such grand narratives as reductive and exclusionary and as having negative social and economic implications for those groups whose "stories" have been erased.

Concepts of space have been similarly transformed. The rapidity of world travel and the visual accessibility of far away places and long-ago times through electronic media are coordinated with changing perceptions and conceptions of physical and social distance. These changes register in our bodily interactions with cultural difference in terms of place and time. The far away may now be physically close and the past may be palpably here through sound and sight technologies. Further, changing perceptions and conceptions of distance draw attention to issues of perspective that affect epistemology. Knowledge is understood as "situated" not "absolute," as Donna Haraway has argued in "Situated Knowledges" (1988). And the bodily basis of knowledge has been articulated through numerous studies in fields ranging from philosophy to gender studies to performance studies (see in, particular, Merleau-Ponty [1962] 1978; Johnson 1987; Case 1996; Phelan 1993).

The epistemological changes that are linked with changing conceptions of time and space have manifested themselves in philosophical thought generally. Conceptions of perspectival knowledge have called into question the idea of truth and more generally the binary nature of understanding. If all knowledge reflects the cultural and historical place and time of the one who knows, then no single perspectival knowledge is privileged and hence no particular way of understanding the world is true in any absolute sense. Such a non-foundational epistemology has resulted in a number of differing philosophical formulations. Derrida demonstrates the implicitly binary nature of thought and identifies its exclusionary and hence negative social implications (see Derrida 1976, 1982). Rorty seeks a philosophical goal in the concept not of "truth" but of "edification" (see Rorty 1979); and a variety of post-phenomenological philosophers offer experiential understanding as sufficiently foundational (Ihde 1976; Casey 1987).

Non-foundational philosophical perspectives have further resulted in a focus on knowing as interpretive. If knowledge is understood as perspectival, then whatever is known must be a result of interpretative understanding. In such a framework, lived experience—in other words, perception of the world—is the embodiment of cultural convention. And while it finds a basis in the world as cultural construct, perception is a creative act, not simply the apprehension of absolute givens. Various authors have taken up issues concerning the interpretive nature of knowledge, linking the change to larger philosophical shifts in the twentieth century that have focused on the constitutive role of language (see Rabinow and Sullivan 1987; Ricoeur 1976; Taylor [1971] 1987). The interpretive function may also be observed in Roland Barthes's landmark essay, "The Death of the Author" (1977), which relocates the source of meaning from the author to an interaction between creator and receiver (reader, listener, viewer), each of whom is understood as part of an intersubjective context that confers meaning.

Another distinct yet related entry into questions of knowledge occurs in Michel Foucault's several influential books. His later work in particular demonstrates in great empirical detail how knowledge arises out of the historically situated discursive practices of social institutions. He argues that social discourses and practices fundamentally shape what can be construed as knowledge and give rise to social power. Foucault's non-foundational epistemology and its focus on social power has become a springboard for various studies of constituencies marginalized by discursive and institutional practices. These include not only human constituencies as exemplified in studies focusing on the construction of gender, on "queer" practices, on ethnicity, and on class, but also hierarchical artistic categories which segregate on the basis of "high" and "low" practices (see, in particular, Foucault 1972, 1979, 1980).

Issues of social power and discursive practices have also focused attention on the nature of representation, that is on how various linguistic, visual, and aural depictions do the work of constructing social attitudes and behaviors. While various authors have shown how linguistic, visual, and aural images work within a discursive practice, one example from gender studies illustrates how behaviors are inscribed in and read from bodily action. In "Throwing Like a Girl," Iris Marion Young (1990) demonstrates both how physical actions of throwing may bear the marks of female embodiment as socially inscribed within a patriarchal culture and how the physical action itself may be read as a sign of physical inferiority within that culture. Her focus on the significances of bodily action and gesture are suggestive for thinking about the aural domain that is often characterized in terms of gesture.

EXCURSIONS INTO MUSIC

This sketch of the central concepts of postmodern thought provides a touchstone for the essays on music included in this volume, each of the which takes up one or more of these issues with respect to the disciplinary concerns of music. For present purposes, these issues may be understood as clustering around a series of questions which I offer here as a way of helping readers to focus the broad range of postmodern thought into sharper points for the excursions into music.

> How might a postmodern musical practice be construed: in terms of aesthetic and stylistic issues, in terms of how people use music, or how music is promoted in consumer culture?

> How has postmodern thought affected modes of musical understanding: have new analytic methodologies been created or have new categories of musical concepts arisen?

> How has postmodern thought affected issues of value with respect to questions of listening and scholarly choices: have listener interests been transformed by postmodern thought, or has the canon been replaced or expanded in music scholarship?

> How has postmodern thinking about time and space affected musical composition or scholarship: do expectations of historical development still operate in our understandings of musical practice, or have expectations about "originality" been overcome with respect to musical creation?

> How has the idea of postmodern interpretation affected issues of creation, performance, and scholarship: does musical understanding still rely on composer-information as the absolute source, do composer/creators build interpretation into their music?

> How have postmodern ideas of social power affected musical creation: are composers and performers less concerned with the expression of an individual voice and more concerned with the idea of music as social communication, or how does a composer write music that flattens the hierarchy between composer and listener?

NOTES

1. McClary's *Feminine Endings* (1991) is notable for its observation of music's role in the operation of social dominance with respect to gender and class. And a noteworthy example of understanding music as a tool of ethnic affirmation occurs in Lipsitz 1990 and 1994.

2. Susan McClary has addressed recently composed music and works of the canonic literature. However, the musicological discipline as a whole responded most vigorously to her writings on the canonic literature, such response itself a signal of a still firmly entrenched canon of music and thought about it.

3. For instance, composers such as Milton Babbitt, Pierre Boulez, Karlheinz Stockhausen, and John Cage have extensive bibliographies. Two notable exceptions from the "Generation of the 1950s" are Wolfgang Rihm and Brian Ferneyhough, each with a substantial body of writings.

4. The conference received financial support from Stony Brook's College of Arts and Sciences, Dean Paul Armstrong, and the Humanities Institute, E. Ann Kaplan, Director.

5. Readers are directed to the other essays in this volume for bibliographies that complement the one given here. See, in particular, Taylor's essay in chapter 5 and Brackett's essay in chapter 10.

WORKS CITED

Augustine. 1977. *Confessions* Translated by R. S. Pine-Coffin. New York: Penguin Books.

Barthes, Roland. 1977. "The Death of the Author." In *Image/Music/Text* Translated by Stephen Heath. New York: Hill and Wang. 142–48.

Case, Sue-Ellen. 1996. *The Domain-Matrix: Performing Lesbian at the End of Print Culture.* Bloomington and Indianapolis: Indiana University Press.

Casey, Edward S. 1987. *Remembering: A Phenomenological Study.* Bloomington and Indianapolis: Indiana University Press.

Derrida, Jacques. 1976. *Of Grammatology* Translated by Gayatri Chakravorty Spivak. Baltimore: Johns Hopkins University Press.

———. 1982. *Margins of Philosophy* Translated by. Alan Bass. Chicago: University of Chicago.

Foster, Hal, ed. [1983] 1998. *The Anti-Aesthetic: Essays on Postmodern Culture.* New York: The New Press.

Foster, Hal. 1996. *Return of the Real: the Avant-Garde at the End of the Century.* Cambridge: MIT Press.

Foucault, Michel. 1972. *The Archaeology of Knowledge and the Discourse on Language* Translated by. A. M. Sheridan Smith. New York: Pantheon Books.

———. 1979. *Discipline and Punish: The Birth of the Prison* Translated by Alan Sheridan. New York: Vintage/Random House.

———. 1980. *The History of Sexuality, Vol. I: An Introduction,* Translated by Robert Hurley. New York: Vintage/Random House.

Goodwin, Andrew. 1987. "Music Video in the (Post) Modern World." *Screen* 28/3: 36–55.

———. [1988] 1990. "Sample and Hold: Pop Music in the Digital Age of Reproduction." In *On Record: Rock, Pop, and the Written Word,* edited by Simon Frith and Andrew Goodwin. New York: Pantheon Books. 258–73. Reprinted from *Critical Quarterly* 30/3.

————. 1992. *Dancing in the Distraction Factory: Music Television and Popular Culture.* Minneapolis: University of Minnesota Press.

Habermas, Jürgen. [1981] 1987. "Modernity—An Incomplete Project." In Rabinow and Sullivan 1987. 141–56. Reprinted from *The New German Critique* 22.

Haraway, Donna J. 1988. "Situated Knowledges: The Science Question in Feminism as a Site of Discourse on the Social Privilege of Partial Perspective." *Feminist Studies* 14/3: 575–600.

Hartwell, Robin. 1993. "Postmodernism and Art Music." In *The Last Post: Music After Modernism,* edited by Simon Miller. Manchester: Manchester Listen University Press, 27–51.

Hermes, Will. 2000. "Rack Jobbing." Review of *Goodbye 20th Century,* by Sonic Youth. *Spin* (March): 155.

Ihde, Don. 1976. *Listening and Voice: A Phenomenology of Sound.* Athens: Ohio University Press.

Johnson, Mark. 1987. *The Body in the Mind: The Bodily Basis of Meaning, Imagination, and Reason.* Chicago and London: University of Chicago Press.

Kaplan, E. Ann. 1987. *Rocking around the Clock: Music Television, Postmodernism, and Consumer Culture.* New York: Routledge.

Kramer, Jonathan D. 1995. "Beyond Unity: Toward an Understanding of Musical Postmodernism." In *Concert Music, Rock, and Jazz since 1945: Essays and Analytical Studies,* edited by Elizabeth West Marvin and Richard Hermann. Rochester: University of Rochester Press. 11–33.

Kramer, Lawrence. 1995. *Classical Music and Postmodern Knowledge.* Berkeley and Los Angeles: University of California Press.

Krauss, Rosalind. 1985. *The Originality of the Avant-Garde and Other Modernist Myths.* Cambridge: MIT Press.

Kuspit, Donald. 1993. *Idiosyncratic Identities: Artists at the End of the Avant-Garde.* Cambridge and New York: Cambridge University Press.

Lipsitz, George. 1990. *Time Passages: Collective Memory and American Popular Culture.* Minneapolis: University of Minnesota Press.

————. 1994. *Dangerous Crossroads: Popular Music, Postmodernism, and the Poetics of Place.* London and New York: Verso.

Lyotard, Jean-François. [1979] 1997. *The Postmodern Condition: A Report on Knowledge.* Translated by Geoff Bennington and Brian Massumi. Theory and History of Literature, volume 10. Minneapolis: University of Minnesota Press.

McClary, Susan. 1989. "Terminal Prestige: the Case of Avant-Garde Music Composition," *Cultural Critique* 12: 57–81.

————. 1991. *Feminine Endings: Music, Gender, Sexuality.* Minneapolis: University of Minnesota Press.

Merleau-Ponty, Maurice. [1962] 1978. *The Phenomenology of Perception* Translated by Colin Smith. London: Routledge & Kegan Paul.

Morgan, Robert. 1992. "Rethinking Musical Culture: Canonic Reformulations in a Post-Tonal Age." In *Disciplining Music: Musicology and Its Canons,* edited by Katherine Bergeron and Philip V. Bohlman. Chicago: University of Chicago Press. 44–63.

Pasler, Jann. 1993. "Postmodernism, Narrativity, and the Art of Memory." *Contemporary Music Review* 7:3–32.

Phelan, Peggy. 1993. *Unmarked: The Politics of Performance*. London and New York: Routledge.

Rabinow, Paul, and William M.Sullivan, eds. 1987. *Interpretive Social Science: A Second Look*. Berkeley and Los Angeles: University of California Press.

Ricouer, Paul. 1976. *Interpretation Theory: Discourse and the Surplus of Meaning*. Fort Worth: Texas Christian University Press.

Rorty, Richard. 1979. *Philosophy and the Mirror of Nature*. Princeton: Princeton University Press.

Straw, Will. [1988] 1993. "Popular Music and Postmodernism in the 1980s," in *Sound and Vision: The Music Video Reader,* edited by Simon Frith, Andrew Goodwin, and Lawrence Grossberg. London and New York: Routledge. 3–21.

Taylor, Charles. [1971] 1987. "Interpretation and the Sciences of Man." In Rabinow and Sullivan 1987. 25–72. Reprinted from *The Review of Metaphysics* 25/1.

Tomlinson, Gary. 1993. *Music in Renaissance Magic*. Chicago: University of Chicago Press.

Watkins, Glenn. 1994. *Pyramids at the Louvre: Music, Culture, and Collage from Stravinsky to the Postmodernists*. Cambridge, Mass., and London: Harvard University Press.

Young, Iris Marion. 1990. "Throwing Like a Girl: A Phenomenology of Feminine Body Comportment, Motility, and Spatiality." In *Throwing Like a Girl and Other Essays in Feminist Philosophy and Social Theory*. Bloomington and Indianapolis: Indiana University Press, 141–59.

CHAPTER 2

The Nature and Origins of Musical Postmodernism

Jonathan D. Kramer

THE POSTMODERN ATTITUDE

Postmodernism is a maddeningly imprecise musical concept. Does the term refer to a period or an aesthetic, a listening attitude or a compositional practice? Is postmodern music still seeking to define itself, or has its time already passed? Does postmodernism react against or continue the project of modernist music? Is it a positive or a negative force? Is postmodern music original, or does it recycle older music? How widespread is it? Why does postmodernism seem to embrace many cultural values previously thought to be inimical to successful art and even to simple good sense? Is postmodern art serious or frivolous?

And, simply, what *is* postmodernism? For some critics, postmodernism's defining compositional practice is its deliberate attempt to reach out by using procedures and materials audiences are believed to relish: diatonicism, singable melodies, metric regularity, foot-tapping rhythms, tonality, and/or consonant harmonies. Nostalgia for the good old days of tunes and tonality, however, is actually opposed to certain strains of postmodernism. It is not so much postmodernist as antimodernist.[1] There is a significant difference between these two aesthetics: antimodernist yearning for the golden ages of classicism and romanticism perpetuates the elitism of art music, while postmodernism claims to be anti-elitist.[2] An important first step in understanding musical postmodernism, therefore, is to divorce it from nostalgic artworks. Only in antimodernist music (such as the flute concertos of Lowell Lieberman, George Rochberg's *Ricordanza* and Viola Sonata, and Michael Torke's piano concerto *Bronze*) is the use of traditional sonorities, gestures, structures, and procedures tantamount to a re-embracing of earlier styles. In contrast to such compositions, postmodernist music is not conservative. Compositions such as Zygmunt Krauze's Second Piano Concerto, John Adams's Violin Concerto, Henryk Górecki's Third Symphony, Alfred Schnittke's First Symphony, George Rochberg's

Third Quartet, Steve Reich's *Tehillim*, John Corigliano's First Symphony, Bernard Rands's . . . *Body and Shadow* . . . ,[3] and Luciano Berio's *Sinfonia* do not so much conserve as radically transform the past, as—each in its own way—they simultaneously embrace and repudiate history.

Many reviewers of the popular press do not distinguish antimodernism from postmodernism. They identify as postmodern any composition that was written recently but sounds as if it were not. Many composers who use the term are not much more enlightened than the reviewers. Most composers I know use "postmodernism" in the corrupted sense of the press, in feigned or real or willful ignorance of the thinking of critical theorists such as Eco or Lyotard. Yet the ideas of such writers *are* relevant to today's postmodern music.

A more subtle and nuanced understanding of postmodernism emerges once we consider it not as a historical period but as an attitude—a current attitude that influences not only today's compositional practices but also how we listen to and use music of other eras. Umberto Eco has written tellingly, "Postmodernism is not a trend to be chronologically defined, but, rather, an ideal category or, better still, a *Kunstwollen*, a way of operating. We could say that every period has its postmodernism" (Eco 1984, 67).[4] Jean-François Lyotard suggests a still more paradoxical view of the chronology of postmodernism: "A work can become modern only if it is first postmodern. Postmodernism thus understood is not modernism at its end but in the nascent state, and this state is constant" (Lyotard 1984, 79). Lyotard seems to believe that before a work can be understood as truly modern, it must challenge a previous modernism. Thus, to take Lyotard's example, Picasso and Braque are postmodern in that their art goes beyond the modernism of Cézanne. Once their art has achieved this postmodern break with the past, it becomes modernist. Similarly, certain music (discussed below) of Mahler, Ives, and Nielsen, for example, becomes postmodern by going beyond the modernist practices of such composers as Berlioz, Liszt, and Wagner.

POSTMODERN VIEWS ON UNITY, INTERTEXTUALITY, AND ECLECTICISM

Beyond the relevance (or lack thereof) of the critical theories of Eco, Lyotard, and others, one other thing that distinguishes antimodernism from postmodernism is the attitude toward the notion of musical unity, cherished by traditionally minded composers as well as by critics, theorists, and analysts.[5] For both antimodernists and modernists, unity is a prerequisite for musical sense; for some postmodernists, unity is an option. I believe that unity is not simply a characteristic of music itself but also a means of understanding music, a value projected onto music. As such, it is necessarily demoted from its previous position of universality. It is no longer a master narrative of musical structure. Many postmodern composers have accordingly embraced conflict and contradiction and have at times eschewed consistency and unity.[6] Similarly, postmodern audiences do not necessarily search for or find unity in the listening experience. They are more willing to accept each passage of music for itself, rather than having—in accordance with the strictures of modernist analysis and criticism—to create a single whole of possibly disparate parts.

Freed from the dictates of structural unity, some of today's postmodern music offers its listeners extraordinary discontinuities that go beyond contrast, variety, consistency, and unity. Such pieces as John Zorn's *Forbidden Fruit* and William Bolcom's Third Symphony, for example, continually challenge their boundaries by redefining their contexts. References to musical styles of any era or of any culture can intrude, possibly unexpectedly. Of course, some modernist (and earlier) music also includes unexpected quotations. One need only recall the sudden appearances of *Tristan und Isolde* in Debussy's *Golliwog's Cakewalk* and in Berg's *Lyric Suite* to understand that quotation and surprise are not the exclusive province of postmodernist composers. Such examples demonstrate one way among several that postmodernism does not necessarily contradict but rather extends ideas of modernism. Intertextuality has become more pervasive as postmodernism has become more widespread: the references in the Zorn and Bolcom works are far more extensive than the isolated Wagner quotations in the Debussy and Berg pieces.

Furthermore, there is a difference in perspective between modernist and postmodernist quotation. Modernist composers often want to take over, to own, to demonstrate their mastery of that which they are quoting, either by placing it in modernist contexts or by distorting it. Postmodernists are more content to let the music they refer to or quote simply be what it is, offered with neither distortion nor musical commentary.[7] Hence postmodern music readily accepts the diversity of music in the world. It cites—in fact, appropriates—many other musics, including that of modernism. In a sense it challenges the notion of the past, since it may include references to music of virtually any era or culture. Wide-ranging quotations are readily included in postmodern works and are easily understood by postmodern listeners because—thanks to recording technology—music of all times and places can be a living force for composers and listeners alike.

Long before postmodernism was widely recognized, and long before recording technology brought distant musics into the present, there were pieces that juxtaposed styles. How does the eclecticism of such music as Ives's *Three Places in New England*, Mahler's Seventh Symphony, or Nielsen's *Sinfonia Semplice*, for example, differ from that of the 1980s and '90s?[8] It is tempting to understand such earlier works as precursors of (but not necessarily formative influences on) today's postmodernism—somewhat as early repetitive works, such as Ravel's *Boléro* or the first movement of Shostakovich's *Leningrad Symphony*, can be understood in retrospect as

precursors of minimalism.⁹ But there is a more intriguing way to view pieces
like those of Ives, Mahler, and Nielsen: they are not so much proto-
postmodern as they are actually postmodern—by which I mean not only
that they exhibit postmodern compositional practices but also that they are
conducive to being understood in accordance with today's postmodernist
musical values and listening strategies.

CHARACTERISTICS OF POSTMODERN MUSIC

Naming music that is nearly a hundred years old postmodern is not will-
fully perverse but rather is a consequence of viewing postmodernism more
as an attitude than as a historical period. This anti-historical stance results
in a blurring of rigid distinctions among modernism, postmodernism, and
antimodernism, resulting in the term "postmodernism" resisting rigorous
definition. Attitudes toward structural unity, intertextuality, and eclecticism, as explained in the previous section, further problematize attempts to
demarcate the word's meaning. Despite such complications, however, it is
possible to enumerate characteristics of postmodern music—by which I
mean music that is understood in a postmodern manner, that calls forth
postmodern listening strategies, that provides postmodern listening experiences, or that exhibits postmodern compositional practices.¹⁰ Postmodern
music:

(1) is not simply a repudiation of modernism or its continuation, but
     has aspects of both a break and an extension;
(2) is, on some level and in some way, ironic;
(3) does not respect boundaries between sonorities and procedures of
     the past and of the present;
(4) challenges barriers between "high" and "low" styles;
(5) shows disdain for the often unquestioned value of structural
     unity;
(6) questions the mutual exclusivity of elitist and populist values;
(7) avoids totalizing forms (e.g., does not want entire pieces to be
     tonal or serial or cast in a prescribed formal mold);
(8) considers music not as autonomous but as relevant to cultural,
     social, and political contexts;
(9) includes quotations of or references to music of many traditions
     and cultures;
(10) considers technology not only as a way to preserve and transmit
     music but also as deeply implicated in the production and essence
     of music;
(11) embraces contradictions;
(12) distrusts binary oppositions;
(13) includes fragmentations and discontinuities;
(14) encompasses pluralism and eclecticism;

(15) presents multiple meanings and multiple temporalities;
(16) locates meaning and even structure in listeners, more than in scores, performances, or composers.

Not many pieces exhibit all these traits, and thus it is futile to label a work as exclusively postmodern. Also, I would find it difficult to locate a work that exhibits none of these traits. I caution the reader, therefore, against using these sixteen traits as a checklist to help identify a given composition as postmodern or not: postmodern music is not a neat category with rigid boundaries.

POSTMODERNISM AND HISTORY

If postmodernism were simply a period, it would be reasonable to search for its origins in earlier times and to understand it as a reaction to and/or a refinement of aesthetic ideas of previous periods. But postmodernism taken as an attitude suggests ways listeners of today can understand music of various eras. It is in the minds of today's listeners, more than in history, that we find clues to the sources of postmodernism. It comes from the present—from ourselves—more than from the past. Music has become postmodern as we, its late twentieth-century listeners, have become postmodern.

To look for historical precedents leading toward postmodernism would be to accept the idea of historical progress, which postmodernists challenge. The literature on postmodernism is full of statements about the death of history, but it is not necessary to go to the extreme of seeing our age as post-historical in order to understand the uneasy relationship between postmodernism and progress. Postmodernism questions the idea that, if one artwork was created after another, the earlier one may have—or even could have—caused or uniquely influenced the creation of the later one. Every artwork reflects many influences, some from its past, some from its present cultural context, some from its creator's personality, and even some from its future (as subsequent generations come to discover or invent new ways to understand it).

Although they reject the linearity of historical progress, postmodern artworks regularly quote from history. How can we understand such a paradox? How can postmodernism both repudiate and use history? Since, as mentioned above, the quotations and references in postmodern music are often presented without distortion, without commentary, and without distancing, composers treat them just as they might use citations of the present. If a musical style of two hundred years ago is employed in the same way—with the same degree of authenticity (that is, composed as it was when it was current) and belief (in its viability as a vehicle for musical expression)—as is a newly developed style, then history is indeed challenged. As the past becomes the present, the concept of historical progress becomes problematic.

The avant-gardists of early modernism (such as Luigi Russolo, Satie, Cowell, and Varèse) sought to escape history, but were hopelessly trapped in the continuity of historical development.[11] To see themselves on the cutting edge, such avant-gardists (and also early modernists like Schoenberg, Webern, and Stravinsky) had to accept history as linear progress. But recent postmodern composers have moved away from the dialectic between past and present that concerned these early avant-gardists and modernists and that continued to plague their mid-century descendants, such as Boulez, Stockhausen, Nono, Cage, Carter, and Babbitt. Because they recognize history as a cultural construct, postmodernists (such as Aaron Kernis, John Tavener, Paul Schoenfield, and Thomas Adès) can enter into a peaceful coexistence with the past, instead of confronting it as latter-day modernists do. For postmodernists, "History is recast as a process of rediscovering what we already are, rather than a linear progression into what we have never been."[12]

The situation for modernists was and is œdipal: they are in conflict with their antecedents, whom they reinterpret in order to possess, shape, and control their legacy. Modernists sought to displace the major figures in their past, because they were in competition with them despite their owing their very (artistic) existence to them. Influence was a critical issue for modernists.[13] Postmodernists, however, are more like adolescents than like children: they have passed beyond their œdipal conflicts with their modernist parents, although they may still have an uneasy relationship with them (thus, postmodernists may accept historical succession even while rejecting the idea of progress). Postmodernists like to feel that they can be whatever they wish. Their music can happily acknowledge the past, without having to demonstrate superiority to it. Postmodern composers understand that their music is different from that of modernism, but they can nonetheless include modernist (and earlier) styles without having to make them something other than what they were or to relegate them to the inferior status of historical artifacts. But, like adolescents, they can maintain ambivalent feelings toward the modernists whom they view as parents. If these attitudes of postmodernists seem naïvely utopian, that quality is certainly consonant with their adolescent nature.[14]

Can we really dismiss history to the extent that we do not look for the origins of the very attitudes that try to turn us away from the concept of the past? We may be willing to accept postmodernism because it exists, but we are also aware that there were times when it did not exist.[15] What happened? What changed? To the limited extent that postmodernism had causes,[16] we should look to recently developed (or at least recently accepted) ideas, perhaps more pervasive in the United States than elsewhere, in order to understand its musical origins. I say this in full realization that I have posited postmodernism in music as far back as that of Ives and Mahler, and believe that there are embryonic postmodernist ideas that can be found in (or projected onto) certain music by Berlioz, Beethoven, and Haydn. However, since I regard postmodernism as an attitude more than as a historical period, and since I believe that an important aspect of that attitude is the placement of meaning in the listener, it is reasonable to suggest that postmodernism did begin rather recently and subsequently spread to the past as listeners of today began to find postmodern meanings in music from earlier periods.

The best place to search for the origins of musical postmodernism is not, therefore, in the history of music. It is wrongheaded to look to those pre-contemporary works I have called postmodernist for influences on today's postmodern attitudes or for sources of the kind of postmodernist thinking that has recently become widespread. Postmodernism *is* a recent phenomenon. It is only now—once it exists, has been experienced, and is to some degree assimilated and understood—that it makes sense to listen to music like Ives's *Putnam's Camp,* Mahler's Seventh Symphony, or Nielsen's *Sinfonia Semplice* in a postmodern manner. But those works and works like them are not the sources of postmodernism.

THE ORIGINS OF POSTMODERNISM IN CONTEMPORARY CULTURE

One source of today's postmodernism, not surprisingly, is the psychological and sociological tenor of our technology-saturated world. Technology has created a context of fragmentation, short attention spans leading to constant discontinuities, and multiplicity—all characteristics not only of contemporary society but also of postmodern thinking. In his book *The Saturated Self,* psychologist Kenneth J. Gergen offers insights into the psychological dimensions of postmodernism. Gergen traces the changing concepts of the self from the romantic age (when each person was thought to possess depth of passion, soul, and creativity) through the modernist age (which particularly valued logic, rationality, and conscious intentions) to the current era of postmodernism, which is characterized by "social saturation" (Gergen 1991, 6).

By "social saturation" Gergen means the condition in which we continually receive messages of all sorts, coming (often electronically) from many corners of the globe, all competing for our attention and involvement. There is no time to reflect, no time to savor, no time for contemplation, no time for depth. Conflicting claims on our attention, as well as constant bombardment with information, lead to the fragmented sensibility associated with postmodern attitudes. Gergen writes:

> The postmodern condition . . . is marked by a plurality of voices vying for the right to reality—to be accepted as legitimate expressions of the true and the good. As the voices expand in power and presence, all that seemed proper, right-minded, and well understood is subverted. In the postmodern

world we become increasingly aware that the objects about which we speak are not so much "in the world" as they are products of perspective. Thus, processes such as emotion and reason cease to be real and significant essences of persons; rather, in the light of pluralism we perceive them to be imposters, the outcome of our ways of conceptualizing them. Under postmodern conditions, persons exist in a state of continuous construction and reconstruction; it is a world where anything goes that can be negotiated. Each reality of self gives way to reflexive questioning, irony, and ultimately the playful probing of yet another reality. (Gergen 1991, 7)

Gergen's concept of the saturated self resonates with my own experiences. In a given afternoon, I may find myself sitting in my office, communicating via e-mail or fax with professional colleagues in London and Perth, advising former students in Warsaw and Taipei, and carrying on personal correspondence with friends in Evanston and San Diego. I may then turn my attention to some journal articles and books, which are rarely read through in their entirety and several of which I find myself studying more or less simultaneously. I may receive phone calls (or messages on my voice mail) from faraway colleagues, old friends, prospective students, performers who are rehearsing my music in distant cities, someone who wants me to do a guest lecture. Each phone call picks up a continuity broken off hours, days, weeks, or even years ago, or else initiates a relationship to be continued in the future. These activities, which continually intrude upon one another, may in turn be interrupted by a knock on my door. A student in need of help? A textbook publisher's representative wanting to convince me to use a certain book in my harmony class? A workman wanting to fix my air conditioner? All of this, and some days still more, within the space of two or three hours! Fragmentation. Discontinuity. Lack of connection. Lack of linear logic. Postmodernism.[17]

Since technology allows me to stay in contact with people I know in many different contexts and those I knew in many periods in my past, the past in a certain sense is no longer as remote as it would have been had I lived before telephones, e-mail, faxes, airplanes, cars, or trains. Two hundred years ago people moved around a lot less and maintained far fewer contacts than they do today. When someone moved from one community to another, acquaintances were lost, relegated to memory and imagination. Not necessarily so today. I am in touch with my first friend (from kindergarten), my high school buddies, my college roommate, my graduate school colleagues, many of my former teachers and students, and people I have met lecturing in several countries. My past lives not only in memory but also through contacts in my present (see Gergen 1991, 62–63). My friends may get older and change, but they are still the same friends. Their identity keeps our shared past alive (although their aging makes me more acutely aware of time's passage than I might have been had I continually traded my friends for newer ones).

The blurring of the distinction between past and present is one postmodern cultural value that is reflected in postmodern music. There are others. Gergen cites as results of social saturation an increasing sense of pastiche and otherness (similar to the way postmodern music refers to or quotes other music). Intertextuality is not solely a condition of postmodern literature or music, but also of the postmodern self. People come into contact with so many other people, with divergent personalities and values, that the self is constantly in flux, always bending under the influence of others.

> As social saturation proceeds we become pastiches, imitative assemblages of each other. In memory we carry others' patterns of being with us. Each of us becomes the other, a representative, or a replacement. To put it more broadly, as the century has progressed selves have become increasingly populated with the characters of others. (Gergen 1991, 71)

Other aspects that social saturation shares with postmodern art are multiplicity and disunity. Gergen again:

> Increasingly we emerge as the possessors of many voices. Each self contains a multiplicity of others. . . . Nor do these many voices necessarily harmonize. . . . Central to the modernist view was a robust commitment to an objective and knowable world. . . . [Yet] as we begin to incorporate the dispositions of the varied others to whom we are exposed, we become capable of taking their positions, adopting their attitudes, talking their language, playing their roles. In effect, one's self becomes populated with others. The result is a steadily accumulating sense of doubt in the objectivity of any position one holds. (Gergen 1991, 83–85)

Robert Morgan has written perceptively on how social forces can shape postmodern music.

> The plurality of styles, techniques, and levels of expression appears both plausible and meaningful in a world increasingly shedding its common beliefs and shared customs, where there is no longer a single given "reality" but only shifting, multiple realities, provisionally constructed out of the unconnected bits and pieces set loose by a world stripped of all attachments. If traditional tonality . . . adequately reflected a culture characterized by a community of purpose and well-developed system of social order and interpersonal regulation, its loss, and the musical atomization that has ensued, reflects a fragmented and defamiliarized world of isolated events and abrupt confrontations. (Morgan 1992, 58)

WHY TODAY'S COMPOSERS WRITE POSTMODERN MUSIC

I would not argue that social saturation, however potent a force in contemporary Western societies, inevitably leads to the creation of postmodern
art. There is always the possibility of protest. Some (indeed, many!) may
find social saturation to be alienating, and seek antidotes or alternatives or
escapes. The persistence of modernism in the arts—and the antimodern
resurgence of traditionalism—can be understood in part as a resistance to
social saturation. But the forces that are transforming the self from a modernist to a postmodernist entity are undeniable. That some artists should
create works expressive of a saturated personality, whether by intention or
not, is hardly surprising. Composers, like others who live in a saturated
society, may have personalities shaped in part by their social contexts. The
same is true of listeners who, immersed in postmodern social values, find
meaningful resonances in musical compositions that reflect postmodern
attitudes and practices.

Uncritically adopting or thoroughly repudiating postmodern values are
not the only possible responses of late-twentieth-century composers to a
socially saturated culture. Some composers—probably more Europeans,
steeped as they tend to be in dialectical thinking, than laid-back, naively
utopian Americans—enter into a struggle with postmodern cultural forces.
It is beyond the scope of this brief article, however, to probe the manner in
which the music of certain composers (such as Bernd Alois Zimmermann
and Louis Andriessen) dialectically grapples and contends with postmodernist ideas, rather than simply accepting or rejecting them.

Various composers respond differently to their postmodern culture.
Whether they accept, deny, or do battle with postmodernism, it is an undeniable force. Even those who embrace it outright may do so for a variety
of reasons. It is appropriate, therefore, to conclude this essay by enumerat-
ing some of the reasons today's composers are drawn to postmodern values in their society.

(1)   Some composers react against modernist styles and values, which
      have become oppressive to them.

(2)   Some composers react against the institutionalism of mod-
      ernism—against, in other words, its position of power within the
      musical establishment, particularly in the United States,
      Germany, France, England, and Italy.

(3)   Some composers respond to what they see as the cultural irrele-
      vance of modernism.

(4)   Some composers (antimodernists as well as postmodernists) are
      motivated by a desire to close the composer-audience gap,
      created—they believe—by the elitism of modernism.

(5)   Some young composers are uncomfortable with pressures from
      their teachers to like and respect one kind of music (tonal) yet

write another (atonal).[18] Like adolescents in the world of post-modernism, they rebel against the values they learn in school. They want to create the music they love, not that which they are told to love.

(6) Some composers today know and enjoy popular music. While there were always "classical" composers who liked pop music, nowadays some composers who appreciate it (such as Steve Martland and Michael Daugherty) see no reason to exclude it from their own stylistic range—a further instance of composing what they love, regardless of how respectable it is.

(7) Some composers are acutely aware that music is a commodity, that it is consumable, and that composers are inevitably part of a materialist social system. Such composers understand postmodernism as an aesthetic whose attitudes and styles reflect the commodification of art. They see postmodern music as concerned with, rather than ignoring (as they see modernism doing) its place in the economy.

(8) Some composers, like their predecessors in earlier eras, want to create music that is new and different. Yet they have become disillusioned with the avant-garde's search for novel sounds, compositional strategies, and formal procedures, and with its adversarial stance with regard to tradition. Rather, they seek originality in the postmodernist acceptance of the past as part of the present, in disunifying fragmentation, in pluralism, and in multiplicity.

(9) All composers live in a multicultural world. While some choose to keep the ubiquitous musics from all parts of the globe out of their own compositions, others are so enthralled by coming in contact with music from very different traditions that they accept it into their own personal idioms. Although such appropriations are sometimes criticized as instances of cultural imperialism, they do abound in postmodern music.

(10) Most contemporary composers are aware of the postmodern values in their culture. These values inform not only the music they produce but also the ways it is heard and used. However varied its musical manifestations may be, and however diverse the reasons for its appeal to composers and listeners, musical postmodernism is—as I have tried to suggest—the all but inevitable expression of a socially saturated civilization.

The reasons behind the creation of postmodern music today are varied. The characteristics of postmodern compositions and postmodern listening are numerous. The origins of the postmodern attitude in music are diverse, as are the responses to it and social uses of it. Hailed by some and reviled by others, postmodern music and postmodern listening are exciting—yet sobering—statements of who and what we are.

NOTES

1. For further discussion of antimodernism vs. modernism vs. postmodernism, see Kramer 1995.

2. Postmodernist music is generally less elitist than modernist music, much of which appeals to a relatively small audience of initiates—people who know how to appreciate atonality, jagged melodies, irregular rhythms, asymmetrical meters, pungent dissonances, and so on. But postmodern music rarely achieves the total overthrow of elitism. By incorporating popular music into symphonic compositions, for example, postmodern composers do not really create pop symphonies so much as they embrace pop while preserving its otherness. Its effectiveness in a symphony derives in part from the fact that it does not totally belong there.

3. I discuss this work in an article forthcoming in *Contemporary Music Review*: "Bernard Rands's . . . *Body and Shadow* . . . : Modernist, Postmodernist, or Traditionalist?"

4. Similarly, Kathleen Higgins writes: "The term 'postmodernism' has an oxymoronic sound. How, if the word 'modern' refers to the present, can currently living people be 'postmodern'? This question arises almost as a gut reaction. The word seems a little uncanny. A 'postmodernist' sounds like one of the living dead or perhaps one of the living unborn—or maybe our sense of temporality is simply offended. We can recall Kurt Vonnegut and conceive of postmodernists as 'unstuck in time'" (Higgins 1990, 189).

5. The postmodern challenge to the concept of unity is the central topic of Kramer 1995.

6. Among postmodern composers whose music is deeply concerned with structural unity are Arvo Pärt and Fred Lerdahl.

7. This distinction, incidentally, helps to explain the difference between two musical aesthetics that are both involved with the past: neoclassic modernists tend to place their own personal stamp on their historical references, whereas postmodernists do not.

8. For a discussion of the postmodern aspects of *Putnam's Camp*, the middle movement of *Three Places*, and of the finale of Mahler's Seventh Symphony, see Kramer 1996, 30–48. For an analysis of the postmodern aspects of Nielsen's *Sinfonia Semplice*, see Kramer 1994.

9. It is impossible to prove lack of influence decisively. However, none of the writings by or interviews with early minimalists with which I am familiar cite either of these works as influences, and I suspect—for aesthetic and stylistic reasons—that the music of Glass and Reich would be unchanged had Ravel and Shostakovich never composed these particular pieces. But I cannot prove this contention. Similarly, I feel (but cannot prove) that postmodernism of today would be essentially unchanged if the cited compositions of Ives, Mahler, and Nielsen did not exist.

10. This list is expanded from one appearing in Kramer 1996, 21–22.

11. I discuss avant-gardism in an article "The Musical Avant-Garde," forthcoming in *Music of the Twentieth-Century Avant-Garde*.

12. I owe this perceptive formulation to an anonymous reviewer of an earlier version of this article.

13. Joseph Straus offers a theory of influence in modernist music, based on the ideas of Harold Bloom, in Straus 1990, 1–20.

14. The adolescence of postmodernism is particularly apparent in traits 3, 5, and 6 in the list of characteristics of postmodern music.

15. While I have suggested that postmodernism is an attitude more than a period, and that instances of postmodern musical practice can be found in compositions of the distant past, I trust that it is clear that I do not believe that postmodernism is ubiquitous throughout history.

16. It is somewhat naive to look only for cultural factors that "caused" postmodernism to develop. Postmodernism shaped as well as was shaped by certain Western cultural ideas.

17. Gergen writes: "We are now bombarded with ever-increasing intensity by the images and actions of others; our range of social participation is expanding exponentially. As we absorb the views, values, and visions of others, and live out the multiple plots in which we are enmeshed, we enter a postmodern consciousness. It is a world in which we no longer experience a secure sense of self, and in which doubt is increasingly placed on the very assumption of a bounded identity with palpable attributes" (Gergen 1991, 15–16).

18. Several students of one well-known modernist composer-teacher have told me how they simultaneously work on two different pieces, one that they truly believe in and one that they think their professor will approve.

WORKS CITED

Eco, Umberto. 1984. *Postscript to the Name of the Rose.* Translated by William Weaver. San Diego: Harcourt Brace Jovanovich.

Gergen, Kenneth J. 1991. *The Saturated Self: Dilemmas of Identity in Contemporary Life.* New York: Basic Books.

Higgins, Kathleen. 1990. "Nietzsche and Postmodern Subjectivity." In *Nietzsche as Postmodernist: Essays Pro and Contra*, edited by Clayton Koelb. Albany: State University of New York Press. 189–216.

Kramer, Jonathan D. 1994. "Unity and Disunity in Carl Nielsen's Sixth Symphony." In *A Nielsen Companion*, edited by Mina Miller. London: Faber and Faber; Portland, Oreg.: Amadeus Press. 293–334.

————. 1995. "Beyond Unity: Toward an Understanding of Musical Postmodernism." In *Concert Music, Rock, and Jazz since 1945: Essays and Analytical Studies*, edited by Elizabeth West Marvin and Richard Hermann. Rochester: University of Rochester Press. 11–33.

————. 1996. "Postmodern Concepts of Musical Time." *Indiana Theory Review* 17/2: 21–61.

————. Forthcoming. "The Musical Avant-Garde." In *Music of the Twentieth-*

Century Avant-Garde, edited by Larry Sitsky. Westport, Conn.: Greenwood Press.

————. Forthcoming. "Bernard Rands's . . . *Body and Shadow* . . . : Modernist, Postmodernist, or Traditionalist?" *Contemporary Music Review.*

Lyotard, Jean-François. [1979] 1984. *The Postmodern Condition: A Report on Knowledge.* Translated by Geoff Bennington and Brian Massumi. Minneapolis: University of Minnesota Press.

Morgan, Robert. 1992. "Rethinking Musical Culture: Canonic Reformulations in a Post-Tonal Age." In *Disciplining Music: Musicology and Its Canons,* edited by Katherine Bergeron and Philip V. Bohlman. Chicago: University of Chicago Press. 44–63.

Straus, Joseph. 1990. *Remaking the Past: Musical Modernism and the Influence of the Tonal Tradition.* Cambridge: Harvard University Press.

CHAPTER 3

Reflections of Surrealism in Postmodern Musics
Anne LeBaron

> ... there exists a certain aspect of the spirit where life and death, the real and the imaginary, past and future, communicable and incommunicable, high and low, cease to be perceived as contradictory. One might search in vain for any other central force in Surrealist activities than the hope of finding this point.
>
> —Breton [1930] 1972, 123–24

Although the surrealist movement and the literary and visual works associated with it have been widely documented, little has been written about surrealist elements that have crossed over into music. A close examination of the history of surrealism reveals two principal components—automatism and collage—which are fundamental to the link between surrealism and some contemporary music, especially some music for which the adjective "postmodern" is appropriate.[1] Here I explore how some recent musical practices sustain and transform early twentieth-century artistic behaviors associated with surrealism.

The founder of surrealism, André Breton, insisted that surrealism embraced far more than literary or visual arts, or politics, or social concerns; it was ultimately a way of knowledge, with the potential for being eternally relevant.[2] In his "official" definition of the term, Breton aligned it closely with automatism (automatic writing): "surrealism, *n.* Psychic automatism in its pure state, by which one proposes to express—verbally, by means of the written word, or in any other manner—the actual functioning of thought" (Breton [1924] 1972, 26). Automatism was so central to the philosophy of surrealism in its early days that the terms "surrealist writing" and "automatism" were used interchangeably. Surrealists were, however, careful to differentiate their use of automatic writing from the mechanical writing engaged in by psychics and hypnotists.[3]

The surrealists were intrigued by automatism since it would assist them in escaping the shackles of supervised thought. Intensive indulgence in automatism could even lead to altered states: "Automatic writing, practised with some fervour, leads directly to visual hallucination" (Breton [1933] 1978, 108). Euphoric with the intoxication of discovery, they "felt like miners who had just struck the mother lode" (Breton [1952] 1993, 44). Breton later stressed the requirement for the detachment of the mind from the external world when engaging in automatism, and made the point that such detachment is closer to Eastern thought, requiring extremely sustained concentration and effort (64–65).

Although automatism existed in surrealism from the outset, the role of collage only developed as surrealism expanded to encompass the visual arts. Breton considered both to be equally viable techniques for producing a surrealist text. The scholar Elsa Adamowicz, in writing about the cutting and flowing natures of collage and automatism, clarifies the primary importance of both techniques to the surrealists: "The spontaneous verbal flow—and later the graphic gesture—which characterizes early automatism on the one hand, and the deliberate cutting up and assembling of disparate elements specific to collage on the other hand, were to be elaborated as the two essential modes of surrealist production, breaking away from traditional codes of mimesis and the aesthetics of coherence, and exploring the language of the irrational and the chance encounter" (Adamowicz 1998, 5).

Surrealist methods of collage became the visual parallel to automatism. Originating from the French word *coller*, it means literally "pasting, sticking, or gluing"—techniques used by artists for centuries. Only in the twentieth century, however, did collage begin to function as a structure of juxtapositions. Lautréamont's verbal collages, such as the celebrated "chance meeting upon a dissecting table of a sewing machine with an umbrella," provided an early model of systematic displacement for the surrealist graphic collagists. As opposed to the formal and aesthetic considerations of cubist *papier collé*, surrealist collage aimed at initiating an unprecedented encounter, to stimulate the imagination and to spark revelation.

The distinction between surrealist collage and other forms of twentieth-century collage, especially cubist collage, is important to understand. Surrealists who worked with collage—and most of them did, either exclusively or peripherally—transcended the literal cutting and pasting techniques so attractive to the cubists. Collage elements in cubism principally functioned as formal units. Surrealist collage, however, reinterpreted familiar fragments—the clichéd images of advertisements, clippings from anatomical textbooks, illustrations from nineteenth-century pulp fiction, ephemera such as bus tickets—manipulating ready-made objects and elements into newly charged works that conjured "the marvelous."[4] Far from merely enriching the palette of the artist, the collage elements in surrealist art were powerfully iconic. *What* was expressed superseded the *means* of expression; the represented object "play[ed] the role of a word" (Aragon [1930] 1965, 44).

The specific visual counterpart to automatic writing was frottage, a variation of collage. Max Ernst, considered the foremost practitioner of surrealist collage, discovered the method of frottage in 1925: "The process of collage resting only on the intensification of the irritability of the spiritual faculties by appropriate and technical means, excluding all conscious mental conduction, reducing to an extreme the active part of what has up till now been called the 'author,' this process is revealed as the veritable equivalent of automatic writing" (Ernst [1938] 1970, 208). In layman's terms, frottage means 'the process of rubbing'—a familiar technique to children, who delight in transferring images of tree leaves or bark in this way. The groundwork for Ernst's discovery began some six years earlier, when he first stumbled upon the potential of unexpected juxtapositions: "One rainy day in 1919, finding myself in a village on the Rhine, I was struck by the obsession which held under my gaze the pages of an illustrated catalogue showing objects designed for anthropologic, microscopic, psychologic, mineralogic, and paleontologic demonstration. There I found brought together elements of figuration so remote that the sheer absurdity of that collection provoked a sudden intensification of the visionary faculties in me and brought forth an illusive succession of contradictory images, double, triple and multiple images, piling up on each other with the persistence and rapidity which are peculiar to love memories and visions of half-sleep. These visions called themselves new planes, because of their meeting in a new unknown (the plane of non-agreement)" (Ernst 1948, 14). As we shall see, what Ernst depicts in his epiphany resembles manifestations of collage in music.

The bridge linking automatism with collage developed through the invention of a game called the Exquisite Corpse,[5] in which different parts of drawings or writings (generally poems) were accomplished by successive individuals, each oblivious to the prior material that had been created. The individual artist relinquishes conscious control, surrendering to a collaborative process that represents the antithesis of the world of assembly-line automatization. Boundaries are dissolved, and a whiplash series of startling juxtapositions emerges, with a "collective" collage as the end result of the game.

A SURREAL SILENCE

Driven by a mixed bag of politics, jealousies, misunderstandings, philosophical differences, and outright naiveté, the predominantly negative attitude of many French surrealists toward music was complicated and fluctuating. Giorgio de Chirico, one of the progenitors of surrealist art, established this tone in his essay of 1913, "No Music." He proclaimed that a picture has a "music of its own," with the implication that music is ultimately superfluous. In the decisive Le Surréalisme et la peinture, published fifteen years later, Breton immediately dismisses music as inferior to the assorted degrees of sensation and "spiritual realizations" made possible by the plastic arts. Imparting "value" to forms of "plastic expression" that he unconditionally refuses to grant to musical expression, he describes music as "the most deeply confusing of all art forms." It gets worse: "Auditive images, in fact, are inferior to visual images not only in clarity but also in strictness, and, with all due respect to a few megalomaniacs, they are not destined to strengthen the idea of human greatness. So may night continue to descend upon the orchestra, and may I, who am still searching for something in this world, be left with open eyes, or with closed eyes in broad daylight, to my silent contemplation" (Breton [1928] 1972, 1–2).

Sixteen years later, Breton's attitude toward music is far more circumspect, even humble. In his sole essay on music, "Silence is Golden," Breton professes his ignorance of music while calling for a *recasting* of certain principles of music and poetry in order to vaporize the antagonism existing between these two arts. "For the first audible diamond to be obtained, it is evident that the fusion of the two elements—music and poetry—into one, could only be accomplished at a very high emotional temperature. And it seems to me that it is in the expression of the passion of love that both music and poetry are most likely to reach this supreme point of incandescence" (Breton 1944, 152).[6]

SATIE AND ANTHEIL

The composers most closely associated with the surrealists did not participate in the game-playing, the dream-dictation, or any of the other activities that were formulating the surrealist aesthetic by empirical process. Erik Satie began his "second career" in 1912 at the age of 48, after being rediscovered by Debussy and Ravel. Satie, known for his eccentric texts that embellish so many of his works for piano, also experimented with other radical departures from the "normal," such as the absence of barlines in the three waltzes, *Precieux Dégouté*. Satie's biographer, Rollo Myers, describes these waltzes, with their displaced stresses, dry harmony, and absurd association of ideas, as a "surrealistic montage" (Myers 1948, 128).

Satie's stage works, projecting collaborative architectures of collage, would be most representative of the transference of surrealist practices into music. *Parade*, for instance—a hybrid of fresh sounds, novel technologies, and new styles—resulted in juxtapositions that would surely appeal to a surrealist. Satie's contribution to the ballet *Parade*, his and Cocteau's collaborative triumph, owed as much to the dada and futurist movements as it did to surrealism. The score was to have included Morse code tickers, lottery wheels, airplane propellers, typewriters, and sirens; due to crowding in the pit and lack of resources, only a typewriter and siren were actually used. *Parade* outraged a large portion of the public, as well as critics, which delighted Satie. The performance "set the tone for the postwar years. It was a serious-humorous exploitation of popular elements in art, a turning to jazz and music hall and to all the paraphernalia of modern life, not in a spirit of realism, but with a sense of exhilaration in the absurd" (Shattuck 1955, 120–21).

Toward the end of his life, Satie went on to write three other works for the stage. The last, *Relâche* (billed as *ballet instantanéiste*), his scandalous swan song that caused a legendary uproar, carries the distinction of being the first ballet to incorporate film.[7] One of his collaborators for *Relâche*, Francis Picabia, deliberately turned his back on the surrealist camp in order to work with Satie. After the 1924 premiere, ironically coinciding with the year of Breton's "First Manifesto" and "birth" of surrealism, Satie fell ill, succumbing to liver failure the following year.

Surprisingly, Satie was shunned by Breton and most of his followers. Breton took exception to Satie's ongoing artistic relationship with Jean Cocteau, whom he despised. Breton's lifelong loathing for Cocteau was fueled by a confused web of resentments, and he was especially opposed to Cocteau's successful pandering to the bourgeoisie art establishment.[8] As a group, the surrealists weren't especially fond of certain forays taken by Satie that were, as it turns out, amazingly prophetic. His *Musique d'ameublement* (furniture music) anticipated a genre steeped in neutrality that had yet to be named, but which now is termed ambient music and its spinoffs—Muzak, dinner party music, new age music conducive to meditation, and so forth. Satie's own description of *Musique d'ameublement* alludes to the pragmatic incentive for its invention—loud restaurant music—for which he proposed the antidote: "I imagine it to be melodious, softening the clatter of knives and forks without dominating them, without imposing itself. It would fill up the awkward silence that occasionally descends upon guests. It would spare them the usual commonplaces. At the same time it would neutralise the street noises that tactlessly force themselves into the picture" (Toop 1995, 198). Surrealists would oppose the bland innocuousness of this new musical genre.

Erik Satie left an ambiguous yet highly visionary legacy. Since so many movements lay claim to him, it is difficult to make the case that he is principally a surrealist composer. Like Picasso and Stravinsky, he never professed allegiance to any movement, although he was familiar with them all. It is ironic that he wasn't recognized during his lifetime as a musical contributor to surrealism, due to Breton's antagonism and also to the fact that musicians in general were not a part of the movement.

Of the other major composers active in France during the 1920s and 1930s—Poulenc, Auric, Antheil, Milhaud, Stravinsky—George Antheil was the most outspoken and proactive in identifying himself with the surrealists: "The Surrealist movement had, from the very beginning, been my friend. In one of its manifestoes it had been declared that all music was unbearable—excepting, possibly, mine—a beautiful and appreciated condescension" (Antheil [1945] 1981, 300). The surrealists promoted Antheil's music, and he even began a collaboration with Breton and Louis Aragon on an opera, *Faust III*.[9] Mechanical repetition, distortions of time, and the incorporation of noise characterized his music. *Ballet mécanique*, originally

scored for eight pianos, one pianola, eight xylophones, two electric door-
bells, and airplane propeller sounds, incited rioting at the Paris premiere in
1925—a surefire sign of a successful surrealist work.

Five years later, Antheil composed a set of thirty-five piano preludes, *La
Femme: 100 têtes*, inspired by Max Ernst's collage novel of the same name.
In her 1992 dissertation, "Surrealism in the Piano Music of Representative
Twentieth-Century American Composers," Kathryn Lea Fouse discusses
several of these preludes, highlighting their burlesque qualities and pointing
out the references to humor, as in *Prelude XVII*, a parody of a traditional
pianistic exercise. These through-composed preludes sometimes depict
Ernst's collages by means of graphic- or text-painting. However, Antheil's
music, even at its most radical extremes, never seems to fully exploit the
techniques of collage and automatism so indispensable to many surrealist
writers and artists.

SURREAL MUSIC?

Poetry, prose, political manifestoes, games, dream imagery, painting, sculpture, collage forms, photography, and cinema converged to form a movement unlike any other in the twentieth century. Why wasn't music an equal
player in this dazzling array of literary, artistic, and political activities?
Many of the surrealists themselves wondered about the relative absence of
music in their vibrant universe, conspicuous in that virtually all other art
forms were welcomed, contributing to a hothouse atmosphere of cross-
fertilization. The Belgian surrealist writer Paul Nougé asks: "Among all the
forces capable of bewitching spirit—forces which it must both submit to
and revolt against—poetry, painting, spectacles, war, misery, debauchery,
revolution, life with its inseparable companion, death—is it possible to
refuse music a place among them, perhaps a very important place" (Nougé
[1947] 1992, 174–75)?[10] François-Bernard Mâche writes of a meeting that
took place at the home of Max Ernst to discuss the permanence of surrealism.[11] The participants concluded, among other things, that the failure of
music to exhibit more fully characteristics of surrealism was not the fault
of the musicians. Speculating on how music might have collaborated in the
ambitions central to surrealism, Ernst proposed the following scenario: "In
Surrealism, manifesting as 'pure psychic automatism,' one can wonder what
role music would play in automatic writing for the texts, in the frictions for
graphics [frottage], or in floating wood for magical objects. The answer is
rather obvious: they are the dictations of actual raw resonances [represen-
tations of raw sound], which would place our unconscious in possession of
this latent music, latent at the same time in itself and in the resonant stimuli that it would accommodate" (Mâche 1974, 42). Composers would have
to wait for technological developments to fully realize the implications of
Ernst's conception.

Surrealism, a supremely inclusive movement, was founded on two fundamental and complementary tenets: automatism and collage. While these techniques existed in isolated examples of music before and after surrealism's peak, they blossomed into full-blown developments only with the advent of postmodernism. Technological tools used to record and process music, along with a more open and pluralistic musical landscape, provided an environment for such surrealist techniques to flourish when placed at the disposal of composers.

Although early experiments with elements of musical surrealism did not immediately take root, they carved out a testing ground for others to eventually build upon.[12] Many of the collage works of Charles Ives—a person about as far removed from the surrealist ferment and its subversive aesthetics as one can imagine—actually predate surrealist developments. Furthermore, the sudden insertions, and more gradual sonic exuviations, of seemingly unrelated music contribute to the surreal effect found in works by Ives that aren't even considered to be collage pieces. Nearly forty years ago, Peter S. Hansen, describing the abrupt hymn quotation and "perky march-tune" in the "Hawthorne" movement from the *Concord Sonata*, remarks that "these allusions to popular music . . . result in an almost *surrealistic* incongruity with the general climate of dissonance" (Hansen 1961, 80; my italics). Further, the aspirations, electronic investigations and experiments of modernist sound pioneers such as Edgard Varèse, Pierre Schaeffer, Pierre Henry, and even John Cage functioned as yet another germination site for musical surrealism.

Experiments with surrealist elements in music in the 1920s and 1930s were isolated, and not substantial enough to participate equally with the literary and visual components so vital to the realization of surrealist ideals. Most composers of this period were preoccupied with the breakdown of tonality, and serialism, the most radical development in music, was far removed from surrealist aesthetics. In America, however, an early and simple "automatistic" rendering of music, incorporating degrees of improvisation, was beginning to find voice in the music of blues musicians and jazz bands.[13] Meanwhile, electronic music, a frontier for radical expansion of multiple parameters in music, was poised at the cusp of its coming evolution, attracting the sonic imagination of Varèse in the 1940s.

By the early 1950s, music began to break free of prior limitations, including the straitjacket of equal temperament. Newly favorable conditions, such as technological and aesthetic developments, made it possible to prioritize sound over notation, creating a fertile environment for the infiltration of surrealistic factors. What began to emerge—surrealist-related elements of displacement, of radical meshings, of intentions recorded instantaneously—reflected the revolutionary effect that recording technology brought to music. Such a connection was not lost on Pierre Boulez, who recognized that electroacoustic tools could provide a means of relating music to the "other arts" of a prior surrealism. Calling for an investigation of the structural relationships possible between the language of music and the language of science (just prior to the construction of IRCAM [Institut de recherche et de coordination acoustique-musique]), he identified problems in the realm of instruments, intervals, and electronic music. With respect to the latter, he asserted: "the electro-acoustic world, which is of course entirely new and has been taken over, in a way, by a kind of curiosity-shop aesthetics, this bastard descendant of a dead Surrealism" (Boulez [1968]1986, 456). The implication: although developments in electronic music *have* provided the tools to create music in the surrealist mold, Boulez opposed the unleashing of prior constraints *if* musicians are exploring new territory for the sheer fun of doing so.

Jacqueline Chénieux-Gendron also suggests a link between the beginnings of electronic music and surrealism. She devotes several paragraphs in her book, *Surrealism,* to the French surrealists' neglect of music as one "system of signs." Citing the electroacoustic explorations of Pierre Schaeffer and Pierre Henry as being close to the spirit of surrealism, she refers to the optimistic statement of the musician François-Bernard Mâche: "Surrealist forms of music could still arise, seeking the gold of sound as Breton sought the gold of time."[14] Yet, she not only concludes that "these suggestions give a very partial analogy with Surrealism," but also asserts that from an historical perspective, the opportunity for any meeting between music and surrealism has been irretrievably missed (Chénieux-Gendron [1984] 1990, 167–68).

On the contrary, I contend that the profound influences of surrealism began to take hold in the late 1950s and that surrealism in music only acheived its full potential in postmodern musics. The more widespread developments in recording and electronic processing technologies, and the abilities of performers and composers to break the molds of a previously limiting syntactical and sonic palette, contributed to a fertile atmosphere that established the necessary conditions for bringing the last major art form into the fold of surrealism.

Did surrealist aesthetics begin to infiltrate modernist musics after World War II? Nicolas Slonimsky, in his essay, "Music and Surrealism," names over a dozen widely divergent examples, after first establishing his ground: "Musical Surrealism arose primarily as a reaction against Contented Music, the music of the salon, the cult of the virtuoso, the art of tonal tranquilization" (Slonimsky 1966, 80). Slonimsky never really defines music that embodies surreal qualities. For instance, in one statement, he implies that settings of surrealist texts qualify as surrealist music, even if the accompanying music remains completely within the sphere of "Contented Music"—such as Poulenc's music for Apollinaire's bizarre *Les Mamelles de Tirésias.* But then, in the next breath, he makes the stark pronouncement: if it's dissonant it must be surreal.

Slonimsky's arguments are occasionally convincing, such as his assertion that Shostakovich's satirical opera, *The Nose*, was surrealistic in its aesthetic derivation. Slonimsky doesn't stop at the synopsis, but goes on to cite musical effects that he interprets as surreal, such as the "octet of janitors in a polyphonic glossolalia" (1966, 80). Claiming that Hindemith contributed to surrealism in musical theater with his operatic sketch, *Hin und Zurück*, he's on the right track.[15] But when he remarks, "The dissonant texture and rhythmic asymmetry of the score contribute to the surrealistic effect of the music," his rationale begins to resemble the proverbial kitchen sink.

Slonimsky takes a far broader approach to defining a musical surrealism than I do, even equating serialism with surrealism. Yet, he brilliantly zeros in on a couple of fundamental issues. He points out the parallels between collage and *musique concrète*: "The basically Surrealistic techniques of montage and collage found their application in *musique concrète*, born in a Paris studio, on a spring day in 1948, where the French radio engineer Pierre Schaeffer amused himself by combining the sounds and noises of the studio and recording them on magnetic tape" (1966, 83).[16] Slonimsky even enlists Charles Ives as an example of a composer practicing his own brand of *musique concrète*. Indeed, Ives was abruptly juxtaposing musical quotations from a hodgepodge of sources—hymns, folk music, classical works, marching band tunes—*before* surrealism was a viable artistic movement. Both Ives and Schaeffer, although separated by decades and mediums, were capable of relentlessly shunning conventions such as harmony, melody, or tonality.

BREAKING THE FAST

The two principal aesthetic components of the surrealist movement, automatism and collage, have been reincarnated in some of the more vibrant music created in the latter half of the twentieth century. The incorporation of these elements does not, however, imply a postmodern surrealist "movement." Rather, I argue that the impact of the original surrealist movement reverberates in certain types of postmodern music. I demonstrate this reverberation by considering the relationship of automatism to improvisation, and of collage to musical simultaneities, pluralities, borrowings, and sudden juxtapositions of unrelated materials.

Many of the composers and musicians I discuss haven't yet been written about critically and deserve greater acknowledgment and wider exposure. More established composers who could easily be discussed in this essay, such as Varèse, Cage, Ligeti, Stockhausen, or Oliveros, are already the subject of considerable critical and analytical study. José Pierre, for instance, writes that Cage was considered to be a surrealist composer in the 1940s (Pierre 1999a, 37). Mâche goes into greater detail: "The fact remains that the complete genesis of surrealism as a historical idea was revived and reincarnated in John Cage. Thirty years after Russolo, Cage created the genuine confused intonations (*intona-rumori*) with his prepared piano" (Mâche 1974, 46).[17] Stockhausen's attempts to advance into the areas of the musical unconscious by means of an "intuitive music" actually grow directly out of surrealist automatic writing techniques; playing instructions for his ensemble piece *Es* (1968) call upon the musician to play only if that player has achieved the status of not thinking (Willenbrink 1985, 155). In many of her works, Pauline Oliveros has investigated music-making that emanates directly from the unconscious. Even Pierre Boulez, taking a typically rigorous approach, documents his own experiment with automatism in the writing of his epochal *Structures* of 1951–52.[18]

I've narrowed my analysis of surrealism and music to only a few musicians and composers, principally people I've performed with or have known personally. I will highlight surrealist elements in my own music and in the music of several of my peers: Davey Williams, LaDonna Smith, John Zorn, John Oswald, Mark Steven Brooks, Shelley Hirsch, Hal Freedman, and Eugene Chadbourne. Additionally, the music of Robert Ashley and Gyimah Labi, composers from previous generations, shares such indelible affinities with aspects of surrealism central to this essay that I must include it as well.[19] The fact that most of the individuals I've elected to discuss are also performers is no accident. Rather, it's a testament to one of the hallmarks of postmodern music, the dynamic breaking-down of the rigid separation of composers from performers (and vice versa). Composer/performers often have the skills and aesthetic desire to engage in improvisation. Such improvisation relates directly to my interpretation of musical automatism and can indirectly fuel collage technique.

In future writings I hope to extend my analyses to a more comprehensive investigation which would include such artists as Christian Marclay, Earl Howard, Alfred Schnittke, Frank Zappa, Captain Beefheart, Oscar Sala, The Residents, Mauricio Kagel, Ornette Coleman, György Ligeti, Micro-ritmia, Ruth Anderson, Karlheinz Stockhausen, Morton Subotnick, Giustino DeGregorio, the Nihilist Spasm Band, Luciano Berio, Pink Floyd, Diamanda Galas, and Sun Ra.[20]

The material that follows represents an inquiry into the myriad ways in which surrealism has infiltrated, invigorated, and informed a variety of music drawn from the last three decades of the twentieth century. Not only have defining elements of surrealism found their way into musics of diverse origins and backgrounds, but technological advancements, in combination with and parallel to energetic developments in non-referential improvisation, have made possible sonic environments that are more receptive to the surrealist aesthetic than ever before. Automatism translated into improvisation; collage transplanted into jump-cuts and cultural and stylistic borrowing (along with its extreme form of appropriation in plunderphonics);[21] the keynote phrase "convulsive beauty"[22] transfused into the wake-up call of the unexpected insertion; dreams and the unconscious fueled by previously unimagined transcultural dialogues; distorted visual imagery (Dali's limp, melting timepieces, for starters) finding a whole new lease on life in the audio realm of infinite possibility—these are some of the more vivid associations breaking the intermittent fast between surrealism and music.

AUTOMATISM/IMPROVISATION

Since automatism is one of the key components of surrealism, it should have a musical counterpart. One might argue that automatism *could* simply be another way of describing a composer's "inspiration." Such an argument would posit that inspiration, particularly if it finds its way onto manuscript without hesitation or subsequent revision, qualifies as an automatistic activity. Virgil Thomson, in his derisive response to Breton, whom he christened "the pope of the surrealist movement in French poetry," claimed that music has always emanated from the subconscious, and that "automatistic" processes hold nothing new for composers. After grudgingly agreeing with certain points made in Breton's essay, "Silence is Golden," he takes issue with Breton's assertion that music trails poetry in its evolution, declaring that music is in fact, in many ways, more advanced. "The right of poets to express themselves by means of spontaneous, subconsciously ordered sequences of material has seemed to many in our century a revolutionary proposition. It is, however, the normal and accepted way of writing music. . . . Most of the Surrealists' psychological devices for provoking spontaneity represent a return to Romantic musical practice. What they do not represent for the musical world is any kind of novelty. Musicians are only too delighted, I am sure, to lend them for a while to poetry, with all good wishes for their continued success" (Thomson [1944] 1967, 118). Thomson might say that Mozart's superb compositional facility and prowess, or Bach's immense genius as an improviser, are equally representative examples of musical automatism. But this assumption ignores two critical factors that would impede the exercise of pure musical automatism: the constraints of musical syntax, coupled with the requirements of style that molded the information emanating from either composer's unconscious into forms defining their respective periods. These interferences serve to slow and shape the realization of the end product. Thus, equating inspiration with automatism misses its true surrealist meaning.

Automatism, the alloy that welded the infrastructure of surrealism, has its most direct musical parallel in free improvisation. I define this as non-idiomatic improvisation embodying a unity of mind and action: musical concept and performance take place simultaneously. In accessing the unconscious by the most direct and immediate means, non-idiomatic musical improvisation[23] might elicit an even speedier transfer from the unconscious into sensory product (sound, in this case) than either visual or literary automatism.[24]

Can an investigation of abstracted thought processes activated during improvisation help to differentiate this pure, non-referential category of improvisation from the dozens of overlapping varieties of musics that incorporate improvisation to varying degrees? One attempt to address this question can be found in Roger Dean's *New Structures in Jazz and Improvised Music since 1960*. Dean cites the work of Johnson-Laird in presenting three possible types of algorithm that might underlie psychological processes during the act of improvisation. The algorithms are based on the idea that in cognitively processing musical ideas there should be no intermediate memory interpolated between the computation and generation of a sound. "On-line" computation should be minimal, leading directly to the note, or sound object, or rhythm. The first algorithm (labeled "Neo-Darwinian") most closely resembles non-idiomatic improvisation: "combine/modify existing elements arbitrarily; constraints filter out nonviable products" (Dean 1992, 202–3). The existing elements that become the musical "object" are selected arbitrarily, originating in the unconscious; filtering of non-viable products simply refers to the musician's decision-making process, at a subconscious level, and is likely bound up with technique and training (or the resistance against such). This algorithm, equally descriptive of automatic writing or drawing, forms a kind of "proof" for the application of surrealist automatism to a variety of artistic genres.

The originality of surrealist language demands an art of risk and the refusal of past accomplishments and proven techniques in favor of delving into the unknown and uncharted. "The first step—one having to be taken over and over again, Surrealists warn—is to avoid developing a style, cliches, mannerisms, and fixed forms of expression such as every Surrealist ascribes contemptuously to 'schools' of literature and art" (Matthews 1986, 9). The composers and musicians who most vividly incorporate surrealistic elements of automatism and collage in their work also demonstrate two essential requirements of surrealism: 1) the desire to investigate new territory at the expense of adhering to a personal style; 2) the avoidance of complacency and the comfort of the familiar, turning instead to expansion at the risk of occasional failure. Each artist amplifies a conception of beauty while transforming a perception of reality.

Just as the experiments with verbal automatism arose from a frustration with the inherited approaches to poetic practices, many improvisers have been propelled by their dissatisfaction with the accepted norms of musical performance. The postmodern principle of avoiding sameness, and of embracing a plurality of styles, methods, and techniques of playing music, is often part and parcel of free improvisation. Many of the musicians I discuss in this article are well acquainted with, if not defined by, improvisation. The performances and recordings of Davey Williams and LaDonna Smith exemplify the ideal of pure non-referential improvisation. And, in their duo collaborations, an axial component of most successful improvisations is ever present: the mode of listening to one another. To place the importance of their contributions to the art and philosophy of improvisation within a context, it's necessary to briefly examine where and how they fit into the parallel streams of the growth of free improvisation in America and in Europe.

In the twentieth century, prior to 1950, improvisation in Western music occurred primarily in some folk musics and in traditional jazz. Much of the composed music from the first half of the twentieth century was more complex than the predictable recycling of harmonic patterns in jazz over a set number of bars. However, during the 1950s the rhythm sections in jazz ensembles were either enlarged or subverted, expanding the role of improvisation. By around 1960, a collective, improvised performance could reach a level of complexity comparable to the composed serial compositions of the previous decades.

In America, the modernist origins of free jazz are commonly considered to reside primarily in the music of John Coltrane, Eric Dolphy, Sun Ra, Miles Davis, Ornette Coleman, and Cecil Taylor.[25] However, Joe Harriot and Shake Keane, two musicians with strong ties to West Indian music, residing in Great Britain and active in the 1950s, should also be counted among the first to explore free improvisation. Many of these artists, essentially the generation coming after the pioneers of bebop, embody postmodern tendencies as well, such as the melding of classical compositional techniques in the music of Davis, Coleman, and Dolphy.[26]

Although free improvisation began to develop in the late 1950s and 1960s almost concurrently among musicians with backgrounds in both jazz and composed music in the United States, Europe, the United Kingdom, Japan, Australia, and Russia, the different ways in which it evolved (especially in Europe and the United States) are striking. With the exception of maverick composer-improviser Anthony Braxton, the Americans maintained closer relationships with conventions associated with traditional jazz (such as repetitive harmonic structures and fixed rhythmic pulses), while "free jazz" in Europe tended to demolish anything smacking of the formulaic. In the liner notes to a 1970 LP recorded with Derek Bailey and Han Bennink, the British saxophonist Evan Parker remarks: "We operate without rules (pre-composed material) or well-defined codes of behavior (fixed tempi, tonalities, serial structures, etc.) and yet are able to distinguish success from failure." He goes on to refer to "rules of play" that could apply to their music, including, "You shall investigate the unfamiliar until it has become familiar."[27] What could be more empathetic with the vision of surrealism?

The abandonment of clichéd conventions in American jazz in the 1960s was more gradual, less radical than in the European free jazz movement. In the former, chord progressions were treated more flexibly or simply discarded; preconceived harmonic structures gave way to a linear, motivic kind of improvisation which could generate its own harmony; and pulses were arranged in non-metered groupings. Change was the word on both sides of the Atlantic, and a surrealist-style purging of the traditional jazz stables was under way.

One of the very earliest forays into textural improvising devoid of motivic direction can be heard on Coltrane's *Ascension*, recorded in 1965. As timbre supersedes single notes or rhythms, dense group textures consume individual instruments. In the following year, two recordings were made in Europe where density, also paramount, *results* from mass motivic direction: *Litany for the 14th June 1966*, by the Dutch composer Willem Breuker and *Globe Unity* by the German Alexander von Schlippenbach. Each of these recordings breaks away from all traditions of improvised music prior to 1960, launching an altogether independent European improvising movement. These two works also mark the beginnings of composer-controlled free improvisation.[28]

American musicians with classical music backgrounds, such as Pauline Oliveros, Richard Teitelbaum, and Lukas Foss's Improvisers Chamber Ensemble (formed in 1957!), were forging new directions with improvisation in the early 1960s. Improvising groups such as the New Music Ensemble (U.S.), Musica Elettronica Viva (Americans in Rome, including Teitelbaum) and AMM (England) began to embrace the realm of electronic music—though several years later than Sun Ra, who had performed with electronics in his Arkestra since the 1950s.

The exploratory nature of improvisation led not only to electronic enhancements, but also to extended instrumental techniques. John Coltrane spearheaded the timbral expansions of the saxophone with both controlled and purposely fractured multiphonics. Harmonic complexities in the music of Cecil Taylor evolved from the late 1950s into the cluster-studded galaxies of sound he came to generate from the piano. The superhuman circular breathing of Evan Parker, the sung and played multiphonics of Vinko Globokar, and related techniques such as microtonal playing, control of sustained simultaneous layers of tones or of multiphonics, and rhythmic innovations, colored the playing of many musicians in the 1960s and 1970s, up through the present.[29]

In the last decade of the twentieth century, a transcultural explosion among improvisers has blurred distinctions that may have been based on ethnicity or race. Derek Bailey, in his book, *Improvisation*, claims that free improvisation resists labeling due to its most consistent characteristic: diversity. However, he goes on to qualify this diversity as resulting from a lack of stylistic or idiomatic commitment, a neutrality intrinsic to free improvisation that is primarily defined by the *sonic* identity of the players involved. Bailey's position, admittedly purist, hooks up beautifully with automatism. Bailey decries "a certain sound which is produced by a saxophone player when his soul is being stirred, which to me freezes the balls, it stops everything in its tracks" (Corbett 1994, 234–35). The "non-viable products" of the previously stated algorithm could, in Bailey's case, represent just this sort of overhumanized, associative sound that he so vehemently rejects.

Free improvisation, for me, has always been a journey into the unknown, a tool for unearthing profound discoveries, and a method for generating complex structures—which can contain referential as well as non-referential sounds and phrases. Although I'm not a "purist," and sometimes have conflicting feelings about improvisation, I've found ways to reconcile composition and improvisation. Musicians who have spent years exploring methods of combining these two ways of music-making sometimes grow ambivalent toward improvisation. For instance, Anthony Braxton equates total improvisation with existential anarchy, implying that he believes *some* structure is necessary to generate the kind of forward motion responsible for any musical evolution (Lock 1988, 236–37). Anthony Davis articulates a similar position in the liner notes to *Episteme* (1981): "I have turned more and more toward precise musical notation to insure that the improviser is consciously and physically tuned in to the overall structure of a piece. On first glance this approach would seem to inhibit the improviser. This is a valid criticism, but I believe that this inhibition is now a real necessity when one perceives that 'free' or 'open' improvisation has become a cliché, a musical dead end." Although I believe that we've attempted to solve similar problems, I can't agree with Davis's conclusion. My philosophy is more attuned to that of Lukas Foss, who writes some twenty years earlier, on the record sleeve to *Time Cycle*, that in "Composition all becomes fate, in Improvisation there remains chance and hazard, which can be corrected by the will (of the improvisors)."[30]

AUTOMATISM IN POSTMODERN MUSIC

Davey Williams and LaDonna Smith, proponents of free improvisation who make their homes in Birmingham, Alabama, have managed to carve out a lively scene for improvisation in a generally inhospitable environment. They've also extensively documented their art as improvisers, in a series of recordings as well as in the journal they cofounded, *the improvisor*. How did they arrive at this point?

We share a common background, having all been involved in the hotbed of creative energy lurking in the crevices of Tuscaloosa, Alabama, during the early 1970s. This groundswell of alternative activity arose from an extraordinary mix of diverse artists and musicians influenced by pataphysics, dada, surrealism, and psychedelic rock. As part of an entire generation experimenting with altered states of consciousness in the late 1960s and early '70s, this group of Tuscaloosa residents used surrealist principles as a basis for improvisational experiment. According to Craig Nutt, one of the chief instigators and documentarians for much of this activity, "The Pataphysical [Musical] Revue, like the Raudelunas [Art] Exposition it opened, was in a sense a showcase of the whole gamut of what was going on in our community at that time" (Nutt 1999).

A vinyl LP recording of the proceedings of the *Raudelunas Pataphysical Revue* was issued on the Say Day-Bew label in 1975, principally for the local audience.[31] This motley collection of covers of standards ("Volare"; "My Kind of Town"; "Chicago"), featuring the Rev. Fred Lane, [32] was sprinkled with Lane's demented monologues and ironic twists— take-offs on bits of stereotypical Master of Ceremony drivel. Responding to an inquiry from me concerning surrealist influences on this recording, Nutt replied: "The big band tunes walk the line between Dada Dixieland and Surreal Swing." Nutt goes on to claim that the stand-up comedy captured on the recording anticipates the work of the late comedian Andy Kaufman. In addition to Lane's send-ups of covers, and the jokes, "serious"music was an equal participant in the *Revue*. It provided the occasion for the premiere of my first collage composition, "Concerto for Active Frogs." This piece uses call-and-response techniques, organized on a graphic score, to bring human musicians together with frog and toad vocalizations. In a collective work, *Captains of Industry*, the entire company of musicians played appliances, televisions, and shavers on stage. Despite an environment entirely uncomprehending of our art forms and indifferent to our experiments, we put on an unforgettable show, arming ourselves with canned applause aimed back at the largely baffled audience.

The Raudelunas recording went through two pressings, and in 1998 was identified in *The Wire* as one of the "100 Records that Set the World On Fire . . . *While No One Was Listening*,"[33] Some choice comments conclude Ed Baxter's review: "No other record has ever come as close to realising Alfred Jarry's desire 'to make the soul monstrous'—or even had the vision or invention to try. It's all over the place. The sleevenotes describe it as 'the best thing ever'—time has not damaged this audacious claim" (Baxter 1998, 35–36).

Some of the musicians involved in the *Pataphysical Revue* met on a weekly basis, stretching the limitations of their instruments and exploring the dynamics of group improvisation.[34] Our collective awareness of the first-generation European improvisers, thanks to the recordings produced by Incus and FMP, was crucial for our morale, as there was *no* audience to speak of for this kind of music at that point time in an Alabama university town obsessed with football and fraternities. The knowledge that kindred spirits across the ocean were making music in a similar vein was immensely empowering.[35] Did we associate the automatism of the surrealist movement with improvisation when we began to pursue this avenue of music-making? Not right away, but we were all avid admirers of surrealist art and writing, and gradually came to comprehend the obvious parallel.

The spirit of free improvisation, I believe, aligns itself squarely with the democratic aesthetic of the surrealists. Breton never retracted his assertion,

"Surrealism is within the compass of *every* unconscious" (my italics), and repeatedly declared that the realm of the surreal was open to anyone.[36] The recording *Dinosaur Time*, also on the Say Day-Bew label, provides a cogent illustration of this ultra-postmodern philosophy of inclusion. Craig Nutt and Nolan Hatcher, neither of whom had learned to play keyboards,[37] were the sole artists on this album of keyboard duets. Not content to limit themselves to two Steinway pianos, they also performed on esoteric reproductions of keyboards, including a seventeenth-century Flemish harpsichord and a triple-fretted clavichord.

The artistic underground in Tuscaloosa in the 1960s and 1970s has yet to be documented and remains ripe for an extensive critical examination. However, this brief portrait sets the stage for the milieu in which Davey Williams and LaDonna Smith hooked up with one another, initiating an intensive development of their unique musical signatures.

Davey Williams, in his recordings and live performances, has created an unparalleled, and much imitated, sonic world bursting with visceral imagery and ironic commentary on the entire history of guitar playing. Williams's extremely personal style was forged by his participation in blues bands led by Johnny Shines. For several years in the late 1960s and intermittently throughout the 1970s, Williams performed with Shines and company in an assortment of juke joints and dives all over the rural and urban South. His fractured playing, studded with the enormously rich vocabulary of the blues, exudes an ever-shifting patina of irony, comedy, and ironic solemnity. His guitar, like a magician's hat, spits out fragmented folk tunes that he instantaneously warps into wry commentary, such as the subversive duet with LaDonna Smith, "Biscuits Mystic Birdhouse Blues" on their duo CD, *Transmutating*.

The fact that Williams also writes (fiction, poetry, criticism) and paints surreal scenes (usually in oil—see the cover to *Charmed, I'm Sure*: a monstrous baseball glove hovers over a sailor and his lover embracing in mid-air), shades and shapes his music in ways that are absolutely unique. His performances are visually compelling, pierced by startling, quicksilver changes. As early as 1970, he was summoning sounds from his guitar with eggbeaters, eventually adding tape measures, electric motors, and all manner of other toys and obscure mechanical gizmos.[38] In playing his electric guitar *with* mechanized or electronic gadgets, he creates a discrete and highly personal universe of original timbral objects. On "Baby's First Words," the last cut on his latest solo recording, *Charmed, I'm Sure*, a standard slide guitar riff over a gently throbbing bass, all very minimal, gives way to the commentary elicited from the guitar by playing it with a cordless drink mixer. It's simultaneously hilarious and unsettling. The "normal" guitar eventually drops out, leaving the rough semi-pitched drink mixer/guitar to be rudely cut off by a cuckoo clock striking nine o'clock. On track 2 of this same recording, he single-handedly conjures a train streaking through the Southern darkness, with ominous overtones, yet drenched in that "convulsive beauty" so central to surrealist aesthetics. "Our Little Sawmill," a superb example of one of Williams's signature sound worlds, seamlessly intertwines exterior mechanical noises with guitar playing to produce striking timbral similarities between the guitar and the saw, each acquiring a distinct personality in the course of the piece.[39]

Williams shatters his vast blues vocabulary into sound objects. Integrating these referential segments into his more abstracted musical language, he sometimes gravitates toward collage forms, found in some selections on *Charmed, I'm Sure*. For example, "New Boots," for bass and two electric guitars, weaves three simultaneous planes of generic fragments from blues (slides, for instance) and rock guitar into an arhythmic fractured collage. The deconstructing of the foundation of the almighty "beat" exposes techniques indigenous to highly identifiable musics (especially, in this case, the blues) but removes the beat/body element, so that the piece seems to float in hyper-space. Williams achieves a similar effect on "The Nomads," for bass, two electric guitars, and toaster oven. By layering three distinct lines—a virtuosic, perpetual-motion figure, a lyrical foreground, and a bass that projects the persona of a sawmill as well as a bass, all punctuated with the toaster-oven as dysfunctional drum machine—Williams refers, albeit obliquely, to the stereotypical ways that guitars tend to be played. Williams's uncanny and exquisite sense of timing, a testament to the potency and generosity of his gift, confers a sense of twisted suspense to his performances. Witnessing his performances, one can truly observe the lightening-quick gestures of an abstracted musical automatism.

LaDonna Smith, violist and vocalist, has collaborated with Davey Williams in their duo, TransMuseq, for more than twenty years, with hundreds of performances principally in Europe and the United States.[40] Also a visual artist, she has created an extensive body of surrealist-inspired sculpture.[41] A propelling force behind the explosion of free improvisation erupting from time to time in Birmingham, Alabama, Smith has devoted a vast amount of time and energy to the journal she cofounded with Williams, *the improvisor*—the only international periodical devoted to improvisation.

In contrast to Williams, Smith was trained as a classical musician and composer. Her playing is somewhat more abstract, less referential. However, her raw energy has a visceral, animalistic quality that keeps her music from ever sounding studied. Her performances are models for sheer stream-of-consciousness playing techniques. The relationship of her instrument to her singing enhances the effect of this "streaming": the viola morphs into a natural extension of her voice.[42]

Smith's playing displays a fiery, freewheeling power. Several pieces from her solo recording, *Eye of the Storm*, illustrate her sleight-of-voice technique: she knits her vocalizations into sounds coaxed from her viola so seamlessly that it's often impossible to know where the voice enters and exits, and even whether it's real or imagined. In "Fire in the Old Growth," she draws strands of harmonics, combination tones, and sub-harmonics out of her viola, weaving them into polyphonies enhanced with and at times triggered by her voice. "Viola Coaster Rainbows" lurches into a wild, vertiginous, swooping ride with shards of vocal pyrotechnics spinning out from rapidly skittering bow work, a totally mad excursion. Smith makes Laurie Anderson sound like a Lawrence Welk act.

Her aggressive, multi-layered playing style results in an astonishing variety of textures that could never be precisely notated, such as the low register peregrinations in "Flash Flood in Downtown Decatur." "Traveling Nimbocumulous" hurdles along with hardly a pause, an amazingly boun-tiful cornucopia of harmonics that are at times inflected to sound eerily like Korean zither music. Smith even reinvents the "drone" composition in "Oceanic Sleep," with its intermittent open C string cushioning a host of progeny. The harmonics, all gyrating out of one primal sound, are so active and multi-linear that it's difficult to believe one person is playing the music.

Williams and Smith have been outspoken in print and in public about the potential inherent in everyone for musical improvisation.[43] Smith chal-lenges trained musicians to "let go of convention and come back to inven-tion." She speaks eloquently for the acceptance of any sound: "All sounds: pure and clean, fuzzed, split and dirty, thick, thin, high, low, loud, soft, free, fat, limited, or loaded belong to the larynx of the soul and the mind's rational counterpart, the imagination" (Smith 1996, 8).

The intense interaction and musical rapport between Smith and Williams are legendary. They claim to communicate telepathically when performing in duo, and it's difficult to harbor any skepticism after witness-ing their joint performances.[44] On their latest duo recording, *Transmutating*, the first and longest piece moves toward a haunting lyricism between low voice and guitar, suddenly veering into screeching voice/viola accompanied by sparse subterranean guitar plunks from the opposite extreme of the registral spectrum. The two instruments merge, swapping positions, and Smith's voice yaps out a parodic imitation of the guitar figuration, sending it up to stratospheric, theremin-like heights. When an exposed circular series of gradually accelerating upward glissando-slides, played by solo gui-tar, culminates in an aggressive and maniacally repetitive texture, the viola re-enters, claiming its own territory, and the piece ends with a multi-hued texture-dialogue. The music-making of Williams and Smith exemplifies the value of automatism in seizing fire and desire, as articulated by Breton: "Automatism has always guaranteed and amplified passion."

Smith and Williams frequently collaborate with other musicians, as well as with dancers and in theatrical environments. *Jewels*, the third recording on the *trans museq* label, was the first recording to feature free improvisa-tion performed on the harp. The instruments played on this recording

(LeBaron: harp, metal rack, gong; Smith: piano, piano harp, viola; Williams: acoustic and electric guitars, mandolin) create a three-way mimesis, resulting in surrealist-derived constellations of *trompe l'oreille* sound objects.

Musicians with jazz, rock, or new music backgrounds have been drawn to free improvisation not only as a mechanism for discovery, but as an exercise to assist in the shedding of learned musical behavior. Free improvisation in large groups can be an exhilarating experience for both performing and listening participants. However, these larger groups often benefit from an imposed structure or direction. Initiating a group improvisation with a verbal or visual image, thereby triggering the collective illumination of the image, is one of the more open-ended and "suggestive" methods of direction. Fred Frith, for instance, in the liner notes to his recording *Stone, Brick, Glass, Wood, Wire*, describes scenarios proposed to a group of unemployed rock musicians in Marseille with whom he was creating an opera. For example, "The music we've been working on is a mirror, the mirror has been smashed into tiny pieces, you have to try and put it back together." The musicians would then accompany these images as though they were creating a film soundtrack. Frith remarks, "The results we achieved from this modest information were amazing, especially compared to what happened when we just tried to play free!"

One of the more intentional explorations of automatism in music exists in a 1979 composition by Robert Ashley, "Automatic Writing."[45] Ashley's fascination with involuntary speech at the time was fueled by his own mild form of Tourette's syndrome. Preoccupied with a quality of "fourness," the four "characters", as Ashley describes them, are forty-six minutes of his own voice caught in automatic speech, another voice providing a French translation of his voice, Moog synthesizer articulations, and background organ harmonies—all as unplanned and uncontrolled as the involuntary speaking itself (see CD liner notes). The resulting intimate, magnetizing texture of simultaneities, although far more static than the automatic "performing" of Smith or Williams, has a distinct charm. Ashley manages to maintain an impersonal distance while simultaneously giving an impression of confiding in the listener, generating an intensely personal environment that the surrealists would likely have immediately embraced.

Other forms of direction in improvisation include graphic scores, games, and invented notational and conducting symbols—such as Lawrence D. "Butch" Morris and his "conduction" method, or John Zorn's game plans used in *Cobra* and its relatives. These techniques begin to move toward the realm of collage forms.

THE EXQUISITE CORPSE

The surrealists were fascinated with collective games, engaging in them for entertainment as well as exploration.[46] One of the most publicized surrealist activities, the parlor game commonly referred to as Exquisite Corpse, involved the intersection of chance with automatic writing.[47] Originating in the home of Marcel Duhamel in 1925, the rules of the game, initially performed with writing, were: 1) write a word or phrase on a piece of paper; 2) fold it so that the writing couldn't be seen; 3) pass it around in this manner until a sentence was completed. A prescribed and carefully followed grammatical structure provided a consistent framework. The first sentence considered worthy of retention was "Le cadavre exquis boira le vin nouveau" ("The exquisite corpse will drink the new wine")—each of five players contributing one of the principal words involved. Hence, the birth of the game Exquisite Corpse.

Breton defended the value of the game, admitting, however, that it was initially a source of entertainment: "If there is one activity in Surrealism which has most invited the derision of imbeciles, it is our playing of games. . . . Although as a defensive measure we sometimes described such activity as "experimental" we were looking to it primarily for entertainment, and those rewarding discoveries it yielded in relation to knowledge only came later" (Breton [1954]1993, 157).[48] Many of these "discoveries" emerged from the visual variant of the game. Instead of a sentence, participants would draw a figure, leaving only the ends of some lines showing to insure continuity. The unexpected results were amusing, disturbing, revealing, and have been compared to the art of madmen and of children. The resulting collage form representing the Exquisite Corpse, born of a collective spirit, has proved to be remarkably enduring.[49]

The trust in the power of the group to blindly fuse fragmentation into a whole (sentence or drawing) reflects a facet of postmodernism embedded in the surrealist sensibility, even though surrealism, as a movement, is far more frequently associated with modernism. Yet another aspect of postmodernism embodied by the surrealists is their democratic attitude toward creating art. In the exhibition catalog for the Nesuhi Ertegun and Daniel Filipacchi collections of surrealist art, shown at the Guggenheim Museum in 1999, José Pierre remarks that the most inventive examples of Exquisite Corpse were not always those created by the most accomplished artists, but were instead produced by the poets Breton, Eluard, and Tzara in collaboration with their wives and mistresses (Pierre 1999b). As we've seen in the prior discussion of automatism in music, Smith and Williams also espouse a philosophy of inclusiveness.

Musical parallels to Exquisite Corpse are problematic, due to the simultaneous dimensions of time and space that it inhabits. In the same year that the Corpse was born, two Belgian surrealists attempted to transfer automatic writing into the musical medium. Modeled on surrealist procedures of collective creation, Paul Hooreman and André Souris wrote *Tombeau de Socrate*, a "monodie in the form of a mazurka" published in the magazine *Musique I* in 1925, to commemorate the death of Erik Satie (Willenbrink 1985, 154). A simple mazurka-like statement with no barlines, it does not begin to convey the abrupt shifts and fantastical associations so prevalent among the Exquisite Corpse–derived works of surrealist art and literature. The syntax of music was not yet expanded sufficiently enough to allow for transmission of the very factors that were so intrinsically identified with the Corpse.

Moving closer to the spirit of disruption, the American composers John Cage, Lou Harrison, Henry Cowell, and Virgil Thomson, all mutual friends, took part in the creation of "sonorous corpses" around the middle of the 1940s. Lou Harrison, in the preface to the collaborative score, *Party Pieces*,[50] explains their procedures, directly derived from the surrealist game. "Each composer present would write a measure, fold the paper at the bar-line and, on the new fresh sheet, put only two notes to guide the next composer in his connection. The next composer would write a bar, fold at the barline and leave two more black spots and so on. It seems to me that we would begin simultaneously and pass them along in rotation in a sort of surrealist assembly line and eagerly await the often incredible outcome." The twenty published pieces display varying degrees of abrupt shifts in motivic and tonal consistency, while projecting a lighthearted, irresistible charm.[51]

Although each participant remained largely unaware of the previous contribution, the end results still seem tame compared to the startling images of the surrealist-produced Exquisite Corpse poetry and drawings. Fast forward some forty years later and the composer John Zorn is briskly capturing the lively spirit of the Corpse, and of postmodernism in music, with the sheer exuberance and stunning collisions that characterize one of his game pieces for improvising musicians, *Cobra*.[52] A self-professed "new Romantic," opposed to neutrality and cold calculation, Zorn describes *Cobra* as a "psychodrama where everybody's personality comes out in very exaggerated ways" (Gagne 1993, 515). A system based on rules, as opposed to a composition, *Cobra* generates a smorgasbord of references run amok, ranging from a shameless appropriation of genres (blues, country, jazz, rock, ambient, traditional Asian/generic pentatonic), to film noir soundtrack stereotypes, warped allusions to Beethoven's Fifth, clucking chickens and ringing phones, fragments of unidentifiable noise, phrases from "Fly Me to the Moon," and on and on. Thick textures of simultaneities alternate with transparent soloistic episodes; random noise improvisations bump up against quotes from Mozart's Concerto for Flute and Harp. The disjunct sonic images that flow from one into another like schizoid dreams simulate the Exquisite Corpse's fondness for unrelated images, and generate those ephemeral yet powerful frictional sparks so coveted by the surrealists.

For the surrealists, the greater the jolt, the greater the value of the image. As André Masson observed in *Le Cadavre exquis: son exaltation*, the important thing for the surrealists engaged in the game of Exquisite Corpse was the "arrival of the surprising image" (Breton 1975, 28)—the consequence of a *group* interaction. Likewise, in Zorn's *Cobra*, the rate of change, the "harmonic rhythm" of the sound blocks, depends upon the complex interplay among a community of musicians who are adept improvisers. Devoid of musical notation, *Cobra*'s structure relies instead upon rules that provide a "linguistic" framework.[53] The unfettered individual contributions must still function within Zorn's strict system of rules, an oxymoronic proposition delivering an organized spontaneity that paradoxically does not sound controlled. By capitalizing upon the unique skills of the chosen performers, who operate at full tilt with the support of a quasi-structured environment, Zorn's *Cobra* advances notions of aleatoric composition into uncharted territory.

The collective, playful, and all-embracing nature of *Cobra* (and of the *cadavre exquis*) opposes modernist principles of singularity, reductiveness, and rigid constraints, and is thus symbolic of a musical postmodernism. In the exhibition catalog, *The Return of the Cadavre Exquis*, Ingrid Schaffner's metaphor, related to consumerism, aligns the Exquisite Corpse with an expansion of modernism's closed systems: "the *cadavre exquis*, surrealism's abject offspring, is a visual department store disgorged of its goods, an assembly line of absurd—at times, sublime—expressions." One could just as easily describe *Cobra* as an "audible department store disgorged of its goods," and, to borrow yet another phrase from Schaffner's discussion of the historic Exquisite Corpses, equally pertinent, "These works exist as uninterpreted records, novel apparitions of *point sublime*, that spot on the distant horizon where everything—rational and irrational, conscious and unconscious, abstract and concrete—converge" (Schaffner 1993, 43).

Although the musicians playing *Cobra* can hear one another in the flow of time (as opposed to the surrealists, from whom fragments of Exquisite Corpse words or drawings were concealed, or the *Party Pieces* composers, who also played the game "blindfolded"), the end result is the same: a collage, assembled in real time. In 1935, one group of surrealists went so far as to introduce a variant, a kind of collage on collage, by making "*cadavres* out of corpses of by-gone publicity until our supply of old magazines was reduced to shreds" (Jean [1983] 1993, 74). This recycling of old material, pruning it and then repotting it in unfamiliar soil, finds its musical twin in the radical technique of plunderphonics.

COLLAGE

Plunderphonics, a form of self-referential audio collage, has been around for some fifty years. The word itself, however, was only recently introduced by one of its foremost practitioners, John Oswald. "Plunderphonics is a term I've coined to cover the counter-covert world of converted sound and retrofitted music, where collective melodic memories of the familiar are minced and rehabilitated to a new life." Oswald elaborates further, "A 'plunderphone' is an unofficial but recognizable musical quote" (Oswald 1995, 89).[54]

When Max Ernst turned to collage as the underlying principle of his art, he inaugurated a new chapter in art history: his own art became unabashedly dependent on previously existing depictions of art, from which he fashioned his fantastic collage-novels. Similarly, Oswald relies on recorded music for his elaborately constructed plunderings. One major difference looms over this Ernst/Oswald analogy: Ernst's collages were constructed from informative matter that wasn't copyrighted and that generally possessed no independent aesthetic value, whereas Oswald deliberately selects portions of audio recordings that have already acquired aesthetic and/or monetary value. Yet, Oswald is hardly beholden to the baggage of values attached to his "found" sound objects. Obviously, he can ignore their origins and treat his found objects as independent chunks of sound. Or, as Chris Cutler recognized in his perceptive article on the subject of plunderphonics, a plundered object can also be exploited. "As a pirated cultural artifact, a found object, as debris from the sonic environment, a plundered sound also holds out an invitation to be used *because* of its cause, and because of all the associations and cultural apparatus that surround it" (Cutler 1995, 74). Cutler goes on to compare "captured" visual images of artists such as Warhol and Rauschenberg, or directly imported objects such as the "Readymades" of Duchamp, with the potential for an analogous lassoing of sound images.

The far more common, and accepted, practice of plundering among visual artists hasn't escaped Oswald's attention. "It's somewhat ironic that in visual arts, there's been all sorts of appropriation issues and dialogues going on for a long time. There's people who do much more extreme things than I do, like take a photograph of a photograph and put their name on it and say 'This is my art.' This sort of transformation is old hat, like Marcel Duchamp painting a moustache on the Mona Lisa" (quoted in Jones 1995, 133).

Plunderphonics may be one of the most complex challenges yet to notions of individuality and ownership. By drawing exclusively upon material created by another individual, the practice itself demands a re-examination and re-evaluation of our understanding of property rights and of originality itself. As practiced by Oswald and others, plunderphonics is totally dependent upon recording technology. As technological developments in the audio field have become more sophisticated, especially with the movement away from analog techniques and into the digital realm, plundering techniques have likewise become increasingly widespread, more refined, and have elicited greater controversy. Cutler makes the salient point that plundered sound, with its unique ability to simultaneously *refer* and to *be*, "offers not just a new means but a new meaning. It is this dual character that confuses the debates about originality which so vex it" (Cutler 1995, 74).

In his fascinating historical synopsis of the use of the gramophone as an instrument, Cutler points out a 1920 dada event where Stefan Wolpe used eight gramophones to simultaneously play recordings at differing speeds. He cites plundering precedents by Schaeffer, Cage, the Beatles, Zappa, the Residents, and Christian Marclay, among others. A brief account of pop applications of plundering emphasizes hip-hop, house, and techno music (some DJ techniques, in fact, are physically reminiscent of frottage). Cutler also addresses the sticky issue of copyright, including salient facts regarding Oswald's *Plunderphonics* recording, and summarizes plundering and its far-reaching tentacles into the five following types of applications.

(1) *There it is*: materials randomly derived from records or radio are manipulated (as in Cage's "Imaginary Landscapes 2 and 4").

(2) *Partial importations*: recordings are built around ethnic music, animal vocalizations, sound effects.

(3) *Total importation*: existing recordings become the simultaneous subject and object of a creative work, raising the issue of originality in the re-contextualisation of existing recordings.

(4) *Sources irrelevant*: sampling of generic 'sounds,' where no self-reflexivity is involved and recognition of plundered parts isn't important.

(5) *Sources untraceable*: plundered sounds are so altered that their sources cannot be ascertained. (Cutler 1995, 67–85)

John Oswald carried the cut and paste technique of collage to its outer limits, shredding and realigning pre-existing materials to form distinctive portraitures of a band, of a pop song and its singer, and of an entire cross-section of pop and rock tunes from the decade spanning 1982–1992. The following three examples illustrate these plunder approaches. The cut and paste method prevails, paralleling montage, the more time-oriented form of collage. "Z," Oswald's plunderphonicized version of Naked City (a band led by John Zorn), represents an extreme form of plunderphonics: in fourteen seconds, he rips through 47 edits of 35 sound slices, each between 1/20 and 1 second long. With his choices of fragments and their ordering, Oswald not only captures the breathless, manic energy of the band, but also invokes a kind of sonic fingerprint that encapsulates the essence of Naked City.

Oswald takes his method of sonic portraiture to the next level with "DAB," from the CD "Plunderphonics."[55] In "Creatigality," his article published in *Sounding Off!* Oswald asserts that transformation can be revitalizing. Indeed, by distilling Michael Jackson's hit "Bad" into a brilliant series of fragments redolent of the song's very marrow, highlighting its iconic markers—syllables and words, falsetto whoops, breathy punctuations, percussive instrumentation, syncopation, and so on—Oswald plays hide and seek with the range of perceptibility and recognition. His skillful surgery proceeds quite naturally into an abstract non-referential sonic realm, as though he were exploring the song's most intimate physical components. This pseudo-revelation of the very atomic structure of a song, exposing its "DNA", was initiated by James Tenney in his classic 1961 realization, "Collage #1 (Blue Suede)", based on Elvis Presley's version of "Blue Suede Shoes."

Just as Oswald's "DAB" evokes Michael Jackson's singing (and, by association, his dancing) in "Bad," Tenney's "Collage #1," with far more limited technical means, opaquely resuscitates Elvis's rendition of "Blue Suede Shoes." Although thirty-two years of aesthetic and technological developments separate these two plunderings, they are each marked, unmistakably, by their source material (Presley and Jackson) as filtered through their re-creators (Tenney and Oswald). In "Collage #1," the identity of the source song, and Elvis himself, remain a mystery until one minute and seventeen seconds into the piece, when the distinct timbre of Presley's voice breaks through the more amorphous sonic material (also formed from "Blue Suede Shoes"). For the remainder of the piece, snippets of phrases such as 'step in my' flutter in and out of the foreground, and are colored by portions of the song that have been processed beyond recognition. Oswald's "DAB", nearly twice as long (seven minutes), also begins without a clue as to its origins, but not for long. At thirteen seconds into the piece, a close listening reveals the repetitive phrase "who's bad." Present as a wordless rhythm only (although a "wh" sound, extracted from the word "who's," triggers the repeating motif), it quickly leads to more readily recognizable repetitions of the word "bad" over a rhythm track and bass line. The technology available to Oswald, as well as the more pronounced syncopation in Jackson's "Bad," contribute to the visceral rhythmic sensibility of "DAB". Interestingly, Oswald chooses to devote the latter half of his rendering to a total deconstruction of the original song, removing all obvious references or radically transforming them, whereas Tenney employed a similar process during the first half of "Collage #1."

What happens when vast collections of different songs are chopped into tiny fragments that contaminate and hybridize one another? Oswald assembles a relentless barrage of such snippets on his CD *Plexure*,[56] featuring dozens of composite artists such as Moody Crue, John Lennoncamp, Sinead O'Connick Jr., They Might Be Grateful, 9 Inch Monkees, Spinal Top—well, you get the idea.[57] This time, whole chunks of boiled-down stereotypical pop images fly out of the speakers, and the result is frequently hilarious as well as illuminating.

The idea for *Plexure* had its origins in Oswald's fascination with perceptual boundaries. And the notion of perceptual limits is bound up with one of the central issues raised by plundering: "At what point does a sound claim ownership" (Jones 1995, 132). This raises yet another point: At what point does a fragment lose its recognizability? Surprisingly, Oswald claims that he can recognize a sliver measuring twenty milliseconds (one-fiftieth of a second), provided that he's already familiar with the piece to which it belongs. In *Plexure*, he primarily works with durations of one-third of a second, but sometimes goes beyond the threshold of recognition with events that are five milliseconds long. Oswald has the seasoned improviser's unerring instinct for fitting together thousands of puzzle pieces in his assemblages for *Plexure*. According to his illuminating article, "Plunderstanding Ecophonomics," he relied upon tempo as the principal organizing device in *Plexure*: "We could measure tempo as an absolute rational value which we could apply to all the pieces" (Oswald 2000, 15).

In the liner notes for *Plexure*, a few visual guideposts are provided for the listener. For instance, an attempt is made to transcribe the fractured lyrics. "I've been, I have weight, I wait, have I half have been, I help hap hip wait, bin wading waiting, way been, whew, for you," reams that little phrase for all it's worth, and, by so doing, reinvigorates a banality.

But how, exactly, can the cutting up of a previously recognizable element serve to rejuvenate it? Derrida, in distinguishing post-critical collage from conventional collage, provides one explanation: "a calculated insemination of the proliferating allogene through which the two texts are transformed, deform each other, contaminate each other's content, tend at times to reject each other, or pass elliptically one into the other and become regenerated in the repetition. . . . Each grafted text continues to radiate back toward the site of its removal, transforming that, too, as it affects the new territory" (cited in Ulmer 1983, 90). Derrida's description can be applied to Oswald's pieces on the *Plexure* recording as long as their elements (sources) can be identified. At the end of the recording, identification becomes a moot exercise as the progressively shortened clips create an effect similar to the closing fusillade of a fireworks display, when explosions come so fast and furiously that they overlap spectacularly in space and time.

As a polemical instrument, Oswald's wielding of plunderphonics to challenge current assumptions regarding proprietary rights constitutes a courageous stance, befitting a pioneer of the genre. Differentiating the blatant appropriation of sound fragments from related techniques of wholesale sampling, of imitation, parody, or allusion, and even of outright theft—that is, Stravinsky's "good composer [who] does not imitate, [but] steals"—Oswald has carved out a legitimate, vital, and inevitable subgenre, linked to the centuries-old practice of creative borrowing among composers. By limiting himself to material of a consistent nature, or to a period from cultural history, Oswald fashions a "complex mnemonic concordance to a decade of number ones with a bullet that skips across the radio waves like a K-Tel album gone insane, channel surfing with a toddler's sense of wonder and an architect's sense of structure" (Jones 1995, 139). *Plexure*, the most ambitious and longest of the three examples cited, sacrifices an articulate syntax for sheer power, a relentless bombardment reminiscent of Phil Spector's grand "wall of sound." "DAB," however, confined to a singular mining site, reflects an original formal structure riddled with multiple levels of signification.

The surrealists frequently imported ordinary ready-made fragments into previously unrelated contexts in their collages. In one of his first texts published on visual art (linked to Ernst's first show in Paris, in 1921), Breton declared that, since human effort could produce nothing new, artists must limit themselves to reapplications of existing materials. A typically dogmatic stance, yet visionary, and confirmed nearly eighty years later by a leading analyst of surrealist collage: "Collage and assemblage, manipulating already existing signs, are a privileged mode of creating the surreal" (Adamowicz 1998, 11). Both writers make their observations within the context of visual art, but they could just as well be referring to the unconventional deployment of familiar music or sounds as raw material. Photography and film, in providing the means for previously unimagined transformations of pre-existing visual (and sonic) elements, parallel the introduction of possibilities for similar transformations in the audio sphere, due to developments in recording technology.

Strategies of selection and combination of the pre-formed elements are paramount to the successful effect of any collage, whether verbal, pictorial, or musical. In my own Concerto for Active Frogs, natural vocalizations of frogs and toads were carefully selected and ordered to achieve maximum theatrical effect. The resulting tapestry of sounds inhabiting the tape collage inspires amphibian-like responses from the human vocalists and instrumentalists, while also strongly influencing the dramatic rhythm.

Electroacoustic music offers a wealth of examples echoing surrealist collage aesthetics. Here, I focus on a single example in which the composer uses signifying units to fashion a sound portrait—or, more to the point, a caricature—of the late composer Morton Feldman. In his dramatic piece for tape, *The King of Buffalo*, Mark Steven Brooks melds choice bits of interview material, both raw and processed, to radical alterations of Feldman's music. In this satirical, yet oddly moving, sonic depiction of Feldman, Brooks imprints his own compositional markings onto the Feldman source materials. The listener can either play the detective—identifying, decoding, and analyzing the disparate elements—or can submit to the inventiveness, the humor, and the dream-like passages.

The piece begins with Feldman's Brooklyn-accented wish, "I want to be the first great composer that is Jewish," setting a tone of unbridled arrogance. Derisive laughter follows (Feldman's own private joke?), and we're suddenly immersed in an amorphous, eerie electronic sound world that converges into a rhythm track, providing stability for an outpouring of fragments and complete sentences that hints at things to come.

The phrase "If I could be presumptuous, I could say that all important things negate the world" begins the next section, unified by a simple percussive motif tinged with reverb. Feldman goes on to complain that people didn't care for his performances, asserting that his music is important. Subsequent processing imbues these same remarks with a plaintive wail, a whine that, paradoxically, reveals the actual *feeling* behind the disappointment and anger of the statements when they're first heard. What might be thought of as a development section follows, ending with the sudden fragment, "There is a fascistic element in the Rolling Stones." A confession of sorts, "I have great problems" precedes the belligerent sounding "I don't agree with you," which abruptly triggers a cascade of activity—almost as though the music itself embodies a "fight or flight" response to Feldman's implicit challenge.

One of the most extraordinary aspects of *The King of Buffalo* is the auto-intertextuality: Feldman's observations and music are manipulated by Brooks so that they ultimately comment upon themselves. Brooks's choice of fragments, processing means, and combinations and juxtapositions are not only essential to the creation of the piece, but are also indicative of a hidden subtext, and imply a difficult personal relationship between the composer and his subject. The resulting hybrid, a biographical/autobiographical snapshot, is infused with ambiguity. The subject becomes portrayed (betrayed?) by his own narcissism, as interpreted by the complex attitude of his portrayer.

Such a richly penetrating sonic portraiture brings to mind the intensely personal work of Shelley Hirsch, who performs as a vocalist primarily in her own compositions.[58] Hirsch's work on recordings, although meticulously constructed, gives the appearance of spontaneity—a testament to her skills as an improviser. Enlarging her palette with electronics, applied live and in studio recordings, she often layers strands of fractured syllabic repetitions with increasingly complete linear phrases, placing the listener into a decidedly non-linear, multi-dimensional space. Yet, her most complex vertical layerings, and her most jarring horizontal juxtapositions, are framed by a listener-friendly transparency. Her distinct brand of slightly jaded optimism and sincerity, spiked with humor, balances the occasional darker implications of her stories.

Going as far back as her childhood, Hirsch relentlessly mines her life experiences, concocting brilliant collage-like reminiscences that are alternately, and sometimes simultaneously, disquieting and euphoric. Embracing archetypal personas such as Blanche Dubois, she weaves their reinvented essences into the maze of associations conjured by her alchemical compositions. Investigating immediate consciousness, memory consciousness, and image-making consciousness, she becomes a producer of sonic images, recycling the discarded and the strange. Her remarkably unfettered access to the mother lode of automatism enhances her gift of spontaneous ingenuity.

Hirsch's command of extended vocal techniques imparts enormous variety to her music. The tone of her voice can range from audacious vulnerability, to charismatic intimacy (especially in the storytelling segments), to hallucinatory excursions floating effortlessly out of the spoken/sung voice and into pure Hirschian singing. Such transitions always remain viscerally connected to the text and *in* context. By judiciously inserting cliched musical phrases and even covers of commonly recognized tunes, like "Blue Moon" in her composition *States,* she exploits a network of culturally-specific "signs," twisting them into a kind of parody that hovers between homage and satire. Quotes from the Banda music of Central Africa and the voices of a Bulgarian chorus are used to globally expand her images in this composition. Skillful underscoring enhances and propels these and other "circular" story/compositions.

A type of cultural anthropology, Hirsch's musical creations embody the essence of surrealism: the division between the real and the imagined dissolves, replaced by an imaginary world that radiates out from a vast dynamic repository of memory and association. Harry Lachner, in the liner notes to Hirsch's recording, *States,* writes eloquently of her non-linear poeticism: "*States* is . . . a pandemonium of resuscitated ghosts from the past, the present, and the future; an illustrious parade of characters; a vocal discourse between various impersonations of imaginary people; an associative stream of the subconscious where Shelley Hirsch's singing in tongues reformulates our own collective nightmares and hopes."

Hirsch's creative transformations of kitschy fragments and her skilled shaping of multiple dimensions suggest a quality central to the surrealist doctrine, the *merveilleux*: "a rupture in the order of reality" (Adamowicz 1998, 11–12). Her methods go beyond conventional definitions of composition and of performance. By violating logical, linear narrative forms, by opposing elements from our known world in disturbing ways, she plunges herself, and her audience, into collective reminiscences so visceral that they seem almost visual—a surreal accomplishment in itself.

In live performances, Hirsch often relies on layering techniques, piling up a swarming multitude of voices while maintaining a distinct function for each independent line. This ancient method of putting several processes into play at once can be subsumed under the rubric of polyphony. Simultaneity, conceived with respect to the thousand-year history of polyphony, refers to concurrent yet unrelated and self-suffcient processes that do not exhibit the organic cooperation of independent strands bound by a common harmony. In the early twentieth century, the principal of simultaneity was applied to the fields of tonality and rhythm. Bartók's Fourteen Bagatelles, written in 1908, represent the earliest examples of two simultaneously played melodic lines written in different keys. Melodic, harmonic, and tonal principles of simultaneity, along with polymetric techniques, were eagerly adopted by leading composers at the turn of the century, including Stravinsky, Satie, Mussorgsky, Prokofiev, Debussy, R. Strauss, Ives, and Milhaud.[59]

How does simultaneity relate to pictorial and verbal collage? It actually preceded collage-technique, influencing the generation of artists and poets of 1910 and foreshadowing the effect collage would exert on all forms of twentieth-century art. In the discordant representational and abstract forms found in Picasso's *Torero*, in Chagall's *I and the Village*, with its depictions of rural life juxtaposed and interwoven in a non-naturalistic fashion, and in the poetry of Apollinaire, juxtaposed simultaneities paradoxically function as unifying elements, while at the same time inducing fragmentation.

Hal Freedman has accomplished a feat analogous to Oswald's kamikaze cut-and-paste, with his extremist application of simultaneity to one of the most monumental works in musical history, Wagner's *Ring Cycle*. Superimposing the entire *Ring* on top of itself over two hundred times, Freedman squeezed it into a three-and-a-half-minute tape, a massive compression one step away from white noise. In the liner notes to the Opus One recording of *Ring Précis*, Freedman summarizes: "In spite of the density, some essence of Wagner can still be heard through all of the layers. Individual lines emerge briefly, only to sink back into the wall of sound." True enough, and its perversely dramatic quality is certainly suggestive for the filmic medium. *Bartók Précis*, a companion piece, reduces the six Bartók String Quartets into four minutes and thirty seconds. This less dense compilation, however, sonically refers more transparently to its original creator.

Ring Précis was choreographed and danced by Alice Farley at the 1977 International Surrealism Festival in Chicago, reinforcing its pedigree as an example of surrealist music. Other performances of the piece have elicited extremely negative audience reactions. According to Freedman, its 1976 Columbia University premiere was simultaneously booed by the faculty and cheered by the students—a reaction befitting a work not only defined *by* the process of simultaneity, but itself defining an expanded concept of simultaneity. The impact wasn't lost on John Cage, quoted in the liner notes of the recording: "I've always had problems with Bartók's larger works and all of Wagner's, but Hal Freedman's *Précis* works remove them. I find them perfectly beautiful."

A highly personalized saga into the realm of simultaneity can be found on Eugene Chadbourne's rough-hewn *Jungle Cookies* recordings. A kind of "sonic diary," these two CDs were heavily inspired by Chadbourne's trips to Amsterdam. The tag in the liner notes hints at their demented nature: "More and more weird noise, combined in a manner to make it as incomprehensible as possible." Chadbourne, an improvising musician, explains that the records represent an attempt to capture the music he listens to in his daily routines and travels. In other words, they are a product of his penchant for listening to, and recording, life—in this case, life on the streets of Amsterdam, combined with tapes and themes already created by Chadbourne from a Pandora's Box of sound artifacts. Listening to *Jungle Cookies*, one can experience the audio analog of the premise behind the film *Being John Malkovich* and, with the flip of a switch, inhabit the ears of Eugene Chadbourne. His entertaining liner notes help the listener to understand what, exactly, is being heard. For instance, one theme began as snippets stolen from a batch of old LPs tossed out by a neighbor suffering from dementia, before being carted away to the sanitarium (an appropriate signification for the deranged effect of these recordings).

Chadbourne professes to organize the *Jungle* pieces based on the time of day. Attempting to capture the 3:00 A.M. slot of eerie quiet, punctuated with occasional chaos, he writes in the liner notes, "led to one of the strangest bits of composing I have done in a lifetime of being bizarre." Unearthing a duet CD by Sammy Davis, Jr., and Laurindo Almeida that had been buried (and consequently damaged) in his backyard for a year, Chadbourne co-opted its endless repeating and skipping as one of his 3:00 A.M. motifs, combining it with a recording of a skipping Stockhausen record. He continues, "A final part of this set of themes was devised by placing our dachshund Otto in a large box which he could not escape from, full of little hand held drum machines and gadgets. As he pranced around in there, no doubt reminding me to feed him, he came up with wonderful drum tracks."

A long segment of one of the recordings is dominated by a texture that starts with a repetitive motor-like sound, randomly shot through with mechanized interjections of "no no no no no no no" (the damaged Sammy Davis, Jr,. CD?). Eventually, another mechanical sound, like a rusty swing, is added to the mix. Five distinct strands gradually evolve, forming a complex polymetric sound object punctuated from time to time with what must be Otto the dachshund's random percussion contributions. This polymetric texture gives way, eventually, to passages of banjo picking and accordion tunes, along with an unrestricted slew of everyday sonic images, either live or processed. The slap-dash of Chadbourne's simultaneities lacks refinement, but makes up for it by the sheer spirit of adventure and enterprise.

Chadbourne's music, redolent of many aspects of surrealism, not to speak of Dada, freely quotes, borrows, and modifies other works. "Hallelujah, I'm a Bum," a parody of the religious song, provides the scaffolding for what sounds like an obnoxious little girl's comments on the modified words. Screeching threats and obscenities while riffing about gambling squads, she'll suddenly jump into a sweet melodic unison with the singer/guitarist, before careening off into another deranged rant. Meanwhile, a sax player dithers around with a totally unrelated tune, and street noises invade, all attempting to obliterate the "theme tune," which keeps returning for more abuse.

Chadbourne spins out multiple layers, plunders and poaches from existing recordings, and has amassed an arsenal of skills that he can apply at will to skewer a familiar tune and adapt it to his own purposes. These techniques have their roots in the creative borrowings, quotations, and allusions traded among composers and musicians for centuries. The seminal figure, of course, of the twentieth century, whose oeuvre would be vastly different had his rampant use of musical quotation been quelled, is Charles Ives.

In his landmark study of Ives's borrowing procedures, *All Made of Tunes*, J. Peter Burkholder divides the composer's uses of existing music into fourteen categories, ranging from direct quotation to paraphrase, and including collage and stylistic allusion. Burkholder describes the reaction that such borrowings may elicit as a kind of "aesthetic dissonance," "violating the expectation that compositions should be original, self-contained, and based on newly invented ideas" (Burkholder 1995, 2). In committing the nihilistic act of dissolving his own boundaries, becoming coexistent with common tunes, Ives foreshadowed the eventual merging of "high" art and "low" art. Not only was Ives essentially the first composer to invent collage procedure, he was very likely the first postmodern composer.[60]

Others, much later, adapted collage and related borrowing techniques for their own purposes. Berio's *Sinfonia*, Stockhausen's *Hymnen*, and Schnittke's Symphony No. 1 are three major works that come to mind. In my own *Southern Ephemera*, originally written for flute, cello, surrogate kithara, and harmonic canon (the latter two instruments built by Harry Partch), the intent was to evoke a dream-like state populated by half-remembered tunes that accompanied my childhood in the South.[61] To accomplish this, I applied techniques of paraphrase, fracturing, quotation with new accompaniment, and simultaneity to seven songs from folk and religious traditions that had special nostalgic meaning for me, weaving them through an independent, non-nostalgic structure. The use of a microtonal system dividing the octave into forty-three discrete tones enhanced the evocation of the ephemeral nature of distant memory. At the beginning of the piece, the players—and audience—are asked to imagine themselves lying in the grass at dusk, watching the stars pop out in the ever-blackening sky. They hear (or play) string instruments being strummed behind the bridge with picks, generating a swarm of random, hard, high pitches.

The opening of *Southern Ephemera*, along with its intentional evocation of childhood memories, has a counterpart in Giorgio de Chirico's writings and paintings from his metaphysical period.[62] The eerily lit objects that almost float in space, seemingly unrelated to one another, evoke a dream world. In *The Lassitude of the Infinite*, a statue of a reclining female figure, surrounded by an expansive piazza, looks out toward a steam train, outlining the distant horizon. In his writings, de Chirico describes memories from his childhood that resonate in the painting: "The whistles of trains, there beyond the wall, beneath the tremendous mystery of the stars" (quoted in Baldacci 1997, 131–32).

What role does nostalgia play in efforts of artists and composers to excavate their past, resuscitating elemental objects, rummaging through old feelings and emotions, reviving the bygone? Neville Wakefield gets to the heart of the matter: "Seeking moments of stability and perspective from within the chaotic and contradictory violence of the present, we increasingly find ourselves seeking refuge in nostalgia—in a vision of the past from which the worst wrinkles of contradiction have been ironed out, in a past that has been domesticated to suit the desperate needs of the present" (Wakefield 1990, 69).

American Icons, my other nostalgia-induced piece, pays homage to pop music from the 1950s and 1960s, but is hardly an exercise in seeking refuge.[63] Snaring stylistic idioms and referring obliquely to familiar songs, it employs allusion far more than quotation to conjure the aural equivalent of perfume.[64] Tiny fragments and larger chunks of referential patterns swarm and swirl over, under, and into a whirlwind of superimposed layers, capturing the sounds of the era. Tim Page, in the *Washington Post* review, highlighted the aspect of simultaneity: "A bright, brash mixture of jazz, pop, folk and 57 other varieties of homegrown music, this might be likened to listening to five radios at the same time, each of them playing a tune you'd like to hear more of" (Page 1996).

A more radical "rebirth," the transferal of music from its origins into a strikingly contrasting realm, is brilliantly carried out by the Ghanaian composer Gyimah Labi in his *Five Dialects in African Pianism*. I first heard this work performed during a conference exploring the concept of African pianism held at the University of Pittsburgh in October 1999.[65] Labi so skillfully insinuates Africanisms into Western harmonic conventions that I *thought* I was hearing quotes from, or near literal allusions to, Western composers ranging from Beethoven to Gershwin to Nancarrow, especially in *Dialect 5*, "The Ancients Revisited." I discovered, instead, that Labi achieves this remarkable effect with his idiosyncratic method of reducing Western functional harmony to a few basic structures. These structures have a dual role: while signifying their origins, they simultaneously support Labi's recasting of African folk elements, such as traditional Akan singing traditions. This striking fusion, cemented with chromatic passages, hymn-like sections, and quartal harmonies, is funneled through carefully constructed rhythmic grids, which are in turn ensconced in a large-scale form replete with the repetitions and sequences commonly found in African drumming.[66] The Ghanaian identity is preserved, while moving *beyond* the confines of ethnicity.

Labi's grafting of Ghanaian and other African musical elements onto a structure that mimes its object of study (Western music) results in a wholly original syntax. From a Western perspective, the *Dialects* are startling. Labi boldly reincarnates clumps of harmonic, motivic, and rhythmic entities common to the Western canon, shaking off the dust of subliminal association by subjecting his constructed illusions to a process of hybridization. This integrative approach used in the *Dialects* mimics the collage process by combining mirages of Western music with African rhythmic techniques, achieving a metamorphosis of the commonplace. A visual analogue might be *L'Annonciation*, one of Magritte's oil paintings where pictorial objects are viewed in disparate scales. "The pictorial elements are articulated in conflicting spaces, meeting on the planar surface of the canvas rather than in the illusory depth of representational space, signaling their origin in collage construction" (Adamowicz 1998, 47). Indeed, the conjunction of Western and African elements in Labi's *Dialects* occurs on the surface of the music, while allusions to Western music and rhythmic applications of Africanisms are expressed in disorienting ways that refresh and renew jaded perceptual habits.

CONCLUSION

The vibrancy of the surrealist aesthetic continues in the present, its impact and longevity and immense impact anticipated by two originating artists. Louis Aragon proclaimed surrealism's commitment to radical change as well as to the future in his collection of poems and prose texts, *Le Libertinage*, published in 1924.[67] In the preface, he remarks, "Let's accept once and for all the epithet 'messianic.' It's silly, it's empty: we didn't choose it. But finally that's what's held against us, we are messianics. Fine. To the traditional idea of beauty and the good, we will oppose our own, however infernal it may appear. Messianics and revolutionaries, I agree" (Aragon 1924, 271–72). Toward the end of his collection of interviews with Breton, André Parinaud asks: "Can a movement such as Surrealism be limited to poetic or pictorial forms? If you had the choice, in which domains would you find it useful to express Surrealism's positions?" Breton's enigmatic answer leaves the door open: "It hardly matters. The main thing is for Surrealism to express itself regularly, and globally. Its incursions in different domains would thus be much more perceptible" (Breton [1952] 1993, 247).

Breton may not have imagined the extent to which surrealism would express itself, especially in the ubiquitous use of the word itself. The term "surreal" has permeated our language (and others) more intensively than any other word representing a major artistic movement in the twentieth century. Unfortunately, it's often slung around without a real understanding of its meaning. Film, theater, literature, poetry, visual arts, fashion, sports, photography, music, politics, economics, wine, breast implants, mass suicide, natural disasters, even health scares, have been described, during the past twenty years or so, with a smorgasbord of surreal-isms.[68]

Octavio Paz defended surrealism as "not merely an esthetic, poetic and philosophical doctrine. It was a vital attitude. A negation of the contemporary world and at the same time an attempt to substitute other values for those of democratic bourgeois society: eroticism, poetry, imagination, liberty, spiritual adventure, vision" (quoted in Kandell 1998). Paz nails the essence of surrealism: a *state of mind*—not just an avant-garde movement, and not a superficial flash in the history of art or literature.

Has the real *become* surreal? The central question here, however, remains: can surrealist aesthetics function in the time-dominated, essentially non-representational realm of music? My answer is an unqualified affirmative: music can, indeed, operate as one of the domains of surrealism, even when composers and musicians are not consciously utilizing surrealist techniques, or deliberately aiming for surrealistic effects. I've shown three things here: 1) how surrealism invaded music when the conditions were finally ripe, 2) how two facets of surrealism were translated into musical expressions, and 3) how postmodern tendencies embedded in surrealism have surfaced in postmodern music. However, my essay also raises questions. Does music basically lag behind the progressiveness of other art forms? Did isolated developments in music, predating but related to elements of surrealism, in any way affect or influence the surrealist movement? In what ways did American jazz musicians influence composers and free jazzers in Europe? How did music and sound events associated with dadaism and futurism intersect with surrealism, and eventually with postmodern musics? What surrealist elements might be commonly associated with postmodern electroacoustic music? How has collage evolved in twentieth-century music? Will collage forms in music eventually attract critical assessments? What about other motifs orbiting the surrealist pantheon—objective chance, convulsive beauty, revolutionary thought—and how these are manifested in music? Will technological advances in music production further expand the application of surrealist techniques in postmodern musics?

The surrealist movement spawned a mammoth and multifaceted network of literary, artistic, and musical manifestations, influenced by and influencing one another. Not just an artistic movement, not just a revolutionary concept, surrealism reached beyond such limitations, and became a way of living. Reverberating with imagination, analogy, and desire—dislodging reality, provoking and challenging the acceptance of everyday routines—this mode of life, of making art, continues to expand, offering itself as a porthole into alternate realities as we move toward unforeseen ways of creating, perceiving, and evolving.

NOTES

I would like to thank Judy Lochhead for encouraging me to contribute to this volume of essays, and to express my gratitude to friends and colleagues for their assistance with and helpful commentary on portions of this essay: James Cassaro, Chris Cutler, Nathan David, Edward Eadon, Cole Gagne, Victor Grauer, Tom Heasley, Susan McClary, Deane Root, Leonora Saavedra, and Steve Whealton.

1. Several elements intrinsic to surrealism, such as aesthetic concepts of the marvelous, of convulsive beauty, and of the found object, the philosophical concept

of objective chance, and the political concept of revolutionary action, reside in twentieth-century music. I focus here on only two elements of surrealism for practical purposes of brevity.

2. Breton, the central force at the vortex of surrealism, wielded a remarkable power that alternately magnetized and repelled the most adventurous and experimental young male artists of the 1920s.

3. The surrealists were apparently unaware of the initial automatic writing experiments of Leon Solomons and Gertrude Stein some thirty years prior to the publication of Breton's "First Manifesto". Breton's instructions nevertheless echoed the original rules of literary automatic writing as identified by Kittler: "First, it is forbidden to reread anything written. . . . Second, the annoying intrusions of an ego are to be put off by repeating prewritten sentences with an obstinacy that matches their meaninglessness" (Kittler [1985] 1990, 227).

4. "The marvelous is always beautiful, anything marvelous is beautiful, in fact only the marvelous is beautiful" (Breton [1924] 1972, 14).

5. The *cadavre exquis* was named after one of the first lines resulting from this game: "The exquisite corpse drinks the new wine."

6. In other words, he wishes to erase the distinction between poetry and song. Interestingly, Wagner's fusion of poetry and music was likely the closest to Breton's professed ideal. It should therefore come as no surprise that the soundtracks to several surrealist films, including two of the most celebrated—Buñuel's *L'âge d'or* and *Un chien andalou*—used music by Wagner.

7. René Clair made a film sequence for the ballet, a fast-moving montage anticipatory of surrealist imagery. Satie's score for the film, *Entr'acte,* was one of the earliest examples of film music.

8. Mark Polizzotti's 1995 biography of Breton, *Revolution of the Mind*, goes into considerable detail about the reasons for Breton's dislike of Cocteau.

9. The opera was never finished, due to the split of the surrealist movement into two factions, one led by Aragon and one by Breton. However, the libretto to four out of five acts had been completed, and was retained by Antheil.

10. The Belgian surrealists were more open toward the inclusion of music in surrealist efforts, as shown by the three-way collaboration among the writer Paul Nougé, the painter René Magritte, and the composer André Souris. Their collaboration resulted in *Clarisse Juranville*, a poem written by Nougé parodying a popular grammar textbook, illustrated by Magritte in a booklet, and set to music in a small cantata by Souris. According to Robert Wangermée in his article, "Magritte and the 'Universe of Sound,'" Souris's piece was sung at a concert in Charleroi in 1929, among an exhibit of nearly two dozen paintings by Magritte, and preceded by a lecture on music by Nougé (Wangermée 1998).

11. The year of the date of this meeting wasn't given, only that it occurred July 6–8.

12. Sound and noise pieces by the dadaist, Kurt Schwitters, and the futurist, Luigi Russolo, became beacons of early twentieth-century musical adventurism, but neither was directly involved with the surrealist movement.

13. Paul Garon praises the surrealists' defense of non-European cultures, the arts of which often confirmed and reinforced their own perspectives, and goes on to say: "It follows that the Surrealists' sympathetic attention could hardly fail to have been attracted by the vibrant and inspired music created by the American blacks, a music which not only recalls African rhythms and chants, but which is also an impassioned revolt against the white bourgeois 'American way of life'" (Garon 1975, 26). Elsewhere in what may be the only book that addresses a musical form in relation to surrealism, *Blues and the Poetic Spirit*, Garon examines, with remarkable insight, the spiritual revolt against repression as embodied in the poetry of the blues.

14. On the rare occasions when music is discussed in books written about surrealism, the discussions invariably center around interactions of composers—usually Satie, Auric, Antheil, Milhaud, Stravinsky—and surrealists during the 1920s and '30s. Chénieux-Gendron, along with Garon, Sandrow, Kahn, and Schiff, were the only authors I found who addressed the *transference* of surrealist elements into music. (Mâche, Pierrepont, and Willenbrink, in their cited articles, go to considerably greater lengths in drawing connections between surrealist techniques and music.)

15. Slonimsky describes this melodramatic palindrome: "The action is reversed after the husband in the play kills his adulterous wife; she comes back to life and the husband backs out of the door" (Slonimsky 1966, 80).

16. Mâche, less than ten years after Slonimsky's article came out, asserted that until the *musique concrète* of the early 1950s, sounds were always filtered through, and affected by, poetic, religious, or aesthetic screens before being 'received' by musicians—and therefore would not qualify as totally surreal. However, those early works of Schaeffer and Henry constituted the first authentic illustrations of a musical surrealism, even though "such works only occasionally joined surrealism in the embodiment of its aesthetic, but never in its ends nor in its techniques" (Mâche 1974, 46).

17. Mâche elaborates further, mentioning Cage's aleatoric devices, launched with dice, and his involvement with collective improvisation. Yet he concludes that Cage's Zen-inspired "return to oneself is in opposition to the surrealist Don Quixotism" (Mâche 1974, 47). Cage's philosophy and approach to aleatoric and chance methods, and how these techniques and their results relate to surrealism, offers a rich territory for further research, as does his association with Marcel Duchamp.

18. "The first piece was written very rapidly, in a single night, because I wanted to use the potential of a given material to find out how far automatism in musical relationships would go, with individual invention appearing only in some really very simple forms of disposition—in the matter of densities for example. For this purpose I borrowed material from Messiaen's *Mode de valeurs et d'intensités*; thus I had material that I had not invented and for whose invention I deliberately rejected all responsibility in order to see just how far it was possible to go. I wrote down all the transpositions, as though it were a mechanical object which moved in every direction, and limited my role to the selection of registers—but even those were completely undifferentiated" (Boulez 1976, cited in Stacey 1987, 23–24).

19. With the exception of Ashley, Williams, and Smith, it appears as though none of the composers and musicians discussed *consciously* employ surrealist techniques.

20. The legitimacy of surrealism in music has a proponent in the writer and scholar Richard Taruskin, whose article, "Thomas Adès: Surrealist Composer Comes to the Rescue of Modernism," appeared in the *New York Times* on December 5, 1999. One response to his article, a letter published a couple of weeks later, claims that musical surrealism is an impossibility.

21. A term coined by composer and musician John Oswald, plunderphonicler supreme, referring to the musical practice of blatantly appropriating segments from recordings of other people's music and, in the process, creating a new musical form.

22. Convulsive beauty can be thought of as action playing against fixity. "The clash between opposed elements, the violence of a departure endlessly halted" (Caws 1981, 89)as projected by the surrealist hieroglyph of a train suddenly stopped dead in a virgin forest.

23. I use the term "non-idiomatic" to discriminate between improvisatory forms tethered to highly identifiable or indigenous styles such as traditional jazz, Indian ragas, the Korean Sanjo (many others could be mentioned) which *are* idiomatic and those that aren't connected to any identifiable indigenous form, style, or tradition.

24. Speed was actually a preoccupation in the process of automatic writing. When Breton collaborated with Philippe Soupault in one of the initial explorations of this technique (culminating in their book, *The Magnetic Fields*), there were lengthy marathon sessions marked by experiments with different writing speeds. Different levels of velocity were described and attempted: Level v, for instance, was to occur several times faster than the 'normal speed at which one could recall child-hood memories.' At the greatest speeds, the images poured forth so quickly that the writers were forced to abbreviate everything. By varying the speeds with which each chapter was written, they attempted to "determine the limits of the bond between thought and expression" (Polizzotti 1995, 106).

25. In his preface to Breton's *Poésie et autre,* Gérard Legrand, a leading figure of postwar surrealism, compares Breton's 'stance' to that of jazz tenor saxophon-ists Coleman Hawkins and John Coltrane (Garon 1975, 27).

26. The coalition of highly abstract jazz musicians with contemporary music techniques and conventional orchestral instrumentation is commonly referred to as Third Stream.

27. These are rules drawn from Desmond Morris's outline in *The Naked Ape* of rules governing all play activities.

28. See Dean 1992, 151–55, for a detailed discussion of both pieces.

29. Other instrumentalists active as early as the 1960s deserve mention for expanding the sonic potentials of their instruments, including Steve Lacy, Don Cherry, Irene Schweitzer, George Lewis, Richard Teitelbaum, Derek Bailey, Tony Oxley, Peter Brotzman, Peter Kowald, Joelle Leandre, Paul Lovens, Joseph Jarman, Albert Mangelsdorff, Leo Smith, Leroy Jenkins, Philip Wachsman, Misha Mengelberg.

30. Ironically, the reservations of Braxton and Davis are the result of far more extensive experience with improvisation and with improvisers than Foss can claim to have had.

31. The recording documents the live stage performance, presented in 1975 at the University of Alabama's Ferguson Theater.

32. Fred Lane, the alter ego of Tim Reed, has become a cult figure, especially following the Shimmy Disc release of his surrealist/vaudevillian recording, From *The One that Cut You*. Craig Nutt observes that "it's impossible to fully appreciate Fred Lane without a knowledge of American pop and advertising culture from 1920 on." According to Nutt, Lane once told a reporter from the *Tuscaloosa News*, when asked where he got his ideas from (he also writes, draws, and creates whirligigs that sell in craft shows, galleries and boutiques): "They fall out of my head and I pick them up and put them in a plastic bag."

33. The list of names that made the final one hundred stretch from Captain Beefheart to Youssou N'Dour to Public Enemy to Glenn Gould—and most were said to break the patterns imposed by their previous successes.

34. Free music, when it becomes a group activity, requires a synergistic approach and a sublimation of the strong ego to insure that the group intuition remains unblocked. At the moment of the conception of the music, all creative parties interact—and therein lies an essential difference between the act of group improvisation and the act of composition. This synergy (and energy) blooms naturally in groups that have performed together for many years, such as Smith and Williams, or the trio with Alex von Schlippenbach, Evan Parker, and Paul Lovens, or the more structured but still highly improvisatory Willem Breuker Kollektief.

35. Exchanges of letters and recordings with Derek Bailey, Peter Kowald, Paul Lovens, Evan Parker, and others eventually led to performances and recordings in Europe (none of our core group had ever been anywhere outside of the South).

36. This generous position of inclusion, a philosophical hallmark of surrealist ideals, was, on the surface, contradicted by Breton's numerous expulsions of individuals from official membership in the movement, often prompted by nasty political infighting among the members.

37. Nutt was a trombonist and Hatcher a bass player.

38. Check out the riveting "Sonata for Motorized Shark, Baseball Glove, and Electric Guitar" on *Transmutating*.

39. "Our Little Sawmill" was performed with three electric guitars, bass pedal, and features a tape of a Dremel tool cutting a French perfume bottle.

40. Smith, like Williams, frequently performs with other musicians as well, and as a soloist.

41. The surrealists often engaged in overlapping artistic disciplines. For example, the painters Giorgio de Chirico and Leonora Carrington each penned novels—the former published *Hebdomeros* and the latter *The Hearing Trumpet*. Pierrepont points out that Smith's sculptures, and Williams's 'hilarious' texts, define them as surrealists as much as their music does (Pierrepont 1997, 126).

42. The origin of music in the body is an important concept for Smith. Decrying the trade-off resulting from the accessibility of all musics through the

media, Smith concludes, "The normal person has lost his own inner vibration as an extension of *himself*" (Smith 1996, 7).

43. "Our uncertain future, in the model of improvising, becomes an adventure; a model of musical dangers and beauties that you *can* try at home" (Williams 1996, 11).

44. The British guitarist Derek Bailey, a purist and great advocate of the power and value of improvisation, writes of the psychic dimensions of group improvisation: "But ultimately the greatest rewards in free improvisation are to be gained in playing with other people. Whatever the advantages to solo playing there is a whole side to improvisation, the more exciting, the more magical side, which can only be discovered by people playing together. The essence of improvisation, its intuitive, telepathic foundation, is best explored in a group situation. And the possible musical dimensions of group playing far outstrip those of solo playing" (quoted in Bosshard 1999).

45. Many of Ashley's works are fueled, in part, by the process, or thought, or ideal, of automatic speech.

46. Breton's first wife, Simone Collinet, justified their collective play as "a method of research, a means of exaltation and stimulation, a gold mine of findings, maybe even a drug" (Breton 1975, 30).

47. Some writers on surrealism believe that chance was the surrealists' preferred method for artistic organization. Their practice of automatism and their application of chance procedures became so intertwined that it is often not possible to differentiate the two, a concept explored by Martin Willenbrink (1985, 151–54).

48. Breton's interpretation of the value of this amusement comes from his only essay on games, quoted in a boxed compilation documenting surrealist games and related collaborative techniques.

49. The timelessness of this game was documented in an exhibit traveling during 1993–1995, "The Return of the Cadavre Exquis," produced by the Drawing Center in New York. More than one thousand artists participated, using the body's anatomy as points for metaphoric departure. Many of their Exquisite Corpses have been documented in the exhibition catalogue of the same name. At least one musician, Christian Marclay (one of the musicians playing on John Zorn's *Cobra*, discussed below), is represented in a striking collaboration with two other artists, in which "a pair of sutured lips, two green stripes, and a pair of legs cemented into one clay foot yields an image of thwarted expression, an evocation of censorship not one of its parts belie" (Schaffner 1993, 55–56).

50. Published by C. F. Peters in 1982, *Party Pieces* exists as a score of twenty brief collaboratively written works, arranged by Robert Hughes for various combinations of flute, clarinet, bassoon, horn, and piano. The front and back covers are illustrated with collective drawings by Thomson, Cage, and Harrison.

51. Interestingly, each of the twenty published works was the result of a collaborative effort among three or fewer composers. Virgil Thomson participated in only five pieces and never shared a collaborative effort with Henry Cowell.

52. Zorn had previously constructed several game pieces in the late '70s: *Lacrosse*, *Fencing*, and *Archery*. The name *Cobra*, designed in 1984, was taken

from a war game. Totally contrasting versions of the piece are represented on the studio and live recordings.

53. The built-in safeguard of a "guerilla" system—akin to a system of checks and balances—allows the players to demolish, subvert, or redirect anything that has become too predictable or otherwise not to their liking.

54. Extensive documentation of Oswald's adventures with plunderphonics can be found at http://www.6q.com.

55. This recording has become notorious, thanks to heavy-handed legal maneuvering by one of the plundered artists. Released on October 31, 1989, the recording *Plunderphonics* represented the culmination of ten years of work, with Oswald drawing upon source material by Michael Jackson, Dolly Parton, Count Basie, Stravinsky, and many others. It was never for sale; releases were directed to radio and other media. CBS Records rapidly pursued the destruction of the CD, and as of January 30, 1990, distribution ceased and all extant copies were destroyed.

56. 'Plexure' is defined in Webster's Third as "the act or process of weaving together."

57. The large number of sources precluded legal negotiations, hence the morphing of artists' names (a playful reflection of the audio morphings).

58. Hirsch also collaborates with many musicians. Her performances take place in a wide variety of venues, including concerts, radio plays, films, recordings, alternative operas, and multimedia events.

59. H. H. Stuckenschmidt devotes a chapter to the concept of simultaneity in his book, *Twentieth Century Music*, discussing excerpts from works of several composers and even comparing polymetric techniques of Mozart to those of Berg. Although he avoids specific citations, Stuckenschmidt doesn't leave visual depictions of simultaneity out in the cold. Elaborating on Berg's embrace of "every aspect of the craft of composition," he writes, "His music is as much governed by the notion of simultaneity as are some of the major paintings of Max Ernst, the Futurists or Picasso" (Stuckenschmidt 1969, 88).

60. Burkholder specifically defines musical collage found in Ives as "a swirl of quoted and paraphrased tunes added to a musical structure based on modeling, paraphrase, cumulative setting, or a narrative program," citing *Overture and March "1776"* and *Country Band March*. (There are many other examples.) Ives's collages, far from being an indiscriminate hodgepodge of tunes, are carefully structured with distinct functions assigned to the borrowed elements.

61. The orchestral version (without any Partch instruments) is written in twelve-tone equal temperament, and adds passages calling for extended techniques.

62. Not thought of as a collage artist, de Chirico was, for the duration of his metaphysical period, highly influential in the development of surrealism. Although once a composer himself, he abandoned music, asserting that it had no meaning.

63. Scored for large orchestra, *American Icons* was commissioned by the National Symphony Orchestra in 1996 to commemorate the twenty-fifth anniversary of the John F. Kennedy Center in Washington, D.C.

64. Everyone has experienced the rush of rediscovering a scent from one's past, triggering a flood of memories and associations. I wanted to attempt the same feat with this piece.

65. The concept of African pianism, pioneered by Akin Euba, is concerned with the transferal of indigenous African rhythmic and tonal languages to the Western acoustic piano.

66. Labi sets forth his theories in his textbook, *Exploring Resources in Creativity: Quartal Generation of Motions*, soon to be published. In this first volume of the projected African Music Theory Series, he explores three topics: meter in African music; the time line as a formal structure in African music; and the quartal basis in Dipo and Yewe music.

67. A banner year for surrealism, 1924 also marked the official founding of the surrealist movement, as well as the publication of Breton's "First Surrealist Manifesto."

68. A quick search through the *New York Times* archives, from 1976 to 1999, excavated a colorful array of variants such as semi-surrealism, cracker-barrel surrealism, sophomore surrealism, along with a host of other adjectives applied to surrealism: cheapo, ghoulish, disorienting, playful, airy, flamboyant, weirdly plausible, deft, pure, pop, and carnival.

WORKS CITED

Adamowicz, Elsa. 1998. *Surrealist Collage in Text and Image: Dissecting the Exquisite Corpse.* Cambridge: Cambridge University Press.

Antheil, George. [1945] 1981. *Bad Boy of Music.* Reprint, New York: Da Capo Press.

Aragon, Louis. 1924. *Le Libertinage.* Paris: Nouvelle revue française.

———. [1930] 1965. *La Peinture au défi in Les Collages.* Paris: Hermann.

Bailey, Derek. 1980. *Improvisation, Its Nature and Practice in Music.* Derbyshire: Moorland Publishing in association with Incus Records.

Baldacci, Paolo. 1997. *De Chirico: The Metaphysical Period.* Boston, New York, Toronto, London: Little, Brown and Company.

Baxter, Ed. 1998. "100 Records That Set the World on Fire while No One Was Listening." *The Wire* (September): 22–41.

Bosshard, Fredi. 1999. Brochure announcement, citing Derek Baily, for *Total Music Meeting*, August 11, 1999.

Boulez, Pierre. [1968] 1986. "Où en est-on?" [Where are we now?]. Transcript of a lecture given at Saint Etienne on May 13, 1968, published in *Points de repère*, 1981. In *Orientations: Collected Writings of Pierre Boulez.* Edited by Jean-Jacques Nattiez, translated by Martin Cooper. Cambridge: Harvard University Press. 445–63.

———. 1976. *Conversations with Célestin Deliège.* London: Eulenberg.

Breton, André. [1924] 1972. "Manifesto of Surrealism." In *Manifestoes of Surrealism*, translated by Richard Seaver and Helen R. Lane. Ann Arbor: University of Michigan Press. 3–47.

———. [1930] 1972. "Second Manifesto of Surrealism." In *Manifestoes of Surrealism*, translated by Richard Seaver and Helen R. Lane. Ann Arbor: University of Michigan Press. 119–94.

———. [1928] 1972. *Surrealism and Painting*. Translated by Simon Watson Taylor. London: Icon Editions; New York: Harper & Row.

———. [1933] 1978. *What Is Surrealism? Selected Writings*. Edited by Franklin Rosemont. London: Pluto Press Limited.

———. 1944. "Silence Is Golden." *Modern Music* 21/5 (March–April): 150–54.

———. [1952] 1993. *Conversations: The Autobiography of Surrealism*. Translated by Mark Polizzotti. New York: Paragon House.

———. [1954] 1993. "Essay on Games." In *Surrealist Games*, edited by Mel Gooding. Boston: Shambhala Redstone Editions. 137.

———.1975. *Le cadavre exquis: son exaltation*. Milan: Chez Arturo Schwartz.

Burkholder, J. Peter. 1995. *All Made of Tunes: Charles Ives and the Uses of Musical Borrowings*. New Haven: Yale University Press.

Caws, Mary Ann. 1981. *A Metapoetics of the Passage*. Hanover, N.H., and London: University Press of New England.

Chénieux-Gendron, Jacqueline. [1984] 1990. *Surrealism*. Translated by Vivian Folkenflik. New York: Columbia University Press.

Corbett, John. 1994. *Sounding Off: From John Cage to D. Funkenstein*. Durham: Duke University Press.

Cutler, Chris. 1995. "Plunderphonics." In *Sounding Off! Music as Subversion/Resistance/Revolution*, edited by Ron Sakolsky and Fred Wei-han Ho. New York: Autonomedia. 67–86.

Dean, Roger. 1992. *New Structures in Jazz and Improvised Music since 1960*. Philadelphia: Open University Press.

Ernst, Max. 1948. *Beyond Painting*. New York: Wittenborn, Schultz, Inc.

———. [1938] 1970. "The Abridged Dictionary of Surrealism." In *Surrealists on Art,*. edited by Lucy R. Lippard. Englewood Cliffs, N.J.: Prentice Hall. 207–11.

Fouse, Kathryn Lea. 1992. "Surrealism in the Piano Music of Representative Twentieth-Century American Composers." D.M.A. diss., University of North Texas.

Gagne, Cole. 1993. *Soundpieces 2: Interviews with American Composers*. Metuchen, N.J.: Scarecrow Press.

Garon, Paul. 1975. *Blues and the Poetic Spirit*. New York: Da Capo Press.

Greer, Thomas Henry. 1969. "Music and Its Relation to Futurism, Cubism, Dadaism and Surrealism, 1905–1950." Ph.D. diss., North Texas State University.

Hansen, Peter S. 1961. *An Introduction to Twentieth-Century Music*. Boston: Allyn and Bacon, Inc.

Jean, Marcel. [1983] 1993. "The Rewards of Leisure." In *The Return of the Cadavre Exquis*, edited by Jane Philbrick. New York: The Drawing Center. 74.

Jones, Andrew. 1995. *Plunderphonics, Pataphysics, and Pop Mechanics: An Introduction to Musique Actuelle.* Wembley, Middlesex, England: SAF Publishing Ltd.

Kahn, Douglas. 1992. "Introduction: Histories of Sounds Once Removed." In *Wireless Imagination: Sound, Radio, and the Avant-Garde*, edited by Douglas Kahn and Gregory Whitehead. Cambridge: MIT Press. 1–30.

Kittler, Friedrich A. [1985] 1990. *Discourse Networks, 1800/1900.* Stanford: Stanford University Press.

Lock, Graham. 1988. *Forces in Motion.* London: Quartet.

Mâche, François-Bernard. 1974. "Surréalisme et musique, remarques et gloses." *La Nouvelle Revue Française.* (December): 34–49.

Matthews, J. H., 1986. *Languages of Surrealism.* Columbia: University of Missouri Press.

Myers, Rollo. 1948. *Erik Satie.* London: Dennis Dobson.

Nadeau, Maurice. [1965] 1989. *The History of Surrealism.* Translated by Richard Howard. New York: Macmillan.

Nougé, Paul. [1947] 1992. "Music Is Dangerous." *View* 7 (March 1947) 23. Cited in Christopher Schiff, "Banging on the Windowpane: Sound in Early Surrealism." In *Wireless Imagination: Sound, Radio, and the Avant-Garde*, edited by Douglas Kahn and Gregory Whitehead. Cambridge: MIT Press. 139–90.

Oswald, John. 1995. "Creatigality." In *Sounding Off! Music as Subversion/ Resistance/Revolution*, edited by Ron Sakolsky and Fred Wei-han Ho. New York: Autonomedia. 87–90.

———. 2000. "Plunderstanding Ecophonomics." In *Arcana: Musicians on Music*, edited by John Zorn. New York: Granary Books. 9–17.

Page, Tim. 1996. "NSO's Stirring Ninth." *Washington Post* (March 22).

Pierre, José, 1999a. "To Be or Not To Be Surrealist." In *Surrealism: Two Private Eyes*, edited by Edward Weisberger. New York: The Solomon R. Guggenheim Foundation. 34–41.

———. 1999b. "The Exquisite Game." In *Surrealism: Two Private Eyes*, edited by Edward Weisberger. New York: The Solomon R. Guggenheim Foundation: 618–19.

Pierrepont, Alexandre. 1997. "Là où la nuit vigoureuse saigne une vitesse de purs végétaux." *Jazz & Littérature* (Automne): 118–35. Paris: Atlantiques/Les Cahiers du Centre Régional des Lettres d'Aquitaine.

Polizzotti, Mark. 1995. *Revolution of the Mind: The Life of André Breton.* New York: Farrar, Straus and Giroux.

Rosemont, Franklin. 1978. *André Breton and the First Principles of Surrealism.* London: Pluto Press Limited.

Sandrow, Nahma. 1972. *Surrealism: Theater, Arts, Ideas.* New York: Harper & Row.

Schaffner, Ingrid. 1993. "Apres Exquis." In *The Return of the Cadavre Exquis*, edited by Jane Philbrick. New York: The Drawing Center. 43–71.

Shattuck, Roger. 1955. *The Banquet Years.* London: Faber and Faber Limited.

Slonimsky, Nicolas. 1966. "Music and Surrealism." *Artforum* (September): 80–85.

Smith, LaDonna. 1996. "The Moment as Teacher." *The Improvisor, The International Journal of Free Improvisation.* 11: 7–8.

Stacey, Peter F. 1987. *Boulez and the Modern Concept.* Lincoln: University of Nebraska Press.

Stuckenschmidt, H. H. 1969. *Twentieth Century Music.* New York: McGraw Hill.

Taruskin, Richard. 1999. "Thomas Adès: Surrealist Composer Comes to the Rescue of Modernism." *New York Times* (December 5).

Thomson, Virgil. [1944] 1967. *Music Reviewed. 1940–1954.* New York: Vintage Books, Random House.

Toop, David. 1995. *Ocean of Sound.* London: Serpent's Tail.

Ulmer, Gregory L. 1983. "The Object of Post-Criticism." In *The Anti-Aesthetic: Essays on Postmodern Culture,* edited by Hal Foster. Seattle: Bay Press. 83–110.

Wakefield, Neville. 1990. *Postmodernism: The Twilight of the Real.* London: Pluto Press.

Wangermée, Robert. 1998. "Magritte and the 'Universe of Sound.'" In *Magritte: 1898–1967,* edited by Giséle Ollinger-Zinque and Frederik Leen. Ghent: Ludion Press. 37–40.

Willenbrink, Martin. 1985. "Zwischen Zufall und Berechnung: Überlegungen zur aleatorischen Music in Europa und Amerika." *Musica Germany* 39/2: 151–55.

Williams, Davey. 1996. "The Hirsch Extrapolation." *The Improvisor, The International Journal of Free Improvisation* 11: 11.

RECORDINGS CITED

Antheil, George. 2000. "Ballet Mécanique." Conducted by Jeffrey Fischer. EMF Media EM120.

———. 1995."La Femme: 100 Tête," on *George Antheil—Bad Boy of Music.* Martha Verbit, piano. Albany Records 146.

Ashley, Robert. 1996. *Automatic Writing.* Lovely Music. CD 1002.

Bartók, Bela. 1999. *Fourteen Bagatelles,* Op. 6. June de Toth, piano. Orchard 3009.

Boulez, Pierre. 1996. *Structures pour deux pianos.* Afons and Aloys Kontarsky. Wergo 6011.

Breuker, Willem. 1966. *Litany for the 14th June 1966.* Relax 33004; Wergo 80002.

Brooks, Mark Steven. 1999. *The King of Buffalo.* MetaSynthia 2, CD <http://members.aol.com/SublimeArt/MetaSynthia/>

Cage, John. 1994. "Imaginary Landscapes No. 2," on *The 25-Year Retrospective Concert of the Music of John Cage.* Wergo 6247.

Chadbourne, Eugene. 1998. *Jungle Cookies.* Old Gold.

Coltrane, John. 1965. *Ascension.* Impulse AS95.

Davis, Anthony. 1981. *Episteme.* Gramavision GR 8101.

Foss, Lukas. 1961. *Time Cycles.* Columbia Symphony, Leonard Bernstein, conductor. Columbia Masterworks Series 6280.

Freedman, Hal. 1982. *Ring Précis and Bartók Précis.* Opus One 58.

Frith, F. 1999. *Stone, Brick, Glass, Wood, Wire: Graphic Scores 1986–96.* I dischi di angelica IDA 014.

Hatcher, Nolan, and Craig Nutt. 1980. *Dinosaur Time.* Say Day-Bew-3.

Hirsch, Shelley. 1997. *States.* Tellus TE C003.

Ives, Charles. 1993. "Sonata for Piano no. 2 'Concord, Mass. 1840–60.'" on *The American Composer Series—Charles Ives.* Nina Deutsch, piano. Vox box 2 #5089.

Lane, Rev. Dr. Fred. 1983. *From the One that Cut You/Car Radio Jerome.* Shimmy Disc Europe SDE 8911, CD.

LeBaron, Anne. 1975. "Concerto for Active Frogs," on *Pataphysical Revue.* Say Day-Bew 1. Also on *Rana, Ritual, and Revelation: The Music of Anne LeBaron* (1992). Mode 30.

———. 1996."Southern Ephemera," on *Newband.* Music and Arts 931, CD.

LeBaron, Anne, L. Donna Smith, and Davey Williams. 1979. *Jewels.* trans museq 3.

Oswald, John. 1993. *Plexure. Avan* 016.

———. 1994. "Z." *The R e R Quarterly*, Vol. 4 No. 1.

———. 1995. "DAB," on CD accompanying. *Sounding Off! Music as Subversion/ Resistance/Revolution*, edited by Ron Sakolsky and Fred Weihan Ho. New York: Autonomedia.

Parker, Evan, Derek Bailey, and Han Bennink. 1970. *The Topography of the Lungs.* Incus 1.

Satie, Erik. 1993. *Parade* and *Relâche.* Utah Symphony Orchestra, Maurice Abravanel, conductor. Vanguard Classics 4030.

Schlippenbach, Alexander von. 1966. *Globe Unity.* Saba 15 109 ST.

Smith, LaDonna. 1992. *Eye of the Storm.* trans museq 11.

Smith, LaDonna, and Davey Williams. 1993. *Transmutating.* trans museq, CD.

Tenney, James. 1992. *Selected Works 1961–1969.* Artifact Recordings 1007.

Williams, Davey. 1985. *Criminal Pursuits.* trans museq 8.

———. 1997. *Charmed, I'm Sure.* Ecstatic Peace.

Zorn, John. 1984 and 1985. *Cobra*, Volumes 1 and 2. Hat Hut Records 60401 and 60402.

CHAPTER 4

Postmodernism and Art Music in the German Debate

Joakim Tillman

> "When I use a word," Humpty Dumpty said, in a rather scorn-
> ful tone, "it means just what I choose it to mean—neither
> more nor less."
> "The question is," said Alice, "whether you can make words
> mean so many different things."
> "The question is," said Humpty Dumpty, "which is to be
> master—that's all."
> —Lewis Carroll, *Through the Looking-Glass*

The discussion and debate on postmodernism and music in Germany started in the early 1980s after the publication of Jürgen Habermas's speech on
receiving the Adorno-prize of the city of Frankfurt (Habermas 1981
[1987]). Initially the term "postmodern" was used consistently as a label
for the young German generation of composers born around 1950
(Wolfgang Rihm, Manfred Trojahn, Hans-Jürgen von Bose, and others),
who made their debut in the middle of the 1970s with music and aesthetics directed against modernism (see de la Motte-Haber [1990] 1995, 77).
This use of the term was inspired by Habermas who viewed postmodernism as a neoconservative, traditionalistic movement. Consequently, the
word "postmodern" was used in a polemic and negative sense when it was
applied to music.

When the general and international postmodern debate made its way
into Germany, the significance of the term became more confused in reference to music. According to Helga de la Motte-Haber there are various reasons for this, and she considers four of them (de la Motte-Haber [1990]
1995, 77–78). First, a concept of such "affected *gravitas* as that of postmodernism seemed too broadly based to characterize a phenomenon
specific to one particular country," even though these works in late-
Romantic style displayed all the characteristics of the theories of Charles
Jencks. Second, the "word soon lost its aesthetic meaning" as a new
"semantic wave spilt over from France and proved difficult to contain within precise musical channels." Third, postmodernism is a compound word,
whose meaning is dependent upon what we mean by modernism. That the
term "postmodernism" is so imprecise is "due not least to the fact that our
understanding of modernism is so varied, so that one sometimes wonders

whether those who theorize about it actually share a common culture."
Fourth, while postmodernism was seen as a label for a new epoch, its relevance was challenged by "the fact that continuity is everywhere in evidence."

While confusion over the meaning of postmodernism increased during
the second half of the 1980s, a more focused debate on musical postmodernism began. Within a time span of five years, three conferences were held
on the subject, resulting in three anthologies of texts: *Das Projekt Moderne
und die Postmoderne* 1989; "Moderne versus Postmoderne: Zur ästhetischen Theorie und Praxis in den Künsten" 1990; *Wiederaneignung und
Neubestimmung: Der Fall "Postmoderne" in der Musik* 1993. For many
participants in this debate, the more positive view of postmodernism articulated by the young German philosopher Wolfgang Welsch proved influential (Welsch [1987] 1993).[1] Welsch considered fundamental pluralism to
be the key concept of postmodernism (xvii). He argued that postmodern
phenomena exist when a fundamental pluralism of languages, models, and
methods are present not only in different works but in a single work
(Welsch 1988, 10).[2] The influence of Welsch's position did not eliminate the
neoconservative, negative view of postmodernism but rather resulted in the
existence of two contrary positions, as Thomas Schäfer has pointed out:

> the first one understands the Postmodernism as a kind of "new façadic
> art"in the epoch of "cultural stiffness," and consequently, as a sign for an
> epoch incompatible with Modernism; the other position, however, under-
> stands Postmodernism as a radicalized continuation of Modernism, freed
> of dogmatism. (Schäfer 1995, 238)

Hermann Danuser introduced the debate in the musicological discourse and since the mid-80s has written several articles on postmodernism
and concert music. Since these texts clearly reflect the changing meanings
of the term "postmodernism" as applied to music, I will use them as a point
of departure, considering some problems they give rise to and comparing
them with the ideas of other participants in the debate.

DANUSER AND THE CONCEPT OF POSTMODERNISM

Danuser, in his handbook on twentieth-century music, *Die Musik des 20.
Jahrhunderts*, defines postmodernism as a countercurrent against modern
music (Danuser 1984, 424). Danuser distinguishes two streams in this
countercurrent. The first is the return in the '70s to premodernist traditions
of European concert music as evident in the music of composers such as
George Rochberg, Krzysztof Penderecki, Ladislav Kupkovic, and the
younger generation of West German composers. Danuser's definition follows the general concept of the term in Germany at the beginning of the
'80s. The second stream is the revitalization of the American avant-garde,

especially the music of John Cage, in minimalism and meditative music. Danuser has two reasons for labeling those trends as postmodern (Danuser 1984, 392–93). First, they avoid the kind of subjectivity that is characteristic of modernism, and second, they abandon the structural complexity of modernism for simpler structures that are immediately comprehensible to the listener.

Four years later in "Zur Kritik der musikalischen Postmoderne," Danuser retains these two movements—the European return to tradition and the American avant-garde—that constitute musical postmodernism (Danuser 1988). As a result of a more thorough conceptual analysis, though, Danuser makes some modifications in his view of musical postmodernism compared to the earlier text. He conceives postmodernism as a relational concept, its meaning dependent partly upon what one means by modernism and partly upon what kind of relation we consider "post" to be (4). The main question in this context regards the relation of postmodernism to modernism: is it a continuation of modernism, a discontinuous opposite of modernism, or something else?

In order to understand Danuser's reasoning it is necessary to know his distinctions between modernism, avant-garde and new music (Danuser 1988, 4). Modernism is a work-oriented, rationally organized and—despite its break with tradition—latently tradition-based kind of new music. Avant-garde, on the other hand, is an experimental new music for a changed life situation and is directed against the work of art and its established institutions. New music is Danuser's general expression for both these movements.

If one uses modernism in this narrower sense as a starting-point—what Danuser calls the tradition of the advanced work from Schoenberg to Boulez—it follows that one possible postmodernism is the experimental avant-garde: the Duchamp-influenced happening, minimalism, and certain trends within pop and rock music, that is, music that negates the European art music tradition (Danuser 1988, 4). In this formulation, John Cage is the most important representative of postmodern music. However, according to Danuser, such use of the word postmodernism in Germany is less convincing since it is not rooted in the thought of German-language writers. But, he continues, when considering the American history of the word postmodernism, one can see that it has been used to designate different avant-garde movements.

If a wider concept of modernism is used as a point of departure, modernism as an umbrella term for new music (serial, post-serial, and avant-garde), which, according to Danuser, is often the case in ordinary language, traditional components figure centrally in a concept of postmodernism. (Danuser 1988, 4–5). Such a postmodern music is associated with a number of older composers who changed style in the '70s and a young generation of composers (born around 1950) who made their debut in the '70s with an aesthetics opposed to modern music: Rihm, Trojahn, von Bose, and others.

So far, Danuser's position in the second article is nearly identical to that of the earlier text. Depending on how one understands modernism, two differing concepts of postmodernism emerge (Danuser 1988, 5); hence, postmodernism is an ambiguous word with two different meanings when applied to music. The second aspect of Danuser's relational notion of post-modernism centers on the question of whether postmodernism constitutes a break with modernism or is its continuation, a question he takes up by comparing the music of three composers: Ladislav Kupkovic, Györgi Ligeti, and George Rochberg (Danuser 1988, 6–9).

Kupkovic (b. 1936) is a Slovak composer whose musical activities in Germany since the early 1970s identified him as avant-garde. Gradually, during the '70s he changed to a style based on nineteenth-century music, employing functional major-minor tonality, genres and forms from the Classic-Romantic repertoire, and an aesthetics corresponding to these tendencies; in other words, all traces of modernism and avant-garde were eliminated. For Danuser, Kupkovic's negation of modernism cannot be considered postmodern because the prefix "post" not only means after in time but also a partial continuation of the principles of aesthetic modernism. If postmodernism is not understood as such an extension, then all non-modern music since the late nineteenth century could be labeled post-modern. Danuser understands Penderecki's music similarly: its negation of modernism disqualifies it as postmodern.

Danuser uses a similar argument when considering Ligeti's Horn Trio (1983). While the strong break with modernism in Kupkovic's music disqualifies it as postmodern, the modification of modernist principles in the Horn Trio is too weak. For Danuser neither a total negation nor a minor modification of modernism qualifies a work as postmodern (Danuser 1988, 7).

On the other hand Danuser believes that the music of George Rochberg is postmodern since there exists both a distance from and a continuity with modernism. Rochberg's Piano Quintet from 1975 exemplifies Danuser's argument. Of the Quintet's seven movements, the first and last are freely atonal, the second and sixth mix atonal and tonal elements, and the third and fifth movements are completely tonal and in a style reminiscent of Brahms. Despite the stylistic mixture, though, the music is unified by the symmetrical formal cycle and by motivic and interval relationships between the movements (Danuser 1988, 8–9).

For Danuser, the postmodern aspect of Rochberg's music depends on the integration of stylistic pluralism into a unified compositional conception that enables an experiential unity). And, in this respect Rochberg's stylistic pluralism differs from the pluralistic conceptions within musical modernism. For instance, the modernist pluralism in the music of Bernd Alois Zimmermann or Luciano Berio, by virtue of collage and montage, results in an aesthetic discontinuity, the purpose of which is to create an artistic work totality in the form of a stream of consciousness as inspired by James Joyce.

QUOTATION AND COLLAGE TECHNIQUES IN THE LIGHT
OF POSTMODERNISM

In his next article—dealing with quotation and collage techniques in the light of postmodernism—Danuser again modifies his view of postmodernism (Danuser 1990). In this text, Danuser takes Charles Jencks, Jean-François Lyotard, and Wolfgang Welsch as his points of departure. To decide if the quotation technique employed is postmodern or not, Danuser uses this criterion: does the music present a fundamental pluralism or is there a unity holding the heterogeneous parts together? Danuser considers this ideal of unity to be common for both modernism and traditionalism (398–99).

In the earlier 1988 article Danuser considers the quotation and collage techniques of Zimmermann and Berio modern since there is no overall unity. In the 1990 article he argues exactly the opposite: it is the presence of unity that makes the quotation and collage techniques modern. Danuser still considers Zimmermann to be a composer of modernist music, but his compositional thinking reaches over toward postmodernism because of its pluralistic roots (Danuser 1990, 402). In a work like Berio's *Sinfonia* one finds both modern and postmodern tendencies. The modern tendency manifests itself in the composer's intention, despite the abundance of different materials, to integrate the different components. The pluralism of musical styles and of spoken or sung texts assumes a dynamic of its own that, despite the integrative attempt, leads to a postmodern aesthetic (403). Danuser takes Stockhausen as an example of a composer who conforms to the ideal of unity in his use of quotation technique. Stockhausen uses national anthems from around the world in *Hymnen,* Danuser does not consider the work postmodern since the music is thoroughly structured in a way typical of musical modernism (402–3).

How then does Danuser account for Rochberg in this article? Can Rochberg's pluralism be considered postmodern when the composer adheres to the ideal of unity? Danuser does consider Rochberg a postmodern composer, arguing that there are different kinds of postmodernism and that the tradional one must not be undervalued in relation to the ones closer to modernism and the avant-garde (Danuser 1990, 405–6). But he does not give any reasons for this claim and it leads to some serious questions. For instance, one might ask whether disunity really is a necessary criterion of postmodern quotation and collage technique when Danuser allows Rochberg's more unified use of stylistic quotations to be called postmodern. And if it is not, how should traditional postmodernism be separated from pure traditionalism? Perhaps Danuser's answer would be that in postmodern music there must be both a distance from and continuity with modernism, as he argued in the 1988 text. But where does this leave the criterion of unity versus disunity? A solution to the problem is to consider the relation between unity and disunity as a matter of degree, and not view them as opposites of each other.[3] Then it would be possible to argue that in traditional postmodernism the music is less unified and more pluralistic than in antimodern traditionalism, but more unified than in avant-garde postmodernism. Danuser, though, never defines what he means by unity, which perhaps is the main cause of the trouble.

Danuser also understands Alfred Schnittke to be a composer who, in breaking with the modernistic ideal of innovative development of the musical material, may be judged postmodern. Schnittke works with stylistic quotation in a way that is continuous with tradition, but that has a new quality due to the manner of elaborating traditional elements (Danuser 1990, 406–7). Here, thus, Danuser explicitly returns the criterion of both distance from and continuity with modernism, but he remains unclear on the issue of unity versus disunity.

Danuser's discussion of Cage refers to Lyotard's understanding of Cage's music as exemplifying a postmodern aesthetic.[4] This assessment is based on Cage's avoidance of an authoritarian ideal of unity which leads to a fundamental pluralism (Danuser 1990, 404). While recognizing Mauricio Kagel as another composer who abandoned the modernist ideal of total organization and unity, Danuser understands his music as belonging to the specific European tradition of modernism due to its reflexivity—a characteristic of modernism—and because it is characterized by a level of complexity that stands in the way of postmodern pluralism (Danuser 1990, 405).

POSTMODERN MUSICAL THINKING—SOLUTION OR ESCAPE?

The last of Danuser's articles to be discussed here also entails a changed perspective (Danuser 1991). Danuser here makes a distinction between two kinds of postmodernism: postmodernism as antimodernism and postmodernism as the modernism of today. Danuser uses Habermas's negative view of postmodernism to describe the first kind, defining it with these characteristics: condemnation of the ideal of rationality, rehabilitation of an irrational and often traditionalistic aesthetic of feeling, abandonment of complexity, retreat from the idea of avant-garde art, return to bourgeois concert music with traditional genres as symphony and string quartet (Danuser 1991, 60).

These characteristics are typical of the music of the young German composers of the mid-1970s. Despite musical distinctions between these composers, their music was typically directed against the previous modernist music which oriented itself toward Adorno's philosophy of history. Danuser calls this the traditional branch of musical postmodernism (Danuser 1991, 60–61). From the perspective of radical modernism, such postmodern music is an escape. But, as Danuser points out, in the context of a historical moment that has rehabilitated pleasure, modernism is on the retreat and the critics of affirmative art are fewer than two decades ago (62).

In a later part of the article Danuser points out that the view of post-modernism and the relation between postmodernism and modernism changed during the second half of the '80s. As Leslie Fiedler, Lyotard, and Welsch gradually became better known during this time, the earlier sense that modernism and postmodernism were opposites disappeared and the concept of postmodernism as today's modernism emerged (Danuser 1991, 63).

Danuser identifies three characteristics of this second type of postmod-ernism (Danuser 1991, 63–64):

1. Making historical elements accessible in a context of double coding.
2. Bridging the gap between high and low art.
3. Rehabilitating the avant-garde through postmodernism.

For Danuser, the concept of postmodernism articulated in these character-istics differs completely from that which Habermas formulated. In its ear-lier guise, postmodernism is a strictly traditional concept opposed to the avant-garde. In the later version, it is an avant-garde concept opposed to tradition and the hidden elements of high, traditional art within modernism. Further, Danuser affirms that a fundamental pluralism of musical languages is central for the second type of postmodernism, as demonstrated by the music of Berio, Crumb, and Rochberg. This formula-tion realigns Rochberg, away from the traditional postmodernism where he was placed in the 1990 article. Danuser does not state any reasons for this realignment, however, and one might indeed ask why Rochberg has changed sides.

The new idea in this text, then, is that avant-garde postmodernism is not only a phenomenon of the '50s and '60s, but also a tendency in the '70s and '80s that exists side by side with a more traditional postmodernism.

ISSUES AND PROBLEMS IN THE GERMAN DEBATE ON ART MUSIC AND POSTMODERNISM

Cage, Minimalism, and Postmodernism

In all his articles on music and postmodernism Danuser considers Cage a postmodernist. At the same time he is aware of the fact that this is not in line with general usage of the term in Germany. What, then, are the causes behind the German usage of the term? Siegfried Mauser writes that while postmodernism was identified with the avant-garde in the USA, Cage was seen as just an avant-garde phenomenon in Europe (Mauser 1990, 369–70). This understanding derived from characteristics common to the Cage/Feldman pole and the Boulez/Stockhausen pole: avoidance of tonal harmony and traditional melody. Therefore the compositional technique of Cage, according to Mauser, was easily assimilated into the progressive orientation of European modernism. This identification causes problems if one employs a concept of postmodernism in historical accounts of twentieth-century music. Mauser would avoid this problem by not utilizing a concept of postmodernism with respect to musical developments in America (371). This convenient escape route takes a curiously ethnocentric view. Should music history only be written from a European point of view? Shall words only be used in the senses they have in Europe? Mauser is not just describing the use of language in his discussion of Cage, he is also trying to regulate it. Like Humpty Dumpty, we might ask; "The question is, which is to be master?"

Danuser's view of musical minimalism as postmodern is also challenged by some writers. Ulrich Dibelius, for instance, writes that when something unmistakingly new is created under new circumstances, such music does not fall under the concept of postmodernism, even if certain features associated with musical postmodernism occur (Dibelius 1989, 7). For Dibelius, this is the case with minimalist music, especially in its early manifestations by Steve Reich.

Wolfgang Rihm and the Young Generation of German Composers

In all of his articles, Danuser considers as postmodern the German generation of composers born around 1950. This group of composers is also central in Helga de la Motte-Haber's texts on music and postmodernism, though she has a more negative stance toward them than Danuser (de la Motte-Haber 1987, 1989, [1990] 1995). As Siegfried Mauser points out there are three features that de la Motte-Haber takes as characteristic of the postmodernism of Wolfgang Rihm and the others (Mauser 1990, 375):
   1. Extreme and excessive use of secondary parameters of tempo, dynamics, and articulation that guarantee the sought-after expressive-hysteric effect.
   2. Quotation of historical styles.
   3. Return to traditional genres and forms.
Mauser is critical of all three features. First, excessive use of secondary parameters is nothing new; it is a characteristic feature in Schoenberg's music from his free atonal period. Second, the return to tonal elements is overrated as a model for the restorative tendencies within postmodernism. Third, the return to traditional genres and forms is also typical of what Mauser calls classical modernism, that is, the twelve-tone music of the Second Viennese School. On the basis of these conceptual difficulties, Mauser argues that we should stop using the concept of postmodernism in connection with the no-longer young German composers and their leading figure, Rihm (Mauser 1990, 376–79).

Mauser's arguments are themselves not beyond criticism. For instance, why does he only discuss the return to tonality when it comes to quotation of historical styles? This is especially puzzling since de la Motte-Haber maintains that tonality is not a necessary criterion. She claims that some recent music, for instance Arvo Pärt's, uses triads and tonality to an extent greater than the neo-Romantic symphonies but does not try to affect listeners' emotions (de la Motte-Haber 1987, 37). For de la Motte-Haber, then, the late romantic element—the extreme effects and the striving after expressivity—are necessary conditions of postmodernism.

Problems arise with respect to Mauser's criticism of de la Motte-Haber's first and third features. Mauser asserts that excessive use of secondary parameters and the return to traditional genres cannot define Rihm's postmodernism since they already appear in Schoenberg's music. However, the control over secondary parameters is characteristic of Schoenberg's free atonal music in which he abandons traditional genres, and the reliance on traditional genres is characteristic of his twelve-tone music which reduces the extreme contrasts and sudden changes of secondary features. As such, one might argue that Rihm's postmodernism arises from the specific combination of the three features not from the presence of any particular one. What makes Rihm postmodern, then, is his idea of inclusive composition, where all materials and techniques are available to the composer, and his claim that music is a free and spontaneous art of expression (see Danuser 1984, 400–1).

Other Composers in the German Debate

Given Mauser's critique, one might well ask which composers are postmodern in Mauser's view? Mauser takes Welsch's idea of a fundamental pluralism of languages, models, and procedures and the double-coding and ambiguity that result as his point of departure (Mauser 1990, 380). Mauser derives the characteristic musical features of this postmodern aesthetic from Ihab Hassan's criteria of postmodernism: fragmentation of musical structure, dissolution of systems and canons (in relation to rules of compositional technique), irony, and entertainment. The most important feature, however, is stylistic pluralism and the double-coding of material that does not lead to a unified work.

The return to tonal structures in the context of a post-tonal historical moment is insufficient for classifying a work as postmodern since this is only one aspect of postmodern aesthetics (Mauser 1990, 381). Thus, the music of, for instance, Kupkovic and Pärt is not postmodern because it does not satisfy the criterion of pluralism and stylistic diversity. Postmodern aesthetics should not be reduced to restorative tendencies.

Mauser concludes his argument by discussing three "outsiders from the older generation," whom he thinks show a certain closeness to postmodern aesthetics: Schnittke, Crumb, and Killmayer (Mauser 1990 381–82). Schnittke's music presents a well-known example of a pluralistic use of materials and techniques in which both traditional and advanced elements provide a means of double-coding. In the instance of Crumb, Mauser considers Horst Weber's analysis of *Music for a Summer Evening*. Weber's analysis focuses on the use of different materials and techniques and the dramatic relationship between tonality and atonality, and concludes that the work does not operate as a unified whole (Weber 1989). Mauser finds Weber's conclusion too conventional. For Weber, integration does not occur in the intended content (Gehalt) of the work. By this he means that the semantic meanings of atonality and tonality are activated in ways that conform to their meanings in reception history: atonality stands for darkness, aggression, and chaos; tonality for light, law, and order (Weber 1989, 206–7). Killmayer, the last composer exemplified by Mauser, creates a music characterized by a virtuosic and constant change among tonal, modal, and atonal materials that are pieced together into a fragmented structure. For Mauser, Killmayer's music approximates a postmodern aesthetic (Mauser 1990, 382).

The music of George Rochberg is also taken up by Horst Weber in another text that charts the American composer's career (Weber 1990). Weber concludes that Rochberg's criticism of technical rationality and the avant-garde is based on postmodern topoi, but that the gradual reduction of pluralism in his music stands in opposition to a postmodern aesthetic, which for Weber (after Lyotard) is characterized by pluralism (Weber 1989, 271). Rochberg's reduction of pluralism is complete in the Oboe Concerto (1983), where he abandons the confrontations between tonal and atonal music (269). But already in the works from the 1970s there is an attempt to unify the music despite the use of both tonal and atonal styles (268).

Schnittke is also singled out by Wolfgang Gratzer, who views the polystylism in the music by Schnittke, Schedrin, and Pärt from the '60s and early '70s as a specific Soviet form of postmodernism. Like Mauser and de la Motte-Haber, Gratzer does not consider Pärt's later music to be postmodern because of its unity and purity (Gratzer 1993, 82–84).

Subjectivity, Authenticity, and Postmodernism

Two of the most problematic areas in the discussion of postmodernism and music reside in issues of subjectivity and authenticity. Some consider subjectivity to be an important characteristic of postmodern music (Dibelius 1989, 7), while others argue that it is the loss of subjectivity that is typical. Helga de la Motte-Haber, for instance, claims that there is no expressive subject in postmodern music (de la Motte-Haber 1987, 37). She considers Richard Strauss's music to be more honest since it does not pretend to express the sincere, an expression she considers impossible in the absence of unique and original stylistic means. She suggests, then, that postmodern music is a façadic art which, with a bombastic mobilization of means, tries to conceal that it has nothing to express that traditional music has not already expressed in a more subtle and beautiful manner (38).

The question of whether music must be new, unique, and original to be subjective, expressive, and sincere remains, however. In his *Postscript to the Name of the Rose*, Umberto Eco writes:

> I think of the postmodern attitude as that of a man who loves a very cultivated woman and knows he cannot say to her, "I love you madly" because he knows that she knows (and that she knows that he knows) that these words have already been written by Barbara Cartland. Still, there is a solution. He can say, "As Barbara Cartland would put it, I love you madly." At this point, having avoided false innocence, having said clearly that it is no longer possible to speak innocently, he will nevertheless have said what he wanted to say to the woman: that he loves her, but he loves her in an age of lost innocence. (Eco [1983] 1984, 67)

If we are to believe Eco, de la Motte-Haber is wrong when she claims that postmodern music cannot be subjective.[5] But of course, postmodern subjectivity differs from that of earlier epochs. Danuser discusses the problems facing composers who would recover musical expressivity in his first text on music and postmodernism (Danuser 1984, 403). Due to the dominance of older music in the present, a free and spontaneous subjectivity after the Sturm und Drang aesthetics of the eighteenth century is no longer possible. Composers are thus forced to return to a historically-mediated expression, and consequently risk recreating a second-hand expression.

Given the problems of expressivity, is it possible for music to be authentic? The idea of authenticity in musical modernism during the '50s and '60s was governed by Adorno's philosophy of music, as Danuser has pointed out (Danuser 1991, 57). Only the composer who used the most advanced musical materials and avoided worn out ideas could claim to be authentic. As postmodern music breaks with the ideal of progress and the modernistic canon of aesthetic prohibitions, it cannot be authentic in Adorno's sense, for obvious reasons. Horst Weber, for instance, writes that Rochberg's striving for expressivity manifests itself in a return to tonal idioms (Weber 1990, 269). The expressivity Rochberg achieves differs from an authentic type, since that is achieved through breaking the norms of a historically defined style. The problem, according to Weber, is whether such norms exist in the present situation and consequently, if an authentic expressivity is at all possible when there are no norms to break.

Thomas Schäfer articulates a different position on the issue of authenticty. He writes about the composer Peter Ruzicka (b. 1948), whose aesthetic was formed in the early 70s from the idea that everything already had been said in the history of music, and that no really new musical material was available anymore (Schäfer 1995, 212). Therefore, authenticity had to be defined in a way different from Adorno's. Schäfer posits that authenticity was understood as a striving for a unique and original personal language (*Eigensprachlichkeit*) (Schäfer 1995, 228). Music should be in the service of expression and find a language that could communicate the subjective emotions of the composer without sacrificing the constructive element. Ruzicka's return to musical expression corresponds to the development of "music about music" which takes as central the relation to tradition. But Schäfer argues that there are two categories that stand in the way of a free-floating use of the material from music history: memory and reflection (230).

Schäfer's views are different from both Danuser's and de la Motte-Haber's. Danuser considers reflection to be characteristic of modernism, and it is this reflective feature that makes the avant-garde music of Kagel modern rather than postmodern. In a similar argument, de la Motte-Haber points out that while the piano piece *An Tasten* by Kagel uses historical material to a greater extent than some pieces by Rihm, it embodies an aesthetic attitude that makes it different from the neo-Romantic works (de la Motte-Haber [1990] 1995, 80–81). This attitude manifests itself in a musical focusing on the discrepancy between historically distinct material which produces alienating and paradoxical effects that afford an intellectual pleasure that contrasts with Rihm's appeal to emotional immediacy. Kagel's juxtapositions create a sense of historical distance, a distance which is neutralized in Rihm's music.[6]

Postmodernism as an Epoch Label

Another issue in the German debate revolves around whether postmodernism constitutes a new epoch in the history of music. Most writers agree that a change took place in the 1970s when both modernism and the avant-garde lost their earlier importance (see, for instance, Danuser 1984, 398; de la Motte-Haber [1990] 1995, 78–79). But they often disagree on the significance of this change and its relation to historical categories. For instance, does a new epoch begin in the '70s, and if so, is postmodernism an adequate laber for this epoch?

Ulrich Dibelius argues that the confusion over labels for musical epochs generally precludes an objection to the use of postmodernism as a label for a certain characteristic development in music since the middle of the '70s (Dibelius 1989, 6). For Dibelius, not all trends in contemporary composition fall under the concept of postmodernism, unless the comprehensive pluralism prevalent in recent compositional practices is understood as a postmodern phenomenon. Such a use of the term "postmodernism," however, just turns it into a confusing slogan that does not help an understanding of the present situation.

Like Dibelius, Danuser argues that postmodernism is not a category that can be used to characterize the Zeitgeist of our present in all its aspects and, as such, cannot be used as an epoch label with clearly defined criteria (Danuser 1988, 5). However, the same problem also applies to the use of modernism as an epoch label. Danuser writes that modernistic composers and their theoreticians have tried to establish modernism as the only relevant musical culture in the twentieth century. But, in the present pluralistic age, modernism appears as only a part of culture (*Teilkultur*), never reaching a dominant status. However, as Danuser writes, modernism and postmodernism are not neutral, descriptive terms but are connected to values that in the concrete historical situation are coupled to questions of institutional power. Use of the concept of modernism to characterize the 1950s and the '60s is justified because the exponents of modernism (including serialism) managed to get the most power in publicity matters and institutions compared to other parts of the culture. So even if serialism did not dominate in a quantitative way, Danuser understands it as dominant in terms of the power it exerted. But in the same way, the discussion on postmodernism dominates the discourse today. This does not, however, eliminate the possibility that neglected modernist composers of the '70s and '80s will be estimated differently in the future.

Philosophy of Language and the Criteria of Postmodern Music

As the English philosopher of language John Searle points out, any analysis of a word's meaning will depend on certain general conceptions "concerning how words mean and how they relate to the world. It is only given some general theory of or approach to language that one can even get started on a particular linguistic analysis" (Searle 1971, 1). His comments provide a context for considering what philosophy of language, explicit or implicit, lies behind the German writers on music and postmodernism.

The word "postmodernism" is often seen as enigmatic in the German texts. Dibelius, for instance, calls it a beautiful, sphinx-like key word (Dibelius 1989, 4). Danuser understands postmodernism as an iridescent concept, a word whose meaning has turned even more obscure the longer the debate has lasted, and further, he argues that, as a word game without rules, the debate on postmodernism itself has postmodern features (Danuser 1988, 4). He cites Peter Bürger's thesis that in postmodern thought signs just refer to other signs and not to something signified.[7] Despite these observations, Danuser concludes not that the debate is a sham battle over pseudo-problems but rather that it is justified, even necessary, as an attempt to understand important tendencies in our time.

The philosopher Wolfgang Welsch, in opposition to those claiming that there are not phenomena justifying the use of a new term, argues that the word "postmodernism" does indeed refer to something new (Welsch [1987] 1993, 9). But, for Welsch, use of the term has been misleading since it suggests that postmodernism is the same as antimodernism (319). Rather, he argues that postmodernism transforms rather than ends modernism. Further, Welsch criticizes conceptual realism, believing that words do not have any immanent meaning, and advocates nominalism instead.[8] The term "postmodernism" is like the term "*Vatermörder*," the German word for choker or

high collar, which literally means "father murderer." No one would seriously contemplate the idea of bringing a *Vatermörderer* to court. Similarly, we
should not understand the word postmodernism too literally since its usefulness arises from crises in which old words no longer fit, and where no adequate new words are in sight.

This part of Welsch's thoughts on postmodernism have not, however,
been very influential in the debate on music and postmodernism. For
instance, as we have seen, both Danuser and de la Motte-Haber claim that
the meaning of the word "postmodernism" is dependent upon what we
mean by modernism and what relation we consider "post" to be, and many
other participants in the debate share this view. They are not necessarily
wrong in this, but the texts are often confusing concerning a view of language. Most writers assume a distinction between term, concept (Begriff),
and object, but they often confuse the categories, especially term and concept. And the question of whether the meaning is immanent or conventional is seldom addressed. The authors also take different approaches to
the issue of definition. The main issues here are what is defined: terms, concepts or objects? And, are definitions stipulative, descriptive, or regulative?
For instance, on one hand, Danuser mixes abstract conceptual analysis
with references to actual language use (Danuser 1988, 4–5). And on the
other, Mauser would regulate the meaning of musical postmodernism
(Mauser 1990, 371 and 379).

Are there, then, any defining characteristics that are considered common for all music labeled postmodern in the German debate? And is it
necessary that all music labeled postmodern has common and specific features? Some have attempted to formulate criteria of postmodern music in
terms of sufficient and necessary conditions. For instance, Danuser maintains that Rochberg, in his criticism of the avant-garde ideal of progress
and novelty, complies with a necessary but not a sufficient condition of
postmodernism (Danuser 1990, 406). De la Motte-Haber, in her discussion of Kagel, claims that the "use of older material does not necessarily
make a piece of music postmodern" (de la Motte-Haber [1990] 1995, 81).
However, no one manages, or finds it possible, to formulate both necessary and sufficient conditions. Consequently, most of the participants in
the German debate (including Danuser) believe that fundamental pluralism, which implies a break with the modernist ideal of unity, is the only
common characteristic of postmodern music. The particular styles and
compositional techniques used are of secondary importance. Welsch, in
one of his few paragraphs on postmodernism and music, argues that postmodernism should not be understood as an essentialist term and that one
has to consider and work with different sets of criteria (Welsch 1990,
362–63). And, in the end, he maintains that, rather than looking for a
common feature uniting all postmodern music, a more satisfactory under-

standing of postmodern phenomena resides in Wittgenstein's notion of family resemblance.

NOTES

1. Welsch also edited an anthology (1988), that made the key texts on post-modernism available in German.

2. On the influence of this concept, see Danuser 1990, 398; Mauser 1990, 380; Schäfer 1995, 221.

3. Jonathan D. Kramer does this in the American debate (Kramer 1995). Danuser's arguments could also have benefited from the kind of distinctions Kramer makes between textual and perceptual unity. In a more general perspective, it is interesting to compare Kramer's distinctions between modernism and post-modernism, antimodernism and postmodernism, and neoconservative and radical postmodernism to Danuser's categories.

4. Lyotard's view of Cage is elaborated in Danuser 1991.

5. De la Motte-Haber refers to Eco's book but does not consider the relevance of this paragraph for her own line of argument. However, she is critical of Eco's idea that ironic quotation is an important characteristic of postmodern art (de la Motte-Haber 1987, 38).

6. Wulf Konold, who wrote one of the first essays on music and postmod-ernism in Germany, expresses a similar view. Konold mentions Penderecki as the most obvious example of a composer who, without reflection, uses music history as a stock-in-trade for plundering (Konold 1982, 83).

7. Curiously, Danuser makes no mention of Saussure and French poststruc-turalist philosophy.

8. Despite his adoption of nominalism, Welsch uses the term concept (Begriff) frequently.

WORKS CITED

Danuser, Hermann. 1984. *Die Musik des 20. Jahrhunderts*. Neues Handbuch der Musikwissenschaft, Band 7. Wiesbaden: Laaber Verlag.

———. 1988. "Zur Kritik der musikalischen Postmoderne." *Neue Zeitschrift für Musik* 149/12: 4–9.

———. 1990. "Musikalische Zitat—und Collageverfahren im Lichte der (Post) Moderne-Diskussion." In *Jahrbuch 4 der Bayerischen Akademie der Schönen Künste*, edited by Oswald Georg Baur and Sylvia Riedmaier. Schaftlach: Oreos Verlag. 395–409.

———. 1991. "Postmodernes Musikdenken—Lösung oder Flucht?" in *Neue Musik im politischem Wandel*. Veröffentlichungen des Instituts für Neue Musik und Musikerziehung Darmstadt, Band 32, edited by Hermann Danuser. Mainz: Schott. 56–66.

Dibelius, Ulrich. 1989. "Postmoderne in der Musik." *Neue Zeitschrift für Musik* 150/2: 4–9.

Eco, Umberto. [1983] 1984. *Postscript to The Name of the Rose.* Translated by Wiiliam Weaver. San Diego: Harcourt Brace Jovanovich.

Gratzer, Wolfgang. 1993. "'Postmoderne' überall? Aktuelle (In)Fragestellungen im Blick auf sowjetische Musik nach 1945." In *Wiederaneignung und Neubestimmung. Der Fall "Postmoderne" in der Musik,* edited by Otto Kolleritsch. Wien, Graz: Universal Edition. 63–86.

Habermas, Jurgen. [1981] 1987. "Modernity—An Incomplete Project." In *Interpretive Social Science: A Second Look,* edited by Paul Rabinow and William M. Sullivan. Berkeley and Los Angeles: University of California Press. 141–56. Reprinted from *The New German Critique 22.*

Konold, Wulf. 1982. "Komponieren in der 'Postmoderne.'" In *Hindemith-Jahrbuch* 1981, Bd. 10. Mainz: Schott. 73–85.

Kramer, Jonathan D. 1995. "Beyond Unity: Toward an Understanding of Musical Postmodernism." In *Concert Music, Rock, and Jazz since 1945: Essays and Analytical Studies,* edited by Elizabeth West Marvin and Richard Hermann. Rochester: University of Rochester Press. 11–33.

Mauser, Siegfried. 1990. "Zur Theoriebildung in der musikalischen Moderne/ Postmoderne-Diskussion." In *Jahrbuch 4 der Bayerischen Akademie der Schönen Künste,* edited by Oswald Georg Baur and Sylvia Riedmaier. Schaftlach: Oreos Verlag. 368–83.

"Moderne versus Postmoderne: Zur ästhetischen Theorie und Praxis in den Künsten." 1990. In *Jahrbuch 4 der Bayerische Akademie der Schönen Künste,* edited by Oswald Georg Bauer and Sylvia Riedmaier. Schaftlach: Oreos Verlag. 241–470.

Motte-Haber, Helga de la. 1987. "Die Gegenaufklärung der Postmoderne." In *Musik und Theorie.* Veröffentlichungen des Instituts für Neue Musik und Musikerziehung Darmstadt, Band 28, edited by Rudolf Stephan. Mainz: Schott. 31-44.

———. 1989. "Merkmale postmoderner Musik." In *Das Projekt Moderne und die Postmoderne,* edited by Wilfried Gruhn. Regensburg: Gustav Bosse Verlag. 53–67.

———. [1990] 1995. "Postmodernism in Music." *Contemporary Music Review,* 12/1: 77–83. First published as "Musikalische Postmoderne: Rückshau als Neubewertung," In *Jahrbuch 4 der Bayerischen Akademie der Schönen Künste,* edited by Oswald Georg Baur and Sylvia Riedmaier. Schaftlach: Oreos Verlag. 384–394.

Das Projekt Moderne und die Postmoderne. 1989. Hochschuldokumentationen zu Musikwissenschaft und Musikpädagogik. Musikhochschule Freiburg, Band 2, edited by Wilfried Gruhn. Regensburg: Gustav Bosse Verlag. 1989.

Schäfer, Thomas. 1995. "Anti-Moderne oder Avantgarde-Konzpet? Überlegungen zur musikalischen Postmoderne." *International Review of the Aesthetics and Sociology of Music* 26/2: 211–38.

Searle, John R. 1971. Introduction, to *The Philosophy of Language*. Oxford Readings in Philosophy, John R. Searle, ed. Oxford: Oxford University Press. 1–12.

Weber, Horst. 1989. "George Crumb: Amplified Piano—Amplified Tradition. Zur Kritik 'Postmodernen' Komponierens." In *Das Projekt Moderne und die Postmoderne*, edited by Wilfried Gruhn. Regensburg: Gustav Bosse Verlag. 197–210.

———. 1990. "George Rochberg oder Vom Verschwinden des kompositorischen Subjekts." In *Bericht über das Internationale Symposium "Charles Ives und die amerikanische Musiktradition bis zur Gegenwart" Köln 1988*. Kölner Beiträge zur Musikforschung, Band 164. Klaus Wolfgang Niemöller, ed. Regensburg: Gustav Bosse Verlag. 265–80.

Welsch, Wolfgang. [1987] 1993. *Unsere postmoderne Moderne*. 4th ed. Berlin: Akademie Verlag.

———. 1990. "Asynchronien: Ein Schlüssel zum Verständnis der Diskussion um Moderne und Postmoderne." In *Jahrbuch 4 der Bayerischen Akademie der Schönen Künste,* edited by Oswald Georg Baur and Sylvia Riedmair. Schaftlach: Oreos Verlag. 347–67.

———, ed. 1988. *Wege aus der Moderne: Schlüsseltexte der Postmoderne-Diskussion*. Weinheim: VCH, Acta Humaniora.

Wiederaneignung und Neubestimmung: Der Fall "Postmoderne" in der Musik. 1993. Studien zur Wertungsforschung Band 26, edited by Otto Kolleritsch. Wien, Graz: Universal Edition.

CHAPTER 5

Music and Musical Practices in Postmodernity
Timothy D. Taylor

> Modernism is modernity experienced as trouble.
> —Stuart Hall (1989, 12)

I BEGIN WITH THE DESIRE TO SPEAK OF THE LIVING

It seems that the world has changed dramatically in recent years. But there is also no question that the world has been changing dramatically since at least the rise of capitalism as the dominant economic system in the West and, at the same time, the West's colonialized and imperialized elsewheres. Still, most would agree that the last couple of decades have changed so much from the past that we seem to be entering into a new historical era. The problem is, nobody can agree on what to call it. Is it postmodern? Postindustrial? Globalized? Transnational? Late capitalist? Multinational capitalist? The Information Age?[1]

Here I examine this contemporary moment partly as "postmodern"—not so much because I think this is the best vantage point, for I don't—but because it is the most frequently invoked term when examining music and/or other contemporary cultural forms, to the extent that the music industry, musicians, fans, and scholars now use the term. Rather than claiming that there is some kind of music out there that we could call post-modern, I am going to argue instead that modes of representation and marketing of music have changed in the last decade or so: classical musicians are more commodified than ever before, and contemporary composers face even greater pressures to make themselves known.

POSTMODERNITY, POSTMODERNISM, POSTMODERN

In getting to the overall argument about (re)presentation and marketing, however, it is necessary at first to sort out the different "postmoderns" by separating postmodern*ity* and postmodern*ism*. In doing this it is important at this point to recall Marshall Berman's argument concerning modernity in *All that is Solid Melts into Air*, for we can take his ideas concerning the modern world and extend them into our own, as Dick Hebdige has done; thus we can think of postmodern*ity* as a period and postmodern*ism* as artistic responses to it (Berman 1988; Hebdige 1994). Such a formulation is crucial and will shape much of the following. I should also note that this overview is mainly concerned with the canonical works of postmodern theory, for these have had the most lasting influence and have most shaped discussions of music.

POSTMODERNISM AS STYLE

In discussions of music, by far the most frequently used sense of "postmodern" refers to style, and many authors compile lists of stylistic traits, lists that include some well-worn words in cultural theory: intertextuality, inter-referentiality, pastiche, bricolage, fragmentation, depthlessness, the fragmentation of the subject, and more. Ihab Hassan includes a table in *The Postmodern Turn* that demonstrates the "list-iness" some authors employ when attempting to capture postmodernism (Figure 5-1).

Such representations can lead (and have led in discussions of music) to problems, as if one can approach any cultural form or event with a checklist: Postmodern? yes/no. Many discussions of postmodernism in music proceed along these lines, with the author wondering if that work or composer is postmodern or not because of its use of pastiche, or its intertextuality, or because it has crossed the great divide.

What great divide? This is another much-discussed feature of postmodernist cultural production, and it concerns the bending of genres and the appropriation of "low" cultural forms into "high." This idea's author, Andreas Huyssen, writes that the discourse of the great divide "is challenged by recent developments in the arts, film, literature, architecture, and criticism" and "goes by the name of postmodernism" (Huyssen 1986, viii). Huyssen's articulation of this phenomenon has been highly influential in many discussions of music, and names such as Philip Glass, Laurie Anderson, and others are often cited as makers of postmodern musics, partly because they seem to represent this crossing. I think that Huyssen's argument is important and I will return to it below.

POSTMODERNITY AS MOMENT

Another use of the term "postmodern" in discussions of music refers to postmodernity as a historical moment. Charles Jencks offers a periodization of modernity and postmodernity in which he considers modernity and postmodernity not just as periods in the arts, or as sets of styles and aesthetic views, but as periods in history. Jencks offers a chart in which he identifies three periods: Pre-Modern, Modern, and Postmodern (Figure 5-2). This has been an influential periodization of the -isms: qualities and/or states contained in temporal boxes:

Modernism	Postmodernism
Romanticism/Symbolism	Pataphysics/Dadaism
Form (conjunctive, closed)	Antiform (disjunctive, open)
Purpose	Play
Design	Chance
Hierarchy	Anarchy
Mastery/Logos	Exhaustion/Silence
Art Object/Finished Work	Process/Performance/Happening
Distance	Participation
Creation/Totalization	Decreation/Deconstruction
Synthesis	Antithesis
Presence	Absence
Centering	Dispersal
Genre/Boundary	Text/Intertext
Semantics	Rhetoric
Paradigm	Syntagm
Hypotaxis	Parataxis
Metaphor	Metonymy
Selection	Combination
Root/Depth	Rhizome/Surface
Interpretation/Reading	Against Interpretation/Misreading
Signified	Signifier
Lisible (Readerly)	*Scriptible* (Writerly)
Narrative/*Grande Histoire*	Anti-narrative/*Petite Histoire*
Master code	Idiolect
Symptom	Desire
Type	Mutant
Genital/Phallic	Polymorphous/Androgynous
Paranoia	Schizophrenia
Origin/Cause	Difference-Différance/Trace
God the Father	The Holy Ghost
Metaphysics	Irony
Determinacy	Indeterminacy
Transcendence	Immanence

Figure 5-1. Ihab Hassan's "Schematic Differences between Modernism and Postmodernism" (Hassan 1987, 91–92).

	Production	Society	Time	Orientation	Culture
PRE-MODERN 10,000 B.C.–1450	Neolithic Revolution Agriculture Handwork Dispersed	Tribal/Feudal Ruling class of Kings, Priests, and Military Peasants	Slow-changing Reversible	Local/City Agrarian	Aristocratic Integrated Style
MODERN 1450–1960	Industrial Revolution Factory Mass-production Centralized	Capitalist Owning class of Bourgeoisie Workers	Linear	Nationalist Rationali-sation of Business Exclusive	Bourgeois Mass-culture Reigning Styles
POST-MODERN 1960–	Information Revolution Office Segmented-production Decentralized	Global Para-class of Cognitariat Office Workers	Fast-changing Cyclical	World/Local Multinational Pluralist Eclectic Inclusive	Taste-cul-tures Many Genres

Figure 5-2. Charles Jencks's "The Three Eras of Civilization" (Jencks 1986, 47).

Fordist Modernity	Flexible Postmodernity
economies of scale/master code/hierarchy	economies of scope/idiolect/anarchy
homogeneity/detail division of labour	diversity/social division of labour
paranoia/alienation/symptom	schizophrenia/decentering/desire
public housing/monopoly capital	homelessness/entrepreneurialism
purpose/design/master/determinacy	play/chance/exhaustion/indeterminacy
production capital/universalism	fictitious capital/localism
state power/trade unions	financial power/individualism
state welfarism/metropolis	neo-conservatism/counterurbanization
ethics/money commodity	aesthetics/moneys of account
God the Father/materiality	The Holy Ghost/immateriality
production/originality/authority	reproduction/pastiche/eclecticism
blue collar/avant-gardism	white collar/commercialism
interest group politics/semantics	charismatic politics/rhetoric
centralization/totalization	decentralization/deconstruction
synthesis/collective bargaining	antithesis/local contracts
operation management/master code	strategic management/idiolect
phallic/single task/origin	androgynous/multiple tasks/trace
metatheory/narrative/depth	language games/image/surface
mass production/class politics	small-batch production/social
technical-scientific rationality	movements/pluralistic otherness
utopia/redemptive art/concentration	heterotopias/spectacle/dispersal
specialized work/collective consumption	flexible worker/symbolic capital
function/representation/signified	fiction/self-reference/signifier
industry/Protestant work ethic	services/temporary contract
mechanical reproduction	electronic reproduction
becoming/epistemology/regulation	being/ontology/deregulation
urban renewal/relative space	urban revitalization/place
state interventionism/industrialization	laissez-faire/deindustrialization
internationalism/permanence/time	geopolitics/ephemerality/space

Figure 5-3. From David Harvey's "Fordist Modernity versus Flexible Postmodernity, or the Interpenetration of Opposed Tendencies in Capitalist Society as a Whole" (Harvey 1989, 340–41).

While it is possible to agree—or disagree—with the dates and characterizations, the problem is that such a schematicization implies that these periods actually ended, and can thus be contained in boxes. Such a table also hides the many ways that ideas and practices from one period survive into the next, just as some ideas from modernity and modernism are alive and well today, as are peoples' practices.

Another tabular characterization comes from David Harvey's *The Condition of Postmodernity*, a book I greatly admire (Figure 5-3). For Harvey, Fordism as the dominant mode of industrial production gives way to "flexible accumulation," which Harvey says is "marked by a direct confrontation with the rigidities of Fordism," resting on "flexibility with respect to labour processes, labour markets, products, and patterns of consumption" (Harvey 1989, 147). Although Harvey's observations are useful and often provocative, their confinement to a list of binary oppositions gives the impression that modernity has given way, has been superseded, that modernity was one state or a collection of states, and that the term "flexible postmodernity" labels a new collection.

Harvey is careful to point out that such oppositions are never so clear-cut. But the danger is that the subtlety of Harvey's thought in his prose, and his caveat will be lost on those who want to view postmodernism as nothing but lists; or, to be fair, something that can be wholly described through the use of binaries and two-handed comparisons. The greater problem may lie in labeling itself, for labels such as "postmodern" imply a fixedness that social processes never have.

COME TOGETHER

In an early attempt to pull together the seemingly divergent tendencies of style and period, Fredric Jameson authored what has become one of the most influential arguments concerning postmodernism in *Postmodernism, or, the Cultural Logic of Late Capitalism* (first published as an article in 1984); given the half-life of theoretical texts, the fact that this one is still influential is worth noting. Jameson wrote of the importance of examining postmodernity not only in terms of style, but as a period as well, and the opening essay in the book (which gives its title to the book) offers a "periodizing hypothesis" of postmodernity. He writes that "it seems to me essential to grasp postmodernism not as a style but rather as a cultural dominant: a conception which allows for the presence and coexistence of a range of very different, yet subordinate, features" (Jameson 1991, 4). So far so good. He continues: "Aesthetic production . . . has become integrated into commodity production generally: the frantic economic urgency of producing fresh waves of ever more novel-seeming goods (from clothing to airplanes), at ever greater rates of turnover, now assigns an increasingly essential structural function and position to aesthetic innovation and experimentation" (Jameson 1991, 4–5).

For Jameson, this era of "multinational capitalism" makes everything available to everyone; shopping represents just another form of recreation; access to other cultures and their artifacts is practically limitless; the juxtapositions of various times, places, and artifacts made possible by technology boggles the mind. Postmodernism for Jameson involves a "new depthlessness," a "weakening of historicity," a "waning of affect," a new culture of the image or simulacrum. And Jameson invokes Jacques Lacan's theory of schizophrenia to help describe the sort of new fractured syntax evident in postmodernism. With this article, Jameson injected some sanity into the discussion, refusing to separate postmoder*nity* as a period and postmodern*ism* as responses to it, though most writings after this influential article have tended to focus on the postmodernism-as-style aspects of his argument.

Finally, in this section, I would be remiss not to note some other influential characterizations of postmodernity; in particular, Jean-François Lyotard's now-classic conception of postmodernity in *The Postmodern Condition* as "incredulity toward metanarratives" has been widely cited, although it raises troubling questions in its seeming denial of the possibility for any kind of change through conventional means: political activism, education, revolution (Lyotard 1984, vii).[2] Lyotard's idea is essentially a pessimistic anti-politics.

Let me note a curious moment in which, drawing partly on Lyotard or misunderstandings of Lyotard, some cultural theorists of music—myself included—conflated this "incredulity toward metanarratives" with oppositionality.[3] This position was taken to extreme lengths in Russell A. Potter's *Spectacular Vernaculars: Hip-Hop and the Politics of Postmodernism*, in which he writes, among other things, that "the postmodernism of hip-hop pushes the boundaries of the political, in the process redefining the very structures of resistance" (Potter 1995, 15). Despite this move by Potter and others, most cultural theorists quickly realized that marginalized subcultures had in some sense *always* been oppositional, and had always employed techniques such as bricolage now generally seen as postmodern as ways of constructing their own realities. Thus for these purposes the chronology implicit in the term "*post*modernism" was misleading.[4] Still, bricolage and pastiche have become important words in the descriptions of the postmodern world, insofar as they are now applied to mainstream culture as well.

At any rate, Lyotard's was an influential formulation; much was made of it, and it has been advanced and championed in even more problematic directions by other theorists, most prominently Jean Baudrillard, who has argued not only that the belief in metanarratives has gone, but that belief itself is missing. "Power is no longer present," he writes, "except to conceal the fact that there is none. . . . Illusion is no longer possible because reality is no longer possible"(quoted in Berman 1992, 45).[5] For theorists such as

Baudrillard, meaning itself is lost in a welter of signs loosed from their moorings.

In concluding this section, it is important to recall what is perhaps the most important lesson to be learned from Jameson: that modernity/modernism and postmodernity/postmodernism are not just temporal, or just stylistic, or even both together. Instead of being no more than a period in which we find ourselves, "postmodernity" refers to a historical moment in which ideologies or sets of ideologies from the past and present can be tapped into by whomever has access to them; some of these are ideologies we would recognize as originating in modernity. So, for example, modernist musical and other aesthetic values are alive and well in the academy, where modern and modernist discourses have also survived. Further, the values of modernity are, for the most part, present in postmodernity, they've just been shuffled, some newly emphasized, some de-emphasized. And this shuffling can make a big difference.

POSTMODERN POLITICAL ECONOMY

To these two postmoderns—postmodernity and postmodernism—I would like to argue for a third. Neither of these two postmoderns just outlined pay all that much attention to social realities, that is to say, political-economic realities, with the exception of David Harvey's (and even Harvey is more concerned with industrial production than the myriad forms of production in everyday life).[6] It is strange to make this plea for considerations of everyday economic realities; once upon a time, (Old) Left-leaning academics *began* at this point. But the cultural studies explosion—which has done more than anything else to introduce academics previously unfamiliar with various cultural theories, including those of postmodernism—has tended to concentrate on cultural forms, not the economic conditions that produced those forms, or the economic conditions of their sales, marketing, and consumption, or, for that matter, any kind of on-the-ground concerns, such as who consumes these forms and what they make of them.[7] It seems that, today, all the world's a text, not a place where people live and work and have fun, and make texts and meanings.

So for the time being I concentrate on one source that foregrounds political economic issues, a lucid and largely overlooked book by English sociologists Scott Lash and Jonathan Urry, *The End of Organized Capitalism* (1987), a book I have found to be crucial. In making their arguments, they isolate several features of the current economic world that are sufficiently different from "organized capitalism" that they introduce the term "disorganized capitalism." At the top level of production, they write, there are now global corporations with an international division of labor; a separation of finance and industry; growth of industry in small communities and rural areas; and transmission of information and knowledge electronically, instead of in print. At the bottom, there is a movement out of the cities to the suburbs and a pursuit of increasingly narrowly defined interests (contemporary American examples would be organizations such as Mothers Against Drunk Drivers or the National Rifle Association), which can find themselves making all kinds of shifting alliances around particular issues.

Whatever we label this condition, it has, according to Lash and Urry, resulted in new social classes in the developed parts of the world, which, like disorganized capitalism, have also been theorized by a few others. Lash and Urry term the most powerful of these new classes the "new bourgeoisie," a social class similar to Barbara and John Ehrenreich's "professional managerial class," or PMC (Ehrenreich and Ehrenreich 1979); Lash and Urry argue that this new bourgeoisie, because of its high economic and cultural capital, is extremely influential on the culture as a whole.

Lash and Urry write that this new bourgeoisie, which in a North American context we call yuppies, both makes and consumes new kinds of cultural forms that we can label as postmodern, and because of the influence of this class, postmodern cultural production is pervasive, both in the Uunited States and other developed countries where "disorganized" or "late" capitalism is the dominant condition. Jameson, in fact, writes on this very issue: "This identification of the class content of postmodern culture does not at all imply that yuppies have become something like a new ruling class, merely that their cultural practices and values, their local ideologies, have articulated a useful dominant ideological and cultural paradigm for this stage of capital" (Jameson 1991, 407). But not all yuppies are postmoderns, not all cultural production is postmodern; Lash and Urry write that postmodern culture could only happen in this moment and is closely related to disorganized capitalism.

As Fred Pfeil has pointed out, there is also a generational aspect to all of this (Pfeil 1990). The new social class I have been discussing—be it the new bourgeoisie, the PMC, the yuppies—is historically locatable within a particular generation, which is of course the baby boomers (that group of people born between 1946 and 1961, or, some reports say, 1963). It is this class that grew up on television, radio, and other forms of mass media; mechanical and electronic reproduction—key features of postmodern cultural production—for this and all subsequent groups is natural, it's the way things are.

Pfeil argues cogently that postmodern cultural forms are mostly made and consumed by the PMC, who have the time, education, money, and power to play with meaninglessness associated by some with postmodern cultural production.[8] It is middle-class musicians and artists with large amounts of cultural capital who are the most free to toy with other identities, sounds, instruments, and participate in the aesthetic(s) that are well-characterized by Jameson's and others' accounts of postmodernism, abbreviated by some in the lists I presented earlier. For these middle-class groups, the more insalubrious effects of postmodernity are avoidable, especially

by members of this PMC who can insulate themselves from much of the
fracturing and fragmentation assumed to be brought by postmodernity.
They can retain their still-universalized (but increasingly challenged) identities. As Sherry B. Ortner reminds us, "Fragmented identities are not
equally distributed over the social landscape, even in late capitalism, nor is
the inability to formulate and enact one's own projects, to narrate oneself
as both a product of a coherent past and an agent of an imaginable future"
(Ortner 1991, 5).[9]

MUSICAL POSTMODERNISM

I made a few references to postmodernism and music earlier but it is now
time to tackle this in greater detail. It has been only in the last few years that
academic musicians have begun to write about postmodernism and music.
Most discussions of postmodernism and music talk about sounds only, and
there is far less attention to what music (as form and practice) in postmodernity might be.[10] If we view postmodernity as a historical moment and
postmodernism as ways of cultural production linked to political and economic realities, as I am advocating here, then we can't just look at musical
texts to understand what postmodernity might be; we need also to look at
the circumstances surrounding the production and reception of those texts.

Despite Jameson's plea for a "periodizing hypothesis" of postmodernity, most commentators on music are primarily concerned with issues of
style. By and large, all of the musicological discussions of postmodernism
and music concentrate on stylistic traits such as those contained in the earlier tables without examining cultural production itself. And many of these
authors cast modernist music and postmodernist music in exclusive, oppositional terms. These discussions of postmodernism and music have largely
centered on the traits discussed earlier with regard to cultural production
in general.

This is all summed up in a list prepared by composer and music theorist, Jonathan D. Kramer (see chapter 2, page 16 of this volume).[11] Such
lists are useful in laying out potential differences between contemporary
musics and earlier ones, but there is a danger, as in the lists discussed earlier, that postmodernism will be conceptualized solely in terms of such lists,
rather than as a more dynamic process as a Jamesonian "cultural dominant" with roots in culture and history.

There is also a literature on popular music and the postmodern that
pursues some of the same paths, though since a good deal of the study of
popular musics is conducted outside of music departments, there are some
differences. Sociological, cultural studies and other methodologies—
methodologies whose practitioners constantly consider questions of
postmodernism—are more often brought to bear on that music, though
too often with little or no reference to what the music may sound like (see
Goodwin 1991; Grossberg 1992; Hayward 1992; Liptsitz 1994).[12] So there
is plenty of literature by non-musicians and non-musicologists about MTV

and its supposed reflection of a decentered youth identity, or a weakening of a sense of history, or what have you (for instance, see Kaplan 1987; Johansson 1992; Mitchell 1989; Pettegrew 1992).

POSTMODERNISM AS MARKETING

Aspects of musical style cannot be dissociated from other factors surrounding the composition, dissemination, and reception of a work, and these other factors contribute to the sound of postmodern musics. So at this point I want to shift away from postmodernism in terms of musical style, and toward an examination of musical *practices* in postmodernity, which, I believe, is a more fruitful avenue to explore if one is seeking the postmodern in music. This is important, for it sidesteps the inevitable dead end that results when attempting to determine whether or not a particular piece or composer is "postmodern."

First, let's recall Huyssen's argument regarding the crossing of the "great divide" separating high and low culture. I think this divide is indeed being crossed today, though not, as so many would have it, so much in the realm of the *production* of forms (though this is happening in some marginal cases, and, indeed, has always happened) as in their (re)presentation, marketing, and consumption. This, I would argue, is as new as some of the music, and perhaps even more a sign that we are living in a changed, or changing, world. As Dick Hebdige (1994) has written, post-Fordist production emphasizes market research, packaging, and representation more than ever before, a point treated in much greater detail in Scott Lash and John Urry's *Economies of Signs and Space*. In this successor to *The End of Organized Capitalism*, the two British sociologists write that "symbolic processes . . . have now permeated both consumption *and* production" (Lash and Urry 1994, 61).

Lash and Urry argue, as did Harvey, that post-Fordist modes of production have become more flexible; they offer many examples from the culture industry, including the publishing and record industries, noting the ways that duties that were once handled in-house by a company are now usually subcontracted out to a variety of different providers, and they write that "the culture industries were post-Fordist avant la lettre"(Lash and Urry 1994, 123). What this means is that the culture industries in some sense anticipated the dominant mode of production that is usually termed post-Fordist or postindustrial. I am not only agreeing with Lash and Urry on this point, but also arguing that cultural production itself has become more flexible, with modes once confined to certain categories of cultural forms—such as "classy" ways of selling classical music—becoming both destabilized and more flexible.

In a similar vein, Manuel Castells has argued that in this era of "informationalism," the main source of productivity is "the action of knowledge upon knowledge itself" (Castells 1996, 17). That is, production today does not result in objects, but rather, in ways of producing knowledge. My position is that not only has production become more flexible, but that modes of representation have become more flexible as well, and I am including marketing here as a form of representation, as well as considering self-representation as a form of marketing, at least in the arena of cultural production.

One of the ramifications of these changes in production in the realm of classical music is that modes of marketing are not as indexed to particular commodities as they once were. So art musicians are increasingly marketed like rock stars (whether the Kronos Quartet, Michael Tilson Thomas, violinist Vanessa-Mae Nicholson, or, recently, the Finnish violinist Linda Lampenius who goes by the name Linda Brava, also know as the "Brahms Bombshell" and who appeared nude in the April 1998 issue of *Playboy* [Figure 5-4]).[13]

Since the 1980s, some ensembles traditionally dedicated to performing and recording "classical" music have begun to seek other kinds of venues and modes of performance.[14] Probably no group better represents this trend than the Kronos Quartet, which combines rock musician clothing and marketing techniques with performances of some of the most difficult contemporary music around, much of which could still be considered "modernist." Some other string quartets, such as Turtle Island and the Greene String Quartet, have followed in their footsteps.[15] And some soloists who specialize in the standard repertoire have followed suit. Violinists Nigel Kennedy (now known simply as "Kennedy") and Nadja Salerno-Sonnenberg, for example, sport rock star personas; other musicians and ensembles have album covers shot in out of the way places, or in front of landscapes that speak of urban decay, or anything else that offers an alternative to the conventional settings of this music.[16]

It isn't just contemporary composers or contemporary music specialty performing groups such as the Greene or Kronos quartets who are hiring publicists and aggressively marketing themselves and their works. Venerable composers are finding themselves on covers of recordings they never could have imagined. In 1996, violinist Lara St. John released a recording of Bach's partitas, appearing on the cover nude from the waist up, her violin covering her breasts(Figure 5-5). St. John is described as a "young looking 25-year-old virtuoso" by *U.S. News and World Report*, which says that sales of her album were nearly 10,000 units, whereas another release by the company were under 1,000 (see Marks 1996).

The cover is pretty tame, if one is not insulated from the kinds of images that float around on magazines catering to younger audiences or that cover popular culture. *Rolling Stone* covers, for example, are routinely more suggestive than this. But then *Rolling Stone* doesn't usually discuss

Figure 5-4. Linda Brava on the cover of *Playboy*, April 1998.
Reproduced by permission of Playboy magazine.
Copyright © 1998 by Playboy. All rights reserved.

Bach. So St. John's cover caused a furor among some in the classical music world. The music director at an Arizona radio station returned it unplayed; the buyer for Tower Records in Seattle refused to stock it; a Canadian commentator called it "jailbait Bach" (Marks 1996, 58). In an interview aired on National Public Radio, St. John relates stories of being labeled a "bedraggled nymphet" (St. John 1996).

St. John and her label clearly had marketing concerns in mind. One was the downturn in sales in 1995; and St. John says, though this photograph wasn't intended to help sell the CD, it was instead "to do something unusual and perhaps breakdown some of this elitism stigma that is inherent in classical music today. And perhaps demystify to become more innovative and to make things more interesting and less highbrow" (St. John 1996). But St. John's next release, *Gypsy* from 1997, continued the theme, more explicitly, showing her in another sexually explicit pose.

This controversy over covers is made more interesting by the fact that there have been fairly suggestive and even salacious covers of classical works before; some cover photographs of Rimsky-Korsakov's *Scheherazade* I have seen are extremely revealing. But Rimsky-Korsakov is not Bach, and old Western stereotypes of the licentious "Oriental" woman unfortunately permit such a depiction.

Another recent controversy focused on the photograph that appeared on the cover of Singaporean violin prodigy Vanessa-Mae Nicholson's single called *Toccata and Fugue: The Mixes* (1995), a single released from her album *The Violin Player* (1995); the Asian release of *The Violin Player* featured the same photograph. The cover shows Nicholson, in a short white dress, playing a white electric violin while standing in the surf. Since Nicholson was sixteen years old when photographed, her record company had to fight off charges of exploitation. Nonetheless, this record sold: it climbed to no. 16 on the U.K. Top 40 singles chart; the album *The Violin Player* debuted at no. 11 on the Top 40 album chart. These are the pop charts, not the classical charts (see Stewart 1995). Nicholson has also been "declared as one of the '50 Most Beautiful People in the World' by *People* magazine, performed on the title track of Janet Jackson's *The Velvet Rope* album, and toured with the likes of Tina Turner and Rod Stewart" (Bessman 1998, 16).

There is also a recent record company–sponsored trend that is revivifying old avant-garde music by attempting to imbue it with the cachet of contemporary popular music. Philips Records, for example, re-re-released Pierre Henry's *Messe pour le temps présent* (1997) after essentially commissioning DJs to make an advertisement for it with their remix album *Métamorphose*. Nonesuch Records picked up the gauntlet and organized a remix album of pieces by Steve Reich which was released as *Reich Remixed*. Like Philips's 1997 release, famous DJs and techno musicians—Coldcut, Howie B, Tranquility Bass, DJ Spooky, Ken Ishii and others—pay homage

Figure 5-5. Lara St. John, *Bach: Works for Violin Solo*, cover.
Reproduced by permission of Well-Tempered Productions.

to their art music predecessor. With respect to the Philips project, the Nonesuch project seems more calculated since each remix is of a different Reich work (as opposed to the Henry remix DJs taking any movement they wanted from Henry's work). And Reich says that "the label is interested in hooking this up to the new recording of *Music for 18 Musicians* that was released in 1998" (Grad 1999, 17–23).[17]

ENTER THE TOTALISTS

When I was a reviewer of contemporary art music recordings, I noticed that, beginning in the early 1990s, the amount of promotional material that accompanied recordings to review grew considerably. A few years ago I was bombarded by a composer's publicist, sending numerous press releases and free recordings on new music. "There's a new -ism on the scene!" the expertly laser-printed letter tells us. "The first one in over twenty years! Totalism!" This letter even includes footnotes to give the look of scholarly authenticity. Totalism, according to the letter, is a new kind of composition that draws, apparently indiscriminately, on musical traditions from all over the place: classical music, world music, popular music; hence the "total."[18] *Village Voice* critic Kyle Gann, the most versed in totalism and its biggest champion in the press, describes it as a music that "attract[s] rock audiences with its highly physical drum beat, while also engaging more sophisticated listeners through a background of great melodic and formal intricacy" (Gann 1993a).[19]

Such advertising and promotion is relatively recent and demonstrates the struggle for attention that all contemporary composers face. Doubtless a more systematic search could push the dates back further, but the point is made: composers in the last decade or so have begun to rely heavily on publicists and other functionaries of the market economy to help make their music known. Postmodernism, then, can take shape partly as self-consciously postmodern stylistic practices in some cultural forms but also, more noticeably, in ways of production, marketing, and selling, practices constructed by and aimed at the PMC, and all of these occur in the historical moment of late capitalism we have called postmodernity.

Totalist composers such as Arthur Jarvinen, Mikel Rouse, Ben Neill, and others often betray a garage-band and/or "world music" background as well as more classical training. Rouse, for example, studied African drumming, has an alternative rock band, and went to the Conservatory of Music at the University of Missouri at Kansas City. He writes in the liner notes to his CD *Soul Menu*, "It has often been said that my music might be better understood if I worked the more conventional avenues of the modern classical tradition, but the great legacy of American music and the experience of playing in my own group has given me an intuition I don't believe would have been possible otherwise." Rouse also says that "it has been one of my goals to write music for instruments normally associated with improvisation," and his Broken Consort (the Renaissance name for a consort of mixed instruments—Rouse has been dipping into his old music history textbook) consists of a bass, electric guitar, drums, keyboards, Ewi woodwinds, synthesizer and woodwinds (Rouse 1993).

Despite Rouse's declared affinity for popular musics, he seems, like some composers who work primarily as composers in the realm of high culture, to hear popular music as sounds rather than meanings. Rouse's music sounds like "art" music modernism: it utilizes sounds for no apparent reason other than that they happen to sound good to the composer, at the same time as he pokes fun at mainstream popular culture. His 1996 opera *Dennis Cleveland*, for example, is about a television talk show host. "The narrative," writes Rouse, "follows Dennis Cleveland through a myriad of encounters chronicling the promise of salvation through popular culture" (Rouse 1996).

No matter the surface resemblance to popular musical styles, Rouse holds on to much older notions of what good music is. In interviews he constantly refers to the complexity of his music and his attention to large-scale structural concerns; of his opera *Failing Kansas* (1995) he says,

"Listen to 'The Corner' [the opera's climax], where it's happening on so many multiple layers you'll never get all of it" (quoted in Gann 1995a, 63). He has also spoken of his interest in large-scale formal structure and complexity, perhaps the two most sacrosanct concerns of modernist music.

His fans among critics have picked up on this. Kyle Gann, in summing up the achievement of *Dennis Cleveland*, focuses on musical/technical issues: "For Rouse himself has something to sell: Rhythmic complexity. Counterpoint. Thematic unity. Aesthetic richness" (Gann 1996b, 64). Gann has written repeatedly of totalism's goal of melding complexity with accessibility, and hopes that music like Rouse's—music that attempts to fuse art music concerns with pop music sounds—will find a broader audience (Gann 1995a, 1995b).

> What I think everyone hopes is that eventually people who like rock will continue to like it, but, also realize that there's something more they could be listening to, that there are other reasons to listen to music than just to dance to it or sing along with the lyrics or something, and Mike gravitated to this music instead of 19th-century European music, which really has no relevance to their own lives. I mean, this music is much more taken from the materials of daily lives. (Glass, Rouse, and Gann 1995)

The phrase "taken from" indicates the possibility of rejection of everything in a classic modern aesthetic maneuver since its relevance *to* people's daily lives is at issue. Popular culture does, however, seem to draw upon people's daily existence. Rouse, and other composers born in the 1950s, bring "with them ideas about rock music, and also ideas about production" (Glass, Rouse, and Gann 1995). These ideas leave traces in the compositional output of this generation of composers, but modernist aesthetic ideas are almost always left intact.

Rouse's music in *Dennis Cleveland* moves through a myriad of encounters with popular music styles, opening with a rap-influenced music, then through minimalist-inspired riffs that occasionally feature a chorus in the background. Like many of the popular and minimalist models Rouse emulates, there is a constant pulse, provided by a drum machine or sequencer. Sampled tidbits flit through, and sometimes the voice of Dennis Cleveland is compressed (sounding as though it is coming through a telephone line), as in some contemporary popular musics. While there are popular music influences, no one would mistake this for popular music. Rouse, the other totalists, and composers such as Michael Daugherty, John Adams, and Paul Dresher are adept at harnessing the surface pleasures of popular music, but to my ears, the results are less satisfying than the musics these composers borrow from.

Lest one think that the sound of *Dennis Cleveland* indicates the absence of a serious theme, Rouse and his proponents are quick to remind us that *Dennis Cleveland* is, in fact, serious. Rouse was reportedly interested in a book by the Canadian novelist, historian, and businessman John Ralston Saul, who writes in his 1992 *Voltaire's Bastards: The Dictatorship of Reason in the West*, according to Gann, "about the corporatist takeover of the Western world, the dismantling of democracy by multinational corporations, and the consequent increased reliance on the illusion of mass culture as a source of personal meaning." Gann then quotes a passage from Saul's book:

> The most accurate context in which to place television programming is that of general religious ritual. Like television, religious rituals eschew surprise, particularly creative surprise. Instead, they flourish on the repetition of known formulas. People are drawn to television as they are to religions by the knowledge that they will find there what they already know. After watching the first minute of any television drama, most viewers could lay out the scenario that will follow, including the conclusion. Given the first line of banter in most scenes, a regular viewer could probably rhyme off the next three or four lines. There is more flexibility in a Catholic mass or in classic Chinese opera. (Quoted in Gann 1996a, 1996b)

Most readers will recognize this kind of tirade as little different than Horkheimer and Adorno in *The Dialectic of the Enlightenment*, or, more recently, Allan Bloom's *The Closing of the American Mind* (Horkheimer and Adorno 1991; Bloom 1987). It is telling that Rouse, who frequently refers to his popular music influences, would draw intellectual inspiration from this book; his discussion of *Dennis Cleveland* uses some of Saul's language, saying that "talk shows were a phenomenon that started 15 years ago, then 10 to seven years ago started going further and further in a ritual direction" (Gann 1996b, 64). Gann, in the liner notes to *Dennis Cleveland*, also tells us that Rouse took some phrases straight out of the book.

Rather than wondering what people who watch and attend tapings of talk shows might get out of them, Rouse hit on the idea of viewing the talk show more as an aesthetic moment; "When I sat there and looked at it as a theatrical experience instead of a live TV taping, it opened up whole new vistas" (Gann 1996b, 64). The result, Rouse says, was to remove the "intellectual snobbery away from opera," but, it seems to me, only to aim it squarely at the talk show format.

Gann thinks that Rouse's lens on the talk show lifts it up and reveals it worked. Gann writes:

> The idea that music can be popular in format and yet still perceptually challenging, that we can, in effect, upgrade the daily discourse of American life. It's a John Ralston Saul idea as well. Rouse hopes that maybe, just maybe, a few of those people in the talk-show audiences will see *Dennis Cleveland* and start to think about the fact that we who com-

plain about what goes on as observers are also participants. We may be watching the show, but we're also the actors. We let the media tell us we're helpless, but we have the power to change the world. (Gann 1996b, 64)

Note Gann's (and, I think, Rouse's) underlying assumption, a very old one in western culture: talk shows, and popular culture, are bad for you, but the redemptive power of art can uplift popular culture, and all of us with it.

I also need to comment on the fungibility of Gann and Rouse in the foregoing passages. If I seem to have been using Gann's words to represent Rouse's positions, it's because Gann is a self-identified booster of Rouse, and totalism in general, and it is clear that Gann knows things about Rouse's music that nobody else does; for example, Rouse never mentions the influence of John Ralston Saul, but he has clearly clued Gann in on this. In some ways, this is scarcely different from the normal state of affairs during the nineteenth century, when certain critics would champion certain composers. What is different today, however, is that, while in the nineteenth century this practice was largely incidental to "the music itself," today it is in some real sense constitutive of the music.

In closing this section, I should note that totalism was barely a flash in the pan; it was discussed for only a year or so in the music press, and none of the composers involved use the term anymore, all of which point out how much it was simply a marketing tool to gain these composers a foot in the door of fame.

CONCLUSIONS: IT AIN'T NECESSARILY POMO

So is this change in marketing a postmodern story? It ought to be clear by this point that, while some things have changed, some remain the same and that, no matter what happens, slapping on a label doesn't tell us much. Mikel Rouse's music, as I pointed out earlier, owes much to art music sounds and procedures that go back several decades and to various kinds of popular musics; but at the same time, the eclecticism of his samples and his treatment of them is indicative of a more recent musical sensibility that delights in the odd juxtaposition.

But even with these new juxtapositions, even with the new forms of marketing and (self)-representation I have been discussing, most of the older ways of selling and consuming Western European art music are still with us, as is modernism as an aesthetic, as is modernism in Marshall Berman and David Harvey's larger sense of the search for meaning and stability. Cultural production and cultural forms display the old and the new in ways that could only happen in the contemporary landscape in which everything is available in commodity form as never before.

It may be that the best way to understand contemporary cultural production by anyone is to throw out the P-word altogether, for in its very popularity it has ceased to be very useful—it obscures more than it reveals.

Instead, there are more specific discourses that can help us understand particular cultural forms and formations (such as theories of globalization, postcolonialism, and many others). I am impressed, for example, by Manuel Castells's monumental *The Information Age: Economy, Society, and Culture*, which cogently analyzes the contemporary world without resorting to rubber-stamp labels or lists, instead identifying a new polarization between "the Net and the Self," that is, global interconnectedness versus the particulate individual in this information age (Castells 1996, 3).

What Castells tells us is the world has changed and that some cultural production has changed with it, as have the ways we understand this cultural production. But I would also point out that, as the case of Mikel Rouse and *Dennis Cleveland* demonstrates, no historical moment is lived in the same ways by all people; the advent of the postindustrial/postmodern/informational world has left some people behind, unfortunately. In a world in which everything is available in commodity form as never before, the crucial question is: Available to whom? Mikel Rouse and other middle-class musicians are, in a sense, dabblers: playing with juxtaposed sounds and fragmented identities in ways that we might be able to call postmodern in terms of style, but at the end of the day, safe as moderns in their stable subject positions.

NOTES

1. There are many sources that advocate or are situated in all of these discourses. The most important of these are: on globalization, Appadurai 1996; on the postindustrial economy, Bell 1973; on late capitalism, Mandel 1980; on the information age, Castells 1996, 1997, and 1998. See also Kumar 1995.

2. Robert Young offers much the same formulation, though at the same time taking us into the reality of the multicultural: postmodernity, he says, "can best be defined as European culture's awareness that it is no longer the unquestioned and dominant centre of the world" (Young 1990, 19).

3. See, for example, Lipsitz 1990; Taylor 1991, 33–48; Tucker 1989.

4. See also an interview with Cornel West, who first describes rap music as postmodern, but then in the next sentence discusses its political—even modern—viewpoint: "A tremendous *articulateness* is syncopated with the African drumbeat, the African funk, into an American postmodernist product: there is no subject expressing originary anguish here but a fragmented subject, pulling from past and present, innovatively producing a heterogeneous product. . . . Otherwise, it is part and parcel of the subversive energies of black underclass youth, energies that are forced to take a cultural mode of articulation because of the political lethargy of American society. The music of Grandmaster Flash and the Furious Five, Kurtis Blow, and Sugar Hill Gang has to take on a deeply political character because, again, they are in the reality that the black underclass *cannot not know*: the brutal

side of American capital, the brutal side of American racism, the brutal side of sexism against black women" (West 1988, 280–81).

5. See also Baudrillard's *In the Shadow of Silent Majorities* (1983) and *Selected Writings* (1988). For criticisms of this argument, see, most importantly, Berman 1992; Eagleton 1996; and Norris 1990, 1992, and 1993.

6. For a similar critique, see Lash and Urry 1994, 60.

7. For similar critiques, see McRobbie 1996, 335–42; also, a special issue of *Monthly Review* on postmodernism included several relevant essays: Wood 1995; Eagleton 1995; and Stabile 1995. In making this critique, I do not want to include one of the very few figures who has, all along, kept his eye on political economic issues: see Lipsitz 1990, 1994.

8. French theorist Jean Baudrillard is the primary culprit in the death of meaning. See Baudrillard 1988.

9. For a superb discussion of the effects of the postmodern world on working-class South Texas Chicanos, see Limón 1994.

10. See Boone 1991; Hartwell 1993; Hermand 1991; Kramer 1995, 1996; Pasler 1993; Watkins 1994. There is also a growing literature on postmodern musicology, which isn't relevant to my arguments here.

11. This list originally appeared in a slightly shorter form in Kramer 1996, 21–22.

12. None of these are by musicologists, ethnomusicologists, or music theorists.

13. For general information on the changes in marketing classical music, see Borzillo 1996; Chang 1993, 1998; Goetzman 1998; Levine 1998; Loader 1990; Stark 1991. For more on the Kronos Quartet, see Elson 1989; Goldberg 1992; Royer 1989. On Vanessa-Mae Nicholson, see Tressider 1995. On Linda Brava, see Vincent 1998.

14. See Lebrecht 1997 for a discussion of the business of classical music that examines this marketing trend I am focusing on here.

15. On Turtle Island, see Gates 1990.

16. For an article on Kennedy, see "Bad Boy."

17. See also Shatz 1999 for more on *Reich Remixed*.

18. Accompanying Mikel Rouse's *Soul Menu* (1993).

19. On totalism, see also Gann 1993b; Rothstein 1993; Woodard 1994.

WORKS CITED

Appadurai, Arjun. 1996. *Modernity at Large: Cultural Dimensions of Globalization.* Public Worlds, no. 1. Minneapolis and London: University of Minnesota Press.

"Bad Boy." 1991. *Economist* 319 (June 22): 102.

Baudrillard, Jean. 1983. *In the Shadow of Silent Majorities.* New York: Semiotext(e).

———. 1988. *Selected Writings.* Edited by Mark Poster. Stanford: Stanford University Press.

Bell, Daniel. 1973. *The Coming of Post-Industrial Society: A Venture in Social Forecasting.* New York: Basic.

Berman, Marshall. 1988. *All that is Solid Melts into Air: The Experience of Modernity.* New York: Penguin.

———. 1992. "Why Modernism Still Matters." In *Modernity and Identity*, edited by Scott Lash and Jonathan Friedman. Oxford and Cambridge, Mass.: Basil Blackwell. 33–58.

Bessman, Jim. 1998. "Violin Virtuoso Vanessa-Mae Furthers Fusion on Virgin Bow." *Billboard* (March 21): 16.

Bloom, Allan. 1987. *The Closing of the American Mind.* New York: Simon and Schuster.

Boone, Charles. 1991. "Has Modernist Music Lost its Power?" In *Zeitgeist in Babel: The Post-Modernist Controversy*, edited by Ingeborg Hoestry. Bloomington and Indianapolis: Indiana University Press.

Borzillo, Carrie. 1996. "Secondary Exploitation: How to Make Catalog Sexy." *Billboard* (September 7): 50.

Castells, Manuel. 1996. *The Rise of Network Society.* Vol. 1 of *The Information Age: Economy, Society and Culture.* Oxford and Cambridge, Mass.: Basil Blackwell.

———. 1997. *The Power of Identity.* Vol. 2 of *The Information Age: Economy, Society and Culture.* Oxford and Cambridge, Mass.: Basil Blackwell.

———. 1998. *End of the Millennium.* Vol. 3 of *The Information Age: Economy, Society and Culture.* Oxford and Cambridge, Mass.: Basil Blackwell.

Chang, Yahlin. 1993. "Classics Go Pop: Publicising Musicians." *Economist* 327 (April 3): 82.

———. 1998. "Cross Over, Beethoven." *Newsweek* (April 20): 60–61.

Eagleton, Terry. 1995. "Where do Postmodernists Come From?" *Monthly Review* 47 (July/August): 59–70.

———. 1996. *The Illusions of Postmodernism.* Oxford and Cambridge, Mass.: Basil Blackwell.

Ehrenreich, Barbara, and John Ehrenreich. 1979. "The Professional-Managerial Class." In *Between Labor and Capital*, edited by Pat Walker. Boston: South End Press. 313–34.

Elson, John. 1989. "Fanatic Champions of the New: The Kronos Quartet Has a Mod Look—and a Mod Repertoire." *Time* (June 26): 86

Gann, Kyle. 1993a. "Noise is Not Enough." *Village Voice* 38 (December 14): 6.

———. 1993b. "The Rhythms of Totalism: Rhys Chatham, Mikel Rouse, Michael Gordon, Kyle Gann, Larry Polansky, Ben Neill." Adapted and expanded from an article, "Downtown Beats for the 1990s." *Contemporary Music Review* 10: 33–50.

———. 1995a. "Shadowing Capote." *Village Voice* (February 7): 63–64.

———. 1995b. "View from the Gap." *Village Voice* (March 21): 74.

———. 1996a. Liner notes to Mikel Rouse, *Dennis Cleveland*, compact disc. New World Records 80506-2.

———. 1996b. "Opera meets Oprah: Mikel Rouse Hawks Salvation in an Opera for Real People." *Village Voice* (November 5): 64.

Gates, David. 1990. "A String Quartet Cuts Loose." *Newsweek* 116 (September 24): 77.

Glass, Philip, Mikel Rouse, and Kyle Gann. 1995. Interview with Tom Vitale, National Public Radio, *Morning Edition* (January 31).

Goetzman, Keith. 1998. "An Orchestrated Push." *Utne Reader* (March/April): 91–93.

Goldberg, Joe. 1992. "The New Chamber Music." *Billboard* (September 19): C4.

Goodwin, Andrew. 1991. "Popular Music and Postmodern Theory." *Cultural Studies* 5 (May 1): 174–90.

Grad, David. 1999. "No Five-Finger Discount." *New York Press* (February 17–23): 21.

Grossberg, Lawrence. 1992. *We Gotta Get Out of This Place: Popular Conservatism and Postmodern Culture*. New York and London: Routledge.

Hall, Stuart. 1989. "Ethnicity: Identity, and Difference." *Radical America* 23 (October–December): 9–20.

Hartwell, Robin. 1993. "Postmodernism and Art Music." In *The Last Post: Music after Modernism*, edited by Simon Miller. Music and Society. Manchester and New York: Manchester University Press.

Harvey, David. 1989. *The Condition of Postmodernity: An Enquiry into the Origins of Cultural Change*. Oxford and Cambridge, Mass.: Basil Blackwell.

Hassan, Ihab. 1987. *The Postmodern Turn: Essays in Postmodern Theory and Culture*. [Columbus] Ohio: Ohio State University Press.

Hayward, Philip, ed. 1992. *From Pop to Punk to Postmodernism: Popular Music and Australian Culture from the 1960s to the 1990s*. Australian Cultural Studies. North Sydney: Allen & Unwin.

Hebdige, Dick. 1994. "After the Masses." In *Culture/Power/History: A Reader in Contemporary Social Theory*, edited by Nicholas B. Dirks, Geoff Eley, and Sherry B. Ortner. Princeton Studies in Culture/Power/History. Princeton: Princeton University Press. 222–35.

Hermand, Jost. 1991. "Avant-Garde, Modern, Postmodern: The Music (Almost) Nobody Wants to Hear." In *Zeitgeist in Babel: The Post-Modernist Controversy*, edited by Ingeborg Hoestry. Bloomington and Indianapolis: Indiana University Press. 192–206.

Horkheimer, Max, and Theodor Adorno. 1991. *Dialectic of Enlightenment*. Translated by John Cumming. New York: Continuum.

Huyssen, Andreas. 1986. *After the Great Divide: Modernism, Mass Culture, Postmodernism*. Theories of Representation and Difference. Bloomington and Indianapolis: University of Indiana Press.

Jameson, Fredric. 1991. *Postmodernism, or, the Cultural Logic of Late Capitalism*. Post-Contemporary Interventions. Durham: Duke University Press.

Jencks, Charles. 1986. *What Is Post-Modernism?* London: Academy Editions.

Johansson, Thomas. 1992. "Music Video, Youth Culture, and Postmodernism." *Popular Music and Society* 16 (Fall): 9–22.

Kaplan, E. Ann. 1987. *Rocking around the Clock: Music Television, Postmodernism, and Consumer Culture*. New York: Routledge.

Kramer, Jonathan D. 1995. "Beyond Unity: Toward an Understanding of Musical Postmodernism." In *Concert Music, Rock, and Jazz since 1945: Essays and*

Analytical Studies, edited by Elizabeth West Marvin and Richard Hermann. *Eastman Studies in Music*. Rochester: University of Rochester Press. 11–33.

———. 1996. "Postmodern Concepts of Musical Time." *Indiana Theory Review* 17/2: 21–61.

———. 2001. "The Nature and Origins of Musical Postmodernism." Chapter 2 in this volume and also in *Current Musicology* 64, forthcoming.

Kumar, Krishan. 1995. *From Post-Industrial to Post-Modern Society: New Theories of the Contemporary World*. Oxford and Cambridge, Mass.: Basil Blackwell.

Lash, Scott, and John Urry. 1987. *The End of Organized Capitalism*. Madison: University of Wisconsin Press.

———. 1994. *Economies of Signs and Space*. Theory, Culture and Society. London and Newbury Park, Calif.: Sage Publications.

Lebrecht, Norman. 1997. *Who Killed Classical Music? Maestros, Managers, and Corporate Politics*. Secaucus, N.J.: Birch Lane Press.

Levine, Robert. 1998. "Cross Over *This*." *Pulse!* (April): 37–39.

Limón, José E. 1994. *Dancing with the Devil: Society and Cultural Poetics in Mexican-American South Texas*. New Directions in Anthropological Writing: History, Poetics, Cultural Criticism. Madison and London: University of Wisconsin Press.

Lipsitz, George. 1990. *Time Passages: Collective Memory and American Popular Culture*. American Culture. Minneapolis: University of Minnesota Press.

———. 1994. *Dangerous Crossroads: Popular Music, Postmodernism, and the Poetics of Place*. London and New York: Verso.

Loader, Kevin. 1990. "A Mongrel of Dubious Pedigree: Classical Music Has Discovered Beat and Style." *New Statesman & Society* (July 13): 26.

Lyotard, Jean-François. 1984. *The Postmodern Condition: A Report on Knowledge*. Translated by Geoff Bennington and Brian Massumi. Theory and History of Literature, 10. Minneapolis: University of Minnesota Press.

Mandel, Ernest. 1980. *Late Capitalism*. Translated by Joris De Bres. London: Verso.

Marks, John. 1996. "Selling 'Jailbait' Bach: Dressing Up Classical CD Sales—by Undressing." *U.S. News and World Report* (November 11): 58.

McRobbie, Angela. 1996. "All the World's a Stage, Screen, or Magazine: When Culture is the Logic of Late Capitalism." *Media, Culture & Society* 18 (April): 335–42.

Mitchell, Tony. 1989. "Performance and the Postmodern in Pop Music." *Theatre Journal* 41 (October): 273–93.

Norris, Christopher. 1990. *What's Wrong with Postmodernism: Critical Theory and the Ends of Philosophy*. Parallax: Re-visions of Culture and Society. Baltimore: Johns Hopkins University Press.

———. 1992. *Uncritical Theory: Postmodernism, Intellectuals, and the Gulf War*. London: Lawrence & Wishart.

———. 1993. *The Truth about Postmodernism*. Oxford and Cambridge, Mass.: Basil Blackwell.

Ortner, Sherry B. 1991. "Narrativity in History, Culture, and Lives." Comparative Study of Social Transformations. Working Papers no. 66. University of Michigan Unpublished.

Pasler, Jann. 1993. "Postmodernism, Narrativity, and the Art of Memory." *Contemporary Music Review* 7: 3–32.

Pettegrew, John. 1992. "A Post-modernist Movement: 1980s Commercial Culture and the Founding of MTV." *Journal of American Culture* 15 (Winter): 57–65.

Pfeil, Fred. 1990. "'Makin' Flippy-Floppy': Postmodernism and the Baby-Boom PMC." In *Another Tale to Tell: Politics and Narrative in Postmodern Culture*. London and New York: Verso.

Potter, Russell A. 1995. *Spectacular Vernaculars: Hip-Hop and the Politics of Postmodernism*. SUNY Series in Postmodern Culture. Albany: State University of New York Press.

Rothstein, Edward. 1993. "Minimalism Pumped Up to the Max." *New York Times* (July 18): H23.

Royer, Mary-Paige. 1989. "Classical Gasp." *American Demographics* (August): 46.

Shatz, Adam. 1999. "Revisiting Steve Reich for the Dance Floor." *New York Times* (March 14): 33.

St. John, Lara. 1996. Interview with Robert Siegel. National Public Radio, *All Things Considered* (November 11).

Stabile, Carol A. 1995. "Postmodernism, Feminism, and Marx: Notes from the Abyss." *Monthly Review* 47 (July/August): 89–106.

Stark, Phyllis. 1991. "Labels Playing Up Contemporary Look of Classical Acts." *Billboard* (May 4): 1.

Stewart, Andrew. 1995. "Image Questioned for Violinist, 16." *Billboard* (March 4): 1.

Taylor, Timothy D. 1991. "Re-signing Mass Culture: Billy Bragg's 'There is Power in a Union.'" *Popular Music and Society* 15 (Summer): 33–48.

Tressider, Megan. 1995. "Fugue What a Scorcher." *Guardian* (May 20): 25.

Tucker, Bruce. 1989. "'Tell Tchaikovsky the News': Postmodernism, Popular Culture, and the Emergence of Rock 'n' Roll." *Black Music Research Journal* 9 (Fall): 271–95.

Vincent, Norah. 1998. "Brava, Brava." *New York Press* (March 4–10): 16.

Watkins, Glenn. 1994. *Pyramids at the Louvre: Music, Culture, and Collage from Stravinsky to the Postmodernists*. Cambridge, Mass., and London: Harvard University Press.

West, Cornel. 1988. Interview with Anders Stephanson. In *Universal Abandon? The Politics of Postmodernism*, edited by Andrew Ross. Minneapolis: University of Minnesota Press.

Wood, Ellen Meiksins. 1995. "What Is the 'Postmodern' Agenda? An Introduction." *Monthly Review* 47 (July/August): 1–12.

Woodard, Josef. 1994. "What is Total Music?" *Jazziz* (June/July): 24.

Young, Robert. 1990. *White Mythologies: Writing History and the West*. New York and London: Routledge.

RECORDINGS CITED

Henry, Pierre. 1997. *Messe pour le Temps Présent*. Philips 456 293–2.

Nicholson, Vanessa-Mae. 1995. *Toccata and Fugue: The Mixes*. EMI Angel 58508.

———. 1995. *The Violin Player*. EMI Angel 55089.

Reich Remixed. 1999. Various artists. Nonesuch 79552-2.

Rouse, Mikel. 1993. *Soul Menu*. New Tone 6716.

———. 1996. *Dennis Cleveland*. New World Records 80506-2.

St. John, Lara. 1996. *J. S. Bach: Works for Violin Solo*. Well-Tempered Productions 1580.

———. 1997. *Gypsy*. Well-Tempered Productions 1585.

CHAPTER 6

Postmodern Architecture/
Postmodern Music

Jane Piper Clendinning

In this essay, I will draw on the established meanings of the terms "modern" and "postmodern" as applied to architecture of the second half of the twentieth century and consider links between the application of these terms in architecture and in music.[1] While the scope of such a comparison could easily run book-length, I will restrict my investigation to a few samples drawn from the many representative buildings (and architects) and pieces of music (and composers) to illustrate the benefits of such an approach.[2]

WHY ARCHITECTURE AND MUSIC?

It has long been customary for music theorists, musicologists, and music critics (and, in some cases, the composers themselves) to label styles in music using terminology first applied to trends in visual art, literature, or other art forms.[3] The linkage of terminology from one art form to another may simply recognize the shared artistic milieu of composers, writers, and visual artists working within the same time frame, but the most useful appropriations of terminology reveal tangible links in practice, technique, method, or aesthetic between the two art forms. In the latter case, the already established meaning of the term in the art form to which it was first applied may be used to illustrate useful features of the second art form by analogy. Although all of the art forms borrow terminology from others on occasion, music is usually the latecomer, reapplying terms from other disciplines to explain our own. In many cases, the primacy of other arts from this terminological perspective stems from the crystallization of new styles in other art forms first, with the analogous transition between styles in music coming later; in others, the change of style was simultaneous, but the musical style was not labeled until after the establishment of terminology for the corresponding style in another art form.

Like many other stylistic terms, the label "postmodern" was widely used in both literature and architecture prior to its appropriation by and application to music. Whereas writers about literary theory date the emergence of postmodernism in their discipline to the mid-1960s, books and articles from the 1970s and '80s by Jean Baudrillard, Jean François Lyotard, Fredric Jameson, and Linda Hutcheon are frequently cited as setting the direction of this trend in literary criticism.[4] The emergence of the concept of postmodernism in architecture is usually dated to the publication of Robert Venturi's *Complexity and Contradiction in Architecture* in 1966 (more about this later), but the first buildings exemplifying the new style date from the 1970s and '80s.

In literary criticism, ideas of postmodernism have been used to describe stylistic or structural features, or postmodernism is used as a way of reading or to describe an interpretative stance. Architecture dwells on the former—the elements and their combination in making the building. Musicologists and music theorists, on the other hand, seem to have been drawn more to the latter—the postmodern point of view in literary criticism—which is summarized by Selden and Widdowson (1993, 174) as follows: "the 'grand narratives' of historical progress initiated by the Enlightenment are discredited" and "any political grounding of these ideas in 'history' or 'reality' is no longer possible."[5] The literary theorist Peter Brooker expands on this critical stance to include "a mood or condition of radical indeterminacy, and a tone of self-conscious, parodic skepticism toward previous certainties," leading to a re-examination of previous ways of thinking about literature (cited in Selden and Widdowson 1993, 175).

That the meaning of "postmodernism" in literary criticism differs in some significant respects from its application in architecture may stem from the concurrent development of the concept in both areas. That there are differences is not surprising, considering that the "objects" of study in the two disciplines—literary works and buildings—are quite different: one uses the meanings of words to build chains of thoughts; the other uses planes, lines, curves, and physical elements to shape an edifice. Music can be compared to a poem, short story, or a play by studying the "narrative" implied by the music or other literary features; however, through the nonverbal aspects of music and its construction by combining specific, identifiable elements, music may be more like a building than a poem, novel, short story, or a play. Both analogies—to literature and to architecture—can reveal interesting aspects of a musical artwork.

MODERNISM AND POSTMODERNISM IN ARCHITECTURE

An understanding of postmodernism in architecture presupposes familiarity with the modernist style that postmodernism purports to react against. While architectural historians mark the beginning of the modernist period in architecture at different points in time between the late 1800s and the 1920s, it is the modernism born in the 1920s—known as the International Style—that was the leading style in architecture for most of the twentieth century.[6] Alfred Barr described the style as having three basic aesthetic principles: "emphasis on volume—space enclosed by thin planes or surfaces as opposed to the suggestion of mass and solidity; regularity as opposed to symmetry or other kinds of obvious balance; and, lastly, dependence upon the intrinsic elegance of materials, technical perfection, and fine proportions, as opposed to applied ornament."[7] International Style, typified by the buildings of Le Corbusier, Gropius, Frank Lloyd Wright, and Mies van der Rohe, achieved near-total dominance among critically recognized architectural firms, commissions, and competitions in the first three decades after World War II.[8]

The International Style is characterized by clean-lined functionality, boxlike or gently curving shapes, minimal decoration, and use of glass, steel, concrete, highly polished stone, and other hard-surfaced building materials (rather than wood, brick, and natural stone). Buildings with stark white concrete exteriors (and white interiors, as well)—either curved, as in Frank Lloyd Wright's design for the Guggenheim Museum (New York, 1956–59), Eero Saarinen's Trans World Airlines Terminal (John F. Kennedy Airport, New York, 1962), and Le Corbusier's Notre-Dame-du-Haut (Ronchamp, France, 1950–54), or box-like, as in Le Corbusier's Villa Savoye (Poissy, near Paris, 1928–31) and Alvar Aalto's Maison Carré (Bazochesw-sur-Guyonne, France, 1956–58)—are typical of this style.[9]

The steel-framed plate glass tower skyscraper—a rectangular column with a flat top—is the most ubiquitous representative of the International Style. Revolutionary in the hands of Mies van der Rohe in the 1950s (for example, the Seagram Building, New York, 1954–58), this design was copied slavishly by many lesser architects in service of corporations wanting an impressive home to tout their success. Rectangular glass towers built in the 1960s, '70s, and '80s are a fixture of most cities around the world that have large buildings constructed during those decades. One of the artistic flaws of the glass box is simply its imitability. With the exception of a few notable towers, each could be anywhere—the design is not tied to place. The tower could belong to any company, with the "everyman" employee living the cubicle life inside.

One element of modernist architecture mentioned by some critics is the influence of machines on design. Trachtenberg and Hyman clarify that

"machine-style buildings only resembled "machines" in a loose, metaphoric way. It was imagined that buildings were being made to function analogously to machines—that is, in a tightly planned, rational manner. . . . Visually, it was never the functioning guts of machines that were reflected by the new architectural mode, but rather their housings and their external hardware—the hulls, railings, gangways, and smokestacks of ships, the shells of cars and turbines, the open framework of early aircraft, and, of course, the new structural 'machinery' of steel and ferroconcrete" (Trachtenberg and Hyman 1986, 487–88).

To the architects, International Style was not merely an aesthetic choice, but part of a utopian vision to improve the human condition through the design of a pure, functional, physical environment. The epitome of this vision was the St. Louis Pruitt-Igoe Public Housing project, built 1952–55. This structure was Bauhaus, utopian, rational—a sleek, modern, complex that won the American Institute of Architect's Award for its designer, Minoru Yamasaki.[10] Unfortunately, the architect's utopian visions made dwelling places that were considered by some to be cold and impersonal. Though houses like Frank Lloyd Wright's Fallingwater (1937), Le Corbusier's Villa Savoye (1928–31) and Philip Johnson's Glass House (1949) are much admired among architecture aficionados, few private homes were built following these designs—the modernist style simply did not achieve popular acceptance among individuals choosing styles for their own homes. It did not provide the personal comfort most people wanted for their families, and the clean-lined, uncluttered style did not seize the public's imagination.

In their search for a utopia in design, International Style architects often ignored the needs of those who would be inhabiting and maintaining the buildings. Time has revealed serious flaws in some of the International Style landmarks. Glass boxes, originally constructed with single-pane glass, became "hot houses in the summer and radiators in the winter" (Roth 1993, 479). Many of the materials used in the construction of the buildings had not been tested by time, and landmark buildings have rapidly decayed or begun to leak.[11] Lack of storage, poor traffic flow, and resistance of the buildings to personalization of one's space has also made some buildings uncomfortable for their users. July 15, 1972, at 3:32 P.M.—the day and time of the implosion of St. Louis's Pruitt-Igoe Public Housing project—is sometimes cited as marking the death of the International Style and the birth of postmodernism (Arnason [1968] 1986, 691). Yamasaki's lauded utopian experiment had not lifted the human spirit of those inhabiting it—just the opposite. The project had become a decaying, neglected, impersonal, crime-ridden hazard (Roth 1993, 479–80).

THE BEGINNINGS OF POSTMODERNISM IN ARCHITECTURE

Many architectural historians (for example: Arnason [1968] 1986, 691–92; Trachtenberg and Hyman 1986, 563; Roth 1993, 505) date the beginnings of postmodernism in architecture to the publication of Robert Venturi's book *Complexity and Contradiction in Architecture* (written 1962, but published 1966), in which Venturi reviews architectural history while presenting his critique of mainstream modernism's sterile glass and steel boxes, reductionism, and over-simplification. In the chapter "Nonstraightforward Architecture: A Gentle Manifesto," Venturi wrote:

I like complexity and contradiction in architecture. . . .

Architects can no longer afford to be intimidated by the puritanically moral language of orthodox modern architecture. I like elements which are hybrid rather than "pure," compromising rather than "clean," distorted rather than "straightforward," ambiguous rather than "articulated," perverse as well as impersonal, boring as well as "interesting," conventional rather than "designed," accommodating rather than excluding, redundant rather than simple, vestigial as well as innovating, inconsistent and equivocal rather than direct and clear. I am for messy vitality over obvious unity. I include the non sequitur and proclaim the duality.

I am for richness of meaning rather than the clarity of meaning; for the implicit function as well as the explicit function. I prefer "both-and" to "either-or," black and white, and sometimes gray, to black or white. A valid architecture evokes many levels of meaning and combinations of focus: its space and its elements become readable and workable in several ways at once.

But an architecture of complexity and contradiction has a special obligation toward the whole: its truth must be in its totality or its implications of totality. It must embody the difficult unity of inclusion rather than the easy unity of exclusion. More is not less. ([1966] 1977, 16)

Guild House	*Crawford Manor*
an architecture of meaning	an architecture of expression
explicit "decorative" symbolism	implicit "connotative" symbolism
applied ornament	integral expressionism
mixed media	pure architecture
decoration by the attaching of superficial elements	unadmitted decoration by the articulation of integral elements
symbolism	abstraction
representational art	"abstract expressionism"
evocative architecture	innovative architecture
societal messages	architectural content
high and low art	high art
evolutionary, using historical precedent	revolutionary, progressive, antiditional
conventional	creative, unique, and original
old words with new meanings	new words
ordinary	extraordinary
inconsistent	consistent
starts from client's value system	tries to elevate client's value system

In his next book, *Learning from Las Vegas* ([1972] 1977, 102), Venturi compares two structures intended as housing for the elderly: the Guild House (Philadelphia, 1960–63), designed by Venturi and Rauch, with Paul Rudolph's Crawford Manor (New Haven, Connecticut, 1962–66). Guild House is not postmodern in the same way as the much later AT&T building (New York, 1978–83) or Michael Graves's Public Service Building (Portland, Oregon; 1980–83) (both discussed later)—it comes essentially before full-blown postmodern architecture[12]—but the comments of Venturi in comparing the two buildings (excerpted below) are instructive:

Venturi's writings (more so than his buildings, of which the Guild House is perhaps the most often discussed) set the direction for the new style. Although some elements of the shift in design from modernism to postmodernism can be traced in buildings from the 1960s, the late 1970s saw the construction of the first buildings that exemplify postmodern style—the style that has, in subsequent years, gradually displaced the International Style on the cutting edge of architectural design. The domination of postmodernism in the last twenty years is noted by Klotz:

> Even though the conflict continues and the defenders of modern and post-modern architecture still confront each other as if the final decision is yet to come, history has already decided. A new kind of architecture prevails today, one that differs fundamentally from Das Neue Bauen of the 1920s. Almost every new architectural idea and every creative architectural form developed since the mid-1970s has stood in opposition to the established authority of the Modern Movement. ([1984] 1988, 2)

CONSIDERING AN ARCHITECTURAL EXAMPLE: PHILIP JOHNSON'S AT&T BUILDING (1978–83)

Philip Johnson's design for the AT&T headquarters, built in midtown Manhattan in 1978–83, brought postmodern architecture to Madison Avenue and to the public's attention. This rectangular tower, rising 647 feet tall to stand among the other landmark buildings of the New York skyline, is composed of three parts—a base, a main shaft with rows of windows, and a scrolled broken pediment—that flow smoothly one into the other. The ten-story base, with its huge Palladian-arched central entrance surrounded by tall, straight columns, reaches the very edge of the lot-line and dwarfs the pedestrians on the sidewalk. The sides of the base feature three rectangular, garage-door shaped openings at ground level, with a circular window aligned above each. Four tall, narrow windows on each side visually balance the top of the arch of the front. The shaft is delineated from the base by its twenty-eight-story grid-work of smaller windows that circle the sides and front of the building. The fenestration grid on the façade divides into three parts—one above the arch and two pilasters above the ground floor columns—further divided by vertical mullions that draw the eye smoothly upward from the columns of the base to the shaft, then to the taller windows of the top floors. A massive broken pediment, whose semicircular division echoes the curves of the oculi and arch below, tops the tower and provides an unmistakable corporate symbol for AT&T. The interior features double-high floors (the ground floor soaring an equivalent of five stories), making only thirty-six stories in what would have normally been a sixty-story tower. The ground floor is a vaulted colonnade with arched doors, with Evelyn Longman's 1917 gilded statue entitled "The Spirit of Communication" (often called the "Golden Boy") rescued from the top of the old AT&T Building prominently displayed (Arnason [1968] 1986, 696–97). The building, inside and out, provides a feast for the eye, with its multiple stylistic references—interesting in themselves—combining to make a structure that is more than the sum of its parts.

Architectural historians writing about the building usually mention their favorite "borrowed" elements. For example, Stern (1988, 84) cites "the arcade from Sant' Andrea in Mantua; the *oculi*, with their deep, chamfered reveals, from the Duomo in Florence; the Carolingian lobby, with its Lutyens-like floor pattern, Roman *opus reticulatum*, and household god—the statue of the AT&T symbol, "Golden Boy."[13] Trachtenberg and Hyman (1986, 575) indicate that "its main façade is the recollection of Brunelleschi's Pazzi Chapel (with a few extra loggia bays), including its telltale coffering and oculus-over-arch motif, blown up to become the giant window fronting the lobby; inside is not the expected Renaissance interior, but a Romanesque confabulation . . . the surrounding loggia carries one off in the opposite historical direction to a French eighteenth-century, coffered hypostyle hall . . ." and "within this provincial, subarchitectural Chippendale is encapsulated the pure Early Renaissance, fronting the grandiose Middle Ages, enveloped by lucid Neoclassicism." Most writers discussing the building (for example, Roth 1993, 506; Stern 1988, 84; Klotz [1984] 1988, 45, 49) also note the links to the New York skyscrapers of the early decades of the twentieth century; the Helmsley Building (architects Warren & Wetmore, 1929), the Municipal Building (architects Kim, Mead & White, 1907–13), the Empire State Building (1931), and the Chrysler Building (architect William Van Alen, 1930) are mentioned in this context.

This building has brought forth a wide range of reactions. Some architecture critics refer to it as a "highboy"—a piece of furniture with legs supporting a series of drawers, topped with a decorative flourish.[14] One of the comments cited by Trachtenberg and Hyman (1986, 574) is that it was the perfect building for "Ma Bell"—it had a pay phone coin slot at the top and a coin return at the bottom. Arnason ([1968] 1986, 697) observes "herein may lie the essence of Post-Modernism, which longs for the monumentality and symbolism of old but, lacking the faith originally embodied in those forms, must inevitably undermine them with ingenious puns and brilliant self-mockery." In any case, the AT&T Building is one of a kind; as Johnson said in an interview about it: "You'll know it is our building."[15] It certainly matches the Chrysler Building and the Empire State Building in its distinctive individuality.

A SECOND EXAMPLE: MICHAEL GRAVES'S PUBLIC SERVICE BUILDING, (1980–83)

White and Robertson (1990, 84) define postmodernism in architecture as a "1970s reaction against International Modern Style's austerity and the commercialization of modern structural techniques. Basically, it returned ornament and decorative motif to building, often in garish colors and illogical juxtaposition." This definition applies well to the Portland Public Service Building (1980–83) by Michael Graves.

This building has a base of three greenish-blue tiled stepped stories, topped by a twelve-story cream-colored near-perfect cube. The front of the building sports a grid of small, square windows, three across and twelve high on either side, surrounding a pair of maroon pilasters—flattened columns six stories high with one story high protruding capitals—imposed on a massive mirror-glass window. The pilasters support a keystone-shaped four-story high lintel. The sides of the building continue the theme of cream walls with a grid of windows, maroon pilasters—four in this case—again overlaid on mirror-glass wall, sporting immense green stylized garlands instead of the capitals of the façade. The garlands, which, as constructed, look like flattened bows and swags, were originally proposed to be in raised relief—like elaborate Baroque floral garlands.

The juxtaposition of historical elements in this building is quite startling, as is the abandonment of the usual scale relationships, and the garish use of color. The cream walls, small square windows, and mirror glass are modernist elements, while the pilasters, capitals, garlands, and keystone evoke much earlier architectural styles without copying them precisely. The huge pilasters and keystone dominate the façade, combining with the surrounding window grids to make an illusion of depth in the flat wall surface. The flattened garlands and columns are like poster-board cutouts—a theatrical substitute for their three-dimensional historical counterparts. Elements of the building are evocative of Art Deco, Pop Art, Greek temples, and Italian Mannerist works—to name but a few of the styles implied—without really being true to any of those styles. Like the AT&T Building, the Portland Building has been fancifully described, in this case as "a huge face with capitals as eyes" and as a "standing figure—a broad shouldered, Atlaslike 'strong man'" (Trachtenberg and Hyman 1986, 573).

Whether this public services building "works" artistically and functionally or not is up for debate. Arnason ([1968] 1988, 696) says: "The Portland [Public Service Building] has become a reality in every sense of the word, a truly civic building imbued with all the dignity of the human past made whole with a boldly asserted, living present." Trachtenberg and Hyman (1986, 573) agree: "The Portland Building is truly a civic building, permeated with dignity, scale, color, vitality, referential layers of ancient civic archetypes of Greek temples and Roman arch, and even with an explicit image of humanity itself." But Roth (1993, 510) takes the opposing stance: "Yet for all the architect's written assertions and visual intimations that this was a return to the gracious public architecture of the turn of the century, the gesture rings hollow, for the ornament is painted plaster, not marble, the entrances are constricting, not inviting, and the interior public spaces are cramped and not generous." Architect and architectural historian Robert A. M. Stern (1988, 82) concurs: "But in reality, the building is more convincing as a billboard for an idea, rather than its embodiment."

WHAT CONSTITUTES POSTMODERNISM IN ARCHITECTURE?

There are several characteristics associated with the postmodern style in architecture, but I will focus on four: disunity, multiple meanings, playfulness, and emphasis on surface decoration. First of all, postmodern buildings are intentionally not in one unified style of architecture—they are *purposefully* disunified.[16] Postmodern architects value the overt presence of older styles—including modernism—by quotation and obvious allusion. Their use of these styles, however, is not a covert "remaking" of the past of the modernists, but a blatant co-opting of the past for their own ends and their own use.[17] Through disunity, the elements of various historical styles juxtaposed therein evoke rich historical references, both to their origins, and in their "commentary" on each other.

One of the delights of these buildings is that they may evoke many meanings at once—they are not limited to one critical viewpoint, one "statement." Viewers tend to focus on different elements of the same building and may not interpret what they are seeing in the same way. Both buildings considered in this essay have been described as social commentary as well as art forms: reviews of the AT&T Building include references to the workers in the "drawers" of the highboy (Trachtenberg and Hyman 1986, 575); on the Portland Public Service Building, there have been comments that the levity of the design mocks its purpose of solemn public service (Roth 1993, 511). There is not a consensus among architectural critics regarding them; both buildings have been reviewed both favorably and critically.

Some critics cite the presence of irony in the inevitable conflict between elements in an eclectic building, while others see the irony as introduced by the comments of the critics themselves. Whether irony is intended by the architect or not, postmodernism in architecture often does displays a spirit of lightheartedness—a lack of willingness to take anything too seriously, including design, historical elements, or the buildings themselves. In contrast with the serious, no-nonsense, industrial nature of the International Style, postmodernism restores an attitude of playfulness to architecture.

The return of surface decoration—the presence of visual elements because they are pleasurable, comforting, familiar, or interesting to look at—serves an aesthetic purpose rather than a practical one. These buildings are not intended to provide utopia—they are simply buildings. While the eclecticism of a postmodern building may not make everyone "comfortable," there is more attention in this style to practical functionality and the needs of users.

Both of the buildings discussed above exemplify these characteristics. Of course, not every building that can be considered postmodern will exhibit all of these "markers" of postmodernism, but the presence of several is typical for buildings classified in this style.

MODERNISM AND POSTMODERNISM IN MUSIC

A critical vocabulary around the idea of modernism has not been as developed in musicology as it has been in architecture, yet the terms and aesthetic positions associated with modernism describe avant-garde music of the first three-quarters of the twentieth century as well as they do architecture of the same time period. The start of modernism in architecture was around 1900—the same time frame as significant stylistic shifts in music. Although Trachtenberg and Hyman (1986, 487) were writing about architecture, if one substitutes the word "music" each place "architecture" appears, their comments apply as well to modernism in music:

> The birth of modern architecture—like the Renaissance—hinged on the recognition of a deep historical discontinuity. One of the great obstacles in the nineteenth century to modernism had been the rigid insistence on the continuity with the past. About 1900, however, the architectural avant-garde severed this bond. The immense spectrum of historical styles, which had been so passionately researched and churned by the nineteenth century in its troubled pursuit of architectural relevance, was now recognized as antithetical or, at best, irrelevant to architectural Modernism. The way to the future, it was suddenly realized, was not through the past. The past was over—an almost unbridgeable void had opened between it and the present.

In breaking with the past, however, modernist architects and composers wanted to be perceived as in a direct line from the past masters, carrying on the tradition of creativity and artistry—a condition that Joseph Straus in his book *Remaking the Past* (1990, 18–19) refers to as the Bloomian "anxiety of influence."

In many ways, musical styles from about 1910 to 1970 have significant resemblances to the International Style of architecture. Looking back at the first half of the twentieth century, and speaking in the broadest terms, Barr's description of the three elements of International Style bring to mind musical compositions as well as buildings. There was an emphasis on a unified approach throughout a building/piece of music—the design was simplified to one primary medium or compositional method. Like architecture, modernist music, particularly after the First World War, emphasized clean lines, with no extraneous elements. Individual composers also come to mind in conjunction with Barr's elements: Varèse and Webern in their development of volume (spans of intervals) as opposed to mass; regularity without symmetry—Stravinsky and Bartók; technically perfect use of materials, without applied decoration or patterning—Webern most of all, but others of the Second Viennese School as well. Many of the compositions now considered classics of the early part of the twentieth century are clean-lined, to some extent machine-like, tightly planned, and (to the ears of some listeners) rational, cold, and impersonal.

Like the modernist architects, the rhetoric of modernist composers rings with a sense of mission; they, too, were seeking utopia, but through music composition. To give only two examples: the writings of Second Viennese School composers emphasize awareness of their goal—to liberate the twelve tones from the hierarchies of tonal music and set forth a new path to musical greatness. Varèse, as early as the 1930s, was looking for a future of music in the invention of electronic instruments that would allow composers to write any sounds they could imagine.[18]

As in architecture, modernist compositional practices continued to dominate the musical avant-garde of the first three decades after World War II. Boulez, Stockhausen, and their colleagues certainly saw themselves as pressing forward into territory that their predecessors had failed to conquer—bringing music, at last, to a freedom from older styles. Although the avant-garde of the immediate post-war period thought of itself as setting out on a totally new direction, in looking back, we can see the compositions of Boulez, Stockhausen, and the others who dabbled with total serialism as continuing the path of modernism—the search begun by Schoenberg, Webern, and Berg to liberate themselves and their music from the hegemony of the past. Their manifestoes declared their independence from the procedures of the pre–World War II composers, while their actions and compositions continued in the older styles.

The post–World War II modernists distilled the elements of earlier representations of this style. These works, more than the pre-1945 ones, had a unity of style and compositional method—emphasizing the employment of only one compositional approach in a piece. Composers of total serialism and early minimalism both strove for unity and purity of elements (perhaps best achieved by the early minimalist works), in their search for perfection in music. Even the compositions of John Cage (whose works have been called both modernist and postmodern) from the 1950s–'60s tend to be consistent in sound materials and style throughout. He, too, was searching for utopia, but in letting "the sounds be themselves"—a common theme in many of his writings.

In their concern for "progress" in music, late modernist composers often neglected the needs of performers and the concerns of listeners. Performers were given rigidly restrictive scores—the extreme example is Boulez's *Structures* (1951)—where the precise durations, dynamics, and articulation were specified to the point that some pieces were almost unplayable. Like modernist buildings that resisted personalization by their users, the specificity of scores for some late-modernist compositions denied performers a role in shaping, developing, or making the music their own. Their pieces were, in many ways, not intended or suited for "inhabitation" by performers. It could seem, at its most extreme, that composers wrote solely for themselves and "did not care if one listened" to paraphrase the title given to Babbitt's famous dictum.[19] The hands of the modernist masters produced works with a special kind of beauty lauded by a small circle of cognoscenti, but which alienated the masses who did not feel comfortable in the presence of the "new music" and did not want to expend the effort to understand the new style. As a result, the modernist style in music, like that in architecture, while appreciated by a few, did not seize the public's imagination.

HOW DID POSTMODERISM IN MUSIC BEGIN?

This is an interesting question—and one whose consideration in depth is unfortunately beyond the scope of this essay—but I will speculate briefly on it here. To my knowledge, there has been no "postmodern manifesto" analogous to that of Venturi's *Complexity and Contradiction in Architecture* in its impact as a touchstone of change. How did postmodernism in music begin? Composers simply started writing pieces that could be characterized as postmodern.

Some of the very earliest post–World War II works that can be considered postmodern are from the pen of Luciano Berio and date back to the late 1960s. While many of his compositions from that decade and the next are unified in style and clearly modernist, the third movement of his *Sinfonia* (1968)—with its swirling, eclectic mixture of music from the Scherzo of Mahler's Second Symphony, quotations and allusions to music from Bach's time to his own, and recitation from Samuel Beckett's play *The Unnamable*—might be taken as an early example of a postmodern composition.

Early minimalist works from the 1960s have a modernist unity, yet, as minimalism entered its second decade, the diversity of elements included in some compositions by Reich, Glass, and Adams led to a style sometimes referred to as "maximal minimalism" in the 1980s and 1990s. Reich's *Tehillim* (1981) and *Different Trains* (1988) and Adams's opera *Nixon in China* (1987) are worthy of consideration as postmodern compositions in the context of architectural developments discussed above. Other works from the 1970s and '80s that come to mind as worthy of investigation as postmodern artworks are György Ligeti's opera *Le Grand Macabre* (1978) and John Corigliano's Clarinet Concerto (1977) and *Pied Piper Fantasy* (1982). We will consider other pieces by these last two composers in the next section.

CONSIDERING A MUSICAL EXAMPLE: CORIGLIANO'S *THE GHOSTS OF VERSAILLES* (1991)

One of the pieces that typifies a postmodernism comparable to architectural examples is John Corigliano's opera *The Ghosts of Versailles* (1991). This expansive opera, running about three hours, is as grand in scope and spectacle as any to grace the stage of the Metropolitan Opera in recent years. In his synopsis to the opera, Corigliano explains that "the *Ghosts of Versailles* is set in the present in the palace of Versailles. It seems that the ghosts of the court of Louis XVI have been haunting the place since their demise during the French Revolution."[20] Louis XVI, Marie Antoinette, and their courtiers (dressed in the Met production in tattered, white-dusted garments and disheveled powdered wigs) occupy the stage as the opera opens. Among the courtiers is the playwright Pierre Augustin Caron de Beaumarchais (1732–99), author of *The Barber of Seville* and *The Marriage of Figaro*, identified in the synopsis as "in love with the ghost of Marie Antoinette for the last two hundred years."

The "present" in the opera, however, is the eternal present—it could be any time since the Revolution.[21] The element that dates the world of the ghosts is the music, which is of a post–World War II vintage. The dissonant and atmospheric lengthy introduction "Bored as an egg, Bored as a potato . . ." both illustrates and inspires the audience to feel the boredom through atonal music reminiscent of Penderecki's compositions from the 1960s.

In order to alleviate the general boredom and the grief of Marie Antoinette, the character Beaumarchais proposes to stage an opera. The libretto of the opera-within-an-opera is drawn in part from the third play of Beaumarchais, *The Guilty Mother* (1792, with later revisions), a sequel to his *The Barber of Seville* (1775) and *The Marriage of Figaro* (1778), but set twenty years later.[22] In *The Guilty Mother*, set in France at the time of the Revolution, the main characters from the Figaro operas return: Count Almaviva and the Countess Rosina, Figaro's wife, Suzanna, and Figaro himself, up to his usual tricks. Cherubino, the page from *The Marriage of Figaro*, appears also in *Ghosts*, but in a flashback scene of his seduction of Rosina, twenty years earlier. Characters new to this play include Florestine, Count Almaviva's illegitimate daughter, whom he has adopted without revealing the connection between them, and León, Countess Rosina's illegitimate son by her liaison with the page Cherubino (result of the aforementioned seduction scene)—young lovers unaware of their past and parentage. The villain Bégearss, confidant of the Count, completes the roster. In its setting as the opera-within-an-opera of *Ghosts*, Beaumarchais's opera is not any ordinary opera; this opera has the power to change history, allowing Beaumarchais to rescue the queen from her historic fate, allowing her to flee with him to America.

This work, unlike other successful contemporary operas from years just previous, such as Philip Glass's *Einstein on the Beach* (1976), engages fully in the tradition of opera. The complexity of the libretto (nothing new to opera fans) provides opportunities for all of the types of entertainment normally associated with opera: there are arias, duets, quartets (sometimes made of pairs), detailed costumes, elaborate sets, puppets (including a many-times life-size Pasha puppet), set pieces, cameos, divas, and showstoppers. Some scenes in the Met production—for example, the trial and execution of Marie Antoinette from the second act—would seem more at home on Broadway than in Lincoln Center, drawing on the spectacle of late-twentieth-century musical theater.

What distinguishes Corigliano's opera from those of previous time periods is the eclecticism of the music and the wide range of references to other works—literary and musical, historical and contemporary, past and present. The mix of music is extraordinary: the ghost music (1960s–'70s); the world of the Figaro opera (harpsichord and Mozart); tonality, modality, and atonality. There is even a touch of world music in the very comical Samira's aria (from the end of Act 1)—Samira is an "Egyptian diva" providing suitable entertainment for the party guests of the Turkish embassy to a nonsensical text made from Arab proverbs.[23]

Although the music of the ghosts places the opera at the end of the twentieth century, the score of the opera-within-the-opera draws on the conventions of Mozart's *opera buffa*—to the casual listener it sounds at times like a Mozart opera—but with a "twist." For example, the quartet "Come Now, My Darling" (actually, a double duet, like many of Mozart's quartets) pairs a duet from the "flashback" scene where Cherubino seduces Rosina from the opera-within-an-opera with another duet in the realm of the ghosts where Beaumarchais attempts the same line of persuasion to seduce Marie Antoinette. The flowing, graceful melodies of the duets are tonal, yet the characters in each duet begin in different keys—not something Mozart would have done this blatantly. The keys themselves, though, correspond to the emotional content of the lines the singers are singing, using key relationships to represent the relationship between characters—an idea often identified with Mozart opera. As the characters come to an agreement, they sing in the same key, modulating several times in a short passage, but going through the keys together. While Corigliano borrows heavily from Mozartean operatic conventions, the music has been "through the looking glass" of the twentieth century—this opera could not date from an earlier period.

The opera plays upon multiple historical references in the libretto as well. The layers of social commentary in the Figaro operas are well known—the impudent character Figaro threatened the social structure of the end of the eighteenth century to such an extent that the real Louis XVI forbade productions of the play *The Marriage of Figaro* in France (Lawrence 1962, iv). (The historical Beaumarchais, assisted by some close to Marie Antoinette, succeeded in getting the play performed in houses of the nobility.) The characters in the Beaumarchais play themselves are drawn from *commedia dell'arte* stock characters—yielding another layer to the whole proceeding—and Figaro is thought to be modeled on elements of the life of Beaumarchais himself.[24] In addition to *The Guilty Mother*, the libretto for *Ghosts* includes text from the trial of Marie Antoinette and a prayer using her own words.

Why does this opera remind me of the Johnson AT&T Building? First, its grand scale. It represents a return to monumentalism—the grand opera as compared to the grand monumental building. Second, it mixes ideas— musical, literary, and theatrical—drawn from a variety of times and places. Although both the building and the opera have features that should appeal to anyone, the more observers/listeners know about the history of the art form, the more references they will recognize. The contrasting elements, while distinct, individual, and identifiable in themselves, seem to comment on each other—making the whole much more than a sum of its parts— and exemplifying the characteristics set out by Venturi.

CONSIDERING A SECOND MUSICAL EXAMPLE: LIGETI'S PIANO CONCERTO (1985–88)

A second example of music that I consider to be postmodern, György Ligeti's five-movement Piano Concerto (1985–88), differs from the first in that it does not have a text—any intertextuality or multiplicity of meaning in the work draws from musical elements alone. The combination of disparate elements is apparent from the up-tempo, percussive, dance-like first movement "Vivace molto ritmico e preciso." A highly rhythmic piano part notated in 12/8 is set against a second rhythmic stream in the strings, notated in 4/4. These two rhythmic patterns are syncopated in relation to their dotted-quarter or quarter note beats, while creating cross-rhythms (duple vs. triple) with each other. The overall effect is quite reminiscent of Bartók's "Bulgarian Rhythms," but the construction of the rhythmic texture is through ostinato duration cycles—an element of Igor Stravinsky's music and of serial techniques, as well as a hallmark of African percussion, which was an interest of Ligeti's in the 1980s. The horn, violin, flute, and other winds attempt to interrupt the rhythmic frenzy by interjecting melodic fragments—at first lyrical, then more strident—but the rhythmic streams prevail, dominating to the end of the movement, where all activity suddenly comes to an end.

The contrasting second movement, "Lento e deserto," begins with a haunting, ethereal flute solo. The flute is eventually joined by a bassoon, slide whistle, ocarina, and piano in an otherworldly counterpoint. The descending tetrachords of the melody settle into the piano part, but are interrupted by the brasses, before yielding to a pitch microcanon (rhythmically free canon with canonic entrances close to each other in time) midway through the movement. At times, the timbres in this movement almost sound electronic, but this effect is achieved with non-traditional instruments (in addition to those mentioned above, add siren whistle, flexatone, chromatic harmonica, alarm whistle, and a full battery of percussion instruments) and unusual instrumental combinations. The ocarina, with its breath-fluctuating tuning, also evokes the Asian spirit of shakuhachi flute.

The third movement, "Vivace cantabile," begins with a pattern-meccanico section featuring several overlaid repeated patterns that grow from dyads into a descending tetrachord—a melodic element that links the movements—then disintegrates into a perpetuum mobile featuring the pianist. The fourth movement, "Allegro risoluto," is a collage of musical fragments—some lyrical, some rhythmic—evoking a wide range of Western and non-Western music through Ligeti's choices of pitch materials and rhythmic patterns. While each of the previous movements featured disunity of small-scale elements within an overall unifying formal design, this movement seems to be disunified in both the juxtaposition of local events and in its overall structure.[25] A brief whirlwind of a fifth movement—a "presto luminoso"—brings the piece to an end.

Many of the musical elements that are combined in this piece are from previous compositional styles of Ligeti himself: the microcanon of *Lux aeterna* (1966) and *Lontano* (1967) in the second movement; the mechanical pattern repetition of *Continuum* (1968) and *Coulée* (1969) in the third movement; the rediscovery of accented surface rhythms from *Hungarian Rock* (1978) in the first movement, especially; and singing melody, prominent in the Trio for Violin, Horn, and Piano (1982), at points in each movement. The music of Bartók, a prevalent influence in Ligeti's compositions prior to 1956 but of little evidence in his works of the 1960s and '70s, returns in this work, particularly in the rhythmic character of the first movement.

Unlike Corigliano's *Ghosts*, the Piano Concerto has no explicit references to previous tonal styles—the entire piece is in a twentieth-century idiom—yet, by Ligeti's own admission, some of his techniques, especially micropolyphony, draw on contrapuntal procedures from Renaissance and eighteenth-century counterpoint.[26] His knowledge of and interest in a wide range of twentieth-century styles is evident: those evoked include serialism and electronic music, as well as hints at elements of Asian and African music.

In addition to the multiple styles and allusions in this work, a characteristic that marks it as postmodern is the juxtaposition of contrasting ideas:

in some cases, contrasting elements are simultaneous and overlaid; other times they follow one another like an extended nonsequitur. The Piano Concerto is indeed well described by Venturi's words: it is "complex and contradictory" and displays a "messy vitality."

WHAT CONSTITUTES POSTMODERNISM IN MUSIC?

Postmodernism in music can be discussed in the same terms as postmodernism in architecture as set out by Venturi: complexity and contradiction, messy vitality, richness over clarity, many levels of meaning, a combination of forms, decoration and ornament for its own sake, mixed media, symbolism, representationalism, and starting with the listener's value system rather than seeking to impose the composer's values on the listener.

Like postmodern buildings, postmodern compositions are purposely disunified. This disunity can be expressed in the surface elements of the piece, with a deeper level organization that provides an overall unity to the compositions, or the form and larger-scale structure of the piece may be disunified as well.[27] Postmodern compositions draw consciously on the past— both the long past and immediately previous styles—mixing techniques and elements from a variety of time periods. Postmodern music tends to be rich in references and meaning: there is no one interpretation or meaning, allowing individual listeners to establish their own ideas of a piece's meaning. Sometimes irony is an element of postmodern music—whether on the part of the composer, or in the perception of the listener or critic. Postmodernism in music heralds a return of ornament for the pleasure of ornamentation and a concern on the part of the composers for those who play and listen— postmodern composers "care who listens," and write interesting, singable/ playable parts appealing to musicians and listeners alike.

Postmodern pieces, in my view, may draw from a constellation of postmodern elements: no one piece is expected to exhibit all of the characteristics of postmodernism; yet pieces that are considered postmodern do prominently employ elements from the list of possibilities associated with the style. Postmodern music, like postmodern architecture, is controversial—some critics love it, some hate it.

CONCLUSIONS

As in architecture in the 1970s and '80s there has been an "uneasy coexistence of latter-day modernism and postmodernism in music composition" (J. Kramer 1995, 14). It seems now, from our restricted viewpoint at the end of the century, but less than thirty years after the beginnings of postmodernism in music, that this style is here to stay. Audiences love it—the Met sold out performances of *Ghosts*, the opera has already received several other performances, and a recording of the Metropolitan Opera performance has been released in both videocassette and laser disk. A telling indicator of the popularity of *Ghosts* is the reaction of graduate and undergraduate students in my Music Since World War II course: primarily novices in the world of post-war music when they begin the class, many declare that they don't like new music; yet, when I play a portion of the video in my class, students stay after, wanting see the rest of it. Like *Ghosts*, the Piano Concerto is a sparking, beautiful, virtuoso work that, from its catchy rhythmic opening, draws listeners in.

The parallels between modernism and postmodernism in architectural styles in the twentieth century and the styles in music of the same time period seem quite clear. Although this study is circumspect in scope—limited to two buildings and two musical compositions—I hope that it has illustrated the promise of recognizing that "musical compositions are sometimes like buildings" and the strength of analogy between the disciplines in considering what it means for an artwork to be modern or postmodern.

NOTES

1. This is not the first essay to draw on these connections. Dibelius (1989), in a brief article, refers to the Graves Portland Public Services Building in the context of Krzysztof Penderecki's change in style from the 1960s to the 1980s. Jonathan D. Kramer (1995) also draws on architectural, as well as literary, ideas of postmodernism in reference to post-1945 music. Although its title seems promising, the article by Kompridis (1993) is primarily philosophical, with little reference to actual music or architecture.

2. At this time, I am working on a more extensive consideration of both modernism and postmodernism in post-1945 music, drawing on the use of these terms in architecture. This essay is a preliminary sketch for that larger project.

3. Examples that come immediately to mind are impressionism and minimalism—both terms were first applied to visual arts, then to music.

4. A basic explanation of postmodernism in literary criticism and a bibliography of the most significant early sources are provided in Selden and Widdowson 1993, 174–88, 197–200. (The discussion of postmodernism was introduced in this edition.) The authors listed do not define postmodernism in a unified way—each sets out on a slightly different path from the others.

5. For two examples of musicologists or music theorists who draw on postmodern approaches from literary criticism to look back at older music, see Lawrence Kramer 1995 and Jonathan D. Kramer 1996, 21–61.

6. The term "International Style" comes from an exhibition of architectural designs and models organized by Philip Johnson and Henry-Russell Hitchcock at the Museum of Modern Art in 1932. This exhibit was the first from this young museum to be sent on tour—to thirteen cities outside New York—introducing the International Style (Schulze 1994, 75–80).

7. From Barr's preface to the catalog for the 1932 Museum of Modern Art

exhibition "International Style: Architecture since 1922" (Hitchcock and Johnson [1932] 1966, 13).

8. Although Frank Lloyd Wright was included in the 1932 exhibition, he was of an older generation and expressed a different artistic aesthetic than the other listed architects. His building materials differed from many of the others—he often used stone, wood, and other vernacular building materials associated with a particular location—but the clean-line functionality of his structures link his designs with the International Style. For these reasons, some architectural historians list him within this group, whereas others do not.

9. Unless otherwise indicated, the dates listed with buildings reflect when the structure was built.

10. Yamasaki was also the designer of the World Trade Center twin towers in New York, 1964–72.

11. For example, the Art and Architecture building at Yale University, a Paul Rudolph design in the late modernist "Brutalist" style built 1959–63, leaked so badly in the mid-1980s (when I was working as a library assistant in the at Art and Architecture Library) that yards of plastic sheeting hung over the book shelving units to be pulled like huge furniture dust covers over the stacks to protect the valuable art and architecture reference books any time there was a forecast of rain. The building had a confusing layout (described as nearly unusable by Trachtenberg and Hyman [1986, 548]), and was also invariably hot in the summer and cold enough in the winter that workers wore their coats and gloves inside.

12. Klotz, however, cites Guild House as "the first large building of postmodern architecture ([1984] 1988, 150)."

13. *Opus reticulatum* refers to brick or stone walls where square pavers are set on their point, in a diamond shape, to form a diagonal net-like patterning.

14. Trachtenberg and Hyman (1986, 574–75) use the image of the Chippendale highboy as a springboard for a lengthy discussion of the building's ironic qualities and visual puns.

15. Stern (1988, 86) cites this remark from an interview of Philip Johnson in *Architecture* 72 (July 1983): 64.

16. This point is discussed by Jonathan D. Kramer (1995, 12–13) in regard to both architecture and music.

17. For a discussion of the "remaking" of the past by musical modernists, and the background of this viewpoint in literary criticism, see Straus (1990, 1–20).

18. For a sampling of his comments on the liberation of sound, see the excerpts of lectures by Edgard Varèse (1967, 196–208).

19. The article referenced is "Who Cares if You Listen?" by Milton Babbitt ([1958] 1998, 1305–11).

20. The synopsis is cited in the introductory materials for each of the extracted arias, ensemble pieces, and excerpts that have been published thus far. This quotation (and that later in this paragraph from the synopsis) was taken from an unnumbered page facing page 1 of John Corigliano, *The Ghosts of Versailles*, Figaro's aria "They Wish They Could Kill Me." Music by John Corigliano; libretto

by William M. Hoffman. New York: G. Schirmer, 1991. The complete opera score is listed as forthcoming from G. Schirmer.

21. The intermingling of past and present in *Ghosts* brings to mind Jonathan D. Kramer's differentiation of modernist and postmodernist approaches to history: "Modernist pastiche acknowledges history: the past is reinterpreted in the present. But postmodern pastiche is anti-historical: the past coexists with, and indeed is indistinguishable from, the present (1995, 26)."

22. As many readers know, the first two plays were adapted long ago as libretti for operas whose fame has eclipsed that of the original plays: *The Barber of Seville* was set by Gioacchino Rossini in 1816 to a libretto by Cesare Sterbini; *The Marriage of Figaro* was set by Wolfgang Amadeus Mozart in 1786 to a libretto by Lorenzo Da Ponte. Regarding the third play, Robert Lawrence, in an introductory essay for a score of Rossini's *The Barber of Seville* (1962, V) remarks: "One regrets that some other great composer, in the tradition or Mozart and Rossini, did not set this play to music, thus completing the cycle operatically." He further suggests that Berlioz or Richard Strauss would have been able to do it justice. Corigliano has done just that—probably not in the way Lawrence envisioned.

23. When the ghosts watch as the Beaumarchais opera characters attend entertainment at the embassy, is it opera within opera within opera?

24. Mentioned by Corigliano in a lecture to students at Florida State University while he was in residence as a Housewright Scholar, February 3, 1999.

25. The fourth and fifth movements of this concerto were composed after the premiere of the first three movements in 1986. In my review of this score for *Notes*, I criticized the fourth movement for "not attain[ing] the level of coherence typical of Ligeti's compositions" (Clendinning 1992, 1455). At this point, I am willing to accept the fourth movement as intentionally disunified—an intensification of the process exhibited at the local level in the three movements he had already composed.

26. This is a common theme in his interviews and writings about his music. See Ligeti [1979] 1983, 30 and passim.

27. This may be another way of expressing a point made by Jonathan D. Kramer (1995, 21–22) in dividing postmodernism into two camps: neo-conservative and radical. According to Kramer, the first maintains organicism as a force but combines pre- and postmodern elements; the second has stylistic juxtapositions, but is not organically unified. While I (like Kramer) see compositions of John Zorn as emblematic of the second type of disunity (Kramer's radical postmodernism), I am not sure we would agree completely on which pieces belong in the first camp. Kramer also sets forth these two "camps" as the primary categories for postmodern music, but I do not see the division as that clear-cut.

WORKS CITED

Arnason, H. H. [1968] 1986. *History of Modern Art: Painting, Sculpture, Architecture, Photography.* 3rd ed., revised and updated by Daniel Wheeler. New York: Harry N. Abrams. Material on postmodernism is new to this edition.

Babbitt, Milton. [1958] 1998. "Who Cares if You Listen?" In *Source Readings in Music History: The Twentieth Century*. Rev. ed., edited by Robert Morgan. New York: W. W. Norton. 1305–10. Originally published in *High Fidelity* 8/2 (February 1958): 38–40 and 126–27.

Clendinning, Jane Piper. 1992. Review of György Ligeti's *Konzert für Klavier und Orchester* in *Notes* (June): 1453–55.

Dibelius, Ulrich. 1989. "Postmoderne in der Musik." *Neue Zeitschrift für Musik* 150/2 (February): 4–9.

Hitchcock, Henry Russell, and Philip Johnson. [1932] 1966. *The International Style*. (Original title, *The International Style: Architecture since 1922*.) Preface by Alfred H. Barr. New York: W. W. Norton.

Klotz, Heinrich. [1984] 1988. *The History of Postmodern Architecture*. Translated by Radka Donnell. Cambridge, Mass., and London: MIT Press.

Kompridis, Nikolas. 1993. "Learning from Architecture: Music in the Aftermath to Postmodernism." *Perspectives of New Music* 31/2 (Summer): 6–23.

Kramer, Jonathan D. 1995. "Beyond Unity: Toward an Understanding of Musical Postmodernism." In *Concert Music, Rock, and Jazz since 1945*, edited by Elizabeth West Marvin and Richard Hermann. Rochester, N.Y.: University of Rochester Press. 11–33.

———. 1996. "Postmodern Concepts of Musical Time." *Indiana Theory Review* 17/2: 21–61.

Kramer, Lawrence. 1995. *Classical Music and Postmodern Knowledge*. Berkeley and Los Angeles: University of California Press.

Lawrence, Robert. 1962. Introductory essay for an edition of Gioacchino Rossini's *Il Barbiere di Siviglia (The Barber of Seville)*. Libretto by Cesare Sterbini. New York: G. Schirmer.

Ligeti, György. [1979] 1983. "Interview with Péter Várnai." In *Ligeti in Conversation*, translated by Gabor J. Schabert. London: Eulenberg. 13–82.

Roth, Leland M. 1993. *Understanding Architecture: Its Elements, History, and Meaning*. New York: HarperCollins.

Schulze, Franz. 1994. *Philip Johnson: Life and Work*. New York: Alfred A. Knopf.

Selden, Raman, and Peter Widdowson. 1993. *A Reader's Guide to Contemporary Literary Theory*. 3rd ed. Lexington: University Press of Kentucky.

Stern, Robert A. M. 1988. *Modern Classicism*. New York: Rizzoli.

Straus, Joseph N. 1990. *Remaking the Past: Musical Modernism and the Influence of the Tonal Tradition*. Cambridge: Harvard University Press.

Trachtenberg, Marvin, and Isabelle Hyman. 1986. *Architecture: From Prehistory to Post-Modernism*. New York: Harry N. Abrams.

Varèse, Edgard. 1967. "The Liberation of Sound." In *Contemporary Composers on Contemporary Music*, edited by Elliott Schwartz and Barney Childs. New York: Holt, Rinehart and Winston. 195–208.

Venturi, Robert. [1966] 1977. *Complexity and Contradiction in Architecture*. With an introduction by Vincent Scully. 2nd ed. New York: Museum of Modern Art Papers on Architecture.

Venturi, Robert, Denise Scott Brown, and Steven Izenour. [1972] 1977. *Learning from Las Vegas: The Forgotten Symbolism of Architectural Form*. Cambridge, Mass., and London: MIT Press.

White, Anthony, and Bruce Robertson. 1990. *Architecture and Ornament: A Visual Guide*. New York: Design Press.

CHAPTER 7

Feminine/Feminist? In Quest of Names with No Experiences (Yet)

Martin Scherzinger

> . . . to be musical without rhythm and rhyme . . .
> —Walter Benjamin, *On Some Motifs in Baudelaire*

> The slightest deviation from the true proportion ... affected me just as violations of abstract truth are wont, on earth, to affect the moral sense.
> —Edgar Allan Poe, "Colloquy of Monos and Una"

I do 4 ½ things in this paper: (1) describe, via the voice of Benjamin Boretz, a music-analytic orientation that I will identify, tentatively enough I hope, with "feminine" hearing; (2) try to listen to various short passages by Mozart under this recommendation; (3) extol some of its values; (4) worry about some of its values; and (4 ½) suggest listening again with this worry in mind. I hope that this work contributes to the deconstruction of a contrast that has become almost canonic in recent critical music studies in the "New Musicology" between, on the one hand, formalist close listening and, on the other, post-structuralist inspired musical interpretation. In part, this will involve outlining some of the theoretical affinities between various music theorists (particularly Benjamin Boretz and Joseph Dubiel) and post-structuralist writers (particularly Gilles Deleuze, Félix Guattari, and Jacques Lacan) who have contributed to postmodern thought generally. At the same time, I hope to show that the methodological resonance between a certain kind of musical formalism and post-structuralism does not necessarily assure the critical efficacy of such formalism. Indeed, I describe the progressive potential of formalism mostly with reference to the modernists Georg Lukács and Theodor Adorno. In the second, more critical, part of the paper, I make an excursion into philosophy proper and outline the limits of the "feminine" mode of listening via a close reading of a section from G. W. F. Hegel's *Phenomenology of Spirit* in conversation with the work of Adorno, Boretz, and Dubiel. I want to mention at the outset that my critique of various forms of music analysis does not herald a new kind of anti-formalism. On the contrary, I embrace the effort to listen to music all the way, but to do so within the context of a political predicament.

FEMININE HEARING AND THE TERRAIN OF MOZART

In step with an attitude found in the writings of Deleuze and Guattari, Boretz advances a listening posture that maximizes experiences not antici- pated by codified analytic models. Suspicious of ascriptions that "holisti- cally pre-empt and remake the ontological interior of what is experienced as . . . music," (Boretz 1992, 281), Boretz's writing about music wants to be maximally "experiential-quality-sensitized" (277) description. While "[no] text captures the experience itself, any more than anyone has described the experience of trance, or conveyed the ontology of mystical experience," such "perpetually in-progress" descriptions of music, at least at their "highest pitch of vividness . . . are swinging doors into and out of focused music-sensing episodes" (276). The contrast case involves a description that mistakenly stabilizes its inherently "metaphorical relation- ship" to the music "into a specifiable localized determinate quality- conferring effect" (281). Such an account becomes "reductively ontologi- cal" (281)—a condition that Boretz associates with the social-ideological problems that beset our field.

> The problem is probably at its most lurid and blatant in the music-devastating ontological transference that typifies traditional ear-training, and most other forms of traditional music-learning, music-studying, music-theorizing practice, all of which lead inex- orably—and familiarly—to musical expression–destroying experien- tial reductiveness: hearing analyses, hearing serial structures, hearing complex time-pattern relationships, hearing motivic transformations, hearing adumbrations internally and intertextually and historically, hearing ideologies, hearing anything that is ontologically in the ver- bal—or symbolic—referential-linguistic domain rather than in its own fully ontologized experiential intellectual language, is not only to freeze and paralyze the cumulating evolution of a person's inner music-experiencing history, but threatens to annihilate the entire intu- itive music-experiencing history a person may have already accumu- lated. (Boretz 1992, 283)

Theoretical discourses, Boretz argues, very often are not descriptive but "aggressively *ascriptive*: They transfer into music itself the very characteris- tics and functions of representation and metaphor they attribute to it. Verbal configurations like 'scale degree chord numbers,' 'Sonata form,' 'Schenker-level,' 'Fibonacci series,' 'combinatorial set structure' do not, in their most pervasive applications, function to represent musical phenomena; nor do metaphors like 'violence,' 'crystallization,' 'loneliness,' in their most pervasive usages, function to describe anything necessarily in the music; most of the time, it seems that music is being conscripted to stand for them" (1999, 4). For Boretz, such "representation-ascriptive" rhetoric, "mostly borrowed from the physical, cognitive, and social sciences," objectifies experience in the service of "social empowerment" (5). Invoking Pierre Bourdieu, he shows how such discourse marches in step with "institutional capital, . . . hierarchization of experts and practitioners, the verification of historical and scholarly accuracy, the enforcement of ideologies, and the whole business of and around music in the 'real world'" (5–6). But most disturbingly, this discourse is totally subversive of the "non-ascriptive description that looks but doesn't touch" (6) the music, which Boretz also calls "unlabelled experience" (3) or "experiences with no names" (Boretz 1992, 272).

While Boretz makes no explicit references to the gendered dimensions of his survey, his analysis of the relation between ascriptive discourse and social power alerts us to a kind of patriarchal anxiety in our institutions about musical interpretation that is figured as somehow private, peculiar, receptive, subjective, experiential, or passive.[1] In his article "Masculine Discourse in Music Theory" Fred Maus raises these dimensions prominently. Without claiming that the "feminine" has a literal referent, Maus shows how some kinds of analytic approaches in our field are belittled because they are perceived as such. For example, John Rahn's figurative pair "'theory-of-experience' vs. 'theory-of-piece' . . . designates a difference in discursive style, with experience-oriented accounts tending toward personal chronicle (gendered feminine), piece-oriented accounts tending toward statement of results and impersonality (gendered masculine)" (Maus 1993, 270). Maus shows how one way to allay the uncomfortable passive aspect of music theory—the central and constitutive role played by listening—has been to infuse one's discourse about music with general and predictive assertions. In the words of Maus: "The generality would situate the individual composition as an instance of the general theory, thereby giving the theory a sort of controlling power over the composition; the predictive conceit would, in a way, reverse the conversational temporality, giving the theorist the opening conversational move" (272). Like Boretz, Maus is disturbed by such discursive formations because of their relation to social power. More specifically, Maus is disturbed because they tend to marginalize alternatives. And like some deconstruction-influenced feminists such as Hélène Cixous and Luce Irigaray, who attack these *modus operandi* under the name "phallogocentrism," Maus resists peripheralizing any particular interpretative activity by menacing the opposition between seemingly "calm, objective writing about music" and seemingly "self-indulgent writing about oneself" (277). Instead of standing in a relation of contrast then, there are bits of both in both of these poles, and, in conclusion, Maus recommends a strategic revaluation of the latter, ostensibly "feminine" pole.

I am attracted to this recommendation; to an analysis that tries to free itself from established modes and from the pressure to stabilize around a principle; to a description that breaks away from the beaten paths; that does not repose on identity as much as ride on difference; that celebrates oscillations, undecidability and immerses itself in the changing state of things; the lateral and circular flights of fact rather than the dichotomous ones; the radically ungeneral, unpredictive, ungiven, adventitious roots instead of tree structures. Listening in this way may produce, in Deleuze and Guattari's terms, a rhizomic "multiple"—not understood as "always adding another dimension" but as "always [at] n-1 [dimensions] (the only way the one belongs to the multiple: always subtracted)" —that never exhausts the subject and delights in the unique, the peculiar, the deterritorialized (Deleuze and Guattari 1996, 6).

Figure 7-1. Adagio of Mozart's Piano Sonata in F Major, K. 280, mm. 1–8.

Listening to the opening measures of the Adagio of Mozart's Piano Sonata in F Major (K. 280), for example, can be a strangely uncertain experience. There is first the unusual spacing of the opening tonic chord that helps to isolate the dotted neighbor-note motive in the upper voice and to emphasize the entry of the inner voice echo in m. 2. Then a third voice sounding the motive enters in m. 3, while the first voice peters out on its own starting note. This is followed by four measures of neighboring motion in the lower voices sounding a kind of back-and-forth movement with no clear direction. It is as if specific pitches fall into the texture and then are given the capacity only for neighboring motion—an odd, hobbled, at once static and dynamic quality. Initially this motion involves only an upper neighbor and then gives way to an oscillation between upper and lower neighboring motion. These oscillations move between two borders alternately striking different harmonic meanings at various levels.[2] Are mm.4 and 6 sounding vii^7, VI or even ii, and is this alternating with i or V^7 (in m. 5 and m. 7)? We are aware of both of these vibrations (within and between measures) at the same time and, in effect, are suspended between alternatives provoked by an undecidable terrain. It is this sense of not-quite-knowing that encourages keeping alive more than one reading at a time and thus settling on a method that sustains such indecision.

But not letting one interpretation trump the other is also subversive. Note that one thing about the C♭ and D♭ in the bass of mm. 4–7 is that they can produce parallel fifths between chords V and VI. Now, the trouble with parallel fifths is that they stand next to one another as equals; they inhibit subordination of one another, and so cast some doubt on their function. Notice that it is precisely the murmuring oscillations in the right hand of mm. 4–7, and the possibility of investing in the neighboring motion otherwise, that inhibits a more vulgar or naive parallel fifth relation here. So, by listening rhizomically—that is, by *not* asserting a principle that reduces to fewer notes (or renders some neighboring and others structural)—we can paradoxically respect the prohibition on fifths! Alternatively, by subordinating the neighboring motion more emphatically, that is, by listening hierarchically, we must slide back and forth in prohibited movement! Is this mischief-making (infusing dullness with finesse, folly with cunning) not a creative deterritorialization that in Deleuze and Guattari's terms "continually escape[s] from the coordinates or punctual systems functioning as musical codes at a given moment" (Deleuze and Guattari 1996, 299)? And do each of these "becomings" not bring about "the deterritorialization of one term and the reterritorialization of the other; the two becomings interlink[ing] and form[ing] relays in a circulation of intensities pushing the deterritorialization ever further" (10)? And is this not a way of making those codes leak by pervading our ears with every minority; with every detail and mutation—"a theme that was a variation from the start" (309)—and even then, always subtracted from any whole, however multiple in appearance?

What is subversive about this kind of hearing is that it marks, and becomes fascinated by, those musical moments that reflect something that is out of kilter with what is readily apparent as a syntactical norm or as a stylistic convention of the piece. For Theodor Adorno, the greatness of Mozart's classical compositions lay in their "powers of self-reflexivity which liberated the mechanical from its inflexibility and transformed the trivial" (Adorno 1992, 305). These are moments that veer away from having the value of archetypes; moments that resist crystallizing into sedimented generality; that (in Boretz's terms) "minimize my discovery-limiting kneejerk habits (such as internalized conditioned impulses)" (269); moments that proliferate, not reduce, laws of combination—for Deleuze and Guattari, "a process that is perpetually prolonging itself, breaking off and starting up again" (Deleuze and Guattari 1996, 20). These are weird moments that overspill a centered automaton (organizing memory or standardized perception) and provide instead "multiple entryways and exits and [their] own lines of flight" (21).

Let me try elaborating this approach further with another example from a piece by Mozart that starts almost like the previous one. The opening piano solo in F♯ minor of the Andante of Mozart's Piano Concerto No.

23 in A Major, K. 488 seems to be strangely preoccupied with the pitch D. To begin with, d^2, as neighbor to $c\sharp^2$ in m. 1, is the only neighboring motion around the constituents of the opening chord that produces another

Figure 7-2. Andante of Mozart's Piano Concerto No. 23 in A Major, K. 488, mm. 1–12.

"consonant" triad. Its presence infuses F$\sharp$ minor with the flavor of D major. Then, D is abruptly left hanging in two prominent places. First, as Joseph Dubiel has pointed out, if we hear the *right* hand of mm. 1–3 as two voices descending in staggered sixths (a^2–$g\sharp^2$–$f\sharp^2$ over $c\sharp^2$–b^1–a^1), d^2 in m. 3 sounds curiously isolated (Dubiel 1996). While the lower line extends forth through $g\sharp^1$–$f\sharp^1$–$e\sharp^1$ to the end of the phrase, the upper line simply jumps to d^2 and then gets stuck there. And then, as if to recoup and resolve to C$\sharp$ after the cadence, the next phrase begins with D major, a chord that sounds like a kind of skewed or stretched version of the opening F$\sharp$ minor chord. Second, d^3 in m. 10, the obviously highest note in the passage, is similarly left hanging with no voice-leading consequences. Most strikingly though, the "displaced" cadences in mm. 6 and 8 involve an uncoordination between D major and F$\sharp$ minor. What sounds like a move to V in D major in m. 6 is transformed into F$\sharp$ minor by the time the upper voice resolves; while what sounds like a move to i in F$\sharp$ minor in m. 8 is similarly transformed into D major. It is as if neither sonority can assert itself unequivocally; as if F$\sharp$ is curiously fixated with D.[3]

The first point I wish to make is that this peculiar expressive feature is heard in moments of normative failure. D was marked for consciousness exactly where it broke a linear pattern (m. 3); where it sounded like it might have been contorting another chord (m. 5); where it hung on an edge in isolation (m. 10); or where it befuddled the timely resolution of a suspension (m. 8). The second point is that an analytic approach that is vigilant about those musical moments that elude normative paradigms shares philosophical ground with post-structuralism. For example, in Lacan's psychoanalytic theory, the *real* is revealed only in those moments that the signifying system in which the subject operates is considered inadequate and the subject is put into a relation of desire to unreachable objects.[4] In a fascinating essay, "Contradictory Criteria in a Work by Brahms," Joseph Dubiel (1994) (without Lacan on his mind) elaborates an exemplary case for this kind of privileging of the negative. He coins the term *abnorm* to capture "definably irregular events that become criteria of prolongation or succession in violation of larger norms of the pieces in which they occur" (82) In the same way that Lacan's *real* is only partially divulged in the moment that signifying systems falter as a result of an ever-elusive *objet a*, the expressive identity of a musical work is partially divulged when an *abnorm* seems to interfere with the network of musical norms. In Judith Butler's more Nietzschian terms, this is a moment of bad conscience—the moment that the "psychic operation of a regulatory norm" fails (Butler 1997, 5).

It is important to recognize that these abnormal moments are experienced and conceptualized in negative terms; when something in the music seems to flounder, bend, stoop, equivocate, hesitate, halt, confound, or protrude. In his account of the anomalous repeated D♯s near the beginning of Beethoven's Violin Concerto in D Major, for example, Dubiel describes an experience that bears the weight of acknowledging what does not happen to the D♯s (Dubiel 1996, 27–37). This permits a hearing that is beholden neither to a paradigm that wants to alleviate what is problematic about the anomalous tones nor to an analysis that anticipates hearing any particular thing, like a "direct connection to the pitch (or pitch class) D♯," for example (44). Instead, this more "ad hoc" than "principled" attitude opens the realm of possibility for what might count as hearing under the influence of those weird D♯s (44). Radically unpredictive and radically ungeneral, Dubiel's approach is awake to events (and non-events) that are not given by stylistic norms, on the one hand, and to descriptions of these that are not given by ready-to-hand music-theoretical paradigms, on the other. This kind of analysis is a critical gesture. Beholden to the radically contingent aspects of a particular musical piece, and thereby to its absolute peculiarity, it dialectically challenges the control of those normative generalities within which the piece operates. Despite its seemingly formalist account of the notes alone then, this interest in marking what is recalcitrant to contextual standards established by musical sounds is, in fact, not far away from Lacan's psychoanalytic interest in the mismatch between the imaginary and the symbolic orders.

I wish to make three points about this. Firstly, I think there is a fairly contiguous historical link between the nineteenth-century philosophical figure of music in German metaphysics and late-twentieth-century French post-structuralism, so that the discursive affinity between a kind of purely musical description and psychoanalysis should not be that surprising.[5]

However, the connection has been routinely overlooked in recent critical musicology partly because the idea of musical autonomy has been figured in ahistorical terms, emphasizing the hermetic and therefore uncritical nature of the musical work. What has been disregarded in these accounts is the provocative side of this formulation of aesthetic autonomy as it was elaborated within a dialectical tradition. Even in its most receding aestheticist moments, the provocation could not be ignored entirely. For instance, when Eduard Hanslick asserted that "the beauty of a piece is specifically musical, that is, is inherent in the tonal relationships without reference to an extraneous, extramusical context," it was framed in dialectical prose and suggested that no description of the musical work could exhaust its meaning (Hanslick 1986, xxiii). Appeals to "feeling," he claimed, for instance, "cannot derive a single musical *law*" (xxii; italics mine). To understand the relation between the work's hermetic receding and contexts outside of itself as inherently reactionary is to overlook the crucial challenge this view posed to appropriation by norms and generalities. That is, the denial of the relevance of "extraneous, extramusical" dimensions was both an escape from *and* a challenge to the social world. It was a rejection of the seemingly solid nature of everyday meanings and thus insisted on rendering the relations between world and work as refractory and broken ones. In short, absolute music was inherently non-discursive and could not be absorbed into the continuum of ordinary representations.

Secondly, the musical interest in marking for consciousness music's radically contingent moments may have a critical role to play in the political sphere. In his essay "Reification and the Consciousness of the Proletariat," Georg Lukács describes the process by which the logic of modern capitalism penetrates social relations between people (Lukács 1971, 83–222). "Reification," he claims, "requires that a society should learn to satisfy all its needs in terms of commodity exchange" (Lukács 1971, 91). With the commodity form as a central referent, Lukács argues that the reification of consciousness involves the atom-like isolation of the individual whose social relations are increasingly mediated by an abstract principle of rational calculability. The impulse to rationalize in this way penetrates all aspects of life and then also regulates them by harnessing reductive, predictive, and general conceits. In the words of Max Weber (on the topic of the legal system): "The modern capitalist concern is based inwardly above all on *calculation*. It requires for its survival a system of justice and an administration whose workings can be rationally calculated, according to fixed general laws, just as a probable performance of a *machine* can be calculated. . . . [T]he judge is more or less an automatic statute-dispensing machine . . . [his] behaviour is on the whole *predictable*" (in Lukács 1971, 96; italics in original). For Lukács, the rational systematization of social relations tends toward a rigid and closed system that is capable of absorbing every possible situation in life into a generalized system. The system, in turn, yields increasingly to the principles of prediction and calculation.[6] Now, these impulses to generalize and predict are the two principal characteristics Maus figures as "masculine" discourse in music theory. In Lukács's scheme, music theory of the "masculine" sort would thus march in direct step with the ideological demands of capitalism. While his views on art, particularly his valorization of nineteenth-century realism, were quite old-fashioned, Lukács's model of relations between base and superstructure was less "reflective" and more "productive" in orientation. In other words, art was not only considered as a mediated reflection of the relations of production (its ideological justification), but also *as* an aspect of production itself. This left open the possibility, however limited, that art could challenge the status quo. In this way, instead of "attemp[ting] to establish a rational system of relations which comprehends the totality of formal possibilities . . . subject[ing] them to an exact calculus," (Lukács 1971, 129) the musical hearing espoused by Boretz, Dubiel, Maus, and others, the value they place on listening for the unique, capricious and open-ended, is also an effort to challenge reification and the formal standardization of experience. Boretz thematizes this social concern thus: "[Those] for whom acts of creative text-making seem mostly to be cartoon-image manifestations of medical, legal, or sanitary problems, can't help us get serious about our own personally real and poignant sociopolitical problems" (Boretz 1992, 264). Challenging the reification of commodified culture, Boretz advances "ongoing discovery rather than . . . the accumulation of a stockpile of marketable facts" (272). Now, while the extent to which hearing music has a purchase on political relations is open to question and in doubt, I want to suggest that the ways of listening advanced by these theorists, at the least, fits awkwardly within the demands of capitalist rationality as Lukács elaborates it.

Although I am primarily concerned with adumbrating the critical potential of allowing the capricious domains of musical experience to be perceptually significant in terms of a late modern predicament, this kind of alertness can be historically illuminating as well. Jamie Currie, in an intriguing unpublished study, demonstrates how the often antagonistic relationships between musical styles in Mozart's eighteenth century betray various dynamics of social and class struggle. For example, in the Allegro assai of Mozart's Piano Concerto No. 19 in F Major, K. 459, *buffa* and learned styles are introduced in stark opposition to one another. The almost caricatured four-square upbeat world of mm. 1–32 is maximally separated from the motet-like world of imitative entries in mm. 33ff., as if the two actively sought out the safety of their hermetic domains. Only the fact of not modulating at this point can stage a rapport between them— unmotivated, fickle, and arbitrary. While the official narrative involving a gradual stylistic resolution within a unified framework can be perceptually sustained in this movement, these styles are also reluctant to blend. I am suggesting that, very often, such irreconciliation can be heard in the weird details of the movement, when one style ostensibly takes on the traits of another but is transformed in the process into something compromised and preposterous. Mozart's composed cadenza, for instance, begins with a statement, in the left hand, of the subject of mm. 33ff., while the right hand

Figure 7-3. Opening of the Piano Cadenza from the Allegro Assai of Mozart's Piano Concerto in F Major, K. 459.

sounds a brilliant accompaniment. But instead of receiving an answer in another voice, the descending portion of the subject is extended into the depths where it is attributed the banal significance of an accompanying scale. Far from achieving reconciliation, this figure becomes a protuberant mask of its former self.[7] And far from becoming enlightened (thereby liberating the subjective dimensions of human beings), this figure becomes a jesting pretense of enlightenment. The point is that opening our ears to unwanted details in the music can alert us to the social struggles that the music otherwise glosses over.

The third point I wish to make is going to take a more critical turn. Briefly stated, I do not hear "experiences with no names" in my descriptions of these musical passages. There are names everywhere: descending motions; triads; suspensions; subjects—just those terms that buttress the hierarchies of stratified rhetoric. My language is conjugated by such territorial discourse; implied by established routines; anticipated by their modes of assembling facts. These are paths that always-already select and organize the possible lines of flight my listening may take. My failure to conjure the freshness of unfettered, unlabeled experience is assured.

And yet—

In K. 488 I hear a contrapuntal line that is no longer one exactly— now it is a zigzag perhaps (a feathery sound in flight); or I hear a D-major triad that is no longer one—now it is an F♯ minor one in drag (or behind an eighteenth-century mask, for the hetero-historically minded); or I hear another sound in that last note in m. 10—now isolated and bristling on a desolate summit (sad as a petrified animal); or I hear the trickster at the cadences beriddling us with twists and turns affirming new proportions in unpredictable places. All these peculiar animals, nomads, sorcerers, birds, and clowns find their earhold in formations that are habitual or patriarchal or, worse still, rigid and sedentary territorialities. But these formations are put to strange new uses in order to open the way for other transformational operations. In the terms of Deleuze and Guattari, these are "microscopic events that can challenge the local balance of power" (Deleuze and Guattari 1996, 15). These may be historically conditioned dualisms, but they are invoked to challenge other dualisms.

But now I am on a quest for names with no experiences yet, not for experiences with no names. Perhaps this is a failure of imagination, but I have to sustain the belief that all facts are theory-laden if only as a safe-guard against the illusion of unmediated hearing, however proliferate and liberating its categories. This is where Boretz's distinctions between our description/their ascription, or our experience/their ontology, not only resists their deconstruction, but represses acknowledging the presence of those ascriptive ontological dimensions necessary for doing and saying any-thing at all. Even his more modernist sounding text—"chink-chink twit-tering G–F♯ over B–D ambiguities" (Boretz 1992, 280) that describes some of the beginning of the first movement of Mahler's 4th symphony, for instance—still advances metaphors that are peculiarities within territorial norms. That is, however deterritorializing in movement, these "ambigui-ties" are in static harmonic territory, while these Gs and F♯'s are in Western standardized tuning territory. The problem with thinking that we are think-ing in no names—in thinking that some things are better done than said— is that we do not come clean with our ascriptions. Not that I am necessar-ily recommending Catholic honesty here, but that, by thinking this way, we shield from view the reasons why some ascriptions (or descriptions) might be more valuable in life than others. Instead, we risk resting on the idea that some are inherently more "experientially-quality-sensitized" (277) than others; perhaps even closer to music's "ontological core" by using "its own fully ontologized experiential-intellecutal language" (281–82) The sustained effort to resist the "ascriptive mode" that ostensibly reifies and reduces this specific and chaotic "fully ontologized experiential-intellectu-al language" to "hearing ideologies" (282) is also a trick because it opposes ideology with a kind of experience, and likewise the masculine with the feminine. Instead of asking which ideological formation might be more useful in the world, it quietly suggests that one formation is not ideological at all (a "category without prejudice," in Boretz's spoken words), and so its moral advantage is assured. What I am suggesting, in contrast to this view, is that the masculine and feminine dimensions of musical experience exist in a continuum. They are gradations of each other—the one a refinement of the other and not its logically opposite.

The occasional reminder in Boretz's text that *non*-ontological-descriptions *also* do not "apply" (Boretz 1999, 6) to the music under consideration, or that "no text can capture the experience" (Boretz 1993, 276) does not sufficiently weigh down the argument at large. It also leaves us with few grounds for choosing one mode of description over another. I am not saying that these grounds do not exist in his text or elsewhere, but that they are premised on a philosophical sleight of hand. Knowing that a description is somehow a case of "mistaken ascriptive use" (282) is also knowing a little bit about what is not mistaken, that is, knowing a little bit about music's "ontological core," or at least of the values you detest and uphold by situating that core beyond the sayable (281). This, as Hegel points out in his opening arguments of the *Phenomenology of Spirit*, in fact amounts to knowing a great deal, and knowing it in a kind of brute, unmediated way. Thus Boretz becomes guilty of just that "raw operation of the gangster-power strategy" (262) that he detests in others. Let me argue this point in detail by using Hegel's opening arguments as an accompanying commentary. In this next section I will read Boretz's analytical project as a kind of philosophical proposition and attempt to point out the unquestioned primitives that ground it. Along the way, I will return to Dubiel's position as an alternative to Boretz before concluding with some thoughts on the terrain of feminism.

A DIALOGUE IN FOUR VOICES:
HEGEL, BORETZ, ADORNO, DUBIEL

Boretz's musical descriptions are interested in muddling the modalities of the experience of music, on the one hand, and the representation of it, on the other. Recall that he favors descriptions that are not "used, or allowed, to invade and holistically pre-empt and remake the ontological interior of what is experienced as those musics" (Boretz 1992, 281). Not quite believing that *any* description of necessity falsifies this interior, Boretz advances the use of language that is "semantic[ally] irregular" and "remain[s] [in] an unfixed, unfixable, dynamically overflowing process of inscrutable co-existence (where existence is travelling, and co-existence fellow-travelling) intensely activating the sentience-space between persistently ontologically distinct objects/texts stubbornly resistant to semantic fusion" (281). Irreducibly split, then, the experience and the description are in optimum accord when the language is irregular, elusive, and metaphoric; in short, when the language approximates the condition of music, when it yields into and becomes other.[8] In other words, the split is best overcome when we "recover the ontology of verbal-expressive phenomena by analogy with music—or, even better, in the form of music" (259). Here Boretz marches in step with Adorno's dictum, "To interpret music means: to make music" (3). In other words, interpretation is an effort to "transcribe" instead of "decode" music's meaning (3–4). But for Boretz, a maximally intense "co-travelling" may also lead to a kind of musical version of an "experience of trance, or . . . of mystical experience" (276) mentioned at the outset. And the intensely subjective dimension, far from rendering the experience relative and unreal, actually approximates the most significantly real: "people actually have mystical experiences. And they actually have trances. And they actually have transcendent inner experiences of music" (253). Occasionally, the epiphany even takes on Schopenhauerian motifs: "Sound is the sensory medium of the interior, of inner life in process; the ontological material of the consciousness of the realities within" (268). Here Adorno would part company with Boretz and claim that such mysticism would be yielding to the temptation one feels "to abstain from all meaning [because of] a sense of [music's] own power" (5). This would be "to act . . . as if [music] were the direct expression of the Name" (5). So, despite the common interpretative orientation between Boretz and Adorno, Boretz's promise of some sort of transcendent experience aligns him more closely with Hegel, to whom I shall now turn.

In the *Phenomenology* Hegel attempts a similar muddling of modalities on the terrain of epistemology. Having inherited the Kantian contrast between the thing-in-itself (a.k.a. "ontological interior" in Boretz's framework) and the thing-as-appearance (a.k.a. "linguistic description" in Boretz), Hegel attempts to show that a certain kind of philosophical work can overcome the gap between them. He calls the poles "science," on the one hand, and "appearing knowledge" on the other. While this overcoming, or superseding, does not lead to a musical epiphany, it does lead to an epistemological one that ultimately ushers in absolute knowledge. What does Hegel mean by "appearing knowledge" and "science," and how does he think they are related to each other and to absolute knowledge? Let me explain.

Unlike his eighteenth-century predecessors, Hegel thinks that appearing knowledge (or knowledge-for-itself) and science (or knowledge-in-itself) are dialectically related. Instead of figuring these poles as irreducibly antithetical, Hegel believes that the former can, through immanent resources, lead to the latter. In fact, appearing knowledge is a necessary starting point on the way to science and is therefore, if not logically then dialectically, entailed in science. This means neither that they are the same kind of knowledge nor that they are related on a continuum, but that, through a series of determinate negations (or enabling contradictions) that expose the inadequacy of what knowledge (or cognition) takes itself to be at various dialectical stages, common sense can ultimately issue forth absolute knowledge.

While he does not define the meaning of these terms at the outset of the *Phenomenology,* Hegel distances his construal of the relation between them from the skepticism he takes to inhere in philosophical discourse that draws a distinction between them very sharply. He "mistrusts this very mistrust" in appearances (Hegel 1977, 47). To polarize knowledge-for-itself rigorously from knowledge-in-itself necessarily involves both skepticism and a dogmatic moment—an inkling, however vestigial or fleeting, of the in-itself. Indeed, the skeptical fear of falling into untruth "takes something—a great deal in fact—for granted as truth, supporting its scruples and inferences on what is itself in need of prior scrutiny to see if it is true. . . . Above all, it presupposes that the Absolute stands on one side and cognition on the other" (47). Either cognition is not entitled to this kind of negative limiting claim, or, insofar as cognition recognizes (*erkennen*) its own inadequacy, the unattainable truth *is* in cognition's grasp, in which case it does not (want to) know what it knows; or stated differently "what calls itself fear of error reveals itself rather as fear of the truth" (47).

Thus Hegel's initial construal of the relation between "appearing knowledge" and "science" takes the form of refuting, or better ignoring, the vividly dichotomous view, and of provisionally permitting a methodological confusion between the two. More specifically, to the extent that "science," however inadequately formed or even unattainable, is initially apparent to us, it must be as "appearing knowledge." One reason for this is that, in its underived arrogation to being true knowledge, its power lies only in, what Hegel calls, its *"being"*; it is merely posited—a "bare *assurance"*—that furthermore cannot be told apart from the mere *"being"* of untrue "appearing knowledge" (49). When science enters "the scene" it has not yet "justified itself as the essence or the in-itself" (52). Such unelaborated assurances cannot capture the desired distinction, and so Hegel begins his inquiry by unsubscribing to it.[9]

While Boretz is scrupulously wary of the scientific claims of music theory on related grounds, he oscillates between two untenable philosophical positions. The first of these finds its critique in Hegel's argument. That is, Boretz's insistence on an ontological core that persistently gives linguistic interpretation the slip betrays the fear of truth to which Hegel alludes. To know about boundaries is already to have crossed them. To know that the musical core lies necessarily outside the realm of the sayable is to be privy to its (paralinguistic) essence; to be in on the core's secret. "Music," Boretz declares, "is *always, necessarily,* a mystery" (Boretz 1992, 253; emphasis added). This is a desire not only for a kind of revelation without concealment, but for naming what lies outside language. And this secret knowledge takes the form of an ostensibly humbling claim about our necessary interpretative failures. But it also *keeps* the secret (that no words can divulge). As Albrecht Wellmer says in a related context: "It expresses the secret . . . but without comprehending it" (73). So, valuing metaphorical descriptive claims about music over pedantically scientific ones becomes a bare assertion—unmediated and arbitrary, or, in Boretz's own terms, "given by authority or taken on faith" (270). An interpretation can either make a leap of faith and embrace this dogmatism or, strictly according to the protocols of the secret, it cannot tell which descriptive mode approximates the core better. Perhaps the scientific tree structures, scale degree chord numbers, Schenker-levels, Fibonacci series, and combinatorial set structures are correct after all. Unutterable mysteries cannot tell.

But what if, as Nietzsche might ask, the unintelligible is not unintelligent; if, despite various not fully thinkable limits, something *can* be known about the ontological core of music? Boretz inhabits a second philosophical position that is open to this possibility, for he advances the possibility, albeit with reservations, of language that "merge[s] with sonic stimuli to produce experienced music things," which he calls "semantic fusion" (Boretz 1992, 274).[10] While such theorizing is "entirely processual in nature, having no meaningful steady-state referential applicability" (275), it leaves open the possibility of overcoming the rift between music's core and its description within discourse. Thus it reintroduces the opportunity to justify one form of writing about music over another. While music is "impervious to discourse, certainly; and impervious in principle to any one-to-one verbal or symbolic metarepresentation," it is not, in principle, "impervious to transcendent forms of creative representation whose own ontologies lie outside the realm of one-to-one cognition—outside the realm, that is, of linear, normal-logical, cognitive-scientific thinking" (257). Instead of contrasting musical experience with language in general then, music's discursive other is now figured as a brand of scientific rationality. Indeed, a creative representation *is* possible through a kind of Lacanian "homeomorphic identification" or "*maximal cohearing*" (257–60)—one that resists "terminating" in scientific thinking and embraces "active-creative feedback interaction" (163). Let me take up this more sophisticated reading of Boretz, one in which linguistic description may productively influence our hearing by approximation, by returning to Hegel's text.

In the *Phenomenology*, Hegel also proposes to justify certain claims over others, this time the claims of science against the naive assumptions of common sense (instead of, say, the claims of metaphor over science). Thus the distinction between science and appearing knowledge is reinstituted within a dialectical context of phenomenal knowledge (*das erscheinende Wissen*) where it is engendered by immanent contradiction instead of assumed. By taking "natural consciousness" (perhaps a kind of "appearing knowledge" not already an inmate of the unprepared contrast to "science") at its word, or as an instance of "real knowledge," he shows how its self-conception, or what it takes itself to be, is out of kilter with its "realization of the Notion," or what it turns out to be when it is articulated.[11] By confronting the inadequacy of the "realization," or acknowledging its contradictory stances, common sense (natural consciousness) loses itself as a candidate for true knowledge. It finds itself on a "pathway of *doubt*, or more precisely [on] the way of despair" (Hegel 1977, 49). But this doubt is not of an abstractly negative sort that will revise its findings in the same terms; an "empty nothing" as Hegel says (56). It is rather a doubt that is negatively privileged because it issues forth new terms or "configurations" for true knowledge from within itself (50). Thus, by contrasting the idea of what it is to know an experience with how that experience effectively is, consciousness is able to supersede (*Aufheben*) one form of cognition with another; and, through this shifting ground of truth-making, consciousness undergoes an education (*Bildung*) that sets it on an inexorable path to science. In short, out of the naive assumptions of common sense, a recognition of its own contradictory nature emerges, whence science begins. The claims of science are justified to the extent that they begin where the logic of common sense falters. Absolute knowledge is given when "Notion" (being-for-another) and "object" (being-for-itself) coincide (51).[12]

While Boretz similarly gestures toward an absolute condition of music-descriptive experience, his repeated, albeit inconsistent, emphasis on the power of music as such to impose itself on the desired description no longer tallies with Hegelian dialectics. The quest for "experiences with no names" (Boretz 1992, 272) betrays a romantic conception that grants music the mystical ability to issue forth a kind of self-announced "unlabelled experience" (Boretz 1999, 3). Now, I do not wish to deny the potential value of behaving *as if* music had such magical power, for the purpose, say, of honing our imaginative consciousness—after all, as Nietzsche might have it, some fictional illusions may concede true concerns. But to posit a zone of untouchable knowledge absolutely, to completely forget the *perhaps* structure of the wholly negative, can only serve to dull our musical and political imaginations. In my view, the unknowable aspect must lead to ongoing discursive elaboration if it is to widen the horizon of the musically/politically possible. Instead of figuring music as an approximation of the hermetic "realities within," (Boretz 1992, 268) one is obliged to posit the non-identity (between music and discourse) as a productive tension that can be critically superseded.

This is where Dubiel provides a more dialectical model for analysis. Dubiel's sustained effort to negotiate the antagonism between the general and particular dimensions of hearing music leads him to "*articulate* th[e] escaping of [music's] categories as part of the piece's sound" (Dubriel 1999, 272; italics mine). For Dubiel, revising and upgrading one's perceptions *constitutes* an optimum hearing of a musical passage. Also, Dubiel locates the dialectical tension less between the (unknowable) music and language and more between different kinds of "mental configuration that determine how [a musical] figure is to be heard" (Dubiel 1999, 269). These configurations, like dialectical poles, are both musical perceptions, albeit in an agonistic relation. In Dubiel's words, "A hearing of [a musical] figure is not attributed to a context as such [a.k.a. Boretz's musical interior], but to a mental configuration that determines how the figure is heard" (269). I would argue that Dubiel's procedure is a case of Hegel's "determinate negation" on the terrain of musical perception. Before doing so, let me describe what Hegel means by "determinate negation" and how this might matter in justifying certain kinds of claims over others.

For Hegel, when consciousness encounters its untruth it recognizes that this negation of itself is not wholly negative, but contingent on that form of consciousness "*from which it results*" (Hegel 1977, 51). This is what Hegel calls a "*determinate [bestimmt] nothingness*," one that does not try to revisit its initial premises, but produces instead a "*content*" or a new form of consciousness. Thus, consciousness passes beyond its own limits by interrogating its knowledge claims to the point of contradiction: "[C]onsciousness . . . suffers violence at its own hands: it spoils its own limited satisfactions" (51). *Aufhebung* has the dual significance of negating the terms producing contradiction *and* ushering in both a new set of criteria/standards to measure what it knows and a new object of knowledge.[13] This is how knowledge claims yield a change in content in the movements of determinate negation: What appears to consciousness as the "object" turned out to be a mere "Notion"—no more than a "way of knowing it" (56). While this mutated object becomes the new content for the phenomenological inquiry, new "patterns" of consciousness are established to interrogate *its* knowledge claims.

While Dubiel does not thematize its Hegelian aspects, the analytic orientation he advances privileges the role of "negative experience" in musical hearing (Dubiel 1999, 277). Like Hegel's "natural consciousness" whose discursive elaboration turns out to be different from what it once took itself to be, Dubiel emphasizes the process of "testing your own hearing against your expected hearing" (277). For Hegel, this kind of disjuncture does not prompt a wholesale revision of one's premises in the manner of an either/or logical commitment, but produces instead the *Aufhebung* that brings about a new level of consciousness. Analogously, Dubiel claims that the disjunctures of musical perceptions (or "hypotheses") result in "gains in knowledge" that are "not necessarily best understood in terms of confirmation or disconfirmation of these hypotheses" (277). The "negative experience" is also a "positive one" because you can "consider your 'hypothesis' (or sonic image) to have been outclassed and upgraded, rather than to have failed as such" (277). The revisability of musical perception has often led critical scholars to believe that such music analysis is inherently unstable and relative and thus fictional. For example, asserting a familiar "gap between our experience and our description of that experience," Jim Samson claims that "in revealing the contingencies of music analysis, we reveal . . . the fictive character of this and other discourse about music" (Samson 1999, 47). What this kind of argumentation fails to take into account is its own dichotomous grounds, about which Hegel was so vigilant. In the words of Adorno: "Of undoubted significance for music theory is Hegel's insight that although all immediacy is mediated and dependent on its opposite, the concept of an unmediated thing—that is, of something which has become or has been set free—is not wholly engulfed by mediation" (Adorno 1992, 299). In other words, for Hegel, the fact of revisability (on account of differently mediated contents of consciousness) does not amount to a wholesale subjectivism even if the resulting knowledge is not verifiable in the robust sense. Similarly, for Dubiel, revising a musical perception (on account of a differently mediated hypothesis) does not amount to hearing something "any way you want to" even if the path to "refining" one's hearing lies outside the logic and grasp of binary (dis)confirmation (Dubiel 1999, 277).

In short, Dubiel's effort to get "beyond what the concepts provided [for]" (Dubiel 1999, 274) is essentially dialectical. Like Hegel's supersession to higher levels of consciousness, "analyses of music are more likely to be valuable as consciousness-raising exercises . . . than as renderings of the content of musical experiences" (274). But, unlike Hegel, Dubiel's project does not terminate in absolute knowledge for it is inherently imaginative and experimental. "What do theories tell me?" he asks. "Not what to do; but what there is to do" (282). This aligns him more with the dialectics of Adorno than with Hegel. In an analysis of musical themes, for instance, Adorno argues that "it is much more important what the themes *become*— what happens to them and *how* they develop—than what the basic elements themselves actually are" (Adorno 1982, 179). Dubiel's analyses of motivic connections in music put this principle to work. Instead of pointing out similarities between motives, themes, pitch-class collections, and the like, Dubiel is interested in "what happens to these themes when they are heard in the context of one another" (Dubiel forthcoming, 9). For Dubiel, the "relationships between passages [are the] source of characteristics of passages" (15). In short, incongruous musical events are as interesting and significant as congruous ones; they indicate what has become of the music. Similarly, Adorno values non-identical musical events, which he calls their "moment of Becoming" (Adorno 1982, 179). In his characterization of "*musique informelle*" (a shorthand for a kind of optimally critical music), for example, Adorno says: "*Musique informelle* would be music in which the ear can hear live from the material what has become of it" (Adorno 1992, 319). Adorno argues that the expressive character of a piece resides in its moments of normative failure (269–322). Subjectivity and expressiveness "only [stand] out where the composition fail[s], temporarily, to match up to its material" (302). Like Dubiel, who urges us to "keep oursel[ves] ready to be struck by aspects of sound that [we] aren't listening for" (Dubiel 1999, 302), Adorno argues that informal music should be music "whose end cannot be foreseen in the course of production" (Adorno 1992, 303).

As I have argued in the context of Lukács, Adorno also grants this negatively dialectical stance a critical role in the world. In an age where culture falls increasingly under the sway of instrumental reason in the form of marketing, styling, and advertising, Adorno maintains that an informal music is a site for promoting critical consciousness. Resisting normative abstractions in musical listening (or "recoil[ing] from the demands of . . . conventions"), recalls the subjective dimension that has been eliminated in a context of reification and alienation (Adorno 1992, 320). The effort to liberate subjectivity, or what Lydia Goehr calls the "quest for voice" (Goehr 1998), while central to the aims of Enlightenment, has paradoxically been increasingly eroded in the modern era. Thus Adorno connects such critical musicality to a social conscience: "Within the all-embracing blindness and delusion [of the culture industry] the only things which inhabit their rightful place in society are those which have broken with communication, instead of seeking to discover its genuine or supposed laws" (Adorno 1992, 320). Adorno (in the manner of Dubiel) places a high premium on musical listening as experimentation. He understands this as a kind of social imagining—an effort to expand the realm of the socially possible. Its relevance is measured to the extent less of its success and more of its longing for another world. "The aim of every artistic utopia today," Adorno writes, "is to make things in ignorance of what they are" (322).

This is where Boretz's fantasy of unlabeled experience bears less of an emancipatory potential (directed against the dominant forms of technical and bureaucratic rationality) than it might have. The utopian perspective of a transdiscursive experience is in a certain sense simply the inversion of formal logic, instrumental reason, and a compulsion to systematize; a "retreat from enlightenment into mythology," to use Adorno's words (Adorno and Horkheimer 1997, xiii). If the musical experience can only be conceived of as being beyond the sphere of conceptual thought, it necessarily falls outside of social praxis. In contrast, if the problem of truncating and prearranging the experience—"conscripting" music, in Boretz's terms, to "stand for" concepts like Schenker-levels, and so on (Boretz 1999, 4)—is attributable not to the concepts as such, but to the *use* to which they are put, then musical imaginings can be made worldly. By returning to music the power to be represented, Dubiel and Adorno hold out the possibility that musical reflections can expand the current limits of meaning. In so doing, musical reflections also expand the boundaries of the world and the subject.

On the other hand, the effort to expand the realm of the musically/socially debatable does not imply an opening gesture without limits. This is where a critique of Dubiel's occasional succumbing to the Boretzian notion that our "mental configurations" are somehow "elicited from us by the piece" (Boretz 1999, 272), instead of dialectically jostling for meaning in an experience of the piece, becomes urgent. The same applies to Adorno's occasional suggestion that the non-identical cannot be retrieved from the world beyond language, or that one must allow the musical composition to "*assert itself* in order to be able to enter its structure analytically" (Adorno 1982, 175). But, aside from these occasional moments, there is a different limitation in the positions held by Dubiel and Adorno, to which I would now like to turn.[14] By asking the question whether Hegel's project is plausible, I want to draw attention to what I will call the problem of "immanentism" in Dubiel and Adorno.

Charles Taylor argues that Hegel's production of evolving contradictions by laying out the linguistic content (or the "effective experience" in Taylor's parlance) of various modes (or "models") of "appearing knowledge" or "certainty" is plausible if it can be shown, beyond question, that (a) "effective experience can be characterized in terms independent of the model of experience we are working with," and (b) that we are "able to identify some basic and pervasive facets of experience independently of our model" (Taylor 1976, 160). If the effective experience is to effectively contradict the model, these basic facets must stand outside of the model. I understand the first of Taylor's points to suggest that, without recourse to independent terms, the contradiction cannot appear. While it may be true that we have developed beyond the constraints of, say, knowledge as sense-certainty, there is no reason to suppose that this development was immanent to sense-certainty as such. Without an appeal to some kind of knowledge that we were already in on, but that is not itself under critical investigation at each dialectical juncture, the supersession cannot get off the ground. As Nietzsche might say, it cannot lift itself into the sky by its own bootstraps (which, incidentally, is not to say that it cannot dance). This leads to the second of Taylor's points which calls for an identification (or a rendering visible) of just those basic facets that seem concealed in the investigation. While Hegel's attempt, by disengaging from the appearance/reality split, to leave open the lineaments in which knowledge may emerge, is laudable, these hidden facets risk functioning as surrogate *absolutes* destabilizing the world of *appearances*. Perhaps this recapitulates the theater world Hegel attempts to elude. At the very least, *something* not inhering in the "certainty" under investigation anticipates its contradiction. The question is whether this is a dogmatic moment—a vestigial "giving . . . over to the thoughts of others"—or not (Hegel 1977, 50).

What I am suggesting is that the dialectical supersession may not be achieved through immanent resources. Contra-Hegel, I am suggesting that

Hegelian dichotomies are not disturbed and contested from wholly *within* their own logical structure. In the context of the music analysis espoused by Dubiel, this means that whatever modality we bring to bear on the musical experience, however "puzzled" its "preoccupation with an oddity" (Dubiel 1999, 270) may be, it is already materially conceived by historical contingencies. What guides Dubiel is an effort to capture the uniqueness of a musical piece: "The theory of *music* interests me less than the theories of *pieces*" (280). "Listening configurations" are harnessed not for their own sake, but "to show that the network of relationships goes *this* way and not *that*" (272). While I applaud the effort to open up the modalities through which musical meaning may emerge on the terrain of the specific, I now want to draw attention to the non-"immanent" criteria upon which this orientation rests.

On the one hand, how do we gauge the value of this rather than that *modality/listening configuration?* Is it valuable when it ceases to produce a determinate negation of itself? If so, does this amount to absolute musical knowledge? Or, if this knowledge is always partial, what guides its gradations? On the other hand, how do we know that our "listening configurations" are appropriately directed—interacting, that is, with the correct "network of relations?" Or how do we even know that we are *listening* at all? What material conception of music *in general* must already be in place before the specific emerges for interaction? While the dialectical relations in Dubiel's model serve to negate self-subsistence on many levels, the conceptual instability of the musical work itself is not considered problematic. And to reside unproblematically (even for a moment) is always also to render something immobile; to close some doors of inquiry; to exert pressure on the contingent to become absolute; to bring something under the rule of the automatic. Marion Guck puts the problem this way: "[B]eliefs about the nature about the relationship between perceiver and work [cannot] be disentangled from beliefs about what musical works are like" (Guck 1998, 159). Boretz, in fact, addresses the question of the work more directly than Dubiel by adding a historical dimension to his theory of theorizing. That is, in an inherently temporal experiential setting, Boretz's musical sounds become a "cumulative evolutionary 'it'" (Boretz 1992, 276) instead of Dubiel's given "piece." But this formulation only postpones the problem. For instance, what is "it" not? Would my fascination with the lips of the conductor shown on the sleeve of my LP record, say, count as part of my hearing of Mahler's 4th symphony? Or the crackle of the gyring vinyl? Or the grain of the singer's voice, as Roland Barthes (1991) might say ? Or the idea that this is a case of Hercules leaving the scene, as Lawrence Kramer might say (1998)? In other words, what definition of the musical work shows our listening the way? And, as a result, what kinds of mental configuration can never count?

I am neither suggesting that we yield to a pluralist maelstrom at this point, nor that we return to Boretz's expansion of the musical into a transcendental experience, nor even, as David Lewin advises, that we "distrust anything that tells [us] not to explore an aural impression [we] have once formed" (Lewin 1986, 359–60). I am also not saying that Dubiel would necessarily advocate such options in all situations. What I am saying is that there is something unthought lodged at the center and the periphery of his musical discoveries. By "unthought" I do not mean so much that which is "unthinkable" or "other" as that which is superlatively familiar. Indeed, its very immediacy conceals its face. In Ludwig Wittgenstein's formulation: "A proposition can only say *how* a thing is, not *what* it is" (Wittgenstein 1998, 49). Now, once we recognize this concealed dimension of the inquiry—the recognition that, even in our most vigilant and vivid musical experiences, there *cannot not* be modalities of hearing that we actively forget and aural impressions that we actively distrust—we are obliged to raise the question of what modalities we *should* so distrust and forget.

I will now discuss one preference that Boretz, Dubiel, and Adorno share, albeit in different ways, namely a high respect for those modalities that flush out the radical particularity of a musical piece. Boretz actively seeks out the "precise," "vivid," "specific," "non-generic detailed extreme" of experienced music (Boretz 1992, 256). More dramatically, he advocates "so much distinctness of identity in one's own experience as to be utterly isolated from the external world" (256). In other words, aesthetic autonomy plays a role in the extent to which one becomes ravished by music (which might also be understood as a sharpening of the imaginative faculty). Adorno, too, advocates the kind of music analysis that corresponds to the status of music by taking upon itself "the demands of its own autonomy" (Adorno 1982, 177). This involves a commitment to the absolutely unique features of music, the "*deviation[s]* to [general] *schema*" on account of the "small but decisive features—little physiognomic characteristics" that ultimately "derive from each work anew" (173, 174, 185). Similarly, albeit without any overt commitment to autonomy, Dubiel favors "mental configurations" that give us "reason to believe that our responsive capacities are being specifically shaped to the [musical] occasion" (Dubiel 1999, 273). Indeed, his fascination with the harmonically invasive D♯ toward the beginning of Beethoven's Violin Concerto, say, cannot be transferred to another musical occasion without considerable strain. Again, this is not unlike Adorno's "thinking of nonidentity," in his *Negative Dialectics*, which "seeks to say what something [uniquely] is," as opposed to "identitarian thinking," which "says what something comes under, what it exemplifies or represents, and what, accordingly, it is not itself" (Adorno 1995, 149). But the premium placed on the "highly idiosyncratic" (Adorno 1999, 269) aspects of a musical piece beckons at least three problems. Let me make this argument with reference to Dubiel's approach.

One problem is that the quest for particularity is in strong tension with the ultra-liberal stance these theorists take toward what kinds of modality are suitable for the analytic scene. In fact, central to Dubiel's project is an effort to find categories that are not institutionally ready-to-hand (precisely the better to articulate/inaugurate the unique dimensions). But what legislates that we are becoming particular? To offer an almost canonic philosophical example, what prevents the Violin Concerto from becoming "Three Blind Mice?" If we have a particular ear for clarinets, we might have heard the opening of the latter three times before D♯ even appears. Or, if we have a particular desire to figure tonality as nature-given, we might hear it across the entire span of the movement—with D♯ very possibly banished from earshot. Strictly according to the protocols of the argument, all of these modalities are permitted. With no guide to what counts as a specific experience, the notion of "specificity" is rendered uselessly unspecific. In other words, specificity morphs into blind generality. And to theoretically permit the concerto to become "Three Blind Mice" (or "Three Deaf Mice" for that matter) is about as far away as one can get from the interest in the radically particular.

The second, related, but more technical, problem is that if the quest for uniqueness is the *only* value that is thematized, then what we desire of our quest easily encounters its wholly intimate other. For example, one very effective way of describing a piece in all its particularity would be to simply list all the immediately recognizable events: "The piece starts with four quarter-note timpani strokes on D at a piano dynamic. Then the woodwinds enter. The oboe plays an A . . . ," and so on. This is about as droll as the drum motive could have been without those D♯s, and it is unlikely that this is what Dubiel wants us to notice. On the contrary, I think Dubiel wants us to notice what is startling and abnormal about the piece; he wants us to become perplexed by it. But to elaborate this interest only in the metaphorics of uniqueness, instead of as a dialectic between, on the one hand, an always-already idealized and habituated general aspect and, on the other, an always-already idealized and eccentric particular, is misleading. Like Hegel's "appearing knowledge," what this analytic orientation takes itself to be is different from what it can turn out to be on reflection. So, to better identify this orientation in *its* particularity, supplemental criteria are called for, and this raises a third problem.

What is the *value* of becoming perplexed, vigilant, startled? Why is it important to be prepared for the unprepared? Without criteria (that unsettle the erroneous claim that certain modalities better render music's particularities), it is hard to adjudicate why, in the experience of Beethoven's concerto, the startling D♯s are more valuable than the humdrum ^3, ^2, ^1. Besides, being startled can take many forms. It might be startling if I hear the four D♯s as an echo-of-the-pre-spirit-of-Charles-Ives-becoming, but is it valuable in the same way that is Dubiel hearing? Although Dubiel is careful to distinguish his analytic disposition from it, the malaise of anything-goes subjectivism must be possible in the absence of an evident horizon of values, however negotiable. In other words, unless certain criteria and their value matter, D♯ may count as optional spice (or less) and still remain squarely within Dubiel's paradigm. Just because "something . . . like empirical resistance [sends you] . . . back to the drawing board," (Dubiel 1999, 277) there is no telling on what sort of board you want (or are able) to draw or by what sort of empire you want (or are able) to be resisted. The point is that not all empires are morally equal.

I am not advocating any absolute values by which we posit criteria for music analysis. Nor am I advocating the vortex of ever more radical critique. Rather, I want to draw attention to the irreducible ethical buttress inaugurating our musical analyses, the better to negotiate ethics in our analytic efforts. In other words, the recognition that our facts are values as well obliges questioning the value of these values. This questioning must go beyond Guck's conclusion that the "fictional" dimension of our analytic stories should be "explicitly stated" (Guck 1998, 174). This is because being "aware of what we ask others to accept" can become a kind of confession that floats free of contextual rationale and thereby takes on absolute value; an eternal return of the same; an "analytic fiction" always-already (174). It is worth remembering that "being aware" can be a hindrance as well. Also, despite Guck's vivid portrayal of a kind of repressed, assembly-line music analysis, mere "awareness" (that the analysis is one possible "fiction" among others) tells us nothing about the value of this fiction. Releasing music analyses from their metaphysical entanglements does not point us toward useful ones.[15] Indeed, while such critical awareness should render certain values negotiable, certain values should also render critical awareness negotiable. It is crucial, at some strategic point, to muzzle the voice of critique as much as that of absolute value.[16] The point is to know when.

Now, in case this is sounding like a dismissal of these musical writers, I now want, firstly, to draw your attention to the kinds of reification produced in launching my own critique, and, secondly, to remind you of the fact that the moments when critique is muzzled in Boretz, Dubiel, and Guck are fascinating and politically useful moments. Only a brazenly formalist stance, disinterested in the changing dynamics of historical conjunctures, will figure the objects of my critique in terms of their singular success or failure. The principle that contradictory positions are only true or false is a formalism that has more in common with the instrumentality of the economic apparatus than it has with the axiomatics of interpretation, let alone with the imagination of music. The point of critique is not to destroy the secrets of their objects by exposure, but to do them justice by revealing their individual usefulness.

It is perilous to think of criticism vindicated of this qualification. For example, one problem with my critique is that its sustained warning against foundationalism can take on the character of a formula. Like the eternally returning formalisms, whose spell on music theory they set out to break, these disenchanting gyres of critique risk making every analytic event their repetition. As Adorno describes it in connection with Kant, this is the failure of "aim[ing] at the new; and yet . . . recogniz[ing] nothing new, since it always merely recalls what reason has always deposited in the object" (Adorno and Horkheimer 1997, 26). Even my "being aware," as it were, of the problems of being aware can also be a return to mythology, made virulent by appearing in the form of critique. In its ogre-like hold on the always-already of phenomena, such critique can take on the character of Adorno's instrumental reason. Unleashed to cleanse music analysis of "demons and their conceptual descendents," it also "assumes the numinous character which the ancient world attributed to demons" (28). For Adorno, the challenge is to move beyond determining the "abstract spatio-temporal relations of the facts which allow them just to be grasped" (whether these relations are embraced in the case of instrumental reason or rejected in the critique of it), and instead to "comprehend the given as such" (26). While my critique puts a prohibition on succumbing to Adorno's "given as such," I want to draw attention to the irreducible proximity of this "given" dimension even at points of maximally critical distance from it. By confronting music analysis with the kind of logical rigor to which it cannot match up, I not only risk investing this *kind* of rigor with legislative authority, but I risk undermining, or at least devaluing, analytic efforts that are driven by conjuncturally apprised experimentation.

On the occasion of Émile Zola's famous pronouncement, "I will not be complicit," Derrida makes a distinction between different kinds of "complicity" (with that which one opposes). Despite his open letter in 1898 to the president of France on behalf of Alfred Dreyfus, the Jewish artillery officer falsely accused and convicted of treason, Zola cannot escape his complicity with the crime in the general, irreducible sense of the term. Only his complicity in the particular, variable sense is open for debate.

> What is the price of this strategy ["I will not be complicit."]? Why does it fatally turn against its "subject"—if one can use this word, as one must, in fact? Because one cannot demarcate oneself from biologism, from naturalism, from racism in its genetic form, one cannot be *opposed* to them except by reinscribing spirit in an oppositional determination, by once again making it a unilaterality of subjectivity. . . . All the pitfalls of the strategy of establishing demarcations belong to this program, whatever place one occupies in it. The only choice is between the terrifying contaminations it assigns. Even if all forms of complicity are not equivalent, they are *irreducible*. (Derrida 1989, 39–40)

For Derrida, because the generalized complicity is irreducible, Zola's specific act of resistance becomes contaminated by what it opposes. Still, such particular, contaminated complicities are *not* equivalent with the general one, even if the only option is to avoid the more terrifying practices of the ruling order, and to adopt the less terrifying ones. This distinction allows us to separate those music analytic practices that are open to judgment, such as their challenge to the balance of power, from those that are not, being their condition of possibility. It behooves us to observe how, despite their inevitable complicity with the discourse of power, some music analyses struggle against the ossification of musical sounds and may fit awkwardly with power's ideological demands. Some musical stories kill powerful notes to make others sing more beautifully; Boretz's stories mythologize to issue forth truths; Guck's stories endorse to challenge; Dubiel's stories generalize to give us that one fortunate insight. While the always-already compromised position of our musical stories unhinges the link between universal reason and moral value, it opens the way to speak of them in particular ethical terms. Beyond good and evil the ethico-political dwells, once more, within our proximity.

CONCLUSION: FROM FEMININE TO FEMINIST HEARING

Let me end by recapitulating my account of the "feminine stance" in music theory and speculate on its problematic relation to feminism. In my argument so far I have interpreted the Boretzian stance less in the self-described terms of musical "looking without touching," and more in terms of the desire to touch music all over. But yielding our bodies wholesale to unfettered sound necessarily involves various openings, fractures and gaps that cannot not enfold as they open: "Necessary enemies," say Deleuze and Guattari, "the furniture we are forever arranging" (Deleuze and Guattari [1988] 1996, 21); "subjection," says Judith Butler, "that initiates and sustains our agency" (Butler 1997, 2). While I hope to have made vivid the re-enclosure that marks the apocalyptic transgression that a kind of feminine stance desires of the musical experience, I do not want to dwell on the apogee of critique. Nor do I want to move in directions for which I am not prepared. For Deleuze and Guattari, "the fact that there is no deterritorialization without a special reterritorialiation should prompt us to rethink the abiding correlation between the molar and the molecular: no flow, no becoming-molecular escapes from a molar formation without molar components accompanying it, forming passages or perceptible landmarks for the imperceptible processes" (Deleuze and Guattari [1988] 1996, 303). Deleuze and Guattari encourage us to follow the imperceptible flows; to heed the distractions; the becoming "woman," becoming what is not implied by established templates: "The quality must be considered from the standpoint of the becoming that grasps it, instead of becoming being considered from the standpoint of intrinsic qualities having its value as archetypes or phylogenetic memories" (306). But even this, quite Humean, formulation of an appropriate frame of mind for interpretation, "unprejudiced" as it were by the inevitable sedimentations of encrusted habit, is an opening gesture alone and cannot institute political commitments even as it opens the horizon of the politically possible. I have argued that "becoming" can be absolutized as well, can become a political slogan. Finally, I have suggested that it is important to dampen the gung-ho spirit of becoming and look "from the standpoint of intrinsic qualities" as well. To factually limit the horizon of becoming no less than to open it from the standpoint of becoming. To fly with trees, no less than to gravitate with birds. To idealize strategically.

My closing question becomes: Why are these and not those openings and blockages valuable in the world? I want to suggest that a feminist hearing only begins with a strategic idealization (which also means a political stand) in mind. And, lest my efforts float free of contextual determination, let me ask these questions plainly: What ways of hearing are going to allay the drastic inequality between men and women in global modernity; the differential axis to mobility; the sexual division of labor—where unpaid domestic labor carries the cost of the capitalist machine; where those women who do serve as a reserve labor force for the marketplace are systematically paid less; and where "woman" is still property? And how do our musical analyses enter the question of what Gayatri Spivak might call transnational economic citizenship-in-finance and exploitation on a global scale?

Hereabouts lie the values for which I seek names for which I seek musical experiences. The barbarism of my text lies in the distance it takes from them.

NOTES

1. In his multimedia work *music/consciousness/gender* for live speaker and prerecorded speakers, musics and images on audio and videotape (Boretz 1994/1995), Boretz thematizes aspects of gender in often highly erotic terms. Statements like "as music enters me it touches me in places of gender" are consistent with the essentially feminine stance advocated in Boretz's written articles. Not mentioned in the articles is the idea that listening to music (in a way that allows it to "touch, probe, open, [and] explore" us) undoes the category of gender altogether, leaving us "gendershorn," or "becoming a sacred one (outside ritual gender naming)." Still, the metaphor of castration (the view that gender categories are somehow cut or clipped by intensive listening) is consistent with the assertion that Boretz's paradigm for ideal listening involves a "feminine" stance—however problematic. On the other hand, as Suzanne Cusick argues in "Gender, Musicology, and Feminism," the notion that we lose our gender identities within musical experience is also a desire to spirit away social injustice and inequality in purely aesthetic terms. In the "free play of pure form," argues Cusick, "we can imagine ourselves to be angels, even gods; for 'the

music itself' is a kind of ether in which we lose our selves. As we do so, we imaginatively lose our genders, our sexualities, our very bodies" (Cusick1999, 494).

2. Is the neighbor note a^{b1} in m.2, say, strictly dissonant, or does it form part of ii^7 of A$^\flat$, an implication taken up by the suggested V^7 of A$^\flat$ on the next beat; and, if it is dissonant and g^1 is consonant, how is the other dissonance f^2 (over g^1) resolved? Does e^{b2} count as its resolution (despite its dissonance over B$^\flat$ and d^{b1}) because it produces a recognizable dominant seventh chord? If so, is this not the very chord that was implied by taking a^{b1} as a chord tone as well? Settling on one determination over the other seems to be inherently contradictory.

3. It is interesting to me that the syntactically felicitous, but absent, A major chord in m.6 sounds a kind of minor (A, B$^\natural$, E) before resolving too late (thus producing another minor chord), while the analogously felicitous F$^\sharp$ minor chord in m. 8 sounds briefly major (F$^\sharp$, A$^\natural$, C$^\sharp$) before resolving too late (and producing another major chord). In this way, the fleeting harmonic yield in a context of carefully uncoordinated counterpoint produces sounds that are not normatively implied.

4. According to Lacan, despite the permanent separation from the mother and from the plenitude of the imaginary order, the subject seeks to fulfill his/her desire through a substitute object. Such an object, which Lacan refers to as the *objet a*, has a metonymic relation to the original experience of union with the mother. It can never lead to the ultimate source of total fulfillment, nor can the subject ever know what this unconscious object-of-partial-fulfillment is. It is the radically contingent thing that interferes with any network of signs that tries to pin it down and is thus necessarily outside of language. Only through an experience of the impossibility of reaching out for or representing the object of desire does the subject gain a vague expectation of the true dimensions of it. Hence the real emerges in a kind of mismatch between the symbolic and the imaginary orders, the moment that the limits of signifying practice issue forth desire.

5. While I realize that this is a strong claim even though I cannot undertake a full investigation of this genealogy in the space of this paper. In "When the Music of Psychoanalysis Becomes the Psychoanalysis of Music" (forthcoming in *Current Musicology*) I describe some of this history:

> Following the invention of aesthetics in the eighteenth century, philosophers have long taken music as a kind of paradigm case for asserting a realm that is beyond the reach of linguistic signification and implicated instead in an ineffable higher truth about the workings of the world. Whether this interest took the form of Wackenroder's idealism (in which music occupied a pure angelic domain independent of the actual world), or Schopenhauer's endlessly striving Will (to which music bore the closest of all possible analogies), or of Nietzsche's Dionysian strain (which represented the rapturous musical frenzy that destroyed the veils of *maya* and freed us from norms, images, rules, and restraint), or Kierkegaard's analysis of the absolutely musical (which best exemplified the highly erotic striving of the pure unmediated life force), music frequently served as a discursive site for speculation on the limits of philosophy, knowledge, and

meaning. A central metaphor for that which resisted epistemological certainty, music in philosophical discourse functioned as a kind of language of the un-image, the non-significant, the unsayable *par excellence*. Less apparent, perhaps, today is the way this kind of theorizing of fundamental negativity (which came out of German metaphysics) has impacted the current French philosophical, psychoanalytic, and literary-theoretical scene. While the explicit reference to music has receded in most post-structuralist writing, the form of the inquiry has not changed all that much. Like the older figure of music, the operations of deconstruction, for example, mark what is semantically slippery and puzzle the divide between hardened historical oppositions. Coming out of the Hegelian principle of non-identity, what counts as meaning in the deconstructive account includes what is not said, what is silenced out of discourse, that which impedes narrative coherence. Still, despite the general evacuation of thought about the purely musical, the metaphor of music is never far away in these later writings either. In his description of the sound of the operatic voice, for instance, Roland Barthes isolates that which imposes a limit on predicative language as the "grain of the voice," the visceral materiality that escapes linguistic significance. Jacques Derrida works out his notion of the *supplement*—the negatively privileged term which marks a semantic excess that cannot be subsumed into the discourse under investigation—in the context of Rousseau's consideration of melody and speech in the *Essai sur l'origine de langue*. And Julia Kristeva points to the musical basis of a non-representational theory of language—one in which the desemanticized "pure signifier" reverberates as if in musical space. This rather complicated path in the history of philosophy via German metaphysics to post-structuralist French theory, (to use shorthands) ought to disconcert both the view that thought about music somehow lags behind the recent theoretical developments in postmodernism, critical theory and cultural studies, and the view that music figured as pure sounding forms in motion, precisely the discourse lacking significance, is somehow the antithesis of these developments. Historically speaking, their discursive affinities are more prominent than their differences.

For another account that links romanticism with postmodernism, see Bowie 1997.

6. Despite appearances, Lukács regards these principles as irrational because hyper-rationalization consists (in part) in leaving unquestioned the necessary grounds of formalistic conceptualization: "The question why and with what justification human reason should elect to regard just these systems as constitutive of its own essence . . . never arises" (Lukács 1971, 112).

7. If anything, it is the masked oblong portion of the "subject" that is imitated by the right hand in quick notes after the left hand finally ends.

8. Elsewhere, Boretz compares "the subjective reality of music" with "the intersubjective realities attributed to it," which implies, perhaps, a less vivid contrast between experience and representation. Still, in order to maintain a critical distance

from the truth claims of the latter, these modalities remain "stubbornly disjunct" (Boretz 1992, 453).

9. In an effort not to anticipate the lineaments in which his objects of consciousness may emerge, Hegel posits the starting point for his *Phenomenology* as a "chance" encounter with an "external" object (Hegel 1977, 55).

10. I am reading Boretz against the grain here. Boretz, in fact, aims to *resist* the ontologizing tendencies of semantic fusion. I do so because, in this second reading of Boretz, I want to avoid the entailed prohibitions (implied by this resistance) against labeling music. Also I want to suggest that there cannot *not* be semantic fusion in any comprehensible account. It might be worth pointing out that, in the *Dialectic of Enlightenment*, Adorno and Horkheimer associate the very split between language and nature with Enlightenment mythology (Adorno and Horkheimer 1997, 19). If art is to play a critical role in the world, it might be worth heeding this warning on the terrain of language and music.

11. It is in this sense that Charles Taylor claims that Hegel's opening argument to the *Phenomenology* is beholden to the idea that "to know is to say" (Taylor 1976, 156), or that Taylor Carman (in a private discussion) likens the dialectic to a kind of Freudian talking cure.

12. The distinction between "being-for-another" and "being-for-itself" parallels, but does not correspond to, Kant's distinction between appearances and things-in-themselves. The former distinction is made in the context of consciousness, and so, unlike the Kantian thing-in-itself, for example, "being-for-itself" is inherently knowable. The standard by which we come to know "being-for-itself" is set up by consciousness. It is this last point that leads Adorno to privilege dialectics on the analytical terrain of music. That is, even more obviously than for epistemology, *art* "move[s] towards a neutral zone between things that exist in themselves and those which exist for us, because this 'for us' is a constitutive elements of [its] existence in [itself]" (Adorno 1992, 308). In short, the distinction between "science" and "appearing knowledge" is still more false in art than in epistemology.

13. Instead of merely bending knowledge to suit the object in the face of a contradiction, Hegel claims that the object of knowledge alters as well (precisely because it was essentially beholden to the earlier knowledge).

14. When I mark the affinities between Adorno and Dubiel, I do not mean to claim that their projects are equivalent; they are not. For example, Dubiel is interested in the act of listening/composing, while Adorno suggests that music's critical potential resides within itself.

15. In case Guck has a pragmatic model in mind, whereby the most compelling or startling story ultimately gains the firmest foothold in analytic discourse, I should mention that even a cursory glance at the discipline should suffice to illustrate the endemic seduction of the power of analysis conceived in factory-like data bytes and fear of social deviation. It might be worth distinguishing those kinds of analysis that resist their irreducible fictional aspect and so concentrate instead their non-fictional aspect—raise it to another power—from those kinds of analysis that do not. In "The Storyteller," Walter Benjamin makes a useful distinction between "information" and "experience" (Benjamin 1968, 83–109). While storytelling

modeled on experience leaves open the "psychological connection of events," information "lays claim to prompt verifiability" (1968, 89). That is, under the rule of information, no event "comes to us without already being shot through with explanation" (Benjamin 1968, 89). Like Benjamin, Guck aims to return to analysis a dimension of subjective choice. But, while Benjamin does not advance a future-oriented alternative to it, he does advance a political critique of information. At the least, this begins to point the way towards a concrete alternative. In contrast, pragmatized thought in apolitical space can be no more than thoughtful wishing.

16. Søren Kierkegaard recognizes the irreducible moment of madness entailed in faithful Christian living, and Derrida recognizes the Kierkegaardian madness entailed in ordinary human living. Derrida describes the irreducible minimal idealization associated with all critique in terms of an "invaginated" metaphysical limit; (Derrida 1985, 273); that is to say, ensheathed within itself; a limit that is twisted and devious, folded back upon itself.

WORKS CITED

Adorno, Theodor. 1982. "On the Problem of Musical Analysis." Translated by Max Paddison. *Music Analysis* 1:2, 169–87.

———. 1992. *Quasi Una Fantasia: Essays on Modern Music.* Translated by Rodney Livingstone. London and New York: Verso.

———. 1995. *Negative Dialectics.* Translated by E. B. Ashton. New York: Continuum.

Adorno, Theodor, and Max Horkheimer. 1997. *Dialectic of Enlightenment.* Translated by John Cumming. New York: Continuum.

Barthes, Roland. 1991. *The Responsibility of Forms: Critical Essays on Music, Art, and Representation.* Translated by Richard Howard. Berkeley and Los Angeles: University of California Press.

Benjamin, Walter. 1968. *Illuminations.* Translated by Harry Zorn. New York: Schocken Books.

Boretz, Benjamin. 1992. "('starting now, from here, . . .') three consecutive occasions of sociomusical reflection: (1) text for the Society for Music Theory, Oakland, California, 9 November 1990, on 'J.K. Randall's Writings During the 1970s'; (2) 'Some things I've Been noticing, Some Things I've Been Doing, Some Things I'm Going to Need to Think more about'; (3) "Experiences with No Names.' *Perspectives of New Music* 30: 250–83.

———. 1995. "music/consciousness/gender: texts, musics, textsoundmusics, images for live speaker and prerecorded speakers, musics and images on audio and videotape." *Open Space.*

———. 1999. "Music, as a Music: A Multitext in Five Movements." Paper delivered as part of the Columbia University music department's colloquium series, April.

Bowie, Andrew. 1997. *From Romanticism to Critical Theory: The Philosophy of German Literary Theory.* London and New York: Routledge.

Butler, Judith. 1997. *The Psychic Life of Power: Theories in Subjection.* Stanford: Stanford University Press.

Cixous, Helene. 1994. *The Helene Cixous Reader.* London and New York: Routledge.

Currie, Jamie. 1999. "'*Viva la libertá*': An Investigation into Tensions in the Interactions between Musical Signs in Late-Eighteenth-Century Music." Paper delivered as part of the Columbia University music department's brown bag series, November.

Cusick, Suzanne G. 1999. "Gender, Musicology, and Feminism." In *Rethinking Music*, edited by Nicholas Cook and Mark Everist. Oxford and New York: Oxford University Press. 471–98.

Deleuze, Gilles, and Felix Guattari. 1984. *Anti-Oedipus: Capitalism and Schizophrenia.* London: Athlone Press.

———. [1988] 1996. *A Thousand Plateaus: Capitalism and Schizophrenia.* London: Athlone Press.

Derrida, Jacques. 1976. *Of Grammatology.* Translated by Gayatri C. Spivak. Baltimore and London: Johns Hopkins University Press.

———. 1985. "Le retrait de la métaphore." *Analecta Husserliana* 14: 273.

———. 1989. *Of Spirit: Heidegger and the Question.* Translated by Geoffrey Bennington and Rachel Bowlby. Chicago: University of Chicago Press.

Dubiel, Joseph. 1994. "Contradictory Criteria in a Work by Brahms." In *Brahms Studies*, edited by David Brodbeck. Lincoln and London: University of Nebraska Press. 81–110.

———. 1996. "Hearing, Remembering, Cold Storage, Purism, Evidence, and Attitude Adjustment." *Current Musicology* 60 and 61: 26–50.

———. 1999. "Composer, Theorist, Composer/Theorist." *Rethinking Music*, edited by Nicholas Cook and Mark Everist. Oxford and New York: Oxford University Press. 262–83.

———. Forthcoming. "Motives for Motives (or I've Got Connections)." Unpublished chapter draft for *Musical Experience and Musical Explanation.* Berkeley and Los Angeles: University of California Press.

Goehr, Lydia. 1998. *The Quest For Voice: Music, Politics, and the Limits of Philosophy.* Berkeley, Los Angeles, and London: University of California Press.

Guck, Marion A. 1998. "Analytic Fictions." In *Music/Ideology: Resisting the Aesthetic*, edited by Adam Krims. Amsterdam: G&B Arts International.

Hanslick, Eduard. 1986. *On the Musically Beautiful: A Contribution Towards the Revision of the Aesthetics of Music.* Translated and edited by Geoffrey Payzant. Indianapolis: Hackett Publishing Company.

Hegel, Georg Wilhelm Friedrich. 1977. *Phenomenology of Spirit.* Translated by A.V. Miller. Oxford, New York, Toronto, and Melbourne: Oxford University Press.

Hume, David. 1985. "Of the Standard of Taste." In *Essays: Moral, Political and Literary*, edited by Eugene F. Miller. Indianapolis: Liberty Fund.

Irigaray, Luce. 1985. *This Sex Which Is Not One.* Translated by Catherine Porter with Carolyn Burke. Ithaca: Cornell University Press.

Kant, Immanuel. 1987. *Critique of Judgment.* Translated by W. S. Pluhar. Indianapolis and Cambridge: Hacket.

Kierkegaard, Søren. 1992. *Either/Or: A Fragment of Life.* Translated by Alastair Hannay. London and New York: Penguin.

Kramer, Lawrence. 1998. "Classical Music and Postmodern Knowledge." Paper presented at the 56th annual meeting of The American Society of Aethetics, Indiana University, November.

Kristeva, Julia. 1980. *Desire in Language: A Semiotic Approach to Literature and Art.* Translated by Thomas Gora, Alice Jardin, and Leon S. Roudiez. New York: Columbia University Press.

Lacan, Jacques. 1977. *Ecrits: A Selection.* Translated by Alan Sheridan. New York: W. W. Norton.

Lee, Jonathan Scott. 1990. *Jacques Lacan.* Boston: Twayne Publishers.

Lewin, David. 1986. "Music Theory, Phenomenology, and Modes of Perception." *Music Perception* 3/4: 327–92.

Lukács, Georg. 1971. *History and Class Consciousness: Studies in Marxist Dialectics.* Translated by Rodney Livingstone. Cambridge: MIT Press.

Maus, Fred Everett. 1993. "Masculine Discourse in Music Theory." *Perspectives of New Music* 31/2: 264–93.

Nietzsche, Friedrich. 1967. *The Birth of Tragedy.* Translated by Walter Kaufmann. New York: Vintage Books.

———. 1989. *On The Genealogy of Morals.* Translated by Walter Kaufmann. New York: Vintage Books.

Rousseau, Jean Jacques. 1997. *The Discourses and Other Early Political Writings.* Edited and translated by Victor Gourevitch. Cambridge: Cambridge University Press.

Samson, Jim. 1999. "Analysis in Context." In *Rethinking Music*, edited by Nicholas Cook and Mark Everist. Oxford and New York: Oxford University Press. 35–54.

Scherzinger, Martin. Forthcoming. "When the Music of Psychoanalysis Becomes the Psychoanalysis of Music: Review Essay: David Schwarz. *Listening Subjects: Music, Psychoanalysis, Culture,*" *Current Musicology* 65.

Schopenhauer, Arthur. 1966. *The World as Will and Representation.* New York: Dover Publications.

Spivak, Gayatri Chakravorty. 1999. *A Critique of Postcolonial Reason: Toward a History of the Vanishing Present.* Cambridge, Mass., and London: Harvard University Press.

Taylor, Charles. 1976. "The Opening Arguments of the *Phenomenology.*" In *Hegel: A Collection of Critical Essays*, edited by Alasdair C. MacIntyre. Notre Dame, Ind.: University of Notre Dame Press.

Wackenroder, Wilhelm Heinrich. 1971. *Confessions and Fantasies.* Translated by Mary Hurst Schuber. University Park: Pennsylvania State University Press.

Wellmer, Albrecht. 1993. *The Persistence of Modernity: Essays on Aesthetics, Ethics, and Postmodernism.* Translated by David Midgley. Cambridge: MIT Press.

Wittgenstein, Ludwig. 1998. *Tractatus Logico-Philosophicus.* Translated by C. K. Ogden. London and New York: Routledge.

Scaling the High / Low Divide

CHAPTER 8

Postmodern Polyamory or Postcolonial Challenge?

Cornershop's Dialogue from West, to East, to West . . .

Renée T. Coulombe

Like all postmodern inquiry, this paper finds its origins in odd and disparate places and represents the intersection of many issues that began as unrelated entities. For the first lecture of a world music class, I wanted to spark a discussion about the differences between musics of non-Western traditions, and music from non-Western traditions packaged for consumption in the West. Since most of the students had not yet heard any of the music for the course, this seemed a good way of finding out what their preconceived notions about "world music" might be.

> " . . . *saturating hegemonic systems* . . . "
> —Said [1978] 1994, 14

It became clear early in the discussion that the music that most of my undergraduate students now associate with non-Western cultures is actually Western in origin. After a few names were offered, someone mentioned a CD I had brought with me as an example. So, I played them a sample: the opening track, "Deep Forest," from the CD of the same name. To further the point, I read them the accompanying liner notes. They begin:

> Imprinted with the ancestral wisdom of the African chants, the music of Deep Forest immediately touches everyone's soul and instinct. The forest of all civilizations is a mysterious place where the yarn of tales and legends is woven. . . . Universal rites and customs have been profoundly marked by the influence of the forest. . . . The chants of Deep Forest, Baka [*sic*] chants of Cameroun, of Burundi, of Senegal and of Pygmies, transmit a part of this important oral tradition gathering all peoples and joining all continents through the universal language of music.

There is no need here to rehearse the work that has been done critiquing such rhetoric.[1] During this particular class discussion, however, these remarks sparked a new curiosity in me. It all seemed so amusing, given the dangerous naiveté embodied in phrases like "universal harmony." Yet I couldn't imagine why I should be so bemused. If we as a society see no problem in setting the work of one of our own medieval composers to a new-age/techno beat, what could ever stop us from taking doing so to the music of other cultures?[2]

What I found funnier still was that, as if anticipating my discomfort, the liner notes in *Deep Forest* go on to assure me that

> *Deep Forest* is the respect of this tradition which humanity should cherish as a treasure which marries world harmony, a harmony often compromised today. That's why the musical creation of Deep Forest has received the support of UNESCO, and of two musicologists, Hugo Zempe [*sic*] and Shima Aron [*sic*], who collected the original documents.

Finally a pop album with the musicologist stamp of approval already present in the CD notes![3] It seems so straightforward on the surface— musicologists in the forest record beautiful "native music." Concerned Western musicians hear this, are inspired, and "bring" this unique sound to the world. Concerned musicians donate money to a fund to help protect the aforementioned "natives." It's a situation we can all feel good about. Right?[4] As a composer, I desperately *want* it to be true that I can use any sound I come across as building materials for my work, and do so with impunity.[5]

> *. . . it is a certain will or intention to understand, in some cases control, manipulate—even to incorporate . . .*
> —Said [1978] 1994, 12

So many mistakes, half-truths, and Western anxieties work themselves out in the rhetoric concerning Western forays into "indigenous" musics. I began to wonder what kind of music would emerge if the positions usually occupied by Westerner and non-Westerner were altered. Is the subject position of those in the West always the most overriding characteristic of their music? More specifically, what do the musicians that inhabit the postcolonial terrain in many parts of the world have to say? What would their work imply when seen in light of the issues of creativity, control, and, above all, individual agency in music?

Those who grew up in the West, but who, due to the racial or ethnic makeup of their families or communities, have not been accepted by whatever Western culture they find themselves swimming in have a unique subject position vis-à-vis Western culture. Being in it, but not fully "of" it, having "legitimate" access to more than one sphere or cultural influence, provides an interesting "fissure" through which to explore issues of ownership, identity, and culture through music.

The 1997 release *When I Was Born for the 7th Time*, by the band Cornershop, offers an ideal opportunity to explore these different subject positions. *7th Time* rides a wave of recent popularity of Indian pop music in the West.[6] The musicians who make up the group, besides Tjinder Singh, who sings, writes most of the songs, and plays guitar and *dholki*, are white and British: Ben Ayres, guitar/tamboura; Anthony Saffery, sitar/keyboards; Nick Simms, drums; Pete Hall, other percussion. But they assume, by virtue of Tjinder's strong creative drive and the rest of the band's interest in and proficiency with non-Western instruments, a stance that is neither Western nor non-Western. Cornershop is somewhat a combination of the two. The identities worked out through the sonic cacophony of the CD occur in a cultural landscape that has been determinedly printed by the experience of colonialism.

Postcolonial theory—with its focus on conceptions of language or place, its themes of exile, hybridity, in-betweenness, and liminality—offers a useful model to discuss the intricate web of subjectivities presented by Cornershop's music. Since my first hearing, *7th Time* has struck me as a sonic record of composer/songwriters Tjinder Singh and Ben Ayres working out complex identities and subject positions with a unique mixture of songwriting and sonic collage. I know that they are both living in the West, but does that perforce make them Western musicians? Can they be more than one thing at once? Can their music speak for more than one identity at once?

In using postcolonial theory to analyze music, I do open myself to the more general criticisms leveled at the discipline. "The term 'postcolonial' has become 'the latest catchall term to dazzle the academic mind' " (Jacoby 1995, 30). "'Postcolonial' [is] becoming shorthand for something (fashionably) marginal" (Loomba 1998, xii). These observations are certainly grounded in the reality that much of the writing on postcolonial issues can be dense, self-referential, and sometimes jingoistic.[7] Also, the rapid construction of a canonical body of postcolonial works has troubled some who fear it will just as quickly founder under the weight of its own rhetoric.

I offer this essay, then, as a meditation on the issues that Cornershop's *7th Time* raises in a context of postcolonial inquiry, occurring as it does at the intersection of race, class, and culture unique because of modern postcolonial history. It proposes a shift away from a model of "exoticism in Western music" to challenge what exactly *is* "exotic" or "Western" in music. This shift must be preceded by a move away from imperialist/orientalist views, and toward a postcolonial model of "hybridity." Cornershop's work is interesting not only for the ways that it *can* be interpreted, but also for the ways in which it is impossible *not* to interpret it.

"IN-BETWEENNESS, DIASPORAS, AND LIMINALITY" (LOOMBA 1995, 173)

Postcolonial theory has been criticized for overlapping with postmodernism or post-structuralism to the end that one can complain always, but do little. "Postmodernism in this view is a specifically Western malaise which breeds angst and despair instead of aiding political action and resistance" (Loomba 1995, xii). To this, Cornershop does offer a refutation. "[T]he reason we started in music wasn't because we wanted to be in a band, it was because we didn't like the industry" (Fricke 1997, 24). Their early notoriety in Britain actually came for political action, when they protested another British pop musician's racist rhetoric and newly articulated fascist remarks vis-à-vis Asians and Asian immigrants.[8] Not surprisingly, Singh's background in England was perfect training for a career postcolonial artist.

Tjinder grew up Tjinder Singh Nurpuri in the north of England in the industrial town of Wolverhampton. His family emigrated from the Punjab, in northern India, and maintained Sikh identity and culture at home. This included participation in the local Sikh temple. Singh's experiences there certainly shaped his world-view: "There would be people who just come up and beat you, who chase you on bikes, because they don't like you." Not all the experiences in Wolverhampton were bad for his musical aesthetic, though. Singh said in an interview:

> We'd go to this local temple, which was hired on Sundays and half of
> it was full of Sikhs playing Punjabi religious music. But the other half
> was black gospel. So I used to sneak in. I was always interested in
> amalgamating ideas and influences rather than having firm, straight-
> forward ideas in my head all the time. (Wiederdorn 1996, 32)

Growing up a Sikh in Britain, playing the *dholki* in his local temple and getting beaten up by the local bullies for being Indian, Tjinder continues to feel threatened to this day in his home city of London—and with justification. One day, late in 1995, when he was walking down a street near his home, hand in hand with his girlfriend, he was punched in the face by a "drunk Irishman," who reportedly took a dislike to the sight of an Indian man with an English woman (Wiederdorn 1996, 32).[9]

When Tjinder and his brother Avtar were toying around with the idea of forming a band during their college days in the early 1990s, they named it Cornershop after the corner stores in England often run by Indian owners. Ben Ayres (one of the earliest bandmembers) answers the assertion that the name was meant to reflect a political stance:

> Perhaps to a small extent. It's more about taking a word or phrase that
> had sort of bad connotations—it's often used in a derogatory way with

Asians in England, that all Asian people were good at doing was running cornershops—and giving it a good meaning. (Hiransomboon 1998)

Being English and, in important ways, not—this is what makes the strongest mark on their 1997 release *When I Was Born for the 7th Time.* Slippery and eliding subject positions, jarring juxtapositions and disjunct narratives, ironic with regards to its own displacement—all of these characteristics could apply if the music was simply postmodern, and not postcolonial. This brings us to the rather thorny issue of overlap of musical postmodernism and postcolonialism—important both for what postmodernism is and what it is not to musical postcolonial studies.

POSTMODERN POLYAMORY

Jonathan Kramer (1996), in his "Postmodern Concepts of Musical Time," offers a list of "postmodern" characteristics he believes help clarify the "aesthetic" for the sake of future discussion and debate.[10] I will quote seven:

- [Postmodern music] includes quotations of or reference to music of many traditions and cultures
- embraces contradictions
- distrusts binary oppositions
- includes fragmentations and discontinuities
- encompasses pluralism and eclecticism
- presents multiple meanings and multiple temporalities
- locates meaning and even structure in listeners, more than in scores, performances, or composers

Many scholars acknowledge that postmodernism and postcolonialism overlap in several important ways, and these could easily be seen as characteristics of postcolonial work as well.[11] While the term "postcolonial" has the implication of a supplanting of colonial fact with something completely new and different, this implication is in some way misleading. "Post-" applies to colonialism the way it does to "modernism" or "structuralism"—incorporating aspects of the old with the new. It is a cohabitation of colonial realities with post-colonial forces in economics, politics, and culture.

Bearing this in mind, I will define "characteristics" or "elements" of the postcolonial in music. Taken mostly from *The Empire Writes Back* (Ashcroft et al. 1989), the list of characteristics below was directed originally at the analysis of literary works. Nonetheless, they translate well for speaking about musical works:

- Postcolonial works incorporate aspects of the previously imposed culture, but subvert them in some way (counter-discursive rather than continuing expression of imperial discourse) (20).
- Such works often manipulate materials in such a way so as to challenge the imperialist hierarchy *and* the fundamental precepts on which it is based (33).
- Language is central to postcolonial thought—specifically the alteration, abrogation, or appropriation in serving to express postcolonial realities. Thus both indigenous languages and the imperial languages imposed on a population become fair game for the postcolonial artist/writer (7).
- The fundamental concept of "exile" or "outsider" is common in postcolonial narratives. "A major feature of postcolonial literatures is the concern for place and displacement. It is here the crisis of identity comes . . ."(8).
- Postcolonial writing "privileges the margins"(41).
- Postcolonialism shares a predilection for simultaneous disjunct or discontinuous narratives with postmodernism. It also shares irony, with a special focus on the "language-place disjunction" in describing the postcolonial predicament.

Simultaneously conflicting realities, multiple viewpoints, layers of sometimes contradictory identities, allowing the assignment of meaning to happen outside the work itself (both in individuals and cultures from which they arise)—all of these characteristics of postcolonialist literature might certainly have a liberating effect on artists who find themselves in this situation.

> The alienating process which initially served to relegate the post-colonial world to the margin turned upon itself and acted to push that world through a kind of mental barrier into a position from which all experience could be viewed as uncentered, pluralistic, and multifarious. Marginality thus became an unprecedented source of creative energy. (Ashcroft et al. 1989, 12)

Singh sums this point up eloquently for himself: "I consider myself more Asian than English because of my color. But I really don't feel either of them" (Fricke 1997, 24). Said has noted, however that this sense of cultural "limbo" is a fertile ground for the artist:

> We can better understand the persistence and the durability of saturating hegemonic systems like culture when we realize that their internal constraints, upon writers and thinkers were productive, not unilaterally inhibiting. (Said [1978] 1994, 14)

Singh says as much himself when he notes that "I've always lived in an intimidating rather than happy atmosphere. It's really fueled my aggression and given me a sense that I don't belong" (Wiederdorn 1996, 32). The fact that he relies on his music in part as tool for the artistic illumination of the listener helps push it from the postmodern to postcolonial camps (which are adjacent enough to begin with).

"All Indian Radio"

When I was Born for the 7th Time contains fifteen tracks, including more instrumentals than "songs," which is not atypical for a dance album. The instrumentals dominate the release and contain some of the most interesting sonic materials ("Butter the Soul," "Chocolat," "What Is Happening," "When the Light Appears Boy," "Coming Up," "It's Indian Tobacco My Friend," "State Troopers"). Most combine lopsided beat loops from various worldwide sources with cheesy, low-fi FM synthesis sounds. Some have the most startling juxtapositions of sonic worlds. Rejecting the "authentic" sound of world music in favor of a hybrid-pop style and incorporating technology, Western and non-Western instruments, divergent genres, and samples side by side may be seen in and of itself to be a certain kind of resistance:

> . . . resistance, far from being merely a reaction to imperialism, is an alternative way of conceiving human history. It is particularly important to see how much this alternative reconception is based on breaking down barriers between cultures. (Said 1993, 216)

Most reviews have contained some reference to the odd juxtapositions in the music with descriptions like "funk meets punk meets raga-and-roll" (Hebert 1998). Jon Pareles, in the *New York Times,* insightfully pointed out that Tjinder "toys with the incongruities of Anglo-Indian identity" through an "East-West fusion [that] is simultaneously self-conscious and cranky, breaking stereotypes while exploring instrumental combinations" (Pareles 1995, 24). One critic even asserted, "Cornershop's seamless concoction of pop-rock, funk, DJ culture, and traditional Punjabi folk music put them well ahead of European pop's present flirtations with South Asian music and culture" (Grant 1997).

The "concoction" of these juxtapositions is a heady mix. Some seem to literally fold the fabric of space and time to juxtapose entire sound worlds—each complete in itself. Upon being thrust together in Tjinder Singh's postcolonial mind, each borrowing seems as appropriate as the other.

One of the most innovative tracks, "When the Light Appears Boy," is named for Allen Ginsberg's poem of the same name. Ginsberg himself is in this track, reading his poem into Singh's tape recorder in the kitchen of his own New York City apartment (Wiederdorn 1996, 32). Though the volume of this recording is low, one can make out the background noises of a non-studio recording, lending an extremely informal "low-tech" air to the piece. At almost equal volume is a recording is a tape of musicians playing in a crowded city street. Decidedly exotic, this is a rather good example of Cornershop nodding toward Asian identity in their use of a recording Singh made of Delhi street musicians. Cornershop did not, like many of their Western colleagues, credit the musicians whose work they recorded and used in their own composition. Their tape recorder is still the locus of Western control and power. But unlike their Western colleagues, their handling of the material in their own work leaves the original startlingly whole and coherent.

What Singh does to create the piece is certainly not to sample each recording and play it back to his own tune on a Western keyboard. Each recording is allowed to continue unhindered for almost the entire piece. The Delhi street musicians provide the only musical continuity in the track, lending a sonic frame to Ginsberg's distinctive voice. The recordings are not edited such that the creative hand of Singh obscures anything evident in the originals. These recordings do not provide "raw materials" but rather the polished building stones of the entire piece. Singh is almost absent here, though one can imagine the affection for each recording in the arrangement. They are lovingly placed side by side, each infecting the other with its unique myriad of associations.

Even the title of the song shows no clear influence of the musicians, named as it is for Ginsberg's poem. Singh creates with his tape recorder, using each recording to frame the other and provide additional meaning through placement. His new context, in which Delhi street musicians complement the rhythmic cadence of the poet's recurring line "when the light appears, boy, when the light appears," leave each feeling equally affected by the other.

Another feature of the cut—it opens with a recording of what sounds to me like a bus station or airport loudspeaker that could have been made anywhere—adds a surreal, yet at the same time quotidian, element to the piece. It sonically illustrates one of the most common "contact zones" of the modern world, the transportation center. Many of us have become accustomed to the languages we hear while traveling in foreign airports, train stations, and so on. They can become a locus for our Western imaginations: a trope of "foreignness." By opening the cut this way, Singh points to the Western imagination of otherness, establishes it firmly. But as the voice drones on in an internationally recognizable monotony, we are lulled into a sense of "familiarity" with the "foreignness." A decidedly unexotic nod toward the exotic.

The voice fades down as a percussive groove fades up not yet to full, yielding the middle ground to a slightly thin, definitely low-fi recording of Ginsberg reading around the table in his kitchen. The recording of the poem is used at low volume and it takes a bit of a sonic "back seat" to the groove, which is peppered with the noises of a crowded street. The groove occupies an exterior landscape, the poem, interior. When the poem ends, the rhythmic groove suddenly stops and then reenters more forcefully with microtonal horn blasts and drums now beating double-time.

This cobbling together of sonic "landscapes" on vastly divergent continents has more precedent in visual art than music—it stands in sharp contrast to the more typical practice of providing exotic "flavoring" to what is basically a formulaic Western pop song. Its structure is disjointed, abrupt, and lopsided. This treatment of disparate "sonic" materials is nothing new to those of us who have listened to (or created) electronic music. Indeed technology has made sampling possible, which has in turn created entirely new musics—and new ways of looking at music. In the hands of Tjinder Singh, recordings are a way of bringing the gospel and Sikh music of his youth together on a much larger scale. The DJ spins culture, in that the primary materials of his/her trade are in themselves cultural artifacts.

Singh and Ayres, in England but not of it, use the sonic fragments of their identities, weaving together the disparate strands to create something unique and striking. If a major feature of postcolonial literatures is the concern with place and displacement, the bringing together of a vast array of sounds sampled from all over the world, and creating something new *without* imposing a system of dominance over the original, is surely a display of mastery over a complex cultural landscape. Similar in conception to John Zorn's *Spillane*, which can be considered a landmark postmodern piece for its sonic juxtapositions of disjunct materials, "When the Light Appears Boy" is far more leisurely in its exposition of materials. Each recording maintains its own coherence, which helps each stand on its own merits while still allowing one to indelibly impress upon the other. Each serves as opposition and complement to the other, creating a postmodern irony that resides outside the piece and becomes present through the audience's associations with each recording. Those familiar with each of the worlds brought together so closely through Singh's tape recorder must surely experience the most ironic pleasure from these mixes.

"It's Indian Tobacco My Friend"

One of the most obvious differences between "English" pop and Cornershop to any first time listener is the plethora of languages present, whether recorded, sung, or spoken. If singing in English is the key to success in the Western pop-music arena, what is one to make of a recording released in the West, sung entirely in Punjabi? Well, almost entirely in Punjabi. The English words "IBM" and "Coca Cola" (in the song "It's Indian Tobacco My Friend") occur in a completely unknown context (unless one speaks Punjabi). The addition of "mutha fucker" after the second appearance of these two American brand names gives us a slight clue as to the sentiments expressed. Nonetheless, by virtue of their recognizability, they actually make the Punjabi text of the song *more* foreign, *more* striking, than it would be if no English were present at all.

Another example of Singh's conflation of "other" and "familiar" makes itself most immediately present in the remake of the Beatles's "Norwegian Wood," here sung entirely in Punjabi. By using a tune that is familiar, he accomplishes the same trick of elision above, but on a strictly musical level. This particular version is significant largely because the familiarity of the tune to Western audiences (as indeed the Beatles' music has become a ubiquitous and obvious symbol of Western popular culture) causes the new language to become a jarring imposition on the original in and of itself. It may as well be in English, as we all know the words, but it isn't.

Thus, in characteristically postmodern fashion, the meaning of the song is located somewhere *between* the original and the new version. Singh's opening for the track, consisting of the somewhat faint background noises of a crowded room, highlights the "in-betweenness" of the tune. By including the stray sounds we imagine to exist outside the context of the song within the track, its placement in some undefined space is emphasized.

Sung in Punjabi, with the sitar line out in the front of the mix (and not George Harrison's Western sitar playing, either), the "squared-off" quality of the original formulaic strophic song is challenged. The syllable-dense lyric pushes and tugs at the ends of the original vocal line, it is most definitely a new version of the tune, produced by someone who is doing their culture surfing from the other side of the map.

The postcolonial implications of this particular song deserve such attention in my opinion, though Ayres and Singh insist that there are no "special" implications ("We thought it was a good song" [Fricke 1997, 24]) behind this recording. They say they intended it more as their spin on an old song, rather than a "jab at the Beatles for their gentleman's adventure in Indian music" (24). An interesting stance, given that at other moments Tjinder himself seems fully cognizant of the postcolonial drive of *7th Time*. He calls it "something for everyone: from country, to brunch with hip-hop, cricket on the lawn with Punjabi folk music and a square dance before dinner with the most righteous beats" (Cornershop 1997).

"The Candyman Is Back"

The very profusion of styles implicated in the above statement is part of what makes Cornershop's position so interesting. Not that they claim privilege to a specific, easily definable tradition, they claim privilege to none, and to all. Their track "Candyman" contains a guest rap by Justin Warfield, which exuberantly reminds the listener, "Automator's on the fader/Cornershop with the boom (mic)/slapping hands with my brothers as we rise to the sun." Subtle inclusions of the audience's presence are sprinkled throughout the CD, effectively obscuring the lines between performer and audience.

In "Butter the Soul," a mix of steady sitar twanging alternates in the foreground with an electronic swooping riff. The riff contains prominent wide pitch bends, the microtonal implication of which references the sitar's sound in a vaguely ironic way. Even more ironically, the harmonic progression slows during the sitar sections, becomes more rapid during the electronic sections. Each is separated from the other by a slow and sometimes lengthy drum break.

The funk groove sustained by, of all things, the Western drum back, breaks down during the drum breaks, seems constantly on the verge of falling apart. At one point, it even disintegrates into a slight flurry of applause, only to resurrect itself to lope along once again. And who is the source of the applause: an appreciative audience, recording engineers, the band themselves? Indeed, who exactly is occupying the audience position is usually suspect on some level in most of the songs. Sometimes it is destabilized by nothing more than Tjinder's references to colonialism with an odd musical smirk.

Why a smirk? If one is not listening closely, it is very possible to hear the Indian influence on the recording, but not the *implications* of that influence for Tjinder. The references to postcolonialism are often prominent (as his "hip-hop brunch" quote above might suggest). Sometimes they are veiled cleverly, in what can only be described as Singh's poetic lyric. In "Sleep on the Left Side," he observes:

> . . . No Asian lyre
> Will leave us dyre [*sic*]
> Born again into Asian line
> There comes no telling
> How it will be
> What gets turned to smoke
> Was in our hearts
> And planets up
> What we have lost
> Sleep on the left side
> Keep the sword hand free
> Arrrh, wuttevess gonna be is
> Gone nu be"[12]

The "keep the sword hand free" gives the chorus a not-so-vaguely aristocratic tone reminiscent of the language of conquest and adventure. That throws the "we" in the song into a slippery position. Does that mean that the line, "and planet's up what we have lost," refers to the actual losing of territory (as in the British losing so much of the planet with the dissolution of the colonies)? Is "we" Singh and his Western audience chatting casually on the lawn? Or does it refer to something more spiritual? Perhaps what he himself has lost? Is the reference to keeping the sword hand free a commentary on needing to always be ready to fight? The origin of the phrase does, after all, refer to keeping one's sword hand free in case of surprise attack in the night—so that one could be instantly ready to fight if awakened by an enemy.

But who is the "we" implied by the imperative tone here, and who should "sleep on the left side" in anticipation of attack? Leaving these questions open helps facilitate the postcolonial stance, a sort of "postmodern polyamory," in which love of things "Indian," "English," and more generally "Western" can remain side by side *without* ever resolving the intense conflicts among them.

He follows with "Brimful of Asha," the homage to Indian film music and singers like Asha Bosle whose movies he watched in England growing up. The lyric "everybody needs a bosom for a pillow/Mine's on the 45 (rpm)" is, despite its subject matter and opening lines spoken in Punjabi, a Western pop creation. The subject matter waxes nostalgic for Indian roots, but the form and genre clarifies a Western position. It is not too surprising that this was the big hit of the album.[13]

More interesting in terms of colonial references is the song, "Funky Days Are Back Again," with its opening sample of someone popping the top on a soda can (an obscure nod to the Coca-Cola of track 5?), and the lyrics:

Well it seems like the funky days, they're back again
Funky funky days are back again
And we're in vogue again
Before the gurkers [*sic*] get called up again

"Before the gurkers get called up again"? This reference was confusing at first, but a quick click on my computer to Microsoft's *Encarta* (and some serious fudging around with spelling) revealed the following:

Gurkhas, Nepalese mercenaries known for their bravery and fighting skills. Gurkha soldiers come from several different ethnic backgrounds within Nepal and have a military tradition dating from the sixteenth century. Their fame spread throughout the world after they fought the British army in the Anglo–Nepalese War (1814–1816) over Nepal's southward and Britain's northward expansion in India. Although the British defeated Nepal, they were so impressed by the Gurkha fighters that they enticed them to enter the British (and subsequently, Indian) army. The Gurkhas, known for carrying razor-sharp curved knives called *kukris,* have fought in nearly all of the world's major wars and have earned Britain's highest service awards, including the Victoria Cross. (*Microsoft® Encarta® Encyclopedia 99*)

Encarta notes that the Gurkhas were "enticed" into the British army to fight for the British; with this one word we are thrown startlingly back full circle to the theoretical underpinnings of postcolonialism. The word "entice" may, and probably does, stand in for a complex web of coercion, complicity, hegemonic construction, or all-out physical threat that marked the experience of the Gurkhas. Certainly the definition implies much about the aspects of economy, status, social order, and political change.

By casually referencing Gurkhas, Singh creates an ironic stance in which once again the term "we" is thrown into question. If the "funky days are back again" until the "Gurkhas get called up again"—what is exactly "funky" about these days? Whereas "Sleep on the Left Side" seems subtly to reference English tradition and "gentleman's adventure," the reference to Gurkhas throws it squarely back into the resistance context. As a result, the line "and we're in vogue again" now can only refer to Singh's Indian identity.

"Being 'Indian' might well be 'in' now," Singh declares, "but five years ago, we started the amalgamation of those ideas and we've still not got the credit. It's very unfortunate. We don't give a fuck about Asian elements, this east-meets-fucking West. That's bullocks. Tacky nonsense" (Grant 1997).

If "language becomes the medium through which a hierarchical structure of power is perpetuated, the medium through which conceptions of 'truth,' 'order,' and 'reality' become established" (Ashcroft et al. 1989, 7), then Singh's wordplay, in the context of his Western-style songs and preternatural elisions of sonic space, can be seen as a commentary in themselves. Conceiving of a world in which all of the musical styles, sonic fragments, and traditional grooves coexist in a flat plain, devoid of barriers, is to fashion "an alternative way of conceiving human history . . . [a] reconception . . . based on breaking down the barriers between cultures" (Said 1993, 216), not "east-meets-fucking west-tacky-nonsense." Using country music ("Good to Be on the Road Back Home") with funk ("Butter the Soul," etc.), or rap ("Candyman") with pop ("Brimful" or "Good Shit"), is perhaps Singh's musical way of saying, "I want you each and all to switch yr [*sic*] tiny mind on."

Singh may certainly claim that he doesn't care much about Asian elements and that nothing he does should be seen in a political context of postcolonial rhetoric. Yet, with this, I believe, he underestimates his listeners, who are going to draw their own conclusions, rather than trusting entirely what Singh, in his haste for ironic detachment, may say. As many of their concert reviews reveal, these guys aren't exactly magic with an audience and quite possibly don't care what conclusions it may draw. Review after review from shows all over the globe refer to Cornershop's practice of "avoiding eye contact with the audience" (Pareles 1996).

Cornershop cheated fans a bit in the entertainment department. On drawn-out instrumental portions of songs, Singh's sidekick Ben Ayers [*sic*] sat languidly and strummed away. Singh abstained from between-song banter, lazily wandering the stage like a weedhead wondering which guitar he should play. (Brown 1998)

Singh would charitably be described as shy and enigmatic; uncharitably as completely lacking in charisma." (Gray 1998, 8)

Perhaps what reviewers and audiences alike perceive is their own superfluity to Singh's music. It is in the end a deeply personal music created by an artist acutely aware (though perhaps in some denial) of his own position in a complicated postcolonial landscape populated by webs of intertwining oppression, conflicting realities, and danger. Indeed, Cornershop's own identity as a musical enterprise is far from set. Their newest release is not under the name "Cornershop" at all, but rather "Clinton."[14] Their willingness to slip out of the name that made them (somewhat) famous, so soon after doing so, is not very common in the music business, where bands or musicians can develop a name that comes close to the recognizability of a Western brand name like "Coca Cola" or "IBM." A name, once established, ensures that one will at least get a hearing, whether in the end the music deserves it or not.

Is this name-switch a final stab at the identity politics that might otherwise essentialize Singh's work into "India Pop?" To align himself with his own personal heritage is to invite an enormous pressure to remain transfixed in the rigid stereotypes that identity implies in the West. His work is in danger of being essentialized by its very existence. Sidestepping that, in part by shifting gears as "Clinton" and putting out more dance records, can be seen as a sign of restless creator working on a "side project" or a sophisticated attempt to avoid being ghettoized as "that Indian DJ."

"If you feel you have been denied the chance to speak your piece, you will try extremely hard to get that chance," Edward Said wrote ([1978] 1994, 335). But in current culture, single chances relegate one to the category of a "one-trick-pony," or, as it is known in the music business, a "one-hit wonder." Struggling against the weight of a saturating hegemonic system, in which his own music conspires against him, leaves Singh in a difficult position. Not only must he struggle to "get that chance," he must, to remain in the spotlight long enough, escape the pressure to remain faithful to a "schizophonic" subject position. Avoiding eye contact with his audience, he avoids staring directly at the biggest threat to his hybridized identity: his audience.

NOTES

1. For an elegant discussion and dissection of the complex web of appropriations which bring the "Pygmies" and their music into the global spotlight, see Feld 1996.

2. I refer, of course, to *Vision: The Music of Hildegard of Bingen* (Angel CDC 7243 1994), which contains "original compositions, arrangements, and interpretations performed by Richard Souther." The liner notes also point out: "The idea was to record Hildegard von Bingen's music in its purest form and marry it to the imaginative concepts of the contemporary American composer Richard Souther, using contemporary pop and world-music sounds that reinvent the startling immediacy, the piercing beauty, and the sublime spirit of Hildegard's art" (see Taylor 1997a). With statements like "*Vision* is a collaboration between two creative artists who never met," Souther reveals that the idea of collaboration with those who cannot possibly have creative say in the process is not only a Western/non-Western phenomenon.

3. The misspelling of these musicologists' names, which should be Zemp and Arom, may give a hint as to the level of their involvement in the project.

4. For a useful discussion about the politics using field recordings, see also Guy n.d. Many thanks to Nancy Guy sharing her draft for this chapter.

5. Timothy Taylor's recent work on a similar recording, Engima's *Return to Innocence*, which also contains indigenous music repackaged in a sort of "new-agey electronica" feel-good skin, provided me with an elegant framework for my dis-ease (Taylor 1997b); see also his work on Paul Simon's 1986 *Graceland* release (Taylor 1993).

6. Recent releases include *OK* by Talvin Singh (no relation to Tjinder), which combines complex talas and Indian classical vocal music with drum 'n' bass/Electronica beats, Asian Dub Federation, and club recordings such as *Bombay the Hard Way: Guns, Cars & Sitars,* by Dan "The Automator" Nakamura (who also produced some tracks on Cornershop's *7th Time*), which uses film music mostly taken from the 1970s B-movies of "Bollywood." The latter release is particularly interesting in that the music is mostly fashioned after the popularity of Western styles of the period, like funk and disco. It is especially worthwhile to note the influence of the 1970s fashion on Tjinder Singh, which will be addressed later in the chapter. The Sabri Brothers have also brought Sufi devotional music (Qawwali) to a wide Western audience. In 1996, it was Cornershop opening for the Sabri Brothers that made critic Jon Pareles note "the Sabri Brothers made the rockers (Cornershop) sound like beginners" (Pareles 1996; see also Pareles 1995).

7. Loomba (1998) offers an excellent introduction to the field. This study would not have been possible without Loomba's work.

8. I speak here specifically about Morrissey, whose *Bengali in Platforms* and *Asian Rut* were seen, in the early 1990s, as evidence of his acceptance of British stereotyping of Indian immigrant culture.

9. I cite this detail here because it is included in the reporting of the story by Jon Wiederdorn in *Rolling Stone* and in order to remain faithful to the report—not because I have any evidence that the man was either drunken or Irish. There are layers of circumstances here which make the inclusion of the fact that the assailant was

"drunk" and "Irish"—a classically English stereotype used to separate the "sober" English subject from the "drunken, Irish colony." The fact that one "colonial subject" would meet another "post colonial" subject on the street and hit him for being there with an English woman is a paper in itself.

10. The complete list is included in chapter 2 of this volume, pages 16–17.

11. Before moving on to define traits I associate with postcolonial music, I should first define some of the terms that will be tossed about. For the sake of discussion, when I speak of colonialism, I refer specifically to the "conquest and control of other people's lands and goods" (Loomba 1998, 2). It is a continuing process that relies on a complex web of physical and social threat (hegemony) to maintain. Imperialism, separate from the fact of colonialism itself, is the political will or drive to overtake others. One can be an imperialist society without actually having colonies outside its borders. Nonetheless, imperialism is always present in one form or another in the act of colonialism.

12. Lyrics from the Luaka Bop home page for Cornershop. Luaka Bop home page at http://www.luakabop.com/cornershop/. For the purposes of this essay, I have relied on the lyrics as printed on the web site, the only place where they are generally available. There are a number of small differences from official lyrics as transmitted by the record label.

"No Asian fire will leave us dire,
born again into Asian line.
There comes no tellin' how it will be,
what's turned to smoke was in our hearts
and planets up what we have lost

Sleep on the left side keep the sword hand free,
oh whatever's gonna be is gonna be"

———

"Well it seems like the funky days they're back again
Funky, funky days they're back again,
and we're en vogue again
before the Gurkhars [*sic*] get called up again"

13. Despite the band's hope for "Butter the Soul" or "Good Shit" (which is a good match for "Brimful" in terms of accessibility by audiences unfamiliar with both Indian pop and electronic music) to follow "Brimful" to the top of the British Pop charts, neither has.

14. They insist that this is also not a tip toward politics, but rather that the word sounds "phat."

WORKS CITED

Ashcroft, Bill, Gareth Griffiths, and Helen Tiffin. 1989. *The Empire Writes Back: Theory and Practice in Postcolonial Literatures.* London: Routledge.

Brown, G. 1998. "Cornershop on Stage Not Quite Record Caliber." *Denver Post* (June 10), Living section: F5.

Feld, Steven. 1996. "pygmy POP: A Genealogy of Schizophonic Mimesis." *Yearbook for Traditional Music* 28: 1–35.

Fricke, David. 1997. "Ragas-a-Go-Go." *Rolling Stone* (October 30): 24

Grant, Kieran. 1997. "Can't Corner Cornershop." *Toronto Sun* (November 15).

Guy, Nancy. n.d. "Trafficking in Taiwan Aboriginal Voices: Dilemmas in the Use of Field Recordings." In *Getting It All Back? Problems, Possibilities, and Dilemmas in Repatriating Ethonographic Field* Materials *to the Pacific*, edited by Sjoerd R. Jaarsma.

Gray, W. Blake. 1998. "On Stage, Singh Squirms." *Yomiuri Shimbun (Daily Yomiuri)* (April 23): 8.

Hebert, James. 1998. "Out-of-This-World Music; Cornershop: A British Band that Just Can't Be Painted into a Corner." *San Diego Union-Tribune* (June 11).

Hiransomboon, Andrew. 1998. "Brimful of Cool: Cornershop Makes Modern Music with Traditional South Asian Accents." *Bangkok Post* (June 5).

Jacoby, Russell. 1995. "Marginal Returns: The Trouble with Postcolonial Theory." *Lingua Franca* (September/October): 30–37.

Kramer, Jonathan D. 1996. "Postmodern Concepts of Musical Time." *Indiana Theory Review* 17/2: 21–61.

Loomba, Ania. 1998. *Colonial/Postcolonial: The New Critical Idiom.* London: Routledge.

Microsoft® Encarta® Encyclopedia 99. "Gurkhas." © 1993–98 . Microsoft Corporation.

Pareles, Jon. 1995. "Working Out Anglo-Indian Rock's Cross-Cultural Options." *New York Times* (November 23): C24.

———. 1996. "Scaling Mystic Heights on a Driving Sufi Beat." *New York Times* (November 5): C18.

Said, Edward. [1978] 1994. *Orientalism.* New York: Routledge.

———. 1993. *Culture and Imperialism.* New York: Alfred A. Knopf.

Taylor, Timothy D. 1993. "The Voracious Muse: Contemporary Cross-Cultural Musical Borrowings, Culture, and Postmodernism." Ph.D. diss., University of Michigan.

———. 1997a. "A Riddle Wrapped in a Mystery: Transnational Music Sampling and Enigma's 'Return to Innocence.'" Paper presented at the meeting of the American Musicological Society, Phoenix, November 1, 1997.

———. 1997b. *Global Pop: World Music, World Markets.* New York: Routledge.

Wiederdorn, Jon. 1996. "Cornershop Curry Western Flavor: London Bridge." *Rolling Stone* (February 22): 32.

CHAPTER 9

Production vs. Reception in Postmodernism:

The Górecki Case

Luke Howard

In February 1993, a new recording of Henryk Górecki's Third Symphony, the "Symphony of Sorrowful Songs," reached the no. 6 position on the British pop album charts, outselling new releases by Madonna and REM.[1] It was twice the fastest climber on that chart, achieving silver and gold record status in the same week, while in the United States it appeared on *Billboard*'s classical charts for 134 consecutive weeks. Never before had a recording of any piece of art music attained such sudden and spectacular success; that it should happen with a slow and somber contemporary symphonic work by a relatively unknown Polish composer was, to many observers, even more bizarre.[2]

In subsequent years, Górecki's symphony has insinuated itself so deeply into the ears and minds of a new, predominantly young audience that the repercussions of that phenomenon continue to sound long after the symphony's notoriety had crested. One of the more unusual manifestations of this phenomenon is in the work of pop musicians who have taken Górecki's popularity and crossover appeal as a point of departure, creating songs that combine pop styles and technologies with quotations or references to Górecki's music.

In the ways that it challenges traditional boundaries between "high" and "low," past and present, elitism and populism, this body of work and the whole Górecki phenomenon might be viewed as quintessentially postmodern. For example, taking Fredric Jameson's essay "Postmodernism and Consumer Society" as a measure, it would be easy to label Górecki's symphony itself as postmodern. Jameson posits two general principles that unite many of the varieties of postmodernisms across the arts: first, an effacement of key boundaries, especially the distinction between high culture and mass culture; and second, a specific reaction against high-modernism (Jameson 1983, 111–12). But if the Górecki phenomenon in general (and not just his symphony specifically) is to be understood as postmodern, then the focus must move beyond the cultural artifact alone to consider issues of reception and the audience.

The task of determining which aspects of the phenomenon may be profitably understood from the vantage point of postmodernism is made even more difficult by the web of myth, media hype, and misinformation that surrounds the Górecki case. Clearly the best-selling recording of the Third Symphony, released on the Elektra–Nonesuch label in 1992, effaced some very obvious and long-standing boundaries. Its level of popular success, especially among young listeners used to MTV and alternative rock, challenged the whole notion of a dichotomy between "high" culture and pop culture to the extent that the composer was labeled by the press a "hero of Generation X" (Croan 1994). Concurrently, Górecki's music began to infiltrate another principal channel of pop culture—the movie industry—where it continued to be associated with pop music. Peter Weir's 1993 film, *Fearless* (starring Jeff Bridges, Isabella Rosellini, and Rosie Perez), uses lengthy excerpts of the Third Symphony alongside tracks by the Gipsy Kings. The soundtrack for Julian Schnabel's *Basquiat* (1996) includes the Third Symphony and songs by Joy Division, Public Image Ltd., and other pop artists. And Bertrand Blier's 1996 soft-core porn film, *Mon Homme*, juxtaposes Górecki's lesser-known Second Symphony with the sultry verbal foreplay of Barry White. Through its appeal to young listeners, and its association with pop musicians and cinema, Górecki's music had clearly entered the realm of popular culture.

Conforming to Jameson's second criteria of postmodernism, the Third Symphony, with its relative consonance and readily coherent form, provocatively challenged the prevailing stylistic traits of high modernism that prevailed in the mid-1970s, when it was composed. Premiered at the 1977 International Festival of Contemporary Art in Royan, France—one of the most important avant-garde festivals of the time—it was largely a critical failure in that venue. Alan Rusbridger (1993) later reported in the *(London) Guardian* that one "prominent French musician" (possibly Boulez, though Górecki doesn't name him specifically) let out a very audible "Merde!" as the symphony's final chords died away. Some of the critics in attendance even questioned whether the work belonged at such a festival, admitting that it was unquestionably "beautiful" but, therefore, not sufficiently avant-garde (Kanski 1977, 15). In a telling comment that positions this work as post–"high modernist," if not expressly postmodernist, Górecki told a reporter for the *(London) Independent* that he considered his symphony the most truly avant-garde piece he heard at the festival.

Though the Third Symphony appears to satisfy Jameson's two criteria cited above, such a case for its "postmodern" status would be misguided. In particular, the "effacement of boundaries" did not begin until years after the work was premiered, suggesting that there was little that might be regarded as inherently postmodern in the music itself, and it was regarded as reactionary only in the very narrow and specific context of a particular avant-garde festival. If there is a case to be made for a postmodernist interpretation of the Górecki phenomenon in general, then it would appear to hinge on the symphony's popularity in the 1990s, and the pop musicians who quote or reference Górecki's music in their own work.

Even before the Third Symphony's phenomenal success in 1993, it had begun to intrigue and influence pop musicians. The English industrial group Test Department played recorded excerpts of the symphony in a pre-concert mixed-media collage during their "Unacceptable Face of Freedom" tour in 1985–86, and in several smaller concerts before then, years before the work had even been given its British concert premiere.[3] Test Department gave a tape of the symphony to the young British composer Steve Martland, who indicated in 1991 that there was a burgeoning underground interest in the work at the time, fueled by young musicians trading pirate copies of the symphony (Martland 1991, 45).

As the Third Symphony's popularity grew in late 1992 in early 1993, its connections with the world of commercial music accelerated. Warner, the parent company for the Elektra–Nonesuch recording label, advertised the symphony as one of its Christmas specials in 1992, alongside Madonna's *Erotica*, REM's *Automatic for the People*, and a re-release of Mike Oldfield's *Tubular Bells*. A more direct interface with pop music occurred in 1993, when the Norwegian "goth"-music band Ildfrost sampled the opening of the Third Symphony on their track "Hearts Perturb" from the *Absolute Supper* album. Over a foundation of cellos and basses quoted from the opening of the symphony's first movement, Ildfrost layered speech fragments, radio noise, synthesized chords, and choral interjections, creating a softly ambient sonic collage. A similar procedure was followed by Faust, the famed *Krautrock* band from the '70s, who in 1994 produced their first studio album in over twenty years, *Rien*. In the track "Eroberung der Stille, Teil 1," the opening orchestral canon from the symphony's first movement serves as a scaffold for Faust's trademark industrial noises and violent vocalizing. Ildfrost's track seems relatively innocuous compared with the political and aesthetic implications of Faust's Górecki quotation. Faust's artistic manifesto, released in 1973, promotes a situationist absurdity whose intent and intensity transcend the blank eclecticism of Ildfrost's collage. The common (though inaccurate) perception of Górecki's Third Symphony as an anti-Nazi work (Howard 1997) resonates with Faust's ongoing attempts to confront Germany's history through music. Rather than being merely a sonic aggregate, Faust's appropriation of Górecki is a tightly constructed anti-fascist political statement that coalesces as the listener connects the disparate sonic layers, linking the sampled screams with the violent subtexts of Górecki's symphony, the helicopter sounds and the industrial noise with the machinery of war. This postmodernist placement of meaning within the listener (as opposed to a meaning situated in the musical work itself) is one of Faust's primary aesthetic goals. As stated in their manifesto:

> Faust have mentioned that working as they do in the space between concept & realisation they are in fact doing nothing. Faust would like to play for you the *sound of yourself listening*.
>
> Then we would have consciousness.
>
> then we could talk about altering that consciousness.
>
> then we could forget about the music.[4]

The same year that Faust issued the *Rien* album, William Orbit recorded electronic versions of some Górecki pieces, alongside works by Satie, Barber, and Arvo Pärt, and planned to release the recording under the title *Pieces in A Modern Style*. The title is a play on Górecki's *Three Pieces in Olden Style* (a favorite "filler" track on many recordings of the Third Symphony), from which Orbit had arranged two pieces for synthesizer. Publishing-house lawyers threatened to file lawsuits over the unauthorized arrangements of the Pärt and Górecki pieces (which were still protected by copyright), and the recording was pulled from the shelves the week of its release.[5]

Repeating Test Department's experiment of a decade earlier, the Smashing Pumpkins played taped excerpts of the Third Symphony as a pre-concert warm-up for audiences during their 1996 world tour. At a concert in Auckland, New Zealand, on May 23, 1996, the mosh-pit became dangerously crowded. Concert management turned on the floodlights and re-broadcast the symphony over the sound system in an effort to calm the audience. A local rock critic, who described the scene as a "crowd crush ballet" continued his account: "Under harsh fluoro lights, hundreds of kids were being pulled out of the steaming, squirming mass of greasy hair and wet t-shirts to the sound of Henryk Górecki's Symphony No. 3. Ominous cellos bellowing out of the speakers as bouncers struggled to save the fearful young kids who got more than they bargained for."[6] This event occurred only days after a teenage girl had been crushed to death at a Smashing Pumpkins concert in Dublin, Ireland. In this case, Górecki's symphony may have helped save some young lives, while recalling in its lyrics the grief of tragically young deaths.

All these examples involve wholesale quotation or sampling, where the audience would be expected to recognize Górecki's music in the new context. But equally as significant as the musical borrowings themselves is the ease with which rock journalists and reviewers refer to these Górecki quotations in their articles, without explanation or elaboration. His music was so well-known among rock/pop audiences that these writers assumed knowledge of Górecki's symphony among their readership.

In addition to these overt quotations, other mainly British pop musicians have produced works where Górecki's influence is much more subtle. Meriel Barham, the lead singer and guitarist for the British group Pale Saints, once said in an interview that Górecki is the only classical composer she listens to.[7] According to the interviewer, Górecki lends name and musical inspiration to the track "Henry" from the Pale Saints' 1994 album *Slow Buildings*. The reference to Górecki is an esoteric one, as the musical style of this song is far removed from that of the Third Symphony, and there are no allusions to him or his music in the lyrics. There are, however, some slight connections that may indicate a subtle influence. At 10'47" it is rather long for a pop song, pushing the envelope of the genre just as the Third Symphony tested the limits of continuous adagio composition. "Henry" is based on a constantly repeating two-chord ostinato, a slow non-cadential progression in a minor key from consonance to slight dissonance that may refer obliquely to the opening of the symphony's third movement, though it's also not out of place in standard pop repertoires.

The closest reference to Górecki's music steals in almost unnoticed at the end of "Henry," where Pale Saints directly sample two orchestral chords from a later passage in the third movement of the Third Symphony. Pale Saints downplay the borrowing by quoting it in a different harmonic context, and not introducing it until the song's final fade is well under way (it is barely perceptible at normal volume levels). Once identified, the reference is unmistakable, though it is deeply buried in the musical form and texture, and not likely to be discernible to most listeners.

The English "future bebop" duo Lamb (Andy Barlow and Louise Rhodes) have had some success with the song "Górecki," from their debut self-titled album, released in 1996. "Górecki" made it into the U.K. pop Top 40 in late 1996, was included on the soundtracks for *Girlstown* and *I Still Know What You Did Last Summer*, and was featured in a third-season episode of *La Femme Nikita*.[8] The instrumental remix became something of a dance-club favorite in the United States and Europe. The Third Symphony's influence on this song is more overt than in the Pale Saints' work, and not merely by virtue of the title. Like "Henry," Lamb's song alternates two slow chords in non-cadential progression in a minor key, but it also features a background arrangement of orchestral strings, along with the Górecki thumbprint of punctuating piano notes sustained by string chords.

The song's opening line of text, "If I should die this very moment, I wouldn't fear," is analogous to the symphony's second movement, which sets the courageous pleas of a young woman facing imminent death. But if Lamb's slightly cryptic lyrics seem more like a love song ("I've found the one I've waited for . . ."), then it is important to remember that the Third Symphony is also inherently about a strong emotional bond, that between a mother and child, as much as it is about death. As in the Pale Saints' song, the clearest musical reference comes in an understated conclusion. The final note of "Górecki" is a low sustained E on the bass: an identical musical gesture (in pitch, register, and instrumentation) to the conclusion of the symphony's first movement.

As this song's popularity was peaking, there were media reports that Lamb, like the Pale Saints, had actually sampled the Third Symphony. While there doesn't appear to be any direct sampling from a recording of the symphony, Lamb's Andy Barlow didn't exactly deny the reports either. He did admit that sometimes he will tape musicians as they play a composition, and then sample those sounds.[9] If this is the case in "Górecki," then the background string arrangements and the song's final low E on bass may have a closer, direct origin in the Third Symphony.[10]

In a 1997 review of Lamb's "Górecki," the reviewer claimed that the Third Symphony had been "more ably and slyly referenced in Tricky's re-imagination of Garbage's 'Milk,'" than it was in Lamb's song.[11] Garbage—a noise-pop band out of Madison, Wisconsin, but led by the sultry Scottish redhead Shirley Manson—recorded "Milk" as the final track on their 1996 self-titled debut album. The popular and critical success of this album prompted the release of a CD single that included two remixes of "Milk," one of them by Tricky, the Bristol-born "trip-hop" musician who had previously worked with the Bristol bands Massive Attack and Portishead (the band with which, incidentally, Lamb is most often compared). The original version of "Milk" shares much in common with Lamb's "Górecki." Both are in the same key (E-minor) as the opening movement of the Third Symphony, and both feature a slow simple harmonic progression as the basis for the song. The repeated refrain in "Milk"—"I'm waiting, I'm waiting for you"—is closely related in textual theme to the refrain of Lamb's "Górecki" ("I've found the one I've waited for").

The repeated text—"I'm waiting"—is set to a three-note motif of a rising minor third, followed by a descending half-step. Adrian Thomas, in his study of Górecki's music, has identified this motif as the "Skierkowski turn" (Thomas 1997, 85, 91), a characteristic figure in Polish folksong and in much of Górecki's oeuvre, but especially apparent in all movements of the Third Symphony. While Garbage's "Milk" might exhibit these similar features with the Third Symphony only coincidentally (there is no evidence to suggest Górecki's music influenced Garbage *directly*), Tricky makes the most of these similarities and explicitly alludes to the symphony in his remix. His whispered doubling of Manson's breathy delivery is juxtaposed against brief snippets of a classically-trained soprano singing a rising four-note scale (from E to A in E-minor). It is precisely the same musical gesture as the first vocal entry in the symphony's first movement. While the soprano voice in Tricky's remix has been altered in the studio, the vowels are identical to those in Górecki's text (*"Synku,"* Polish for "my son"), and the halo of orchestral strings that surround this vocal excerpt further suggest that it might be an actual sample from the symphony.

The other remix of "Milk" on this CD single is by the British jungle/drum 'n' bass musician, Goldie, who would later release his own tribute to Górecki on his 1998 *Saturnz Return* album. Issued as a double CD set, the first disc of *Saturnz Return* consists almost entirely of the track "Mother," Goldie's tribute not only to his own mother, but to Górecki and the Third Symphony. He had been introduced to the symphony by fellow musician and former girlfriend Björk. Goldie later admitted, "Björk showed me Górecki, and Górecki showed me something else. Don't fuck with Górecki. I love him so much. I just went and smashed his head with a sledge-hammer and pulled out his whole brain, and that's what "Mother" is."[12]

In this song, Goldie works completely outside of his idiom.[13] He eschews the jungle rhythms and rapid drum 'n' bass tempi that made his *Timeless* album so popular. Instead, he writes a slow track for thirty-piece string orchestra, with added ambient synthesized sound and digital echo. Described by one critic as "monstrously long, desperately ambitious," "Mother" is, at over an hour in length, actually longer than the symphony that inspired it.[14]

Over sustained string clusters (borrowing another Górecki thumbprint), Goldie repeats a call to his mother using the three-note motif of the "Skierkowski turn," as well as a variation on it consisting of just the descending half-step. Often in Górecki's music, this motif and its variant represent a call for divine help, though in the second movement of the Third Symphony it is used explicitly for the word *"Mamo,"* a Polish word for "mother." This seems to be the passage that provided the most direct inspiration for Goldie's "Mother."

Goldie has been severely criticized for what might be regarded as this self-indulgent, hypertrophic work. Steven Segerman wrote, "This spooky and esoteric piece tells us very little about Goldie's mom but I'm sure that every time he hears or plays it, it serves some Oedipal-curative function in his subconscious and that's sweet."[15] But in this regard Goldie also mimics Górecki, who has manifested a fixation with the maternal in several of his compositions. Górecki's mother died on his second birthday, and his sense of loss is plainly expressed in works such as the Three Songs (Op. 3), *Ad matrem*, and of course the Third Symphony.[16]

It was the grieving emotional focus of the Third Symphony that influenced the work of Craig Armstrong, a classically-trained Scottish composer who has also done orchestral arrangements for Madonna, U2, Massive Attack, and other prominent pop artists. Górecki's influence is most conspicuous in Armstrong's work on Baz Luhrman's 1996 film *William Shakespeare's "Romeo and Juliet,"*[17] which also included pop songs by Des'ree, Butthole Surfers, and (significantly, in this context) Garbage. In Armstrong's underscoring for the young lovers' double suicide at the climax of the movie (titled "Death Scene" on the soundtrack), the allusion to Górecki's symphony is overt and obviously intentional. Armstrong imitates the vocal climax of the symphony's first movement, resonating with the soprano soloist's text in that passage: "Because you are already leaving me, my cherished hope." Both the passage from the symphony and Armstrong's cue begin with an open octave in the orchestral strings, and a sustained pedal-point as a soprano sings a rising minor-mode scale (Phrygian in the symphony, harmonic minor in Armstrong's cue). Both feature a huge orchestral crescendo as the singer reaches the end of her phrase, and both resolve this crescendo into an intricate web of *fortissimo* orchestral counterpoint at the climax. Armstrong must have known that the audience for this movie would include many of the young consumers who had responded so enthusiastically to Górecki's symphony, and who continued to enjoy the music of Lamb, Goldie, Garbage, and Tricky. The reference is therefore not merely coincidental or opportune, but an astutely placed symbol of the acceptance of Górecki's music within the idioms of pop culture; a connection that many in the movie theater would have recognized immediately.

Each of these examples—the symphony itself and the commercial music that alludes to it—have clearly challenged the boundaries between high art and mass culture, thus satisfying one of Jameson's postmodern principles. The issue becomes a little more complex when we consider what Jameson suggests is the *practice* of postmodernism: namely, "pastiche" and "temporal schizophrenia." He defines pastiche as "the imitation, or better still, the mimicry of other styles and particularly the mannerisms and stylistic twitches of other styles" (Jameson 1983, 113). It's exactly the mannerisms of Górecki's music—the alternating chords, the Skierkowski turn, the rich string-dominated orchestrations—that Pale Saints, Lamb, Tricky, Goldie, and Armstrong have mimicked, and that Ildfrost, Faust, and Orbit have borrowed. But Jameson outlines only two possible motivations for stylistic imitation: one that mocks the original model (which he labels "parody") and one that is emotionally neutral, or "pastiche," which he describes as "blank parody; parody that has lost its sense of humor" (114). Convinced that contemporary culture—"a world in which stylistic innovation is no longer possible" (115)—has lost the ability or inclination to admire, Jameson fails to acknowledge another kind of mimicry, namely, that which functions as *hommage*. The primary reason, I would argue, that each of these commercial musicians, from Test Department in the mid-'80s to Goldie in the late-'90s, appropriated Górecki's music is that they had been deeply affected by it, just as Górecki himself appropriated Chopin and Beethoven out of sincere respect.

When Jameson talks about the second of his criteria for postmodern practice, "temporal schizophrenia," he uses the term not in the clinical sense, but as it is understood by Lacan: the discontinuity of linear time and an uncertainty about the historical past (Jameson 1983, 118–19). He states, "Our entire contemporary social system has little by little begun to lose its capacity to retain its own past, and has begun to live in a perpetual present. . . . [The media] serve as the very agents and mechanisms for our historical amnesia" (125).

Just one small example from the Górecki phenomenon suffices to suggest this may not be entirely true. Each of the three texts from the Third Symphony is historical, and unapologetically so. The first movement sets a fifteenth-century text based on the theme of Mary at the foot of the cross, the second is a graffito from a Gestapo prison cell wall, and the third an early twentieth-century Polish folk text about a political uprising. Each of these texts has tremendous immediacy, especially for Poles but also for the many others who have interpreted the symphony as a memorial or a cathartic expression of grief. Górecki's musical setting aids the listener in understanding the texts' historical narrative, and confirms that his approach to the past remains essentially linear. The oldest text, that of the first movement, is preceded by a lengthy canonic exposition in the orchestra. After the short text, the canon starts up again and proceeds to unravel itself in reverse, ending exactly where it started, with a low E in the double basses. It is as if Górecki uses the orchestral prelude and postlude as a kind of musical time-machine to carry listeners to the distant past, then bring them back to the present.[18] The most recent text, the second movement, has the shortest orchestral introduction and conclusion. The third movement continues the pattern, suggesting that the composer used this technique consciously to represent the texts' relative historical distance. Additionally, the composer quotes the symphony's oldest musical sources (Polish hymn and folksong) in the first movement, which sets the oldest of the three texts. The second oldest text quotes Chopin and Beethoven, and the most recent text makes no direct use of pre-existent music. Thus, in this composition that was so widely disseminated through mass media, Jameson's blanket claim for historical amnesia appears somewhat overstated.

The divisions between "high" art and mass culture (however permeable or imaginary they may be in the first place) have clearly been breached. The key issue is one that Jameson points to in the title of his essay: the "consumer society." It was the collective consumer, not the composer, who crossed traditional boundaries in listening and responding to the recording of the symphony. It was the *reception* of the symphony, rather than its *production*, that initiated this crossing of boundaries and the subsequent amalgamation of symphony with pop song. If we continue to emphasize cultural production in our understanding of postmodernism, then it will remain merely a function of artistic intention and the art object itself. But if we acknowledge the role of cultural consumption, then Górecki's symphony and the commercial music that references it become part of a much larger experiential phenomenon, a postmodernism that we, the audience, define and create.

NOTES

1. As indicated in the list of recordings, at least three earlier recordings (and several reissues on various labels) were already available in commercial release at the time Elektra-Nonesuch released their version in 1992.

2. For a more comprehensive discussion of the "Górecki phenomenon" and the reception of the Third Symphony, see Howard 1997.

3. The first concert performance of the Third Symphony in England was given on September 20, 1988, by the City of Birmingham Symphony Orchestra, with David Atherton conducting and Margaret Field as soprano soloist.

4. from the website http://195.92.248.101:802/faust/manifesto.asp.

5. Orbit subsequently received permission to include the Górecki tracks; *Pieces in a Modern Style* (though still without the Pärt arrangements) was released February 2000.

6. This concert review was published online at http://www.iwi.net.nikki/ripup.htm (this URL no longer functions).

7. Interview and recording review published online under the pseudonym "Yellow Peril," http://www.cia.com.au/peril/texts/features/pale.htm.

8. Episode 306, "Cat and Mouse."

9. Sam Quicksilver, "Fabulous Fusion," http://www.letitberecords.com/zine/archives/features/lamb.html.

10. Significantly, the two-chord ostinato that Górecki uses in the third movement of the symphony is borrowed from the opening of Chopin's A-minor Mazurka, Op. 17/4, and the piano punctuations in the same movement are a subtle reference to the crunching climax in Beethoven's "Eroica" Symphony (Thomas 1997, 92–93). It seems that Górecki "samples" in precisely the same way the Lamb does, with an almost transparent subtlety that still manages to keep the allusion intact.

11. P. N. Bryant, "Circa," http://alivewired.com/19970703/music/html.

12. http://web.ict.nsk.su/house/interviews/goldie_1.html.

13. Goldie later remixed "Mother" as an eight-minute drum 'n' bass dance track on the EP album *Ring of Saturn*, released in 1999.

14. http://web.ict.nsk.su/house/interviews/goldie_1.html. Another critic, apparently unaware of the direct connection to Górecki's Third Symphony, wrote that the main orchestral motive in "Mother" is "as darkly emotive and starkly spiritual as anything by Górecki or Tavener." (See Steven Dalton's review at http://www.nme.com/reviews/reviews/19980101000236reviews.html.)

15. Steven Segerman, online review of *Saturnz Return*, http://home.intekom.com/intenew/Exlore/Entertainment/Reviews/Goldie.html.

16. For a more detailed discussion of Górecki and the maternal bond, see Harley 1998.

17. The various interactions between Górecki and Shakespeare are so numerous they perhaps merit an entirely separate study. For instance, Armstrong's reference to Górecki in this movie parallels Górecki's own admission that he was an ardent fan of the film version of Bernstein's *West Side Story*, which is based on the same Shakespeare play. (Coincidentally, Dawn Upshaw, the soprano soloist on Elektra–Nonesuch's recording of the Third Symphony, is likewise a fan of *West Side Story*, having sung the role of Maria numerous times.) The song "Maria," from *West Side Story*, sets that name with a motif very similar to the Skierkowski turn (in fact, Górecki's choral work *Totus tuus* sets the same name identically). The Naxos label recorded and released their own version of the Third Symphony in 1994, but later included excerpts from the symphony as incidental music on their "audiobook" reading of Shakespeare's *Hamlet*. Predictably, the symphonic excerpts accompany the scenes that deal most vividly with death and mortality, including Hamlet's monologue and the final death scene: "Goodnight sweet prince, and flights of angels sing thee to thy rest." Górecki had earlier set this very text in his *Good Night* (1990) for soprano, flute, piano, and tam-tams. Dawn Upshaw has recorded *Good Night* for Elektra–Nonesuch.

18. Lidia Rappoport-Gelfand similarly appeals to an experience of history in her suggestion that the orchestral canons on either side of the central vocal section are designed to give the listener "a sense of the emotional experiences of participants in [the] ancient mystery [of the Crucifixion]" (Rappoport-Gelfand, 1991, 129).

WORKS CITED

Additional internet sources are provided in the Notes.

Croan, Robert. 1994. "'Elektra' Electrifies the Screen." *Pittsburgh Post-Gazette* (September 12): C2.

Harley, Maria Anna. 1998. "Górecki and the Paradigm of the 'Maternal.'" *Musical Quarterly* 82/1 (Spring): 82–130.

Howard, Luke. 1997. "A Reluctant Requiem: The History and Reception of Henryk M. Górecki's Symphony No. 3 in Britain and the United States." Ph.D. diss., University of Michigan.

Jameson, Fredric. 1983. "Postmodernism and Consumer Society." In *The Anti-Aesthetic: Essays on Postmodern Culture*, edited by Hal Foster. Seattle: Bay Press 111–25.

Kanski, Józef. 1977. "XIV Festiwal w Royan." *Ruch Muzyczny* 21/13: 14–15.

Martland, Steve. 1991. "Invisible Jukebox." *Wire Magazine*: 44–46.

Rappoport-Gelfand, Lidia. 1991. *Musical Life in Poland: The Post-War Years, 1945–1977*. Translated by Irina Lasoff. New York: Gordon and Breach.

Rusbridger, Alan. 1993. "The Pole who Remains Apart." *(London) Guardian* (February 13).

Thomas, Adrian. 1997. *Górecki*. Oxford: Clarendon Press.

RECORDINGS CITED

Armstrong, Craig. 1997. "Death Scene," from *William Shakespeare's Romeo and Juliet: Music from the Motion Picture, Volume 2*. Capitol CDP 7243 8 55567 2.

Faust. 1996. "Eroberung der Stille, Teil I," from *Rien*. Table of the Elements 24.

Garbage. 1996. "Milk—The Wicked Mix" (with Tricky), from *Garbage: Milk*. CD single. Mushroom D1494.

Goldie. 1998. "Mother" from *Saturnz Return*. FFRR 422 828 983-2.

———. "Mother VIP (vocal mix)," from *Ring of Saturn*. FFRR 314 566 079-2.

Górecki, Henryk M. 1992. *Symphony No. 3*. Elektra–Nonesuch 9 79282-2.

Ildfrost. 1993. "Hearts Perturb," from *Absolute Supper*. Cold Meat Industry CMI.50.

Lamb. 1996. "Górecki," from *Lamb*. Mercury 314 532 928-2. (A CD single that included four remixes of "Górecki" was released by Mercury in 1997.)

Orbit, William. [1996] 2000. "Pieces in Olden Style I, II," from *Pieces in a Modern Style*. N-Gram. (Withdrawn from sale, but re-released in 2000).

Pale Saints. 1994. "Henry," from *Slow Buildings*. 4AD CAD4014.

CHAPTER 10

"Where's It At?":
Postmodern Theory and the
Contemporary Musical Field

David Brackett

> When the real is no longer what it was, nostalgia assumes its
> full meaning.
>
> —Jean Baudrillard, "The Precession of
> Simulacra" [1981] 1994

A major thread in discussions of postmodernism over the past twenty-five years has been the erosion of boundaries between high and low cultural production in the West. While this thread appears in much writing about postmodernism in music, there have been as yet few attempts to theorize postmodernism across different registers of music-making, including both high art and popular musics, in order to examine how this erosion might actually be occurring (important exceptions to this include the work of McClary 1989, 1991; Goodwin 1991; Born 1987, 1995; and Taylor 2001).[1]

In contrast to the tendency to read the increasing exchange of materials between popular and art musics as signifying the implosion of these categories, my central premise is that the reciprocal influence of economic and technological determinations with musical style has not merged the spheres of "high" and "low" musics, even though it may have created shifts in production and consumption across the musical field that have affected the delimitation of these spheres. In fact, it is only possible to contend that the musical categories associated with "high" and "low" culture have dissolved if one ignores several aspects of contemporary musical production and consumption: first, the continued centrality of categories to the marketing of music, a practice that has a corresponding effect on the way consumers make distinctions; second, that categories are marked by differences in the way that different types of music are funded; third, that differences between categories persist in differing relationships between composers, performers, and audiences, as do their relationship to official institutions (for example, art music receives frequent government/university subsidies, while popular music rarely does); fourth, that distinctions persist in formal processes between types of music that are separate sociologically, even if there are some well-known instances of a new kind of eclecticism occurring between and within categories that were previously perceived as distinct; and fifth, at the level of everyday discourse about music, the fact that one is speaking of "art music" rather than "popular music" recognizes the persistence of a distinction.[2]

Following from these assertions, I would like to propose a historical model that takes into account some notion of relatively autonomous categories, and to clarify how the concept of postmodernism operates within these historical categories. This is important because a term such as "postmodernism," if used simply as a periodizing label across categories, threatens to be totalizing in the same way as a term such as "modernism." The relationship of postmodernism to modernism cannot, then, be a matter of simple succession, for this implies a straightforward teleology that is untenable. While it may not be a case of simple succession, postmodernism as a concept is still most useful when understood as having become prominent after the heyday of modernism, even if it already existed as a (largely) latent aspect of it.[3] I would like to retain some sense of the historicity of "postmodernism" in order to counter the usage of the term both as a free-floating, ahistorical aesthetic attribute or as a way of describing an underlying "spirit of the age." However, rejecting its usage to describe a "spirit of the age" does not exclude the possibility of using "postmodernism" to clarify the articulation either of institutional discourses with musical practices (assuming for the moment their separability), or of economic and technological factors with discourses pertaining to music.

In order simultaneously to resist both historical totalization and an ahistorical use of the term, I have found it useful to theorize musical postmodernism through a notion of differentiated histories with their own peculiar temporalities delimited by a series of relations that refer to, or produce, a concept or group of concepts.[4] The "concept" that marks a particular historical formation emerges from groupings of statements that constitute a discourse: everyday conversation, critical writing, academic writing, and mass media writing and speech. Musical styles also participate in their own semi-autonomous histories through a field of intertextual references. Thus art and popular music are separated by sociological concepts such as how they are funded, their relationship to official institutions, and differing conventions of performance, as well as by musical style. Within popular music, the familiar "sub-categories" of R&B, country, and pop (and their numerous offshoots) define themselves and each other through the modalities of race, class, place, constructions of gender and sexuality, as well as specific musical practices. At the same time, these categories are fluid, shifting, overlapping, and impure. Each has a relation of contemporaneity (the relation to other musics of its time), and of historicity (the relation to musics that preceded it or followed it) that signals its identity and defines it.

One possible use of theoretical constructs such as modernism and postmodernism is to reveal differences between the semi-autonomous histories of musical categories. This implies that a postmodern turn occurs in different historical series at different times, in different ways, and that the most meaningful way to understand postmodernism is to identify the specific practices that signal a modern/postmodern shift within each relatively autonomous history.

We cannot explain these implications, however, without a sense of what constitutes "modernism" in music. I want to resist listing a series of traits, for presenting such a list risks perpetuating the notion that modernism (or postmodernism) exists "out there" somewhere in the objects under discussion rather than as a theoretical construct that enables the understanding of phenomena in a particular way. Nevertheless, it is useful to state what that theoretical construct might consist of: in this case, I include aesthetic values such as "truth to materials," "logical consistency" (Jencks 1986), and technical complexity, along with philosophical/sociological values such as an opposition to consumerism, a belief in progress/evolution created by ever-increasing technical skill and refinement, and the critical belief that (in the words of Clement Greenberg) the "work be judged as a hermetic, internally related world where the meanings are self-referential" (Jencks 1986, 19, 32, 39)—in other words, a belief in the autonomy of art from social function.[5] The application of these attributes is readily apparent in the realm of Western art music, where they map onto musical practices covering a period of almost a hundred years in an apparently effortless fashion, but they are more difficult to apply to Western popular music, let alone any form of non-Western music (but it is not impossible, for reasons that I will discuss later). This may be due to the development of the term "modernism" in the very milieu in which Western high art forms were cultivated, and to the historically intertwined and agonistic relationship between *modernist* art music and popular music, a relationship with no real parallel in the other arts (see Born 1987).

Architectural critic Charles Jencks has referred to postmodernism as "the continuation of modernism and its transcendence" (Jencks 1986, 15). Most other theorists agree that postmodernism is on the one hand a reaction to the formalism and stylistic purity of modernism, and, on the other hand, a reaction to the absorption of modernism into official high culture (Foster 1985, 121). Both of these descriptions stress the relationship of postmodernism to modernism, and indeed, the imbrication of the two terms with one another, if not the continuity between them which is present most strikingly in an aesthetics of negation.[6] To these relational aspects of postmodernism can be added aesthetic features such as Jameson's (1984) "depthlessness" and "pastiche," Jencks's (1986) "double-coding," Hal Foster's (1985) "eclectic historicism," and Grossberg's (1992) "authentic inauthenticity." In opposition to the idea of the modernist self-contained work, "within the postmodernist text . . . the space of closure is that of the surrounding cultural context, now reduced to the existing repertory of

historical styles and pre-texts" (Straw [1988] 1993, 16). Features less clearly tied to aesthetics may also enhance an understanding of postmodernism;
these include changing notions of authorship and performance, as well as
the mediating effects of "disorganized capitalism" (Lash and Urry 1987),
"incredulity toward meta-narratives," (Lyotard [1979] 1984), "space-time
compression" (Harvey 1989), "increased global flows of information"
(Appadurai 1996), new technologies, and the saturation effect produced by
living in "media culture" (Kellner 1995) or "technoculture" (Penley and
Ross 1991). I want to be clear that no style or genre is simply postmodernist, but rather displays specific registers or elements that are arguably
postmodernist. Another common way of understanding pieces or types of
music as "postmodern," in contrast to looking for specific "postmodern"
elements, is to analyze how their position within the contemporary musical field reveals a particular manifestation of postmodernism as "cultural
dominant" (in Jameson's [1991] famous phrase). While this risks subsum-
ing all contemporary phenomena under a totalizing rubric, which can then
become so vague as to be almost meaningless, it is also a convenient term
for labeling the peculiarly "new" effects of much contemporary music.

IS "POSTMODERN ART MUSIC" AN OXYMORON?

Writers claiming that categories have collapsed frequently follow evidence
attesting to the persistence of categories with a "yes, but" type of response.
A good example of this is Joseph Horowitz's recent article in the *New York
Times*. He observes that "albums are still segregated by genre [at] Tower
Records . . . , *but* as a cultural phenomenon, Western classical music refers
to the past" (Horowitz 1999, 38; my italics). This statement implies that
classical music has lost its distinction as a genre in the present moment.
Tellingly, Horowitz never informs readers why they should ignore the
material evidence presented. The idea of this collapse remains a phantasm.
Thus, the subtitle of this section: "Postmodern Art Music" is an oxymoron
if the idea of postmodernism depends on the collapse of high and low
because the idea of "art music" relies on its difference from popular music
for its identity.

Of course, within the category of art music, there is a wide range of
formal processes, composer-performer-audience relationships, and relationships to commercial, government, and educational institutions.[7] The
music of Michael Daugherty, for example, is often identified with the
concept of postmodernism. And with good reason, at least from the
standpoint of aesthetics. The score of a piece such as his recent opera
Jackie O (1997) is brimming with eclectic references: different styles are
constantly contrasted with one another, both during specific numbers and
between them, as well as occasionally superimposed on one another.

Through all this, Daugherty always maintains an ironic, "distanced" attitude toward his material, conveyed through exaggerating mannerisms and through surprising and absurd juxtapositions, which, because they are devoted to the celebration of a now-faded icon (the namesake of the opera), conjure up an overall "camp" aesthetic (see Sontag [1966] 1990, 275–92 and Ross 1989, 135–70). This combination of camp with extreme eclecticism evokes many of the most commonly cited attributes of postmodernism. It is hard to argue that *Jackie O* is not emblematic of new attitudes toward stylistic eclecticism that have emerged only since the early 1970s. When compared to earlier composers such as Stravinsky, Mahler, or Ives, Daugherty draws on a wider range of source material: "classical music " of many historical epochs as well as "popular" music, both Western and non-Western; and the juxtapositions come more rapidly than in the works of these earlier composers, heightening the sense of pastiche/camp.

Another way of understanding the difference between these earlier forms of eclecticism and the postmodernism of Daugherty is to consider Baudrillard's distinction between surrealism and the hyperreal:

> Surrealism was still in solidarity with the realism it contested, but which it doubled and ruptured in the Imaginary. The hyperreal represents a much more advanced phase insofar as it effaces the contradiction of the real and the imaginary. Irreality no longer belongs to the dream or the phantasm, to a beyond or a hidden interiority, but to *the hallucinatory resemblance of the real to itself.* (Baudrillard [1976] 1993, 72)

That is, in the work of Ives or Mahler, it is possible to hear the quotations as "dreams" or departures from the real which is represented by the music that surrounds the quotations.[8] In music such as Daugherty's there is no longer the sense of what might constitute the real. This description of the hyperreal has much in common with Jameson's notion of "pastiche": a practice of mimicry, like parody, but "without any of parody's ulterior motives . . . devoid . . . of any conviction that alongside the abnormal tongue you have momentarily borrowed, some healthy linguistic normality still exists" (Jameson 1991, 17).

In terms of musical style, Daugherty's music would seem to reject modernist beliefs in textual consistency and organicism. Yet modernist habits can prove surprisingly tenacious. In its emphasis on the negation of modernist aesthetics, postmodernism, as represented by *Jackie O*, repeats the emphasis on negation found in modernism. In terms of its "function," *Jackie O* also does not break with modernism in any significant way. That is, in its acceptance of its "non-functional" status, *Jackie O* does not reproduce the attack on the "institution of art" that, according to Peter Bürger (1984), characterized the "historical avant-garde" in its attempt to break with the modernist/romantic embrace of autonomy. In terms of authorship, *Jackie O* is still clearly the *original* work (however eclectic) of a single composer, who has notated a score which is interpreted by performers, who then "deliver" this work to the audience.

Formal processes reinforce the sense that *Jackie O*, however eclectic it might be, lies within the orbit of Western art music. The score is through-composed, rather than based on continuous variation over a repetitive framework as in most twentieth-century Western popular music (see Middleton 1990, 267–92, 1996). Daugherty's liner notes for *Jackie O* bear this out: when he mentions the "leitmotiv" that forms the "compositional core for many of the melodies and harmonies," and the "arch form" that "forms an important part of the compositional structure," one begins to suspect that concepts of organicism and closure are still very much in play. As Daugherty informs us, "All the musical numbers are rigorously structured, with a central motif or 'hook' that I transform through polyrhythmic counterpoint and unusual orchestrations." While Daugherty emphasizes the score's eclecticism at other points, in noting the "continual juxtaposition and intersection of different styles, rhythms, and melodies" in the score, his other comments attest to the persistence of an overall emphasis on what Chester (1970) would term the "extensional" mode of musical construction.

Music associated with the Bang on a Can (BOAC) festival presents a vivid contrast to Daugherty's while incorporating some of the same references. In aesthetic terms, a work such as David Lang's "Cheating, Lying, Stealing" represents the opposite extreme from *Jackie O*, relying on long sections in which the texture remains static. The idiom here is clearly most indebted to minimalism, and might fit into categories used by Kyle Gann (1997) such as "postminimalism" or "totalism." In terms of textual unity, then, "Cheating" offers a challenge to the Classic/Romantic paradigm only by being, if anything, *more* consistent than high modernist works. However, if one associates "postmodernism" only with stylistic eclecticism, one will miss the ways in which "Cheating" and others of its ilk represent a reaction to modernism. First of all, there is the BOAC composers' much flaunted relationship to rhythms derived from post–rock 'n' roll popular music, the (self-) conscious blending of rock and classical musics (as fusion rather than as pastiche or parody), as well as a tendency in the promotional literature of the festival to emphasize the affinity of the festival's organizers with "the" rock 'n' roll *attitude*:

> Since we began the Bang on a Can festivals in 1987, we have merged and synthesized these worlds (rock and classical), putting together programs of seemingly contradictory pieces. . . .
>   The three of us often talk about how when you look for where content lies in music, it's found in the rough edges, in the dirt. All the pieces

on this CD are gritty and uncompromising, yet also optimistic. Antithesis is a big part of the Bang on a Can aesthetic. . . . (Gordon et al. 1996)

The specifics of the musical reaction to modernism in much of the music associated with BOAC are manifested in the large role played by clear pulse-based rhythms against which syncopations and polyrhythms can be felt. Diatonicism also plays a large, though not exclusive, role in the music. And many of the compositions featured in the BOAC festival use the same performing ensemble, working with musicians with a strong commitment to the style, a relationship that simulates aspects of a "rock band." In addition to this, the ensemble, unlike the typical new music ensemble, features electric guitar, electronic keyboards, and occasionally electric bass, again, resembling a rock ensemble. Some of the pieces emphasize their affinity or indebtedness to types of music originating outside of Western Europe or North America.[9] These negations of modernism are adopted more or less wholesale from "classic" minimalists such as Riley, Glass, and Reich, except that those composers usually performed with their ensembles, blurring the roles of composer and performer more than do their BOAC descendants. Remnants of modernism can be felt in the BOAC pieces in their emphasis on consistency and gradual transformation of texture. As with *Jackie O*, musics outside of Western art music are used as "sources," rather than being entered into on their own terms, reinforcing the sense of difference between art music and other musics (see Born 1987, 55, 69).

In some respects, BOAC's relationship to official institutions could not be more a part of institutionalized art: for example, its yearly festivals between 1994 and 1998 were held at Alice Tully Hall at Lincoln Center. During performances, the relationship between performers and audience is identical to that of any other classical music event (one of separation and calm concentration, with applause and response confined to the conclusion of the piece as the audience sits silently in their seats). However, it is very likely that the constitution of the audience is *not* for the most part identical to that found at other classical music concerts, and probably consists largely of young intellectuals interested in other forms of "downtown" avant-garde art. In terms of funding, a close perusal of the credits for the CD *Cheating Lying Stealing* and the program booklet from their 1997 Alice Tully Hall concert also reveals the similarity between the way in which BOAC and other "classical music" organizations are funded: while revenue from ticket sales undoubtedly generates significant income, the list of funding agencies and private businesses that support the concert takes up half a page of very fine print.

Viewed from both sociological and musicological perspectives, the work of John Zorn comes closer to an actual blurring of boundaries than do the other examples discussed above that feature stylistic eclecticism. Zorn takes a variety of approaches in his work, from free improvisation to "game pieces," from "file card compositions" to works that are completely composed. He works with a variety of ensembles, all of which (excepting the fully notated pieces) feature some degree of improvisation, and thus rely on active collaboration with the other performers involved (in most contexts, Zorn also performs). The majority of his work from the mid-'80s through the early '90s involves rapid cuts between different styles of music, each section typically lasting less than thirty seconds, an approach that has often been compared to someone with a short attention span watching TV with a remote control. The styles involved are quite diverse, although many appear in almost every piece of Zorn's: swing-type jazz at a variety of tempos, bluesy shuffles, "noise" of different densities and types, punk rock, film music from the '60s and '70s, *Klangfarbenmelodie*, quotations of eighteenth- and nineteenth-century art music, New Orleans–style funk, jazz fusion, country music, cartoon music, and so on. While he does rely on the improvisatory abilities of the performers, and even uses styles that rely on a specific improvisational rhetoric (such as jazz and blues), the effect of the improvised sections is ultimately predictable, similar to the use of improvisation and "ad lib" sections by some composers dating back to the late 1950s and 1960s such as Witold Lutoslawski, Krzysztof Penderecki, or Karlheinz Stockhausen. That is, while Zorn needs musicians skilled in particular improvisatory styles (unlike Lutoslawski), one gets no sense of their "voices" as improvisers in the way one would in a jazz piece. In a piece such as *Forbidden Fruit* (1987), or in his "small group" CD, *Naked City* (1989), the styles fly by so rapidly that the voices of the individual improvisers are subsumed in Zorn's compositional concept. Nevertheless, Zorn (and other "downtown" composer/performers such as Anthony Coleman) goes decisively beyond mere "stylistic" eclecticism in moving toward merging the roles of composer and performer, even if he ultimately retains some of the conventional authority of the "composer" and receives the conventional type of credit. Zorn, interestingly, still sees his approach to music as based more in the world of art music than in popular music or jazz, as he self-consciously situates himself in the "American maverick tradition" (Duckworth 1995, 470), rejects stylistic hierarchy, and embraces quotation.

This blurring of boundaries occurs in Zorn's approach to the performance situation as well: while occasionally performing his work or receiving performances in classical music venues, he usually performs in a milieu midway between a "jazz club" and a classical music performance space, eschewing the formality of the performer/audience separation found at Lincoln Center. Zorn also stands somewhere between the typical popular and art music approaches to funding, relying on recording company contracts, revenue from club dates and concerts, and a small amount of grants. Interestingly, grants from the Shifting Foundation in Chicago gave him the artistic freedom (or maybe simply the time) to create the "file card" approach to composition (perhaps the most critically celebrated aspect of his activity), thus implying that a relationship may still exist between the exigencies of commercial music-making and the ability (or lack thereof) to make demanding, avant-garde music.

Zorn's music, then, does represent an ambiguous position in terms of its relationship to the official institutions of art, its approach to performance, and by extension, to authorship; and this is combined with stylistic eclecticism through both juxtaposition and superimposition. In this sense, it can be understood as the heir to the legacy established by both the American experimentalists of the late 1950s and '60s (Cage, Tudor, and others), minimalists such as Glass, and free jazz collectives such as the Association for the Advancement of Creative Musicians (AACM) and the Jazz Composers Orchestra Association, as well as European experimental rock of the early 1970s and early punk in the late 1970s.[10] Yet Zorn's music and that of other downtown composers cannot be considered "popular music" except by the willful fantasy of the postmodern critic. Its impact on popular music is negligible, its audience is infinitesimal, and in terms of its function, it is closer to the "autonomy" of art music than to the "entertainment" function provided by popular music.

BETWEEN THE AVANT-GARDE AND TINKERBELL: THE DISNEY COMMISSION

The type of historical/stylistic eclecticism I have been discussing thus far in recent art music occurs in other ways as well. One result of historicism, in addition to mixing styles within a single piece, is a now radical plurality of styles. At a contemporary music concert nowadays, one might hear high modernist serialism (which has become a historical relic itself), neo-Romanticism, quotations/usages of popular music/jazz/non-Western music, "textural" music (à la Ligeti or Lutoslawski), or pieces that resemble throughout the style of another (usually early-) twentieth-century composer. Another type of eclecticism may be found in the work of one of the most successful composers of art music in the United States today, Aaron Jay Kernis. His work features both eclecticism between pieces—the Air for Violin (1995) is consistently neo-Romantic, while other pieces are not—as well as within pieces—the Double Concerto for Violin and Guitar (1996) mixes Romanticism with modernist flourishes and "jazzy" rhythms and percussion. However, Kernis eschews both the rapid cutting of Zorn or Daugherty between styles, and the persistent association with rock 'n' roll of the BOAC-associated composers, although his earlier *Symphony in Waves* (1989) did reference funk and early rock 'n' roll. Despite the eclecticism of his work, the overall patina of quasi-cinematic romanticism in his recent works—technically supported by unproblematic modality, pulse-oriented rhythms, and long, emotive melodies—suggests that, unlike Daugherty and Zorn, "some healthy linguistic normality still exists" (although this is admittedly a matter of degree). This projection of stability (alluding to some underlying notion of the real) has undoubtedly aided Kernis in being promoted in a way enjoyed by few recent composers. The connection of his music to postmodernism, in what may seem like a contradiction, is nowhere clearer than in its most blatantly neo-Romantic passages, drenched as they are in nostalgia, which (as stated in the epigraph) "assumes its full meaning . . . when the real is no longer what it was."

It is not surprising, therefore, that Kernis has been central to the latest spectacle attesting to the continuing penetration of the commodity into the heart of the high art realm: the Disney commission, of which Kernis was one of two recipients (the other being Michael Torke). This event signals unequivocally that Adorno's dream for modernist art music to resist commodification is definitely over, now replaced by the dreams of children as imagined by adults. The idea of the commission came to Disney chairman Michael Eisner as he witnessed a performance of Mahler's Eighth Symphony. Eisner's response to the work heralds the arrival of a new era for classical music: "Wow, somebody did that before Disney. It was very Disney-esque."[11] Here again, Baudrillard's comments are quite apt:

> Disneyland: a space of the regeneration of the imaginary as waste-treatment plants are elsewhere, and even here. Everywhere today one must recycle waste, and the dreams, the phantasms, the historical, fairylike, legendary imaginary of children and adults is a waste product, the first great toxic excrement of a hyperreal civilization. (Baudrillard [1981] 1994, 13)

The cross-marketing planned for the commissioned pieces—which may include distributing excerpts arranged for marching bands at Disney theme parks and inclusion in *Fantasia III*—differs little from the approach used for contemporary popular music that is featured concurrently in movies, soundtrack recordings, and promotional videos (this approach was used for the "classical" soundtrack for *The Red Violin* [1998], composed by John Corigliano).

The examples considered thus far view postmodernism in art music in terms of aesthetic features (Daugherty), a combination of sociological and aesthetic factors (BOAC, Zorn), and the positioning of style within the larger field of current Western art music (Kernis). The coexistence of these styles attests to the failure of a narrative of progress in which one style smoothly follows the previous one in ever-increasing waves of technical complexity. The extreme plurality of styles is, however, indisputably new (and hence represents a kind of progress), even if for both sociological and aesthetic reasons this plurality still resides clearly in the category of art music. In all of these examples, it is far easier to grasp how they constitute "the continuation of modernism and its transcendence" (to quote Jencks again) than in examples in which the music comes from elsewhere in the musical field.

THE CASE OF POPULAR MUSIC (OR, IS POSTMODERNISM POSSIBLE WITHOUT MODERNISM?)

In order to discuss postmodernism in popular music, one must first determine what "modernist" popular music is/was. The development of the "aesthetic gaze" among segments of the popular music audience beginning around 1964–65 points to the way in which certain forms of popular music (notably "rock") were understood as having values opposed to commercialism (with little awareness at the time of the obvious contradictions involved); and it was during this time that forms of aesthetic criticism developed to understand popular music as a self-contained entity (Brackett [1995] 2000, 157–71; Gendron n.d.).[12] Contributing to this were university educated musicians and critics familiar with New Criticism and the modernist ideals of the self-contained work. A belief in the importance of anticommercialism arrived from the urban folk music revival of the late '50s and early '60s (Frith 1981). In the United Kingdom, this attitude came from art school students, well-versed in modernist art theory, as well as record enthusiasts (Frith and Horne 1987). A quote from a 1971 review of the Jefferson Airplane gives some indication of the critical predilections of the era:

> The Jefferson Airplane has always been one of my very favorite rock bands of the non-blues-playing, white, American variety, and it has always been my contention that they were perhaps fated to advance what has come to be called rock into yet-unexplored areas in much the same way as the Beatles and Cream have done. This unexplored region, my reasoning went, would involve a kind of tonality (an area in which rock has done some amazing things), a further development of polyrhythmics in the rhythm section, and of course, more of those tone-cluster vocal harmonies that the combined forces of Balin, Slick, and Kantner were getting so good at. (Ward 1971)

If this period represents a modernist moment for popular music (or for rock, at any rate), postmodernism would register through the proliferation of those qualities mentioned earlier: both in "the continuation of modernism and its transcendence," but most especially in elements such as "depthlessness," "pastiche," "double-coding," "eclectic historicism," and "authentic inauthenticity." The last of these is most important, as 1960s popular music based its opposition to commerce on a kind of emotional authenticity, a "truth to self," that was perceived to be beyond the manipulations of commerce (Grossberg 1992, 201–9). Beyond such virtuosic displays of parodic eclecticism as the late '60s work of Frank Zappa, the most obvious break in this ideology of authenticity occurred in glam rock in the early 1970s, with its flaunting of artifice and depthlessness (continued in a somewhat different manner in post-punk bands such as the Talking Heads and various artists associated with the "New Romantic" movement of the early '80s). Other aspects of authenticity have weakened since then, from performance conventions (occurring first most notably in disco, with its displacement of the skill of performing singers and instrumentalists), to overt stylistic impurity (evident in the increasing use of quotation, often employing recent technologies, especially sampling), to the overall proliferation of styles and the concomitant sense of the impossibility of technical progress and stylistic evolution, resulting in numerous "retro" styles.[13]

The term "postmodernism" began seeping into mass media critical discourse on popular music in the late 1980s, coinciding with the use of the term by MTV in its "postmodern video" show. It continues to be used, and, if a recent article by Jon Pareles is any example, the music critic's understanding of "postmodernism" is pretty straightforward: postmodern pop music is stylistically eclectic and projects a sense of "parody/irony." This is how Pareles characterizes Beck, one of the most recently celebrated exemplars of postmodern pop:

> On previous albums [to his 1998 release, *Mutations*], Beck has been a quizzical but resourceful post-modernist, sorting through the fragments and juxtapositions of an era that offers a surfeit of information with no clear hierarchies or boundaries. (Pareles 1998, 33)

This characterization is difficult to dispute; on Beck's two previous major label albums, *Mellow Gold* and *Odelay*, the list of styles compares to that found in Daugherty's *Jackie O*: late '60s psychedelia, industrial noise and distortion, early '70s country rock, late '60s–early '70s soul, "ambient" sounds, "raga-rock," funk, hip-hop, blues, urban folk, Dylan, bossa nova. Although the range is broad, it is mostly focused in two historical periods: the mid-1960s to the early 1970s, and the 1990s—that is, prior to the modern/postmodern shift in popular music, and "the present." Beck certainly gives new meaning to the idea of "blank parody" with no hint of homage or deprecation toward the material. Moreover, there are many self-reflexive moves within the recordings that "denaturalize" the act of producing the song (which consequently invokes "authentic inauthenticity"): in "Where It's At" from *Odelay*, a voice intones "that was a good drum break" after an ostentatiously pedestrian drum fill, and later says "that's beautiful dad" in a deadpan voice. "Pay No Mind" from *Loser* announces at the beginning, "This's song two on the album/This is the album right here/put on the album," and later pastiches "poetic" lyrics such as those found in much "folk-rock" from the mid-'60s to the present: "Give the finger to the rock 'n' roll singer/As he's dancing upon your paycheck/The sales climb high through the garbage pail sky/Like a giant dildo crushing the sun." This might seem like straightforward parody, yet the performance style, voice, acoustic guitar, and sound effects—which sound as if the recording has been slowed down—are oddly expressive of a generalized "slacker" affect: "The insects are huge and the poison's all been used/And the drugs won't kill your day job/Honey, that's why/I pay no mind/I pay no mind."

The music differs from the extreme collage of Daugherty's *Jackie O* or Zorn's *Forbidden Fruit* in several crucial respects: first of all, most of the songs present a fairly continuous texture or groove, with the majority of the quick cuts coming at the beginning or ending of the songs. Moreover, the tempo usually remains constant throughout a cut, with only brief interruptions (except for the beginnings and endings); and the rhythm section uses multiple, simultaneous ostinati while the song forms feature a regular, sectional repetition, both elements resembling conventional pop song practice rather than the through-composed, art music practice of Daugherty, Zorn, Kernis, or the BOAC composers. His albums following *Odelay*, *Mutations* (1998) and *Midnite Vultures* (1999), have focused more on individual styles, or style clusters—psychedelic and folk rock for the former, soul, funk, and hip-hop for the latter. *Midnite Vultures* raises questions about how "blank" blank parody might be when the races of the parodist and the parodied resurrect the historical associations and power relations of blackface minstrelsy.

In contrast to Beck, the Icelandic singer Björk has attracted less attention as "postmodern." However, her second album was, in fact, titled *Post* (1995), and a recent article in *Rolling Stone* stated that her "music is 'post'—post-rock, post-apocalyptic" (Fricke et al. 1999, 61). Her work does feature some of the wide-ranging "ad hoc eclecticism" (Jencks 1977) of "aesthetic" postmodernism, though she doesn't strike a particularly ironic or parodic stance. In contrast to Beck, the stylistic diversity in Björk's work tends to manifest itself either as extreme heterogeneity between different songs or as heterogeneity within a single song which occurs *simultaneously* rather than through eclectic collage or rapid "cross-cutting." Another way to put it is that Björk's eclecticism presents a type of stratification that is more "spatial" than temporal. Her aesthetic, especially in the recent *Homogenic* (1997), is typified by layering: bringing sounds together from radically different places and thereby creating a sense of contrasting, yet coexisting levels. She also self-consciously mixes the "natural" and the "technological," making the "natural" sound "artificial" and "mechanical," while making the "technological" sound spontaneous and vibrant without resolving these antinomies in an organic or textually consistent manner.[14] It is, in fact, precisely the possibilities afforded by recent technology as well as the aesthetic choices made available through "space-time compression" that mark Björk's work as postmodern; this includes using a large range of materials from all over the world, both high and low, employing languages other than English (or Spanish), and collaborating with musicians from widely varying backgrounds.

Half of the songs on *Homogenic* heighten this mixing of opposites by featuring a string ensemble that is combined with distorted, electronically generated grooves which recall the sound of "industrial" music or some rap recordings. In these songs, Björk quite explicitly blurs the opposition between nature and technology. The effect is disquieting due to the interference caused by the "noisiness" of the beats with what would otherwise seem like the straightforward "expressiveness" of her voice and the strings, an expressiveness that might by itself evoke the '60s rock music aesthetic of emotional "authenticity."

This creative strategy of layering diverse sounds has resonances with the types of social mediations that involve Björk most directly: she not only brings together sounds from different times and places, but she consciously chooses to work with people who in an earlier era would have been unlikely to come together (different immigrants and children of immigrants in London), marking a kind of postcolonial moment.[15] She comes from Iceland, quite on the periphery of the U.S.–U.K. dominant axis of post-Beatles pop music. More importantly, she *sounds* Icelandic, or, at any rate, she is clearly from neither North America nor the British Isles. Her lyrics are the product of her own polycultural background: she writes them first in English, then translates them into Icelandic, and then finally translates them back into English, with phrases remaining in Icelandic or sometimes turning into language-less vocal sounds. In addition to this, the lyrics express a kind of postmodern perspective, particularly in their questioning of a unidirectional temporality or a unified identity.[16] Her gendered, public persona points to an expanded horizon of possibilities that has opened up only in the last twenty years or so: she is neither a "girl singer" with a band, nor a sensitive singer-songwriter, nor an R&B diva, nor a pop diva, nor "one of the boys," nor a Riot Grrrl; she neither overtly emphasizes nor denies her gender or sexuality. She writes and arranges the songs, is involved with production, sings but does not play an instrument on stage, and is one of the few female stars to draw mainly on techno and other electronic genres.

THE CASE OF RAP (OR, CAN POSTMODERN THEORY AVOID THE TENDENCY TO TOTALIZE?)

In speaking of rap as "postmodern," one wanders onto treacherous terrain. Paul Gilroy (1993, 41–46) has critiqued cultural theorists of modernity and postmodernity for the way in which their formulations have frequently occluded racism as a constitutive element of modernity, and have ignored the effect of membership in a dominant or subjugated group on experiences of modernity.[17] A critic such as Tricia Rose (1994) speaks about rap in terms that evoke those of postmodernism, specifically in her emphasis on rupture, layering, and the emergence of rap within the sociohistorical framework of the "postindustrial" city. Yet she avoids tying rap to "postmodernism" based on these factors, perhaps because to do so might deny what some have called the "strategic essentialism" of insisting upon a specifically African-American historical trajectory, or because to do so would subscribe to monolithic and monocultural periodizations of modernity. On the other hand, George Lipsitz has emphasized the "postmodernism" or "post coloniality" of hip-hop due to the ways in which its "strategies of signification and grammars of opposition . . . speak powerfully to the paradoxically fragmented and interconnected world created by new structures of commerce culture and technology" (Lipsitz 1994, 30; see also Hall [1991] 1997). Lipsitz has sought to harmonize what might be termed the particularist stance of Gilroy and Rose with theories of postmodernism by carefully emphasizing that these "strategies of signification" resonate in particularly powerful ways within the African diaspora.

As indicated earlier, the postmodern turn I am describing occurs within an historical trajectory of African-American popular music including R&B, soul, funk, and disco, and it is through rap's referencing of these styles as well as its association with similar institutional/discursive sites that a notion of postmodernism in rap becomes meaningful yet distinctive to Afro-diasporic history.[18] The range of rap recordings is vast, and any single recording that I might choose would affect perceptions of the genre as postmodern. Yet, almost all rap recordings self-consciously highlight the fact that they are produced in an electronically/digitally reproducible context, that they use sounds which are already mass-mediated in some sense, and that they emerge from within a social matrix that has access to cultural forms produced in widely separated contexts. I have chosen to discuss the music of the Wu Tang Clan because of the extreme way in which they exploit the electronic potential of sound, and for the wide range of sonic and cultural forms that they employ (especially in their recordings between 1993 and 1995).

"Bring da Ruckus" from *Enter the Wu-Tang (36 Chambers)* illustrates several ways in which the Wu Tang Clan develop creative strategies that exemplify what Lipsitz termed the "fragmented and interconnected world created by new structures of commerce culture and technology." The song has a strong sense of rupture, noise, and "time-space compression," as sounds from widely separated historical periods, geographical regions, and media are brought together via sampling. Sounds from earlier musics such as soul and funk inhabit this recording but not to create a consistent style as they would have in a previous era, but rather to create a dissonant musical context for a narrative of "hard life on the streets." A further point of interest is the way in which the chorus of the song celebrates the noisiness of its sonic context, glorifying an aspect of the music that non-rap fans find particularly abrasive and alienating (see Walser 1995; Brackett 1999, 135–38). The narrative and mise-en-scène of the lyric in turn clashes with the voices sampled from a kung fu movie, voices which were themselves "dubbed" over the Chinese in which the dialogue of the film was undoubtedly originally recorded. At the same time, the language used by the rappers speaks in an idiolect that isn't necessarily modified for people outside of their specific geographical and class location.[19] As with Björk's use of Icelandic, this points to the increasing plurality of subject positions that have become available to performers and listeners in recent music, which further erodes the sense of a (white, male) "meta-narrative" for popular music history or for the music industry's conception of the "audience," and which undermines the Enlightenment myth of the possibility/desirability of achieving artistic universality.[20]

In general, then, these examples of pop music compared to, say, pre-'70s pop music, feature a greater emphasis on new uses of technology to employ "noise" in a musical context, or to create "new" sounds divorced from what can be produced acoustically, or to transplant sounds out of their most familiar contexts (often to signify "naturalness," or, alternatively, to use instruments or the human body to sound "artificial"), or to juxtapose sounds from wildly contrasting geo-social-historical locations (see Théberge 1997, 204–6). Despite lacking the eclectic pastiche of the most overtly postmodern art music, these pop styles can also be heard as reactions to their own "modernist" predecessors—psychedelia, urban folk music, soul and lounge music for Beck; psychedelia, "intellectual" pop-rock, and singer-songwriter for Björk; soul and funk for the Wu Tang Clan—within their own semi-autonomous historical trajectories of modernism–postmodernism.

TWO MORE POINTS ON A POSTMODERN MAP

Gilroy's critique discussed earlier raises the idea that terms such as modernism/postmodernism are implicitly concerned with the aesthetics and history of dominant groups in the West. Examples of music from other parts of the world, therefore, have the potential to disrupt such attempts at classification, and the genre of Hindi film song, long one of the most popular musics in the world, performs such a disruption admirably. Hindi film music dating back to the 1940s resists assignations of cultural purity in its dizzying juxtaposition of musical styles associated with widely separated geographical areas and historical periods. Indeed, some of the aesthetic/cultural debates in India during the late 1960s and early 1970s, accusing eclectic composers such as R. D. Burman of lacking originality, eerily anticipate contemporary discussions in the West around musicians who "sample" the work of other musicians. As Anthony D. King has observed, certain forms of cultural mixing which have been recently celebrated in the West as postmodernist, occurred first not "in the European or North American 'core' cities of London, Los Angeles, or New York, but probably in 'peripheral' ones of Rio, Calcutta, or Mombasa" (King 1995, 114). It is important to remember, however, important differences in the conditions of production: the juxtapositions created by the violent encounters of colonialism are a far cry from the postmodern play performed by those with large amounts of cultural capital in Western metropoles.[21] The latter phenomenon is exemplified by a group such as Deep Forest (winner of the 1995 Grammy award in the "World Music" category) who absorb a multitude of non-Western traditional musics via sampling into their New Age–inflected form of ambient-techno dance music in a process described by René T. A. Lysloff (after John Oswald) as "plunderphonics" (Lysloff 1997, 212–15; see also Taylor 1997; Hesmondhalgh 1997).

The second and last issue is a form of self-critique: the Western popular music examples I discussed earlier—Beck, Björk, Wu Tang Clan—are all vulnerable to the criticisms Andrew Goodwin (1991, 180) leveled against earlier writers on postmodernism in pop: that they confused the margins for the mainstream, discussing phenomena as typical that were actually relatively esoteric. While all the artists I discussed are extremely popular in statistical terms, none represent the popular music most widely heard at the time of this writing, which consists of "teeny pop"—the Backstreet Boys, the Spice Girls, Britney Spears, and so on. In general, teeny pop doesn't work in terms of the historical model I have been proposing (when was the "modernist" moment in teen pop?), but it displays its postmodernism within the generalized economy of current pop music in the irruption of an unprecedented pluralism and the failure of any meta-narrative of historical progress (see Frith 1988, 5; Straw 1991, 370–73).

This unprecedented pluralism, this failure of a critically-sanctioned "center" to progress, therefore, suggests a view of the total musical field in North America today as a series of simulations in which the most obviously "fake" products exist to disguise the hyperreality of the others.[20] One may construct a chain of simulations that represents degrees to which musical products produce a "reality effect": thus teen pop masks the contrivance of dance-pop and R&B lite; dance-pop and R&B lite mask the contrivance of alternative lite, pop-rap, and singer-songwriters; alternative lite, pop rap, and singer-songwriters mask the contrivance of grunge-alternative, punk and hardcore rap; and, at the end of the chain, we have classical music and world music (or even more extreme, avant-garde jazz and classical), which, however extreme they may be, produce a sense of "difference" which is always already contained.

Finally, although I'm wary of what are often uncritical uses of the term "postmodernism," I'm reluctant to jettison it entirely. While many continuities with modernism can be found, important changes have occurred as well. Most importantly, while categories and hierarchies may not have disappeared, categories have shifted and hierarchies have eroded, especially among those with large amounts of cultural capital, though that doesn't prevent new hierarchies from springing up in place of the old ones. This is to say that as long as there is a culture industry, and as long as music is "marketed" in some sense, marketing categories are unlikely to collapse, no matter how quickly they may rearrange themselves. Rather than the collapse of categories, it seems to me that one of the explanatory uses of a term like postmodernism is to shed light on new relationships within and between categories, and new ways in which those relationships are articulated with shifts in the economic and technological levels of cultural production.

NOTES

I would like to thank the many people who commented on presentations of earlier versions of this essay. In particular, I would like to thank Joseph Auner, Lisa Barg, Susan Cook, Bernard Gendron, Judy Lochhead, Anthony D. King, Richard Middleton, Promita Sengupta, Timothy D. Taylor, and Lloyd Whitesell for discussing many of the ideas presented here, and for their encouragement.

1. However, there have been several essays that discuss postmodernism in terms of either art music (including Hermand [1991] 1994; Hartwell 1993; Pasler 1993; Watkins 1994; J. Kramer 1995, 1996), or popular music (including Stratton 1989; Tucker 1989; Lipsitz 1990, 1994; Grossberg 1992; Hamm 1995; Potter 1995; and Nehring 1997). This list, of course, does not mention the one area of music in which there has been a perhaps more than ample exploration of postmodernism: that of music video. For a representative sampling of writings on the subject, see the special issue of the *Journal of Communication Inquiry* 10/1 (1986); Kaplan 1987; Straw [1988] 1993; Goodwin 1992; Frith et al. 1993. "Postmodernism" has even started to creep into textbooks, most notably in Grout and Palisca (1996, 800–2). The presence of "postmodernism" in Grout and Palisca, the most widely used history textbook for music majors, might indicate, somewhat deceptively, its widespread acceptance in the musicological community. That relatively few musicologists have studied it may be due to the fact that twentieth-century music in general, and late-twentieth-century music in particular, are still fighting to be accepted into what Don Randel (1992) deemed the "canon of acceptable dissertation topics" for musicology. There is also a self-avowedly "postmodern turn" within musicology itself (see L. Kramer 1995), in which music from the Western art music canon is viewed through the lens of various structuralist and post-structuralist theories.

2. See Frith 1996 for a discussion of the ways discourses of value operate between and across different categories of contemporary music.

3. I am aware that the terms "postmodernity" and "postmodernism" are often used distinctly, the former as a historical phenomenon, the latter as an aesthetic one, and that I am combining the two usages here. Opinions on the historical com-

ponent of postmodernism sharply divide many writers. The usage here is probably closest to that described by Huyssen (1984).

4. This notion of history is derived primarily from Althusser [1970] 1999 (99–100) and Foucault [1969] 1972. See Young 1990 for a genealogy of this concept leading from Bachelard and Canguilhem to Lévi-Strauss, Althusser, and Foucault.

5. See Bürger 1984 on the modernist and "historical" avant-garde movements, differentiated primarily through the historical avant-garde's attack on the autonomy status of art.

6. Born (1987, 1995) stresses this continuity.

7. I will not be discussing here one aspect of what is arguably an additional aspect of postmodernism in contemporary art music: the "crossover marketing" phenomenon in which pieces that are not postmodern in an aesthetic sense, such as Górecki's Third Symphony or *Chant* by the Benedictine Monks of Santo Domingo de Silos, are promoted using techniques from popular music on their way to selling millions of copies (see Howard 2001 and Bergeron 1995).

8. See Morgan 1978 for similarities in the compositional approaches of Ives and Mahler with respect to quotation, and stylistic juxtapostion and superimposition, and how they in some respects anticipate recent developments in art music.

9. This is especially true on the BOAC CD *Cheating Lying Stealing* in the work of Ziporyn and Vierk. The early minimalists similarly claimed to have been influenced by non-Western traditional musics, particularly those of West Africa, the Indian subcontinent, and Indonesia.

10. These latter four entities are listed by Born (1987, 71–73). For more on the AACM, see Radano 1993, 77–116. On Zorn's tendency to perpetuate exotic notions of otherness in his work, see Hisama 1993. Laurie Anderson is an example of a contemporary of Zorn's who effects a similar blurring of boundaries, but with far more commercial success (see McClary 1991, 132–47).

11. From an NPR interview, October 12, 1999. For more on the Disney commission, see also Keller (1999).

12. The argument in Brackett [1995] 2000 relies on the idea that those with large amounts of cultural capital became increasingly involved with popular music during the 1960s (see Bourdieu [1979] 1984). Lash and Urry (1987, 285–300) similarly describe this shift in the expenditure of cultural capital resulting in a redirection of a modernist mode of reception. Pfeil (1990) has argued that postmodernism is largely a type of consumption/reception, rooted in a particular generational experience (that of the baby boom).

13. This does not negate the fact that the search for authenticity remains important for vast segments of the popular music audience as witnessed by the enormous success in the '90s of alternative rock and hardcore rap (with it central trope of "keeping it real"), along with the continued viability of punk (see Nehring 1997).

14. For more on this, see Melissa West and Charity Marsh, "Gender and Technology as Read Through Madonna and Björk" (n.d.), which in turn draws heavily on Donna Haraway's theory of the cyborg (1990). Susan McClary has discussed Laurie Anderson's work in similar terms (1991, 132–47).

15. From an interview with Björk in *Portrait: Björk*, broadcast in 1998 on the Bravo network.

16. See, in particular, "Modern Things" from *Post,* which descries modern technologies like cars as having always existed ("they've just been waiting in a mountain/for the right moment/to come out"), and "Alarm Call" from *Homogenic* ("Today has never happened and it doesn't frighten me").

17. Drawing on Gilroy, Russell Potter has argued for a "postmodernism of resistance" in rap music, rooted "in a deeply historical and resonantly informed *vernacular* articulation of *anti*-modernism" (Potter 1995, 6). See also bell hooks (1990).

18. Nelson George (1994) develops a similar idea of historical specificity, using the term "post-soul" to describe the post-'70s turn in African-American music and identity. On the emergence of a culturally specific "Afro-modernism" in the 1940s, see Ramsey (forthcoming).

19. Although this also becomes involved in a complex web of commodification as people outside the initial sociocultural context are lured by the "exotic." For another view of the complexity of discussing rap as postmodern, see Manuel 1995, 232–34.

20. For more on the displacement of the unitary subject in contemporary Western art, see Owens 1983.

21. For further comments on connections between "globalization" and musical postmodernism, see Manuel 1995; Mitchell 1996; Erlmann 1996; and Taylor 1997.

22. And who are the Backstreet Boys but the latest simulacrum of the Osmond Brothers (with the New Kids on the Block as an important intermediary image)? Or, perhaps, another instance of the dreams of children as imagined by adults?

WORKS CITED

Althusser, Louis, with Étienne Balibar. [1970] 1999. *Reading Capital.* Translated by Ben Brewster. London and New York: Verso.

Appadurai, Arjun. 1996. *Modernity at Large: Cultural Dimensions of Globalization.* Minneapolis: University of Minnesota Press.

Baudrillard, Jean. [1976] 1993. *Symbolic Exchange and Death.* Translated by Iain Hamilton Grant. London and Thousand Oaks, Calif.: Sage Publications.

———. [1981] 1994. *Simulacra and Simulation.* Translated by Shelia Faria Glaser. Ann Arbor: University of Michigan Press.

Bergeron, Katherine. 1995. "The Virtual Sacred: Finding God at Tower Records." *New Republic* 212 (February 27): 29–34.

Born, Georgina 1987. "Modern Music Culture: On Shock, Pop, and Synthesis." *New Formations* 2 (Summer): 51–78.

———.1995. *Rationalizing Culture: IRCAM, Boulez, and the Institutionalization of the Musical Avant-Garde.* Berkeley and Los Angeles: University of California Press.

Bourdieu, Pierre. [1979] 1984. *Distinction: A Social Critique of the Judgement of Taste.* Translated by Richard Nice. Cambridge: Harvard University Press.

Brackett, David. [1995] 2000. *Interpreting Popular Music*. Berkeley and Los Angeles: University of California Press.

———. 1999. "Music." In *Key Terms in Popular Music and Culture*, edited by Bruce Horner and Thomas Swiss. Malden, Mass., and Oxford: Blackwell Publishers. 124–40.

Bürger, Peter. 1984. *Theory of the Avant-Garde*. Translated by Michael Shaw. Minneapolis: University of Minnesota Press.

Chester, Andrew. 1970. "Second Thoughts on a Rock Aesthetic: The Band." *New Left Review* 62: 75–82.

Duckworth, William. 1995. *Talking Music: Conversations with John Cage, Philip Glass, Laurie Anderson, and Five Generations of American Experimental Composers*. New York: Schirmer Books.

Erlmann, Veit. 1996. "The Aesthetics of the Global Imagination: Reflections on World Music in the 1990s." *Public Culture* 8/3: 467–87.

Foster, Hal. 1985. *Recodings: Art, Spectacle, Cultural Politics*. Seattle: Bay Press.

Foucault, Michel. [1969] 1972. *The Archaeology of Knowledge*. Translated by A. M. Sheridan. New York: Pantheon Books.

Fricke, David, Rob Sheffield, Ann Powers, and James Hunter. 1999. "Alternative" (subsection of "The Essential Recordings of the '90s"). *Rolling Stone* 812 (May 13): 48–66.

Frith, Simon. 1981. "'The Magic That Can Set You Free': The Ideology of Folk and the Myth of the Rock Community." In *Popular Music 1: Folk or Popular? Distinctions, Influences, Continuities*, edited by David Horn and Richard Middleton. Cambridge: Cambridge University Press. 159–68.

———. 1988. *Music for Pleasure: Essays in the Sociology of Pop*. New York: Routledge.

———. 1996. *Performing Rites: On the Value of Popular Music*. Cambridge: Harvard University Press.

Frith, Simon, and Howard Horne. 1987. *Art into Pop*. London: Methuen.

Frith, Simon, Andrew Goodwin, and Lawrence Grossberg, eds. 1993. *Sound and Vision: The Music Video Reader*. London and New York: Routledge.

Gann, Kyle. 1997. *American Music in the Twentieth Century*. New York: Schirmer Books.

Gendron, Bernard. n.d. *Between Montmartre and the Mudd Club: Popular Music and the Avant-Garde*. Forthcoming.

George, Nelson. 1994. *Buppies, B-Boys, Baps and Bohos: Notes on Post-Soul Black Culture*. New York: HarperCollins.

Gilroy, Paul. 1993. *The Black Atlantic: Modernity and Double Consciousness*. Cambridge: Harvard University Press.

Goodwin, Andrew. 1991. "Popular Music and Postmodern Theory." *Cultural Studies*, 5/2 (May): 174–90.

———. 1992. *Dancing in the Distraction Factory: Music Television and Popular Culture*. Minneapolis: University of Minnesota Press.

Gordon, Michael, David Lang, and Julia Wolfe. 1996. Liner notes for Bang on a Can, *Cheating Lying Stealing*. Sony Classical SK 62254.

Grossberg, Lawrence. 1992. *We Gotta Get Out of This Place: Popular Conservatism and Postmodern Culture*. New York: Routledge.

Grout, Donald Jay, and Claude V. Palisca. 1996. *A History of Western Music*. 5th ed. New York: W. W. Norton.

Hall, Stuart. [1991] 1997. "The Local and the Global: Globalization and Ethnicity." In *Culture, Globalization and the World-System: Contemporary Conditions for the Representation of Identity*, edited by Anthony D. King. Minneapolis: University of Minnesota Press. 19–39.

Hamm, Charles. 1995. "Modernist Narratives and Popular Music." In *Putting Popular Music in Its Place*. Cambridge: Cambridge University Press. 1–40.

Haraway, Donna. 1990. "A Manifesto for Cyborgs: Science, Technology, and Socialist Feminism in the 1980s." In *Feminism/Postmodernism*, edited by Linda J. Nicholson. New York and London: Routledge. 190–234.

Hartwell, Robin. 1993. "Postmodernism and Art Music." In *The Last Post: Music after Modernism*, edited by Simon Miller. Manchester: Manchester University Press.

Harvey, David. 1989. *The Condition of Postmodernity: An Enquiry into the Origins of Cultural Change*. Cambridge, Mass., and Oxford: Basil Blackwell.

Hermand, Jost. [1991] 1994. "Avant-Garde, Modern, Postmodern: The Music (Almost) Nobody Wants to Hear." In *German Essays on Music*, edited by Jost Hermand and Michael Gilbert. New York: Continuum. 282–99.

Hesmondhalgh, David. 1997. "Nation and Primitivism: Multiculturalism in Recent British Dance Music." In *Music on Show: Issues of Performance*, edited by Tarja Hautamäki and Helmi Järviluoma. Tampere, Finland: Department of Folk Tradition, Publication 25. 137–41.

Hisama, Ellie M. 1993. "Postcolonialism on the Make: The Music of John Mellencamp, David Bowie, and John Zorn." *Popular Music*, 12/2 (May): 91–104.

hooks, bell. 1990. "Postmodern Blackness." *Postmodern Culture*, 1/1. http://www.lath.virginia.edu/pmc/text-only/issue.990/hooks.990.

Horowitz, Joseph. 1999. "Learning to Live in a Post-Classical World." *New York Times*, Arts and Leisure section (February 28): 38, 41.

Howard, Luke. 2001. "Production vs. Reception in Postmodernism: The Górecki Case." Chapter 9 of this volume.

Huyssen, Andreas. 1984. "Mapping the Postmodern." *New German Critique* 33 (Fall): 5–52. Reprinted in Huyssen 1986.

Huyssen, Andreas. 1986. *After the Great Divide: Modernism, Mass Culture, Postmodernism*. Bloomington and Indianapolis: Indiana University Press.

Jameson, Fredric. 1984. "Postmodernism, Or, The Cultural Logic of Late Capitalism," *New Left Review* 146 (July–August): 59–92. Reprinted in Jameson 1991.

———. 1991. *Postmodernism, or, The Cultural Logic of Late Capitalism*. Durham: Duke University Press.

Jencks, Charles. 1977. *The Language of Post-Modern Architecture*. New York: Rizzoli International Publications, Inc.

———. 1986. *What Is Post-Modernism?* London: Academy Editions.

Kaplan, E. Ann. 1987. *Rocking around the Clock: Music Television, Postmodernism, and Consumer Culture*. New York: Routledge.

Keller, Johanna. 1999. "Well, It All Began When Mahler Got Disney Thinking." *New York Times*, Arts and Leisure section (October 3).

Kellner, Douglas. 1995. *Media Culture: Cultural Studies, Identity and Politics Between the Modern and the Postmodern*. London and New York: Routledge.

King, Anthony D. 1995. "The Times and Spaces of Modernity (Or Who Needs Postmodernism?)." In *Global Modernities*, edited by Mike Featherstone, Scott Lash, and Roland Robertson. London and Thousand Oaks, Calif.: Sage Publications. 108–23.

Kramer, Jonathan D. 1995. "Beyond Unity: Toward an Understanding of Musical Postmodernism." In *Concert Music, Rock, and Jazz since 1945: Essays and Analytical Studies*, edited by Elizabeth West Marvin and Richard Hermann. Rochester: University of Rochester Press. 11–33.

———. 1996. "Postmodern Concepts of Musical Time." *Indiana Theory Review* 17/2: 21–61.

Kramer, Lawrence. 1995. *Classical Music and Postmodern Knowledge*. Berkeley and Los Angeles: University of California Press.

Lash, Scott, and John Urry. 1987. *The End of Organized Capitalism*. Cambridge: Polity Press.

Lipsitz, George. 1990. *Time Passages: Collective Memory and American Popular Culture*. Minneapolis: University of Minnesota Press.

———. 1994. *Dangerous Crossroads: Popular Music, Postmodernism and the Poetics of Place*. London and New York: Verso.

Lyotard, Jean-François. [1979] 1984. *The Postmodern Condition: A Report on Knowledge*. Translated by Geoff Bennington and Brian Massumi. Minneapolis: University of Minnesota Press.

Lysloff, René T. A. 1997. "Mozart in Mirrorshades: Ethnomusicology, Technology, and the Politics of Representation." *Ethnomusicology* 41/2 (Spring–Summer): 206–19.

Manuel, Peter. 1995. "Music as Symbol, Music as Simulacrum: Postmodern, Pre-modern, and Modern Aesthetics in Subcultural Popular Music." *Popular Music* 14/2 (May): 227–39.

McClary, Susan. 1989. "Terminal Prestige: The Case of Avant-Garde Music Composition." *Cultural Critique* 12 (1989): 57–81. Reprinted in *Keeping Score: Music, Disciplinarity, Cuture*, edited by David Schwarz, Anahid Kassabian, and Lawrence Siegel. Charlottesville: University of Virginia Press, 1997. 54–74.

———. 1991. *Feminine Endings: Music, Gender, and Sexuality*. Minneapolis: University of Minnesota Press.

Middleton, Richard. 1990. *Studying Popular Music*. Milton Keynes, England, and Philadelphia: Open University Press.

———. 1996. "Over and Over: Notes Towards a Politics of Repetition." http://www2.rz.hu-berlin.de/inside/fpm/texte/middle.htm.

Mitchell, Tony. 1996. *Popular Music and Local Identity: Rock, Pop, and Rap in Europe and Oceania*. London and New York: Leicester University Press.

Morgan, Robert. 1978. "Ives and Mahler: Mutual Responses at the End of an Era." *19th-Century Music* 2/1 (July): 72–81.

Nehring, Neil. 1997. *Popular Music, Gender, and Postmodernism: Anger Is an Energy*. Thousand Oaks, Calif., and London: Sage Publications.

Owens, Craig. 1983. "The Discourse of Others: Feminists and Postmodernism." In *The Anti-Aesthetic: Essays on Postmodern Culture*, edited by Hal Foster. Port Townsend, Wash.: Bay Press. 57–82.

Pareles, Jon. 1998. "A Pop Post-Modernist Gives Up on Irony," *New York Times*, Arts and Leisure section (November 8): 33, 40.

Pasler, Jann. 1993. "Postmodernism, Narrativity, and the Art of Memory." *Contemporary Music Review* 7 (1993): 3–32.

Penley, Constance, and Andrew Ross, eds. 1991. *Technoculture*. Minneapolis: University of Minnesota Press.

Pfeil, Fred. 1990. *Another Tale to Tell: Politics and Narrative in Postmodern Culture*. London and New York: Verso.

Potter, Russell. 1995. *Spectacular Vernaculars: Hip-Hop and the Politics of Postmodernism*. Albany: State University of New York Press.

Radano, Ronald M. 1993. *New Musical Figurations: Anthony Braxton's Cultural Critique*. Chicago and London: University of Chicago Press.

Ramsey, Guthrie P. Forthcoming. "We Called Ourselves Modern: Music and Afro-modernism in the 1940s." In *Race Music: Post–World War II Black Musical Style from Bebop to Hip Hop*. Berkeley and Los Angeles: University of California Press.

Randel, Don. 1992. "Canons in the Musicological Toolbox." In *Disciplining Music*, edited by Katherine Bergeron and Philip V. Bohlman. Chicago: University of Chicago Press. 10–22.

Rose, Tricia. 1994. *Black Noise: Rap Music and Black Culture in Contemporary America*. Middletown, Conn.: Wesleyan University Press.

Ross, Andrew. 1989. *No Respect: Intellectuals and Popular Culture*. New York and London: Routledge.

Sontag, Susan. [1966] 1990. *Against Interpretation and Other Essays*. New York and London: Anchor Books.

Stratton, Jon. 1989. "Beyond Art: Postmodernism and the Case of Popular Music." *Theory, Culture and Society* 6/1 (February): 31–57.

Straw, Will. [1988] 1993. "Popular Music and Postmodernism in the 1980s." In *Sound and Vision: The Music Video Reader*, edited by Simon Frith, Andrew Goodwin, and Lawrence Grossberg. London and New York: Routledge. 3–21.

———. 1991. "Systems of Articulation, Logics of Change: Communities and Scenes in Popular Music." *Cultural Studies* 5/3: 368–88.

Taylor, Timothy D. 1997. *Global Pop: World Music, World Markets*. New York and London: Routledge.

———. 2001. "Music and Musical Practices in Postmodernity." Chapter 5 in this volume.

Théberge, Paul. 1997. *Any Sound You Can Imagine: Making Music/Consuming Technology.* Hanover, N.H., and London: Wesleyan University Press.

Tucker, Bruce. 1989. "'Tell Tchaikovsky the News': Postmodernism, Popular Culture, and the Emergence of Rock 'n' Roll," *Black Music Research Journal* 9 (Fall): 271–95.

Walser, Robert. 1995. "Rhythm, Rhyme, and Rhetoric in the Music of Public Enemy." *Ethnomusicology* 39/2 (Spring–Summer): 193–217

Ward, Ed. 1971. "Review of *The Worst of the Jefferson Airplane.*" *Rolling Stone* (February 4).

Watkins, Glenn. 1994. *Pyramids at the Louvre: Music, Culture, and Collage from Stravinsky to the Postmodernists.* Cambridge: Harvard University Press.

West, Melissa, and Charity Marsh. n.d. "Gender and Technology as Read Through Madonna and Björk." Unpublished paper.

Young, Robert. 1990. *White Mythologies: Writing History and the West.* London and New York: Routledge.

RECORDINGS CITED

Bang on a Can. 1996. *Cheating Lying Stealing.* Sony Classical SK 62254.

Beck. 1994. *Mellow Gold.* Geffen Records. DGCD-24634.

———. 1996. *Odelay.* Geffen Records. DGCD-24823.

———. 1998. *Mutations.* Geffen Records. DGCSD-25309.

———. 1999. *Midnite Vultures.* Geffen Records. DGC06949-0485-2.

Björk. 1995. *Post.* Elektra 61740-2.

———. 1997. *Homogenic.* Elektra 62061-2.

Daugherty, Michael/Houston Grand Opera. 1997. *Jackie O.* Argo 455 591-2.

Kernis, Aaron Jay. 1999. *Air for Violin, Double Concerto for Violin and Guitar, Lament and Prayer.* Argo 289 460 226-2.

Wu Tang Clan. 1993. *Enter the Wu-Tang (36 Chambers).* RCA 07863-66336-4.

Zorn, John. 1987. "Forbidden Fruit," on *Spillane.* Nonesuch 9 79172-1.

———. 1989. *Naked City.* Elektra/Nonesuch 9 79238-2.

SECTION III

COMPOSITIONAL VOICES

CHAPTER 11

Music, Postmodernism, and George Rochberg's Third String Quartet

Mark Berry

Music scholars have recently begun to use postmodernism as a basis for critical accounts of contemporary concert music and in their discussions, George Rochberg's Third String Quartet inevitably enters as an example. Many of these writers have turned to a binary conceptual model adapted from scholarship in art criticism that divides postmodern works into radical and reactionary categories. Typically, Rochberg's quartet is described as a "neoconservative" type of postmodernism whose use of a tonal art music genre and stylistic allusions to past historical styles indicates a nostalgic yearning for an imagined cultural golden age in Western civilization. Scholars contrast the "reactionary" neoconservatism of Rochberg with a "radical" strand of musical postmodernism that juxtaposes different styles and genres in an attempt to criticize accepted cultural standards. Although it has gained a degree of currency within musicological circles, this binary model of postmodernism is not without problems, and the characterization of Rochberg's Third Quartet exemplifies its limitations. In particular, it provides no understanding of the quartet contemporary to its composition and early reception; the question arises as to whether a critical conceptual model that ignores historically-grounded perspectives sufficiently explains a piece of music. An examination of Rochberg's writings from the time that he completed the quartet in 1972 reveal a composer who advocates using styles from all historical periods in the making of new music, an approach which he labeled as *ars combinatoria*. This conception of composition may be understood as part of a larger intellectual discourse in which historical cultural forms have currency in the living present. Within this discourse, the Third Quartet is not a regression into the past but rather an expression of contemporary historical concepts. This tension between a historical interpretation of Rochberg's Third String Quartet and the notion of the piece as neoconservative postmodernism can be used as a starting point in the reconsideration of this binary model and its implementation to the study of concert music.

In their work on music and postmodernism, Jann Pasler (1993) and Jonathan Kramer (1995) both employ a binary conceptual model, derived from the work of art critic Hal Foster, that identifies radical and neoconservative types of postmodernism. The radical strand critiques cultural norms inherited from modernism, including "organic unity" and stylistic homogeneity. An example is John Zorn's *Forbidden Fruit*:

> *Forbidden Fruit* . . . offers a considerable dose of postmodern chaos. . . . Listening to *Forbidden Fruit* can be as dizzying as it is electrifying. You never know what is coming next, nor when. The stylistic juxtapositions are amazingly bold. If there is any discernible thread of continuity, the music would surely be more tame, more predictable, more ordinary. But there is not. (Kramer 1995, 22)

For Kramer, *Forbidden Fruit* embodies the defining features of radical postmodernism. Its contrasting musical excerpts constantly interrupt each other, precluding a regular temporal flow and destroying any pre-conceived expectations of how music should function: the "postmodern chaos" awakens listeners from their own complacency. Through the "postmodern chaos" of their music, the radical postmodernists restore the element of shock to composition that was present in the activities of early-twentieth-century composers such as Anton Webern and Arnold Schoenberg, but do so by questioning these earlier composers' obsession with structural continuity. Neoconservative postmodernism, the second strand, also critically engages modernism, but rejects it out of hand. Neoconservative composers employ premodern styles in an attempt to bring a new type of coherence to the "heterogeneous present" and re-establish the dominance of Western musical practice. Jann Pasler notes the musical characteristics that are indicative of a neoconservative postmodernism:

> In music, we all know about the nostalgia that has gripped composers in recent years, resulting in neo-romantic works . . . the sudden popularity of writing operas and symphonies again, of construing one's ideas in tonal terms. . . . Many of those returning to romantic sentiment, narrative curve, or simple melody wish to entice audiences back to the concert hall. To the extent that these developments are a true "about face," they represent a postmodernism of reaction, a return to pre-modernist musical thinking. (Pasler 1993, 17)

It is through the use of established art music genres and the evocation of various musical characteristics from nineteenth-century-era common practice that a neoconservative, or reactionary, postmodernism manifests itself musically. The conventional musical syntax contributes to the creation of a more accessible music, presumably to please those who find the work of composers such as Schoenberg, Webern, or later serialists like Milton Babbitt, Pierre Boulez, and Karlheinz Stockhausen, too demanding. Reactionary postmodernism represents a return to music that people find "pretty" and easy to understand.

Kramer and Pasler both describe George Rochberg as the "quintessential" neoconservative postmodernist composer and identify the Third String Quartet as the epitome of his reactionary aesthetic. Although neither discusses the characterization in great detail, Kramer supports his point by referring to Rochberg's "Can the Arts Survive Modernism?" in which the composer criticizes musical modernism as a serious artistic gaffe committed by Western culture and perceives the contemporary pluralism of the musical scene as potentially hazardous to social stability (Rochberg 1984). Rochberg argues that the only option is to look to music of the past Western classical tradition as a model of articulate artistic expression.

> The hope, now, is the growing demand to reclaim the past, to bring into existence by an intense exercise of will and self-consciousness languages which embrace the traditions of the premodern and modern periods. To bring into balance again the polarities of heart and mind, or what lies within and what lies without in the experience of man, is a sign that, once again, the arts may be pointing the way to a time when these qualities and characteristics will, perhaps, again appear as new values on the visible plane of a new social, economic, racial, and political order. (Rochberg 1984, 338)

Rochberg's comments substantiate Pasler's sense that the invocation of tonal music represents a reversion to a nineteenth-century notion of the composer as romantic hero, and justifies the judgment on the piece as antimodern and reactionary (Pasler 1993, 18).

Kramer and Pasler rely on the statements of the composer to legitimate their classification, but they use an article written over ten years after Rochberg completed his quartet. An examination of writings from the time that Rochberg composed the Third Quartet reveals a distinctly different aesthetic stance that introduces a possible new interpretation of the piece. In his writings from the late 1960s and early 1970s, Rochberg advocates a "stylistic pluralism" in music. He believes that in contemporary culture, the past and present exist all around artists, allowing them to use techniques and styles from different historical periods. Rochberg labels this new approach as *ars combinatoria* and describes it as:

> . . . the use of every device and every technique appropriate to its specific gestural repertory in combination with every other device and technique,

until theoretically all that we are and all that we know is bodied forth in the richest, most diverse music ever known to man. (Rochberg [1972] 1984, 238)

His concept of *ars combinatoria* amounts to a critical commentary on the accepted teleological approach to history and its implications in the study of music. When musicians develop a teleological view toward music, they assign particular works to the epoch of their creation and ignore their validity as cultural forms in the present. Rochberg adopts a different approach to history that underscores the relevance of past art to the contemporary composer:

> I stand in a circle of time, not a line. 360 degrees of past, present, future. All around me. I can look in any direction I want to. Bella Vista. (Rochberg [1969] 1984, 158)

Standing in the middle of this "circle of time," the artist can make use of all the different techniques and styles of different artistic periods to create a rich and diverse *ars combinatoria* Rochberg presents a different approach to history that would underscore the relevance of past art to the contemporary artist and usher in a new type of musical composition based on figuring out ways in which to integrate different historical styles.

> On the contrary, the twentieth century has pointed—however reluctant we may be to accept it in all areas of life, social as well as political, cultural, as well as intellectual—toward a difficult-to-define pluralism, a world of new mixtures and combinations of everything we have inherited from the past and we individually or collectively value in the inventions of our own present, replete with juxtapositions of opposites (or seeming opposites) and contraries. (Rochberg [1974] 1984, 240)

Composers can use past artistic styles as a repertoire of possibilities that they can combine, reconstruct, or juxtapose in the light of the present. They draw upon musical gestures that already exist in the cultural domain, and play off that knowledge to create something that is new, yet meaningful to their audience. While composers from past historical periods have been aware of historical predecessors and have even attempted to synthesize techniques of previous composers into their own music, few have articulated an aesthetic that resulted in the juxtaposition and integration of recognizable styles within one contemporary piece. The composers of this twentieth-century *ars combinatoria*, for Rochberg, could do just that, embracing the presence of past historical styles in the pluralistic contemporary culture and use it to their advantage.

Rochberg advocated a renewed "contact with the tradition and means of the past" in contemporary composition, but only from the perspective of a pluralistic present (Rochberg [1974] 1984, 242). For Rochberg the educated composer actively confronted the pluralistic mélange of styles in an active way, located artistic similarities that will allow for their integration, and used these compatibilities to bring a fresh new way of organizing a composition.

> Pluralism, as I understand it, does not mean a simplistic array of different things somehow stuck together in arbitrary fashion but a way of seeing new possibilities of relationships; of discovering and uncovering hidden connections and working with them structurally; of joining antipodes without boiling out their tensions. . . . We struggle for clarity and order, to gain not a permanent certainty (which is not possible anyhow) but a momentary insight into how it is possible to resolve the chaos of existence into a shape or form which takes on beauty, perhaps meaning, certainly strength. (Rochberg [1974] 1984, 241)

Rochberg perceived a pluralism that was the result of an acute historical awareness, embraced it, and developed an *ars combinatoria* aesthetic to deal with it. At this point in his life, Rochberg was not acting as a musical conservative who wished to nostalgically revive a past method of composition, but was attempting to create a new compositional outlook that would respond to the cultural condition of the late twentieth century.

Rochberg's comments can be understood as part of a larger public discourse on the arts and society in the 1960s and 1970s. Writers at that time begin to identify particular features of contemporary society and examine their implications for cultural output in ways that are similar to the manner in which Rochberg discusses the relationship between a pluralistic world and his *ars combinatoria*. The published work of these authors, while having different foci and methodologies, were all concerned with the tenor of the times and helped to steer the intellectual conversation on such issues into a direction that focused on social and cultural pluralism. One of the most famous examples of this public discourse is the work of Canadian media analyst Marshall McLuhan. In his book *Understanding Media*, McLuhan presents his concept of human society as a "global village" of diverse groups brought together by electronic communication technology into a synchronic, eternal present (McLuhan 1964, 3–4). The electronic media operated as an external nervous system that connected people worldwide, allowing geographically distant communities to share information by radio, phone, or television; this rapid communication synchronized international events and abolished traditional notions of linear time and spatial distance:

> Today, after more than a century of electric technology, we have extended our central nervous system itself in a global embrace, abolishing both space and time as far as our planet is concerned. Rapidly, we approach the

final phase of the extensions of man—the technological simulation of consciousness, when the creative process of knowing will be collectively and corporately extended to the whole of human society, much as we have already extended our senses and our nerves by the various media. (McLuhan 1964, 3–4; see also McLuhan and Fiore 1967)

According to McLuhan, the creation of a global village had profound positive implications in the political structure of society. Once-ignored factions such as "the teen-ager" and "the Negro" were now connected to the dominant cultural groups by that surrogate central nervous system, the electronic media. The world was in the midst of a new era of cooperative pluralism in which everyone was empowered:

> As electronically contracted, the globe is no more than a village. Electric speed in bringing all social and political functions together in a sudden implosion has heightened human awareness of responsibility to an intense degree. It is this implosive factor that alters the position of the Negro, the teen-ager, and some other groups. They can no longer be *contained*, in the political sense of limited association. They are now *involved* in our lives, as we in theirs, thanks to the electric media. (McLuhan 1964, 5)

The global village is a multicultural mélange of different peoples living within a synchronic, eternal present. Electronic media do not blend the mix into a homogeneous texture, but wrap the separate groups in a "global embrace." Because of the electronic nervous system, an event that occurs in one part of the world is a "simultaneous happening" that is received immediately by everyone everywhere (McLuhan and Fiore 1967, 63). Society is, according to McLuhan, a heterogeneous bundle of peoples united in time and space by the electronic media.

Five years before McLuhan published his pronouncements on how the media would change society, historian and economist Robert L. Heilbroner predicted that the tendency toward historical stasis would be a key characteristic of society in the 1960s (Heilbroner 1959, 195). Heilbroner that history demonstrates as many eras defined by stasis as those by the desire to move forward through revolutions, battles, and upheavals. He predicted that the 1960s would be a time of historical stasis.

> Taking into account the human condition as it now exists, the laggard slowness with which improvements in institutions are followed by improvements in "life," the blurred and ambiguous fashion in which history passes from problem to problem, it is certain enough that the tenor of world history will remain much as it is for a long while to come. (Heilbroner 1959, 205)

While he does not deny the possibility that historical progress exists,

Heilbroner does concede that, at the very least, it will not exist in American life in the 1960s. The author sees the institutional configuration of American society and the random nature in which important problems are dealt with as two important contributing factors to this stasis. This prediction does sound much less optimistic than the concept of the "global village," but what it shares with McLuhan's work is an understanding of the world as being involved in a synchronous world event and its continuation in this state. Just as McLuhan was thinking of the world as a "global village," so was Heilbroner predicting a time in which no significant change would occur, when historical time would—at least temporarily—stop moving forward.

Heilbroner's and McLuhan's focus on political and social situations in their evaluations of contemporary life find a parallel in the work of Leonard Meyer, who considers how changes in society affect the production of cultural artifacts in the 1960s. In *Music, the Arts, and Ideas*, Meyer describes life in the late twentieth century as "perplexing and fragmented," and identifies a period of "cultural stasis" in which various styles of artistic media are practiced simultaneously (Meyer 1967, v, 134).

> Perhaps our time would be characterized, not by the cumulative development of a single style, but by the coexistence of a number of alternative styles in a kind of "dynamic steady-state." It is the exploration of this hypothesis which forms the central core of my book. (Meyer 1967, v)

One reason for this artistic pluralism is the changing notion of history and the role of artworks from the past in contemporary society. Society no longer views history as a progression of distinct epochs, and artists no longer believe that artistic styles can only be meaningful within the historical context in which they were originally created. Artists are now free to use styles of the past as a "repository" of material for the creation of works in the present:

> History is no longer a dialectic succession of necessary stages, but an objective ordering of recorded evidence; and truth is no longer single and ultimate, but provisional and pluralistic. Thus the ideological and psychological conditions which have hitherto precluded the free and open use of past means and materials no longer prevail. The present may now incorporate the past. (Meyer 1967, 190)

Elsewhere, Meyer emphasizes paradigm shifts within the academic community and their importance in changing the way people think. And he links new attitudes toward the use of historical musical material with changes in the fields of history and philosophy. Unlike Heilbroner and in alignment with the utopian vision of McLuhan, Meyer sees this condition as a positive development. The intellectual freedom from older modes of thought allow the artist to make new decisions about their work that were never ever available before.

In light of Meyer's ideas of artistic pluralism, Rochberg may be understood as decidedly au courant, and not at all conservative or retro. His *ars combinatoria* embodies a desire to come to terms compositionally with the larger social situation that McLuhan, Heilbroner, and Meyer articulate in verbal terms. Not advocating the reconstruction of any glorified imagined past, Rochberg articulated a compositional approach compatible with the way we lived in the world. In fact, Rochberg advocated an aesthetic stance that has more in common with the radical postmodernism that Kramer and Pasler describe. The point here is not to reclaim Rochberg as a radical postmodernist, but rather to demonstrate the confusion that results when a different historical perspective other than the one presented by Kramer and Pasler is considered. Given the discrepancy between the ideas Rochberg verbally articulates in the 1960s and 1970s and those of the 1980s, the question must be raised whether it is possible to understand the piece and its allusions to past musical styles as an attempt to realize the *ars combinatoria* principle with respect to its contemporary intellectual context.

Stylistic allusion pervades the Third String Quartet; what is interesting about this feature is the way Rochberg organizes the music to create a sense of diversity that precludes any understanding of the piece as being unified by any one comprehensive compositional style. The first movement has no obvious stylistic allusions—it is written in a non-tonal style—but is a gradually unfolding aural mosaic of musical fragments whose organization sets the pluralistic tone for the rest of the piece (see Figure 11-1).

Figure 11-1. Presentation of Gestural Units George Rochberg, Third String Quartet, first movement.

The first movement contains six distinct musical units whose temporal succession is characterized by juxtaposition. Unit A—a repetition of loud, quick gestures separated by short moments of silence—is interrupted by B, a progression of non-tonal chords introduced by an ascending sixteenth-note figure. As B fades away to *pianissimo* at m. 39, the A unit returns to continue its contrasting music. This is not a repetition of the original statement but rather its continuation. The second A music at mm 40–62 begins with the music that ends the first statement of A, not with its distinctive opening gesture. The connection between the two units allows for the recognition of section A as a continuation of the first, and B can be heard as an interruption in the musical flow. To invoke a spatial metaphor, B breaks A into two individual fragments. The cleavage of unit A by B is indicative of the musical juxtapositions and fragmentations of the rest of the movement and piece.

As the presentation of disparate musical material continues in the first movement, two new gestural units are presented: C at mm. 75–80, and D at mm. 81–102. C is a repetition of one three-bar phrase constructed of eighth-note tritones in the violins, while D consists of a recurring major second motive superimposed upon a tonal chorale in B major played in double-stops by the viola and cello. Unit C returns in mm. 103–5, but only the first phrase is presented before yet another distinct passage—unit E— pre-empts it. The final phase occurs at mm. 109–11, creating a separation of C by E that is similar to the fracturing of section A that occurred in the opening measures of the movement. When music of the D unit returns at mm 128–48, there is also a sense that these measures belong to the earlier D music, that they continue the earlier presentation. The first occurrence of D, at mm. 81–102, ended on the dominant chord of $F^{\#}$ major; the recurrence continues the tonal progression at m 128 with a vi chord that eventually settles into a clear B-major tonic key. Although tonality is used here, its usual sense of forward motion is stymied by both the fracturing of the unit into two parts—at mm. 81–102 and 128–48—and by the context in which it operates; D is just one fragmented unit within a larger whole of autonomous musical segments. In the midst of this musical mélange is unit F, mm. 114–17 and 121–24, which alternates with repetitions of unit E in mm. 112–13 and 118–20. The movement ends with a restatement of units A and B in mm. 149–235, the music that began this onslaught of different musical fragments.

The allusions to past composers' work begins in the second movement and continues to the end of the quartet. At almost every point in the quartet, one can compare what is heard to other music in the western classical repertoire: non-tonal passages evoke the work of such composers as Bartók, Stravinsky, and Schoenberg, while other sections incorporating common practice tonality are written in styles characteristic of Beethoven and Mahler. These moments of music are constantly being introduced, abandoned, and revisited with no overt continuity between them; they operate together within one piece of music, but have only limited connections (see Figure 11-2).

Second Movement	Third Movement	Fourth Movement	Fifth Movement
March	Variations in A Major	March	Scherzo
Stravinsky/Schoenberg	Beethoven	(continuation)	Bartók/Beethoven
			Serenade
			Mahler

Figure 11-2. Juxtaposition of Stylistic Allusions. Rochberg, Third String Quartet.

The second movement is an atonal march that calls to mind the opening of Stravinsky's *L'Histoire du Soldat* or Schoenberg's *Serenade*, Op. 24. Contrasting with the rhythmic drive and parodic intensity of the march music, the third movement is a set of variations in A major that calls to mind Beethoven's late string quartets, particularly Op. 131. The fourth movement continues with music from the second movment's march: the relation is enacted through similar motivic material and identical performance directions—both are to be played "spirited; but grotesque" at precisely the same tempo. The continuation of the march here creates an interesting relationship between the second, third, and fourth movements that is similar to the juxtaposition of material in the first movement. The slow Beethovenesque third movement temporarily interrupts the intense march music. There is no attempt to integrate the two sections in any way—the two manifestations of the march and the slow movement exist independently.

The fifth movement continues the onslaught of allusions, containing scherzo music reminiscent of Bartók and Beethoven, as well as a D-major serenade that evokes the *gemütliche* sentimentality of Gustav Mahler. Again in this fifth movement we hear the juxtaposition of individual musical moments of music, as the scherzo music and serenade alternate. It is as if one is constantly interrupting the other throughout the movement.

The Third Quartet, with its plethora of different styles, is an artistic realization of Rochberg's *ars combinatoria* aesthetic, and an analysis from this perspective calls into question the characterization of the piece as a neoconservative manifestation of nostalgia. Rochberg used musical material marked as past for his own, "present-ist" composition. Kramer and Pasler, working within a binary model of postmodernism, do not acknowledge such an interpretation; their critical assessment is predicated on binary and non-historical framework which disallows the understanding I propose here.

While analytical discussion based in Rochberg's aesthetic stance in the 1960s and '70s and in the larger intellectual context precludes a neoconservative interpretation, some might still say that the piece exhibits neoconservative characteristics since its stylistic allusions refer only to canonical concert music composers. But it would help to keep three points in mind. The first is that Rochberg was a composer who worked in an American university music department, and his music was at least in part a reaction to the institutional paradigm of composition as quasi-scientific research (see Davis 1992, 1993; Brody 1996). Rochberg began his career as a strict serial composer, working within a post-Schoenbergian atonal style and under the shadow of composers like Milton Babbitt. Measured against the music that was written under that paradigm, Rochberg's music does sound stylistically pluralistic. The second point is that he wanted to reconnect with music from the past because it was also the music of the present, enjoyed by many people through concert performances and recordings. Third, Rochberg conceived his compositional practices in terms of "possibility," not of establishing "a permanent certainty (which is not possible anyhow) but a momentary insight into how it is possible to resolve the chaos of existence into a shape or form which takes on beauty, perhaps meaning, certainly strength" (Rochberg [1974] 1984, 241). Rochberg conceived of the world as a mixture of cultures from the past and present; his approach to composition was one way of acknowledging the pluralism and creating music that can successfully operate as part of it.

An investigation of Rochberg's allusion to the style of one particular composer—Gustav Mahler—demonstrates how the Third Quartet constructs an understanding of music from the past as part of the present. Rochberg evokes Mahler's music in the fifth movement, the "Finale: Scherzos and Serenades." Jay Reise notes the evocation, comparing mm. 240–243 of the quartet with m. 75 from the final movement of Mahler's Ninth Symphony (Reise 1980/1981, 404; and see Figure 11-1). Reise lists particular aspects of Mahler's music that are present in the quartet: "the double-changing note figure, the harmonic progression, the pedals, the mood, the dramatic leap of the minor seventh" (405). When hearing Rochberg's piece, I am struck by how evocative these characteristics are. Especially distinctive are the sixteenth-note turn, which Reise calls the "double-changing note figure," and the large descending melodic leaps, two musical elements that have become synonymous with Mahler's style and appear in many of his other works. A second comparison between the Third Quartet and the Ninth Symphony strengthens the connection between the two. In both excerpts an opening two-note motive slowly develops into a full-fledged melody. Both also have counter melodies—in the Ninth it is the horn, in the Quartet it is the first violin—and share a similar diatonic accompaniment figuration in D major. The tempos and dynamics are similar as well.

Rochberg's adoption of Mahler's style in his Third Quartet depends for its meaning on the audience's knowledge of that style. At the time that the quartet was composed, Mahler's music was particularly popular and listeners would surely have understood the reference. They would have probably also had a particular opinion of Mahler's music and would have been aware of its popularity. The Third Quartet highlights the importance of Mahler's oeuvre as part of the musical culture in the here-and-now, emphasizing the presentness of this past musical style as a music that is actively engaged by

the contemporary audience. Already versed in the style of the older composer's music, listeners bring their own meanings to bear on the allusions:

> If, as Rochberg claims, the past is indelibly printed in each of our psyches,
> and each of us is ". . . part of a vast physical-mental-spiritual web of pre-
> vious lives, existences, modes of thought, behavior, and perception . . . of
> actions and feelings . . . ," then our past experiences of the Mahler Ninth
> are a part of that web. (Reise 1980/1981, 405)

When a composer alludes to a historical style, there is usually the assumption that it will be understood and that the audience will have some sort of
reaction to it. The popularity of Mahler's music in the early 1970s when
Rochberg wrote his Third Quartet emphasizes this point. In 1971 movie
director Visconti used music from Mahler's Third and Fifth Symphonies as
the soundtrack to *Death in Venice*. Granted larger exposure through
soundtrack highlight albums, this music was enjoyed by many who never
really followed orchestral music:

> People who do not listen to much other classical music do listen to
> Mahler. . . . Conversely, a person ignorant of or indifferent to Mahler's
> music is apt to get disqualified as a feeling human being. In other words,
> Mahler arouses more than ordinary emotions in his listeners, who form
> intimate relationships with his music and identify themselves by their alle-
> giances to it. (Hoffman 1975, 52)

The exposure provided by *Death in Venice* was actually the commercial crest of a large wave of popularity that began in the 1960s. By the early
1970s, "Mahler . . . is *in*, he is *heavy*" (Gross 1973, 484; see also Danuser
1991; Tibbs 1977). The Third Quartet builds upon this popularity and uses
it to emphasize the existence of past music in our present. This approach
to the past is not "an attempt to reverse time's arrow, to return to the
untroubled virtue of an idealized past" (Meyer 1967, 1993). It involves the
compositional use of past styles relevant in the present. This material is
clearly recognizable as being similar to a historical style, allowing the audience to make that connection. When allusions are juxtaposed, as in the case
of the Third String Quartet, the effect makes one aware of how the past fits
into present-day life as music to be consumed.

My argument so far has been that a binary model of postmodernism
provides a less than satisfactory understanding of Rochberg's music by
ignoring historical evidence and alternative analytical approaches. Another
effect of a binary model manifests itself in Kramer's and Pasler's work. The
binary model derives from a desire to demonstrate the presence of a contemporary avant-garde that is the historical successor to early twentieth-
century composers. By focusing on the similarities and differences between

modern and postmodern music in relation only to each other, writers are attempting to expand the imagined lineage of art music history. Such a limited approach—one that disregards or downplays how the composer understood the piece, critical reaction to it, and how the music might resonate with other cultural forms and discourses—sidesteps important evidence that contributes to a more comprehensive understanding of a piece of music and its existence as an event experienced by people in a historical situation. I myself have certain biases and interests in my research: I personally feel that the use of historical evidence—composer's comments and early criticism—from the time in which a piece was written and first performed can be an effective basis for an analysis. But whatever analytical approach we take, we must always be aware that there are other strategies to be employed. In the case of Rochberg's Third String Quartet, it may not simply be enough to call it neoconservative.

WORKS CITED

Brody, Martin. 1996. "'Music for the Masses': Milton Babbitt's Cold War Music Theory." *Musical Quarterly*, 161–92.

Danuser, Hermann. 1991. "'My Time Will Yet Come.' Die Amerikanische Mahler-Rezeption im spiegel der Zeitschrift 'Chord and Discord.'" *Gustav Mahler und Seine Zeit*. Laabe: Laaber-Verlag. 275–85.

Davis, James A. 1992. "Positivism, Logic, and Atonal Analysis." *Music Review* 53/3 (August): 210–20.

———. 1993. "Positivistic Philosophy and the Foundations of Atonal Music Theory." Ph.D. diss., Boston University.

Gross, Harvey. 1973. "Gustav Mahler: Fad, or Fullness of Time?" *The American Scholar* 42/3: 484–88.

Heilbroner, Robert L. 1959. *The Future as History*. New York: Harper and Brothers.

Hoffman, Eva. 1975. "Mahler for Moderns." *Commentary* 59/6: 52–59.

Kramer, Jonathan D. 1995. "Beyond Unity: Toward an Understanding of Musical Postmodernism." In *Concert Music, Rock, and Jazz since 1945*, edited by Elizabeth West Marvin and Richard Hermann. Rocheste, NY: University of Rochester Press, 11–33.

McLuhan, Marshall. 1964. *Understanding Media: The Extensions of Man*. New York: McGraw-Hill.

McLuhan, Marshall, and Quentin Fiore. 1967. *The Medium is the Massage*. New York, London, and Toronto: Simon and Schuster.

Meyer, Leonard B. 1967. *Music, the Arts, and Ideas*. Chicago and London: University of Chicago Press.

Pasler, Jann. 1993. "Postmodernism, Narrativity, and the Art of Memory." *Contemporary Music Review* 7: 3–32.

Reise, Jay. 1980/81. "Rochberg the Progressive." *Perspectives of New Music* 19: 395–407.

Rochberg, George. [1969] 1984. "No Center." In *Aesthetics of Survival*, edited with an introduction by William Bolcom. Ann Arbor: University of Michigan Press, 155–60.

———. 1984 [1972]. "Reflections on the Renewal of Music" In *Aesthetics of Survival,* edited with an introduction by William Bolcom. Ann Arbor: University of Michigan Press. 232–38.

———. 1984 [1974]. "On the Third String Quartet." In *Aesthetics of Surival,* edited with an introduction by William Bolcom. Ann Arbor: University of Michigan Press. 239–42.

———. 1984. "Can the Arts Survive Modernism?" *Critical Inquiry* 11 (December) 317–40.

Tibbs, Monika. 1977. "Anmerkungen zur Mahler-Rezeption." In *Mahler: Eine Herausforderung,* edited by Peter Ruzicka. Wiesbaden: Breitkopf und Härtel. 85–100.

CHAPTER 12

Resistant Strains of Postmodernism:
The Music of Helmut Lachenmann and Brian Ferneyhough
Ross Feller

In the 1960s, as the hegemony of total serialism waned, the German composer Helmut Lachenmann and the British composer Brian Ferneyhough began writing pieces that posed extreme solutions to the compositional cul-de-sac young composers faced at that time. John Cage had already "invaded" Europe with his ideas about indeterminacy and aleatoricism in music. His presence at the Internationale Ferienkurse für Neue Musik at Darmstadt in 1958 encouraged many European composers to question and re-examine certain types of modernist practice such as serialism. Many opted to explore indeterminate forms and other types of perceived freedom. Lachenmann and Ferneyhough, however, pursued different paths in their respective efforts to move beyond the serial impasse. Each sought to reinject vitality back into the idea of closed-form composition through integrating excessive, unstable, and chaotic structures. Almost three and a half decades later, they continue to develop these issues in their work, issues that foreground qualities that make art a human endeavor.

Throughout this essay several binary distinctions are employed, not in order to demonstrate invariant separation, but instead to unleash the friction or contradiction that results from their points of contact. Rub two sticks together long enough and you'll begin to see a fire.

THE MILLENNIAL DIVIDE

On one side there are dreamers, poets, and inventors whose activities demonstrate a commitment to transcendence, infinity, and the sublime. They may resist pressures to quantify, package, and sort, by creating things that quantify, package, and sort in the extreme. Thus, opportunities are created for breakdowns and failures, requiring new categories, languages, and thoughts. On the other side are bureaucrats, preachers, and a few old-school scientists, who pay homage to the concept of truth, in a world which they see as moving toward total explanation and accountability.

Quantification and packaging are also their tools, but they use them to erect the ultimate reductionism. Millennialism is once again upon us, demonstrating, in full force, the ancient bifurcation between those who aggressively seek the salvation of a secure and comprehensive view of the world, and those who realize that the impossibility of such a program has caused much bloodshed, strife, and poverty.

THE SHIFT

The new music world is populated with a heterogeneous mix of musicians, some with very little in common. One possible subgroup of this world contains composers, performers, and listeners who try to resist the confines of slackening, pastiche, and reified appropriation. On one level they are part of a larger cultural move toward radical expression (e.g., extreme sports), ever faster forms of artistic communication (e.g., speed metal and rap), risk-taking (e.g., tornado following), and wider sexual boundaries (e.g., gender bending). On another level their "resistance" requires an aesthetic of excess, which is, according to Jean-François Lyotard, a condition of postmodernism ([1979] 1984, 81).

POSTMODERNISM

Postmodernism, as has been often pointed out, is a term fraught with contradiction. If modernism can be characterized as an ideology of constant crisis and transgression what would it mean to move beyond it? The inherent contradictions in the term "postmodernism" have spawned a plethora of competing definitions. Part of the problem is that there are at least as many types of postmodernism as modernism. We should recall that modernism itself was vast and by no means consistent. Some types of modernism are easier to grasp, less controversial or contradictory than others. Some are readily accepted as mainstream beacons of their represented objects, while others float toward the margins, resisting the pull toward the center. In perhaps its best-known form, as put forth by the art historian Clement Greenberg, modernism was a defense against what we now call postmodernism (see Silliman 1990, 84). Thus, it laments the erosion of the distinction between high culture and commercial or popular culture. This explains Lyotard's well-known, paradoxical claim that postmodernism does not signal the end of modernism but rather a new beginning (Lyotard 1984, 79).

So, what *is* the definition of postmodernism? Hal Foster and others (e.g., Norris 1990) have parsed the term according to a fundamental opposition between a "postmodernism which seeks to deconstruct modernism and resist the status quo," and a "postmodernism which repudiates the former to celebrate the latter" (Foster 1983, xi). The former strategy which he calls a "postmodernism of resistance" appropriates modernist devices or materials and transforms them by deliberately exposing the inherent contradictions they contain. This strand is thus more closely related to the experimental writing of the Language Poets than to the pop art of Andy Warhol. It attempts a critical deconstruction of tradition wherever it is found, explicitly following Lyotard's motto that "invention is always born of dissension" (Lyotard 1984, xxv). The latter strategy, which Foster calls a "postmodernism of reaction," accuses modernism of being unnatural or elitist and blames it for the unfortunate consequences of modernization. It seeks an absolute break with modernism. Paradoxically, a defining characteristic of modernism is that it is necessary to break with the old in order to initiate the new. According to Lyotard the break required of a postmodernism of reaction is simply "a way of forgetting or repressing the past" (Lyotard 1993, 75), often repeating rather than surpassing it. In its most sinister form it can be characterized, as the Australian musicologist Richard Toop said in regards to the New Simplicity composers, as a "longing for a new millenarian totalitarianism, in which the works of radical and even semiradical modernism can once again be proscribed as 'decadent art' (definitively, this time)" (Toop 1993, 53). Whatever the case, before taking up arms one should remember that the two aforementioned types of postmodernism are not necessarily mutually exclusive. Most composers, in fact, partake of aspects of both.

LACHENMANN AND FERNEYHOUGH

Compositions by Lachenmann and Ferneyhough are largely incomparable, yet they do share some common ground. Adorno differentiated types of music by their relationship to their status as a commodity, some accepting this fate, others rejecting it. Both Lachenmann's and Ferneyhough's compositions reside within the latter type. In a world where almost everything is susceptible to commodification their intentional resistance stems from an idealistic, utopian vision about what music could become.

Both composers have developed consistent, personal styles, consciously reassessed tradition, and critically deconstructed performance practice. Both also incorporate counter-intuitive or counter-habitual mechanisms within a framework that nourishes the chaotic and the complex. Elke Hockings has pointed out that often the stimulus behind Lachenmann's and Ferneyhough's music is a contradictory impulse. They are careful to compose structures that nourish contradiction rather than "solve" it with some kind of false synthesis. Their work thus bridges the philosophical gap between German generalizing and English positivism (Hockings 1995, 14).

This contradictory impulse in their use of rigorous compositional procedures may be linked to their studies with unorthodox serialists. Lachenmann studied with Karlheinz Stockhausen and Luigi Nono, and was very much taken with the latter composer's vision of what Western music might become in the aftermath of the Holocaust, *the* pivotal demonstration of the failure of reason to stand up to fascist power. Lachenmann was influenced by Nono's rejection of nineteenth-century bourgeois elements and his basic concern for the social and political functions of music. In Lachenmann's own compositions the result is, according to David Alberman, "nothing less than a Cartesian reassessment of Western music and art in general. Central tenets such as the unconditional pursuit of beauty, standardised definitions of beauty, or the notion that music should only soothe the human mind, and not disturb it . . . come under critical scrutiny" (Alberman 1995, 15).

Ferneyhough studied with the Swiss composer Klaus Huber and was influenced by Huber's sense of transcendentalism. Ferneyhough, according to Toop, is one of the few composers to "remain faithful to the idea of art as the endless search for the transcendental, and of music as potential revelation" (Toop 1993, 54). Unlike some of the orthodox serialists, his compositions don't seek to exhaust material but rather to unleash its future potential. Speaking in general terms, a total serial piece, like much process-oriented music, begins with the initiation of a process and ends when the process ends, usually after most, if not all, permutations have been used. Ferneyhough's compositional approach is much broader in scope and more narrowly focused on systemic procedure in order to create, or uncover, inherent contradictions in the system itself. It is certainly true, as Jonathan Harvey puts it, that "Ferneyhough has absorbed the discoveries of total serialism to a profounder degree than almost anyone else of his generation, without actually subscribing to its orthodoxies in his music" (Harvey 1979, 123). Ferneyhough distinguishes between three types of serialism (Ferneyhough 1995, 227). The first is simply used to generate the material of a piece. The second involves a kind of sedimentation process from a given set of initial elements. The third type, in which he includes his own works, involves a pressurized channeling of materials through a series of gridlike filters. The pressure is caused by resistance as one element is pressed up against another. Often in his music one can locate a dichotomy between strict or automatic and informal or intuitive structural approaches. For example, complex webs of polyphony are harnessed with organic, high-profile gestures. The friction between these approaches results in the extreme types of musical expression for which he is known.

Both composers appropriate some accoutrements of serial and avant-garde practice, but compositionally integrate them through decentering and dispersion, two hallmarks of postmodern technique. For example, they often utilize extended, instrumental techniques as an integral part of a work's fabric, rather than as special effects. With the possibility open for any sound, they meticulously shape their respective sound worlds with a variety of resources, excluding only reified takes on previous styles. It is instructive to repeat Ferneyhough's take on the post–World War II move to aleatoricism, which he discusses in an essay entitled "Parallel Universes." In it he says that the assumption that "the increasingly threatening discrepancy between process and perception which lay at the heart of advanced serial practice could be annulled via recourse to the blatantly uncritical mimeticism of the aleatoric, in which the problematic nature of the fracture was naively celebrated rather than rigorously probed" (Ferneyhough 1994, 18). He goes on to link this assumption with a kind of postmodern powerplay in which one metadiscourse of repression merely replaces another (20). The work of Ferneyhough and Lachenmann is often mistaken for serialism or avant-gardism but it more closely resembles Foster's postmodernism of resistance.

Lachenmann and Ferneyhough are controversial figures bent on making the most out of music. They employ a diverse range of instrumental and compositional techniques. In their music one frequently encounters what Ferneyhough has called "too muchness" (Ferneyhough 1995, 451). In reference to Lachenmann's music, instruments are played in every conceivable manner. In a sense his music is about the collision between performers' bodies and their instruments. His performers must learn how to connect anew with their instruments. In Ferneyhough's music, "too muchness" is brought about through the intentional overloading of informational/instructional layers. In both cases the performer's responsibility increases.

Both composers privilege the act of writing and are fastidious notators. But, whereas Ferneyhough minutely details almost every musical parameter, Lachenmann is more concerned with detailing the methods for producing sound. Their *écriture* (that is, the act of writing/notating musical ideas) points to Jacques Derrida's notion of *play* which he defines as the disruption of presence (Derrida 1978, 292). Things are rendered unstable through processes of substitution, leading to the excessive, overabundance of the signifier. Signifiers are literally the basic sonic stuff of music. Lachenmann's and Ferneyhough's scores require that their performers *play*, not merely play.

By injecting their music with excesses of all kinds, Lachenmann and Ferneyhough attempt to forestall the closure inherent in all acts of recognition. One primary example involves the concept of noise, whether sonic or semiotic. Sonic noise masks or mutates sound and is a primary tool of Lachenmann's compositional technique. One might think of semiotic noise as involving interference in the process of signification itself. They both incorporate this noise in their music.

LACHENMANN

Lachenmann's early work was in a post-Webern, serial style. Although he borrowed Nono's pointillist technique, his primary focus was on the sonic potential of his materials (see Gottwald 1980). In the late 1960s he began to explore radically unconventional instrumental writing, and developed a compositional technique that he calls "rigidly constructed denial"

(Lachenmann 1989b, 8). At its core it involves the intentional exclusion of unquestioned or habitual standards, brought into *play* through the use of devices such as fragmentation and masking. But, what is ultimately impressive about his music is the powerful demonstration of expression and the personal vision behind it. Thus, his negative dialectic is transformed into a positive affirmation of the human spirit.

Much of his recent work is involved with forms which reintegrate historical convention. On occasion the pressure of tradition surfaces as an audible reference point. For example in works such as *Mouvement* (1982–84) for mixed chamber ensemble, or *Tanzsuite mit Deutschlandlied* (1979/80) for orchestra and string quartet, folk music, the German national anthem, and J. S. Bach serve as a kind of naked frame on which to hang his idiosyncratic sound material. Each reference is transformed via scratching, breathing, and drumming, so that only the rhythms remain partially recognizable.

In Lachenmann's compositions noise is so well integrated that distinctions between noise and music break down. For him composition involves "a confrontation with the interconnections and necessities of musical substance" (Clements 1994, 13) through a re-examination of the fundamentals of sound production. He foregrounds the act of making sound, exposing rather than concealing the effort and technique of production. At times the instruments he writes for seem to take on human qualities, sounding as if they breathe, shout, and groan. And as they do this they become part of new virtual instruments compositely mixed in order to, as he puts it, "fracture the familiar" (13). The Russian formalist Viktor Schlovsky has described this process with the term *ostranenie* (making the familiar strange). The principle aim of poetry was, for him, to use language in order to defamiliarize that which we don't "see" anymore (Hawkes 1977, 62). Translated into musical terms this concept is behind much of Lachenmann's compositional practice.

Like many contemporary composers, Lachenmann's acoustic, instrumental writing is indebted to the groundbreaking experimentation of electroacoustic music, itself born of technological necessity. Transferred into the acoustic realm, a new type of *écriture* is born that doesn't fit comfortably with traditional instrumental design or technique. He calls this simply "instrumental *musique concrète*." It is defined in his music through timbre, tone, and the concept of echo (see Hockings 1995, 12). For instance, in *Dal Niente* (1970) the clarinet soloist performs as a kind of airflow filter. In *Pression* (1969) the cello is used as a transmitter of different kinds of pressurized noise. Figure 12-1 contains the first page of *Pression*. The notation indicates physical movements and rhythms, coordinated spatially with a "bridge clef," which depicts the strings, fingerboard, bridge, and tailpiece of the cello. More recently in *Allegro Sostenuto* (1986/88) for clarinet, cello, and piano he employs the instru-

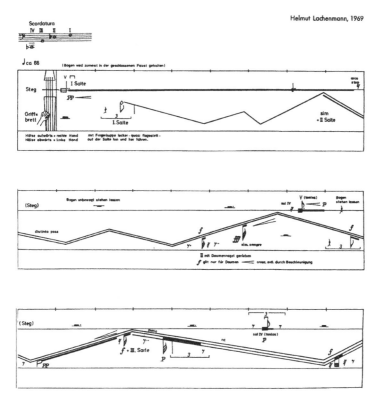

'Figure 12-1. Helmut Lachenmann, Pression (1969), p. 1. Used by Permission of Breitkopf & Härtel. © 1969 by Musikverlag Hans Gerig, Köln. 1980 assigned to Breitkopf & Härtel, Wiesbaden.

ments in combination to make a single virtual instrument by mixing their attacks and sustains. Interestingly, the clarinet and cello are used to defeat the piano's natural *diminuendo* characteristic. This piece partakes in instrumental *musique concrète*, but also uses triadic harmonies as a foil to the more unfamiliar sounds.

In *Gran Torso* (1971–72, 1976, 1988) for string quartet Lachenmann explores an almost inaudible region as the players bow virtually every part of their instruments. In the process of composing it, the structural areas for this piece became so overdeveloped that it would have been impossible, given a concert performance, to perform them all. Thus, he utilized only the torso of the piece. Here we encounter an especially potent form of Derrida's notion of *play*, put into practice. Figure 12–2 shows a section of the cello part. Once again he utilizes the "bridge clef" in addition to rec-tangular notes to indicate approximate finger locations; hollow, diamond

Figure 12-2. Helmut Lachenmann, Gran Torso (1971–72, 1976, 1988), excerpt of cello part. Used by Permission of the Paul Sacher Foundation.

notes to indicate a pinched string, noise harmonic; and many other graphic notation conventions.

Lachenmann's predilection for breaking music down into its basic components is manifest in his incorporation of childlike gesture. In *Pression* it is not hard to imagine that what we hear is the result of the first meeting of a very inquisitive child with a cello. *Ein Kinderspiel* (1980), a set of seven short piano pieces, was written for his own children. In it he combines structural, acoustic processes with pre-existent materials such as children's songs, dance forms, and simple fingering exercises. For example, in one of the pieces he incorporates a compound-duple dance rhythm played loudly on the top two notes of the keyboard. As the hammers hit the strings one's attention is drawn to the action of the instrument and the sounding board. In another piece from this collection, a chord in the upper register is initially struck and sustained. Then, one finger at a time is lifted from the keyboard causing the harmonic content of the chord's decay to vary. These pieces do not only serve pedagogical purposes, nor are they only for children. As Lachenmann points out, "childhood and musical experiences related to it are an essential part of every adult's inner world." One of his most recent pieces is an opera based on a children's story by Hans Christian Andersen called *The Little Match Girl*. According to Alberman, Lachenmann's "life's work as a compose . . . has always been to open up a dialogue between the child and the adult in all of us (Alberman 1995, 16).

FERNEYHOUGH

Since the late 1960s Ferneyhough's work has come to "embody the energy of dichotomy or contradiction" (from the sketches for *Mnemosyne*, Paul Sacher Stiftung Collection). For example, there's often tension between strict or automatic and informal or intuitive approaches to composition. Complex webs of polyphony and parametric subdivision are combined with organic, gestural, or sonic development. The friction between these approaches results in extreme types of musical expression. Ferneyhough is clearly influenced by the hyper-expressivity of the early music of Pierre Boulez, but also by the static sound blocks of Edgard Varèse. Like most postmodernists Ferneyhough seeks to project actively the idea of multiplicity in his work. He does this, however, through incorporating competing, occasionally contradictory, layers of material.

At its best, Ferneyhough's music includes what Jonathan Kramer has called "multiply-directed time" (Kramer 1988, 46). This is a musical motion that is continuously interrupted in an effort to present the unexpected. One of the ways Ferneyhough achieves this is through what he's called "interruptive polyphony" or "interference form," a device employed in his solo works, or for solo parts in ensemble works. Figure 12-3 contains the first page of *Trittico per G. S.* (1989) for solo double bass wherein this device is consistently and comprehensively employed. It involves two or more separate layers of material each notated on its own staff. The staves are arranged in a variable but hierarchical order. The materials from one staff interrupt those from another, shortening the durations from the first staff. In order to clarify these points of interruption he draws horizontal lines to indicate the flow of events, and vertical lines to show interruptions to the flow. This device has clear psychological, implications, for as Ferneyhough claims, "a note begun *as if* it were going to continue for its full written length . . . is going to have a considerably different effect when interrupted than a note written as having an identical real duration" (Ferneyhough 1995, 5). The layers shown in Figure 12-3 are further distinguished through the application of contrasting texture types. At the beginning the top layer contains only double-stops while the bottom layer contains glissandi. He also uses dynamic, registral, and rhythmic contrasts to achieve the same effect.

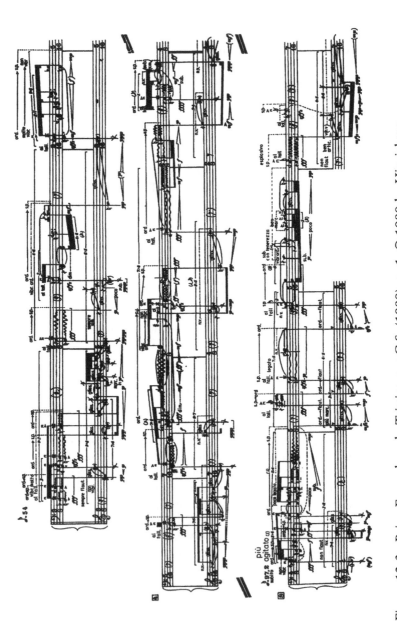

Figure 12-3. Brian Ferneyhough, Trittico per G.S. (1989), p. 1. © 1989 by Hinrichsen Edition, Peters Edition Limited, London. Reproduced by kind permission.

Ferneyhough has employed multiple-line projection in other solo works such as *Time and Motion Study I* and *II* (1971–77, 1973–76) for solo bass clarinet and solo cello, and in *Unity Capsule* (1975–76) for solo flute. But in these pieces the lines work together, in tandem, whereas in his more recent work the lines almost always interrupt each other. Figure 12-4 contains the first page of *Time and Motion Study I*. Here he oscillates between two contrasting types of material. The first is characterized by static, fluid, perpetual motion, the other by dynamic, diverse, and expansive motives.

Ferneyhough's music resists sightreading. Thus, performers must take a step back before learning to play his music. From this very basic point Ferneyhough's performers face the question of how to reintegrate their bodies into radically unfamiliar gestural profiles. Ferneyhough's overnotational practice slows down the process of decoding, thereby delaying habit formation. His performers are enticed into developing unique, strategic approaches in order to overcome the disorientation they face. Percussionist Steven Schick and cellist Taco Koostra have both said that the effort to work through and execute Ferneyhough's complex rhythmic subdivisions results in intense, razor-sharp performances. The point is not merely to play the so-called exact notated rhythms (which any computer could do) but instead to have a human performer make the attempt. Of the standard objections to Ferneyhough's music and notational usage, perhaps the most common is the vehemently held belief that the whole endeavor is pointless because many musical details are inaudible. But, as many writers point out (for example, Dahlhaus 1987; Kramer 1988) what is audible is often illusive and in no way absolute. There are many degrees of audibility, each dependent upon psychological, physiological, and aesthetic factors. It may be difficult to tell the difference between what is completely inaudible and what is barely perceptible. Some music is intentionally pushed to the periphery of consciousness to do its work. The complex rhythms Ferneyhough uses such as a nested tuplet three or four levels "deep" clearly is impossible to sightread but is it really also impossible to perform or hear? One must separate the physically impossible from the merely difficult. According to Henry Cowell, any three-level nested tuplet could be accurately produced if a performer would simply devote fifteen minutes a day, for five months, to such matters (Cowell 1969, 64). The gap between score and result, a fact of all live performance, is radically foregrounded in Ferneyhough's music. Performers routinely fill this gap with performance practice. The less explicit a notation is the more performers must rely upon these kinds of conventional supplements. The accusation that artworks contained superfluous intentions, it is interesting to note, was originally part of Classicism's polemic against Baroque or mannered art (Dahlhaus 1987, 54). Symbols that simply illustrated were praised, whereas allegory was rejected. For Ferneyhough, an aesthetically adequate performance of his music depends upon "the extent to which the performer is technically and spiritually able to recognize and embody the demands of fidelity (*not* 'exactitude'!)" (Ferneyhough 1995, 19; emphasis his).

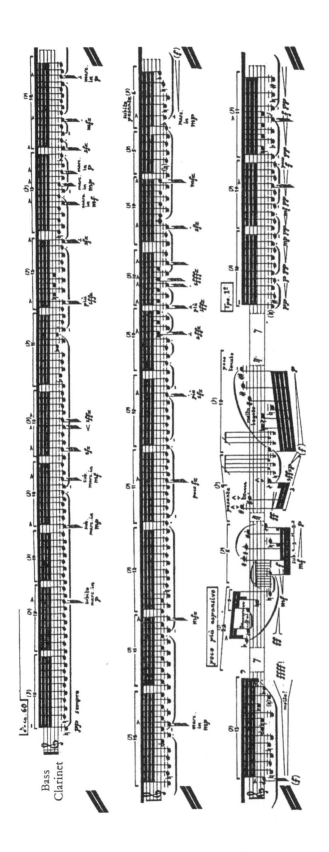

Figure 12-4. Brian Ferneyhough, Time and Motion Study I (1971–77), p. 1. © 1977 by Hinrichsen Edition, Peters Edition Limited, London. Reproduced by kind permission.

The formal principles in Ferneyhough's scores define an environment in which informal, spontaneous generation can re-engage the formal in a meaningful dialogue. His aesthetic emphasizes the human agent not only as the generator of systems, but, also as the catalyst for the system's demise and subsequent regeneration.

CONCLUSION

At its best postmodernism refines our sensibility to difference and reinforces our ability to tolerate the incommensurable (see Lyotard [1979] 1984, xxv). If postmodernism compels us to consider pluralism and alternate worlds, then surely this must include all types no matter how difficult they are to comprehend, even forms of postmodernism that break with modernism in complicated ways due to their partially severed ties or close resemblance to modernist practice. As the poet Ron Silliman points it, postmodernism is not necessarily a style but rather a cultural situation wherein very different forms coexist (Silliman 1990, 90).

According to Lyotard the postmodern condition exhibits excess and complexity far beyond that found in any other period in history. Lachenmann's and Ferneyhough's music reflects this condition, demonstrating how the attributes of excess or complexity might be played out in the world of composed sound. Their work is being performed more now than ever before. Perhaps this is because they foreground many important issues relevant to contemporary musicians such as: the role of the score, inventive notational uses, and the significance of closed-form composition to performance freedom.

Lachenmann ultimately desires "a music which is . . . able to reflect everything—including the illusion of progressiveness. Art as a foretaste of freedom in an age without freedom" (Lachenmann 1989a, 9). His statement could easily serve as a maxim for a postmodernism of resistance.

WORKS CITED

Alberman, David. 1995. "Helmut Lachenmann." Liner notes to compact disc *Helmut Lachenmann 3*. France: Montaigne Auvidis (MO 782075). 15–18.

Barrett, Richard. 1992. "Brian Ferneyhough." In *Contemporary Composers*, edited by Brian Morton and Pamela Collins. London: St. James Press. 285–87.

Carl, Robert. 1990. "Six Case Studies in New American Music: A Postmodern Portrait Gallery." *College Music Symposium*, 30/1: 46–48.

Clements, Andrew. 1994. "Helmut Lachenmann: Truth, Beauty and Relevance." Liner notes to compact disc *Helmut Lachenmann 2*. France: Montaigne Auvidis (MO 782023). 12–13.

Cowell, Henry. 1969. *New Musical Resources*. New York: Something Else Press.

Dahlhaus, Carl. 1987. *Analysis and Value Judgment*. Translated by Siegmund Levarie. Stuyvesant, N.Y.: Pendragon Press.

Derrida, Jacques. 1978. *Writing and Difference*. Chicago: University of Chicago Press.

Ferneyhough, Brian. 1994. "Parallel Universes." In *Asthetik und Komposition zur Aktualität der Darmstadter Ferienkursarbeit,* Internationales Musikinstitut Darmstadt, edited by Gianmario Borio and Ulrich Mosch. Mainz: Schott. 17–22.

———. 1995. *Collected Writings.* Edited by James Boros and Richard Toop. Amsterdam: Harwood Academic Publishers.

Foster, Hal, ed. 1983. *The Anti-Aesthetic: Essays on Postmodern Culture.* Port Townsend, Wash.: Bay Press. ix–xvi.

Gottwald, Clytus. 1980. "Brian Ferneyhough." In *The New Grove Dictionary of Music and Musicians.* London: Macmillan Publishers. 397.

Harvey, Jonathan. 1979. "Brian Ferneyhough." *The Musical Times,* 120/1639: 723–28.

Hawkes. Terence. 1977. *Structuralism and Semiotics.* Berkeley and Los Angeles: University of California Press.

Hockings, Elke. 1995. "Helmut Lachenmann's Concept of Rejection." *Tempo* 193. 4–14.

Koostra, Taco. 1990. Questionnaire response in *Complexity?* Edited by Joel Bons. Rotterdam: Job Press. 27.

Kramer, Jonathan D. 1988. *The Time of Music: New Meanings, New Temporalities, New Listening Strategies.* New York and London: Schirmer Books.

Lachenmann, Helmut. 1997. Program Note, Krannert Center for The Performing Arts. University of Illinois at Urbana Champaign, November 19, 1997.

———. 1989a. "Gesprach mit Ursula Stürzbecher." In *Helmut Lachenmann,* translated by Roger Clément. Wiesbaden: Breitkopf und Härtel.

———. 1989b. "Selbstportrait." In *Helmut Lachenmann,* translated by Roger Clément. Wiesbaden: Breitkopf und Härtel.

Lyotard, Jean-François. [1979] 1984. *The Postmodern Condition: A Report on Knowledge.* Translated by Geoff Bennington and Brian Massumi. Minneapolis: University of Minnesota Press.

———. 1993. *The Postmodern Explained. Correspondence 1982–1985.* Edited by Julian Pefanis and Morgan Thomas, translated by Don Barry, Bernadette Maher, Julian Pefanis, Virginia Spate, and Morgan Thomas. Minneapolis: University of Minnesota Press.

Norris, Christopher. 1990. *What's Wrong with Postmodernism: Critical Theory and the Ends of Philosophy.* Baltimore: Johns Hopkins University Press.

Schick, Steven. 1994. "Developing an Interpretive Context: Learning Brian Ferneyhough's *Bone Alphabet.*" *Perspectives of New Music* 32: 132–53.

Silliman, Ron. 1990. "Postmodernism: Sign for a Struggle for the Sign." In *Conversant Essays,* edited by James McCorkle. Detroit: Wayne State University Press. 79–97.

Toop, Richard. 1988. "Four Facets of 'The New Complexity.'" *Context* 32: 4–50.

———. 1993. "On Complexity." *Perspectives of New Music* 31/1: 42–57.

CHAPTER 13

Imploding the System:
Kagel and the Deconstruction of Modernism
Paul Attinello

Mauricio Kagel has created a large number of works noted for their unusual conceptual and theatrical forms over the past forty years. These forms present remarkably consistent philosophical and cultural views and processes that subvert and dismantle various existing systems in distinctly similar ways. In addition, those processes seem parallel to some of the more self-conscious philosophies of postmodernism, including deconstruction, through their implosion of existing hierarchies and narratives. Although the comparison with deconstruction may seem ahistorical, if one invokes the possibility of cultural ideas emerging from a Zeitgeist rather than from the ideas of individuals, Kagel was just a bit ahead of his time: an essentially sarcastic reaction to one's surroundings—colleagues, works and training—can overturn the modernist universe, and create a consciousness that can never forget that it is permanently "post."

INSTRUMENTAL PREDECESSORS

Processes of subversion are evident in the compositional choices made in Kagel's early works, even those that involve a nearly normal musical score such as the *Sexteto de cuerdas* (1953, revised 1957) and *Transición II* (1958–59). The *Sexteto* was originally composed in Buenos Aires, then revised in Köln under the influence of European musical concepts circulating at the time (Kagel [1962] 1992, ii–ix). It is a highly sophisticated contrapuntal string sextet that recalls Berg's *Lyric Suite* more than anything else. What is remarkable about the *Sexteto* is that its complex determinate elements are mixed with indeterminate and transitional elements at several levels—which means that Kagel's first mature work and first major experiment in serialism already represented a confounding of serial control, an eruption of elements which could not be completely ordered into a serial fabric.

Kagel's analytical statements on the *Sexteto* include the following:

> The consistently rational construction of the piece serves to communicate
> direct expressivity. From the start, this was the aim of the piece—not the
> omnipresent acoustic exposition of the methods in putting together notes
> and durations. Thus the musical language of the work may often give the
> impression of being dominated by rhapsodic, improvisatory gestures. . . .
> But in any case, it should be borne in mind that the player has the possi-
> bility of shaping dynamics, articulation, and the kinds of expression
> through his own individual decisions. Finally, one should note that the
> work incorporates quarter-tones; their contribution is to make the harmo-
> ny more chromatic, rather than to enrich the pitch series. (Kagel [1962]
> 1992, v)

Thus, a certain kind of serialism—"the omnipresent acoustic exposition of the methods in putting together notes and durations"—is placed
under implicit critique; Kagel even points out that the quarter-tones are *not*
intended "to enrich the pitch series." The composer does not mention the
tempo and rhythm transformations, dynamic transitions, or noise-based
sound production techniques, but all of these also tend to blur the identity
of the serialized elements (Schnebel 1970, 13–14). Schnebel's discussion of
this piece focuses on the processes and density of elements, and the ways in
which they erode the serial relation between elements, resulting in something more "stochastic" like the works of Xenakis: "Syncopated, complicated, often irrational divisions smudge [sections] and give them a 'statistical character'" (12). But I would claim that Kagel goes further than this:
Xenakis's "statistical" textures continue to have a certain formal consistency, but even these early works present music that calls itself into doubt.

TRANSICIÓN II (1958–59)

A more elaborate presentation of "subverted" serialism is the combination
of a hyper-difficult performance score with arbitrary operations in Kagel's
first electronic work, *Transición II* (1958–59) for piano, percussionist, and
two electronic tapes (Kagel 1963c).[1] This chamber work begins with pages
of extraordinarily complex instructions for the making of decisions by the
two performers, both beforehand (in the production of the tapes) and during the performance of the piece. The instructions also state that "it should
be difficult to tell the tape from live piano" (note that the percussionist is
restricted to playing on the body and strings of the piano, and there are no
other instruments played).

This is a "moment" form piece, with aleatoric ordering of different sections; more importantly, it is *notationally* in "moment" form, as each page
is different, its technique selected from a number of sophisticated variations
on a schematic approach to musical graphics. The piece is a catalog or

anthology, that is, a set of modules representing a selection of then-current serial styles. The most unusual recurrent aspect of these modules is that they frequently combine a mass of carefully specified serial detail with highly arbitrary graphic signs, and then overlay that combination with elaborate methods of chance interpretation. Thus a precisely drawn set of pitches, with dynamics and accents, is placed on a circular card which is turned arbitrarily on the page, each slight turn reinterpreting the pitches on the adjacent staves in a completely different way. As Paul Griffiths says, Kagel tended

> to view the behavior of the investigatory performer with a certain ironic detachment, and to enjoy the other irony of highly detailed notation giving rise to impure results. In its outlandish sophistication, with rotatable discs and moveable slides, the score of his *Transición II* proceeds from that of Boulez's Third Sonata, while its promised intention to fuse "in one single declension" the musical present (heard in performance) with the past (returning on tape) and the future ("pre-experienced" in the form of previously prepared recordings of music to come) suggests a Stockhausen-like will to compose with time itself. And yet in performance the work could hardly fail to seem an absurd spectacle in which two musicians, operating on a piano, undertake meticulous actions in the service of musical aims which remain obscure, and in that respect the piece—as much as *Anagrama*—presents itself as a caricature of contemporary avant-garde endeavor. (Griffiths 1995, 139)

A difficult question arises about this piece, more than it does with any of Kagel's early work: Is this a joke? Is this piece a parody, or was it meant seriously?—or are there blended levels of irony that makes answering this question impossible? Wilhelm Schlüter, librarian at Darmstadt, commented in conversation that the score *must* have been intended seriously (at least for the most part), as percussionist Christoph Caskel (who played in the premiere) would never have been willing to perform something silly that required so much work. This can, of course, be seen as wishful thinking—the hope that the infection of satire and frivolity has not damaged, at least too much, the citadel of serialism. Erhard Karkoschka has pointed out in conversation that the transitions from free improvisation to very exact notation are extremely difficult, and he remembers that, when Kontarsky once made a single mistake in performance, Kagel insulted (*geschimpft*) him. We may suppose that the stress of performance was intended to be part of the piece.

A different problem is that the one recording, an unpublished tape in the Internationales Musikinstitut Darmstadt archives, suggests that the piece is merely a rather arid expanse of pointillism for various parts of a piano. In fact, there seems to be no way that the complex processes of decoding, interpreting, and choosing notational passages can be perceived by any listener, as the different virtuoso notations and concepts all sound basically the same. Is the piece, perhaps, suggesting something about the impossibility of communication between a composer, performers, and an audience? The peculiarity of the graphic transformations—turning circles, shifting pieces of paper—pull *Transición II* out into a self-consciously bizarre world where one cannot really trust that there is a "deep intention" that informs the surface. Such an interface between complexity and the impossibility of adequately realizing that complexity is paradigmatically ironic in structure; in fact, the piece marks the moment when the earnestness of serialism becomes indistinguishable from a joke.

ANAGRAMA (1957–58)

Anagrama (Spanish, "anagram") is composed for four vocal soloists and speaking chorus (both SATB, although the speaking chorus performs only unpitched material) and a chamber ensemble of three woodwinds, three keyboards, two harps, and three players of (mostly traditional) percussion. The text was prepared by the composer in Buenos Aires in 1955–56, consisting of anagrams based on the medieval palindrome "IN GIRUM IMUS NOCTE ET CONSUMIMUR IGNI," which translates as: "We circle in the night and are consumed by fire." The score was composed between February 1957 and November 1958, after Kagel moved from Argentina to Germany; the premiere occurred in Cologne on June 11, 1960 (Schnebel 1970, 15), and the dense, detailed score was finally published in 1965 (Kagel 1965a).

The text was apparently chosen, not because of its expressive image of the behavior of moths (one might think of Scriabin's *Vers la flamme*), but because of its technical complexity and cryptically suggestive quality. Kagel uses the palindrome as raw material in a quasi-serial fashion, splitting it into its component letters (c, e, g, i, m, n, o, r, s, t, and u, which amount to four vowels and eight consonants, a convenient total of twelve) and rearranging them into words and phrases in various languages. As in *Transición II*, the formal serial technique is confounded by the system's built-in flaws; unlike Boulez and Stockhausen, who agonized over what control meant and whether it was possible, Kagel was already subverting his own serial techniques in his first mature works. In this case, the flaw at the textual level is that twelve *letters* (rather than phonemes) are recomposed into words in different languages without regard for their actual sound; that is, 'u' does not represent the phoneme [u], but represents the various sounds that that letter can represent in different languages. Kagel also allows any diacritics, such that various vowel alterations can be added to the possible sounds. Finally, certain letters are interpreted as representing various sounds which Kagel allows himself to re-spell, detaching symbol from sound after it has been itself detached from symbol. As a result, what may appear on paper as the clearly serial manipulation of a limited set of sounds is treated more as a word game (or more exactly a letter game), with Kagel's very liberal rules virtually disconnecting the network of audible sounds from its source material, or at least greatly blurring the connection between them.

> In speaking of an earlier work, Kagel's *Palimpsestos* (1950), Schnebel says that Kagel chose fragments [of text] . . . , musically worked out so that the words were pulled far apart. He allowed such deformed lines of speech to set off in simultaneous superimposition. As in palimpsests many layers of writing lie on top of each other, except that only one of these can really be readable, so it is with these texts. The polyphony of independent speech lines makes possible multiple layers of speech itself. The texts interrupt each other, but also come into unexpected connections, and the whole allows a new course to begin. This kind of speech composition becomes more extensively developed in *Anagrama*. (Schnebel 1970, 9)

The serial organization of the musical materials is blurred in a comparable way in *Anagrama* by the extensive use of unpitched or approximately pitched phrases in all of the voices. The speaking chorus, as one might expect, has no pitches at all, but performs at pitch levels approximately notated above and below a single-line "middle" throughout; the four soloists perform exact pitches, approximate pitches, and unpitched rising and falling phrases. The instrumental ensemble uses an unusually large number of "noise" techniques, which appear not as special accents or variations to a pitched "text" but instead as constituent of the musical material (Knockaert 1976).

Larger formal structures can basically be dismissed in this piece (as is often true in Kagel's work before 1985). The constant degradation of systems results in products that appear to have no overriding organization of any kind. Knockaert's elaborate attempt to find order in *Anagrama* led merely to these conclusions:

> Kagel prefers a quasi-improvisatory development, without a well-determined scheme, to some classic formal outline by which he would have to introduce severe limitations in the course of the work. We could not discover any "overarching" musical form . . . , neither in the complete work nor in one of the components nor in any particular part (Knockaert 1976, 180).

This lack of an overarching system does not necessarily obviate *textural* consistency; Klüppelholz maintains that the palindrome's

> completely symmetrical structure is the equivalent of Webern's late twelve-tone rows. This is not a superficial comparison, for this piece . . . represents no less than an attempt to match in vocal music the standard of

synthetic sound differentiation based on Webern's work achieved in electronic music of that period. (Deutscher Musikrat [n.d.]a, 38)

It is important, however, that he later qualifies this suggestion of organization with its own reversal: "The form of the work is an implied criticism of the rigid formal structures of serial music; its ideal is constant transition even in the smallest elements" (Deutscher Musikrat [n.d.]a, 38), a comment that reflects a strong similarity between *Anagrama* and the *Sexteto*.

The score of *Anagrama* had a large impact on the composers of the Darmstadt circle. However, interest in the work largely ended when the piece was finally heard[2] (as happened later with *Staatstheater*) and no commercial recording was released until the archival release by the Deutscher Musikrat (Muggler 1973). Since the five sections of the piece use different selections of performers and techniques, it is difficult to find a representative page; the example chosen here is the first page of part IV, which includes instrumentalists, soloists, and speaking chorus, with some of the anagram texts and unpitched glissandi characteristic of the whole (Figure 13-1).

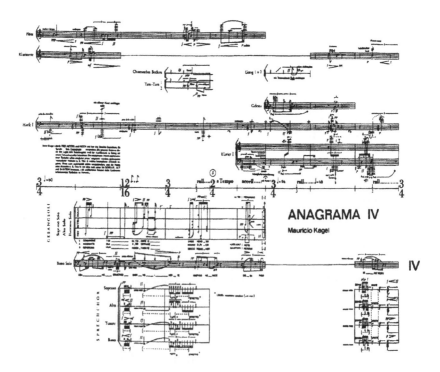

Figure 13-1. Kagel, *Anagrama*, p. 27 (part IV, p. 1). © 1989 by Hinrichsen Edition, Peters Edition Limited, London. Reproduced by kind permission. Note different techniques of sound production and their varied levels of precision.

Schnebel speaks of *Anagrama* in a passage subtitled "Undomesticated Sound": This music has a certain disorder in many places: the chorus howls, screams, flings abuse, and the instrumentalists strike out into it all. But cultivated passages also seem undomesticated: the glissandi of the opening or various accumulations of consonants sound *a modo barbaro*. There things break out with verve and thereby also with great energy, destroying obstructions, and from them fly far to uncivilized lands. This music resounds with the din of such activity. And besides the sounds coming out of new territory don't always sound refined, protest rings out in them, as it is no longer sustained anywhere else. (Schnebel 1970, 15)

In considering the violence imagined by Schnebel for this piece, it is worth thinking of a later comment by Kagel: "If these screams should awaken in the listener an impression that these are injured, suffering persons, then the chorus is to be heartily congratulated" (Deutscher Musikrat [n.d.]a, 38). I have seen no reference to the Spanish Civil War in relation to this piece, and it would be tendentious to make too specific an interpretation; but I think it is safe to say that the composer is thinking, at least approximately, of some of the news of suffering that originally turned him toward political anarchism.[3] Oddly enough, it is difficult to hear the only available recording of the work (Deutscher Musikrat [n.d.]a) as especially violent; if this is not a matter of it being a timid performance, perhaps it is simply a matter of historical hearing, as we have heard so many more overwhelming sounds performed since then. It is possible that, at the time, the constant breaking through of boundaries and fragmentation of elements gave an impression of extreme intensity, at least to the Darmstadt composers examining the score. Indeed, the fact that the actual sound of *Anagrama* is confused and almost formless, even rather messy, may have been a disappointment to those same composers when the work was finally heard.

Knockaert's analysis of *Anagrama* manages to turn up frequent references to death, night, restlessness, and various kinds of uproar among the scattered words of the text. Although he points out that Kagel would probably laugh at any close analysis of his intentions, he quotes Kagel as saying, "Misunderstandings and contradictions are for me something enormously creative" (Knockaert 1976, 185–86). Knockaert's analysis is ultimately inconclusive, more of a catalog of descriptions than an interpretation. Some of his impressions bear perhaps more weight than his analysis:

A listener gets the impression of a very complicated and especially very chaotic work. He certainly is deterred by the impression. Generally speaking one may say that the elements testify to a great simplicity, the complexity resulting from the way in which they are employed. (Knockaert 1976, 186)

It may be useful to reinterpret the earlier impressions of violence in *Anagrama* in this context as more appropriately to be named *chaos*, which could only seem violent in an intellectual context where the regulated hierarchy of ideas is an important aspect of their power and aesthetic effect. In explaining the elements that lead to his impression of complexity, Knockaert names:

> the very great number of different vocal and instrumental techniques. . . . When comparing this with other vocal works which originated about the same time, it strikes us that it is Kagel who performs the boldest experiments with the sound-material: he uses much more different vocal techniques than other composers (such as Berio, Nono, Ligeti, Penderecki . . .) and he subjects those vocal techniques to an endless series of variations and combinations. (Knockaert 1976, 187)

This comparison is not closely analyzed, but seems plausible. Knockaert's final paragraph attempts to establish aspects of *Anagrama* that are typical of Kagel's work, including the element of playfulness, the rejection of rigid patterns, and the difficulty and complexity of the resultant musical score. These conclusions are suggestive of certain solutions, and also of certain problems; of course, *Anagrama* aims to be explosive and revolutionary in a way that shows up in Kagel's later works, but does this perhaps too tamely, too much in the already existing serial style. *Anagrama* has, in fact, a peculiar historical flaw: its density is difficult to distinguish from the density of the more rigid, determinate abstractions that represented serialism, and so the work is not generally perceived as a reaction against that rigidity or abstraction, or as a possibly productive new direction for composition.

SUR SCÈNE (1960)—JOKES, SARCASM, AND THE IMPLOSION OF TRADITIONS

Paradox is a rhetorical gesture whose simplest form is the oxymoron. It can develop in several directions such as creating irony, indicating an unconcealed truth, or manufacturing the surrealistic shock of pure contradiction. Irony itself subverts the believability of a text or statement through connotative gestures such as mockery, sarcasm, and false naiveté; it can also be seen in more formal moves such as euphemism, punning, parody, understatement (litotes), overstatement (hyperbole), and opposite terms (antiphrasis). All of these can be seen tumbling over each other in Kagel's works, where endlessly ironical presentations may be seen as crucial in the process of undermining the avant-garde belief in its own procedures, a process which eventually led to the polymorphous techniques of the '60s and '70s.

Kagel's *Sur scène,* written in 1959–60 and premiered in 1962, is in this context the apex of his early work. The title means "on stage" or "on the scene"; the libretto introduces an elaborately ironical stance in the paradoxical dedication: "For Anonyma, in undying gratitude" (Kagel 1965b). The piece is actually an extended parody of rhetorical discussions of avant-garde music, as though modernism is mocking itself: the central figure gives a speech, accompanied by a (mostly wordless) singer, three instrumentalists on keyboards and percussion, and a mime. The five "accompanists" shadow the speaker's words in a specific series of gestures, sometimes expressive, sometimes nonsensical. The speech itself, a remarkable accretive parody of the many thoughtful, pompous, scathing, and glowing speeches presented by critics and officials in the context of European music after the war (especially, of course, in introducing or critiquing the Darmstadt courses), frequently descends from carefully articulated jargon into nonsense of several varieties, including altered and semi-intelligible words. One of Kagel's favorite rhetorical tricks is a kind of grammatical cul-de-sac, linking up a series of dependent clauses that imply an eventual independent clause or basic thought—which then never appears. This process is used to subvert the arguments of entire paragraphs; an example is this passage from Cornelius Cardew's translation:

> The crisis which today has befallen the musical situation must be viewed, for the time being, as an ultimate consequence of alienation and selfho[o]d, . . . in which musicians—[short pause]—after all we cannot, with this never-ending talk about a crisis, lay bare all the problematic constituents of its problematic essence and simply bypass them, and yet we cannot get around the fact, to employ a consideration, again we take cognizance of the fact that this obscurity, impenetrability, this absence of resonance in extreme situations is something which—under these circumstances we cannot but reach a conclusion which sound common sense had indicated from the beginning: our perception at the end of the sound spectrum is by nature dim. I am sitting in the smallest room of my house.

Thus, a process of extended, disconnected nonsense is brought into grammatical focus for a single, rather tangential statement on perceptual acoustics. Kagel ends the passage with his first concrete sentence, a famous euphemism (Slonimsky 1953, 139)[4] overlaid by ellipsis and disjunction. All these gestures serve to confound the narrative and erase the object of discussion, which appears to be the validity or meaning of avant-garde music. This is appropriately presented in the accompanying sounds of the opening of the piece, which overlaps a parody of instrumental "practicing" with vocal manipulations by the speaker. In fact, unlike the "libretto," the score for three instrumentalists is not engraved, is available on rental only, and in places is barely readable; this suggests that, for the publisher, composer, and (possibly) listeners, the text was the most interesting and viable aspect of the work.

Kagel has said that this textual work is meant to highlight the "utter ambiguity of role behavior and the universe of discourse" (Deutscher Musikrat [n.d.]b, 30). As *Sur scène* continues,

> The piece disintegrates. We hear chit-chat about music—clichés continually being produced by the world of music. Then we hear music which. . . fails to escape deliberate inanity. We see the condition of alienation existing among people in the world of music. (Deutscher Musikrat [n.d.]b, 30)

Serious as such an explanation sounds, it doesn't completely account for the wild humor of the piece itself, which perhaps recalls the stance of the mid-1960s Theater of the Ridiculous, that campy response to the existential seriousness of the Theater of the Absurd. A famous quotation from that movement, which illustrates the distinction between the comedy of modernism and that of postmodernism, stated: "We have passed beyond the absurd; our situation is absolutely preposterous" (Ludlam 1989, xi).

HALLELUJAH (1967–1968)

Kagel's *Hallelujah* (1967–68), an anti-sacred work for voices, exists in at least four major versions, including the original loose handwritten sheets (distributed for a time as rental scores), the engraved and bound version published by Universal Edition, a performing version recomposed by Clytus Gottwald, and the reconstruction with visuals made for the film version. All of these works differ somewhat from each other, sometimes a great deal; but, in all cases, the piece is a collection of a number of musical modules. The sixteen to thirty-two singers who share the roles of soloists, speaking choristers, and "protest" choristers operate in a consistently organized musical space: coherence is maintained by the relative identity of materials, as the vocal lines repeatedly refer to baroque vocal ornamentation.[5] Chaotically free solo foregrounds contrast with droning "chordal" backgrounds, all operating without any metric relation to each other.

The main modules that make up the materials of the score include a set of sixteen *Gesangsoli*, or vocal solos, and eight tutti sections of varying lengths. The solos and tutti sections consist of sets of musical phrases, meant to be performed in any order; of course, the timing and order of the tutti phrases must be decided in advance. Some phrases are pitched, some unpitched, some grouped as "mobiles," where the performer moves from place to place on the page rather than through ordered or contiguous phrases (as in the works of Haubenstock-Ramati, among others). Many of the tutti sections have a strong continuous pulsation, which helps to glue the various elements together. In addition, there are three short sections for speaking chorus, three rather longer "Protestchöre" or protest choruses, and a section of instrumental score (to be performed on eight-note pan-pipes by the singers). The printed score adds an extended soprano solo on the word "Hallelujah" to this collection of materials.

The entire open structure can be seen as ironic and iconoclastic in terms of its relation both to hierarchic choral traditions and to the controlling precompositional superstructures of serial works (compare, for instance, Nono's *Il canto sospeso*). The relation between modules, deliberately disconnected and inconsistent, establishes a universe that seems permanently unfinished, and one that could not be created by a single God—instead by irregular and unplanned forces. This non-structure, however, might refer to a different kind of secret program than is usual in serial works; Metzger says that

> Kagel's compositorial techniques are often secretly based on Jewish theology; musical analysis can occasionally trace analogies to, for instance, the forty-nine stages of meaning in the explanation of every place in the Torah as taught by Talmudic tradition. The composition *Hallelujah* might be entirely understood as a masterpiece of rabbinical expounding . . . from the purely compositional-technical aspect it is a Kol Nidre for a Yom Kippur without atonement. (Metzger [n.d.])

Another important irony is the text itself. Although the text is derived from a German/Latin text found by Kagel in a second-hand bookstore, he has recomposed parts of it to include both created and real words. For example, the entire text of the first soprano's solo part runs:

> Sic / sum complexus otium ut abeo di velli vix queam / aut libris delector, quorum habeo / amasiae festivam copiam / aut fluctus / lahnae fluvii / numero / aut tau tua uat / clavachardia clovochordie cano. (Kagel 1970b, 2–3)

Note the phrase "aut tau tua uat," which is merely three phonemes reordered arbitrarily, and which is followed by the vowel alterations of "clavachardia clovochordie," both of which recall the vowel transformations written into the text of *Sur scène*.

Some texts not in the solo parts are in the vernacular (German, of course), notably an extended monologue on vocal problems spoken by the conductor in the first *Tuttiabschnitt* (section A) and the mass of monosyllabic words voiced by the soloists in the second *Protestchor* (section N). It is interesting that these two texts, probably the only ones comprehensible by the work's intended audience, are remarkably malevolent. In his monologue, the conductor seems to be practically strangling his singers, making it impossible for them to do other than croak and hiss:

The note stays stuck in the throat, breaks off, is pitched too deep (in spite of a good ear), is sharpened up, made intermittent (sounds broken, sort of shaken), is pitched too high, tremoloed (wobbles to and fro as if between two points), is thick, flickers (gets no flowing line of development and stops uncomfortably), is flat, is forced, is strained, is doughy, is palatal, is nasal, is coarse, is fluffy, is pungent, is stuck. (Kagel 1970b, 103–5; translation edited)

The sadistic chain of adjectives that ends this speech finds its parallel in the second *Protestchor* which, after its initial statement of the word "autonomy," presents a hallucinatory bad dream which could pass as an alienated post-war prose poem. The text of the *Protestchor* includes depressing bureaucratic references in the soprano's text, more primitive miseries suggested by the alto, a recurrence of the word "dead" in both the men's voices, fear expressed in the tenor's text, and psychotic violence in the bass text.

The dense tangle of possible meanings in *Hallelujah* is even more complex in the existing recordings. Two commercial recordings, one produced in the early 1970s (DGG 137 010) and one from a concert on April 26, 1990, were made by the Schola Cantorum Stuttgart under Clytus Gottwald. The various radio stations of Germany, especially the Süddeutsches Rundfunk in Stuttgart and the Westdeutsches Rundfunk in Köln, also have tapes of various performances by the Schola Cantorum, as well as a few performances by the more recently established Neue Vocalsolisten Stuttgart (Jahnke 1977, 596).[6]

The first recording, which is probably selected from the performances of the early 1970s, is remarkably tense and aggressive, producing the image of a chaos that virtually attacks the listener (or at least the listener's expectations). Its final phrases, in the last three minutes of a performance that is approximately 28'20" long, are gradually overcome by a harsh, shrill wailing in one of the women's voices (section Q, the final soprano solo). This solo is the only module that is "placed" by the composer (the score states, "This section may only be performed as the *end*"). However, the entire performance seems somehow too balanced and clear, almost organized, which does not seem to be the intent of the score.

It is possible that this organized quality is explained by the 1990 recording, which is clearly modeled on an actual recomposition by Gottwald for the Schola Cantorum, using fragments of the original handwritten version in what is actually a new score, and one that does not perhaps fairly reproduce the intent of the original. This smoother, wittier performance, more than twenty years after the premiere, produces an image of chaos that is sardonic and bizarre, yet somehow harmless in comparison to the earlier version. Perhaps one can compare this with Berio's complaint about recent performances by the Swingle Singers of his *Sinfonia*, that they have become "mannered" and somewhat unreal. One might conclude that the fact that this music did not have any political or cultural effect in the first years of its existence has positioned it in a permanently ineffective niche of dated avant-garde production; it may be impossible to retrieve the fierce aggression and demented panic of its premieres.

Hallelujah is ultimately a less specifically determined, but I think more successful, work than *Anagrama*. Clytus Gottwald claims, in his article on *Hallelujah* interpreted in terms of Habermas's communicative theory (Klüppelholz 1991a, 155–67; Gottwald 1998, 135–47), that the piece cannot even be read as a score: it is instead a problem in communication.

STAATSTHEATER (1967–70)

> It was Kagel, almost inevitably, who created the anti-opera that Ligeti had anticipated and been obliged to go beyond, for Kagel's amused, ironic eye could hardly fail to turn the opera house inside out. His *Staatstheater* . . . uses all the resources of such an institution—principals, chorus, orchestra, corps de ballet, scenery, costumes—in activities that satirize, ignore or contravene customary purpose, the soloists being brought together in a crazy sixteen-part ensemble, the dancers put through their paces in gymnastic exercises. (Griffiths 1995, 181)

Kagel was allowed to present his innovative practices on a larger and more prestigious scale than ever before when the Hamburg National Opera commissioned a full-length opera from him for its 1971 season. He chose to create the sardonically titled *Staatstheater* ("National Theater," with implicit ambiguity between building, institution, and genre), a "scenic composition" in nine sets of modules, most of which can also be performed independently. Actual composition of the work took place as early as 1967; in fact, the two vocal module sets were begun well before the others (*Ensemble* in 1967 and *Debüt* in 1968). The rest of the sets were written in 1970, and the "opera" premiered to a remarkable explosion of cheers and boos on April 25, 1971. The large, carefully handwritten score of 470 pages was published in an expensive fabric-bound edition that same year. Deutsche Grammophon released an eighty-five-minute recording made on the night of the premiere, which included a program booklet rich in photographs and interpretations of the work (Kagel 1971).

Staatstheater is self-evidently an aggressive inversion of the entire world of opera production and performance. Klüppelholz clarifies this when he says,

> *Staatstheater*, a work overflowing with scenic and musical wealth, is simply and utterly a radical negation: no specification of space and time. No libretto. No sung text. No vocal soloists. No accompanying orchestra. No musical description of internal or external action. Also therefore absent is

all sympathy for the dramatic presentation, every comfortable amusement via ballets, disguises, masquerades, neither statutory gravity nor affirmative ostentation, none of any of this, which constituted the species of opera through every change in historical preferences. (Klüppelholz 1981, 31)

In fact, Kagel became somewhat of a hero to some composers because of his ability to carry rebellion and a truly different approach into even the most institutionalized of commissions. If this was not only because of *Staatstheater*, it was nevertheless that work which was the most public and most striking of his rebellions. Younger composer Konrad Boehmer explained the contrast:

Naturally, the musical development of the Köln composers—with the exception of Kagel—did not tend directly towards the theatrical. They were too hermetic for that, and concerned with immanently musical problems. Just as some of the great masters always organized their curtains serially or grew their vegetables in perfect row order, the comprehensive claim of serialism failed in the expansion of its principle into non-musical parameters. The essential initiative for the renewal of the music theater also came especially from composers in whose work serialism plays no, or only a marginal, role. Stockhausen's *Originale*, in which the outside world had been refined and cleaned up, constrained in the serial corset, yawned with boredom. Already, by that time. . . . (Boehmer 1993, 22)

THE VOCAL SECTIONS OF *STAATSTHEATER*

Ensemble for sixteen voices and *Debüt* for sixty voices were both the first module sets to be written and also the sets that most closely resemble the contemporaneous *Hallelujah*. The individual parts for sixteen soloists in *Ensemble*, the third set of modules, are extremely similar to those of the *Gesangsoli* in *Hallelujah*, consisting similarly of two pages of vocal material for each voice. One main difference is that the modules on each page are considerably longer and fewer in number; thus, the Soprano I part for *Hallelujah* consists of nine phrases, of which the longest is equivalent to three normal bars in length, but the Soprano I part in *Staatstheater* consists of a single module eighty bars long (in normally pitched notation), and the Soprano II part of just four fairly lengthy modules (of which three are unpitched). This change reflects pragmatic common sense, as Kagel undoubtedly realized that the repertory opera singers of the Hamburg Opera would not have the flexibility, rehearsal time, or background in avant-garde practice that were available from the Schola Cantorum Stuttgart. It is also notable that the vocal model for *Hallelujah* is one of baroque vocal ornamentation, whereas that for *Staatstheater* is the bel canto opera tradition; as in the earlier work, bel canto exercises and phrases that recall famous arias serve to cement together a wide variety of fragmentary musical gestures. This cementing is particularly necessary since so many other "normal" (traditional or modernist) relationships have been inverted, dismantled or dissolved in the work as a whole (Figure 13-2).

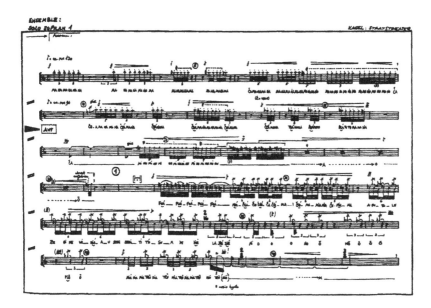

Figure 13-2. Kagel, *Staatstheater: Ensemble*, Soprano I. Used by permission of Universal Edition. Unremarkable notation, but virtually a mass of bel canto exercises.

Debüt, a fourth set of modules written for an opera chorus of sixty voices offering sixty separate one-page sets of modules, is similarly comparable to the *Tutti* sections of *Hallelujah*. However, most parts are unpitched, although most phrases include clear notation of phonemes, general height, articulation and dynamics. In *Staatstheater*, the soloists of the opera house are compelled to sing an *Ensemble*, while the chorus sings soloistic fragments. This makes sense when the vocal exercises of *Ensemble* are compared with the more expressive, soloistic phrases of *Debüt*. As in other ways, Kagel's plan for *Staatstheater* is to invert or deconstruct the traditional relation between elements in an opera house (Figure 13-3).

THE OTHER SECTIONS, AND THE WHOLE OF *STAATSTHEATER*

It is simple enough to analyze all of the sets of modules, with brief notes as to what makes each one an attack on a particular set of ideas or expectations (Table 13-1).

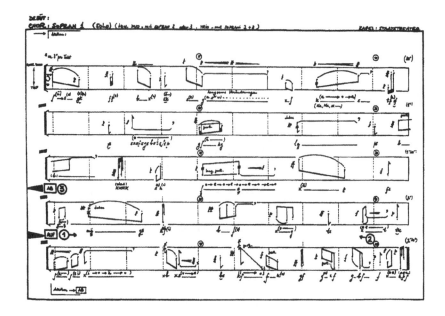

Figure 13-3. Kagel, *Staatstheater: Debüt*, Soprano I. Used by permisison of Universal Edition. Unpitched notation and distinctly expressive, soloistic phrases.

The largest, and according to most writers the most important, set of modules in *Staatstheater* is *Repertoire*, a "scenic concert piece." It consists of a number of single, textless, music-less activities using various distorted instruments and pieces of equipment. "The word 'repertoire' here means, not the meager canon of stories that are circled through by the provincial urban opera houses of today, but instead a tendential, endless universe of fragments of actions" (Klüppelholz 1981, 31). *Repertoire* is given particular emphasis by being both the first part of the "opera" and also its most unavoidable: a performance of the entire work must begin with a performance of most of *Repertoire*, subjecting the audience to what must be one of the most irritating and frustrating experiences ever created in an opera house. *Repertoire* is intentionally trivial in tone and oblique in meaning, a number of fragments of performance art with no evident richness of gesture or sound. This overlapping play of strange little movements that create small, peculiar noises goes on for fully the first twenty minutes of the work, and for the entire first side of the recorded LPs. This experience is difficult to reconcile with elaborate political and cultural interpretations, such as are printed in the recording program booklet:

Table 13-1.

Set of Modules	Description	Notable Aspects
Repertoire, scenic concert piece	Actions with various objects, mostly visual symbolism with slight sounds	No singing or story, no "operatic" activity at all; designed to be "empty" in terms of operatic tradition
Einspielungen (practicing), music for loudspeakers	Material for tape to be played during other segments	A simple background organized around the twelve possible intervals; planes of sound overlapping
Ensemble for sixteen voices	Vocal exercises for the soloists	Soloists forced to sing as an ensemble, kept away from emotive or narrative music
Debüt (début) for sixty voices	Phrases for the chorus	Choristers made to be more expressive and less homogenous than soloists
Saison (season), Singspiel in sixty-five pictures	Scenes parodying opera references, using music from *Debüt*	Classic scenes are inverted or emptied of meaning: Siegfried strikes foam anvil while glockenspiel rings, etc.
Spielplan (program), instrumental music in action	Musical actions (similar to *Repertoire*, but all with sound)	(similar to Repertoire)

Kontra-Danse (contradanse, 'against dance'), ballet for non-dancers	Diagrams and rhythms of movement	Inverts modern dance, where everyday gestures are done gracefully by professionals; these dance moves are done awkwardly by amateurs
Freifahrt (free ride), gliding chamber music	Music for instrumentalists passing back and forth in mechanized chairs	Instrumentalists, not accompanying or as ensemble, move across stage
Parkett (stalls), concerted mass scenes	Large-scale scenes otherwise similar to *Repertoire* or *Saison*, ending in calisthenics	Using the grandiosity of opera against itself, magnification of near-nonsense magnifies contrast of expectations and reality

Alarm. While a siren sounds backstage on a one-sided tambourine, the player comes onstage, his mouth and nose covered by a sort of gas mask. In his hand he carries a guitar case opened towards the audience. . . . *Alarm* is one of those numbers which show the catastrophic effect of musical noises (sirens) on people under certain circumstances: the essential (face, guitar) gets lost, only the husk is left. (Kagel 1971)

There are twenty-odd such descriptions in the booklet, all of which reach an Adornian pitch of dramatic interpretation. While I do not doubt that such an explanation reflects, at least partially, both the composer's intentions and perhaps even some of the experience of perceiving the work,[7] I suggest that the large-scale perception of the entire "opera"—as beginning with a lengthy period of tiny, trivial motions, developing through various kinds of individual and group chaos to a massive, even intimidating ending—is more important in the aesthetic of the work. Indeed, despite the apparently symbolic intention of *Repertoire*, I would suggest that it is no more than a continuation or possibly a final climax of Kagel's invention of "instrumental theater," already established in such works as *Sonant* (1960), *Match für drei Spieler* (1964) and a host of other chamber works.

The most important innovation in *Staatstheater* is not the presentation of instrumental theater on the opera stage, nor is it an escalation of the move to *épater le bourgeois* up to a higher level of cultural privilege. It is instead the creation of a more massive and powerful statement of difference, the signal that even the world of opera can be completely dismantled and recreated in a way that makes it unrecognizable, and that all of the people and mechanisms involved can thus exist completely differently than they have heretofore. This is, I suggest, a move that represents basic deconstructive method. That move is made particularly powerful by the combination of grandiose, malevolently dark, slowly changing sounds (from *Einspielungen*, the music coming from speakers during the piece) and the group calisthenics toward the end which, although absurd in themselves, intensify the presentational power of the massed singers. It is no wonder that the commercial recording of opening night ends in a storm of whistles, cheers, and boos, as members of the audience react in a way unusual in German opera houses.

It is interesting to compare this with Ligeti's opera *Le Grand Macabre* (1975–76), which was of course vastly more successful with both critics and audiences, but which is also "against the grain" of normal operatic practice. The Ligeti opera is easier to accept, I suggest, because the bizarre noises—car horns, shrieking, instrumental farts—were all embedded in a fantastic narrative taking place on another world between strange characters who elaborately parodied normal human activity. It was easy for any audience to distance itself from that narrative; but this is not true of *Staatstheater*, which mercilessly shows that it is happening right here, right now, with people who are, unavoidably, exactly like the members of the audience. *Staatstheater*, in its reflection of the insane fragments of the offstage world, was perhaps too direct a confrontation to be palatable.

THE CATALOG AS MUSICAL WORK

Staatstheater is one of many examples among Kagel's music of the *catalog* as musical work. It appears that many of the composer's works are written by a "modular" technique, where the material was constructed out of amassing index cards of gesture or sound, and the interchangeability of modules is often emphasized. Some form of index card was clearly used in such works as *Kommentar und Extempore* and *Staatstheater*; indeed, in many of his works, the final score seems barely developed beyond the simple iteration of cards. *Anagrama* is evidently constructed as a number of *overlapping* modules composed into a fabric of music, as *Hallelujah* is one of modules presented adjacently and simultaneously.

This method of construction is itself subversive of the existing understanding of the process of composition which, even according to Cage, involves some kind of control over time. The modular structure of such works as *Hallelujah* and *Staatstheater* produces a powerful shift in the meaning of the work *qua* work. If it is perpetually difficult to clarify or specify the identity of a classic work of music among the many shadows of manuscripts, score versions and performances, it is vastly more so when the "score" is really only a collection of materials to create a score, and each performance is vastly different and, by its very nature, unrecognizable (Ingarden 1986). At this distant point in the development of possibilities, the musical work becomes only the locus of human interactions, which is perhaps the most radical shift of all. The musical work, and its technique, become a kind of formalized subversion of existing ideologies, including ideologies of music, politics, and even what it means to relate to other human beings.

GENERALIZED AND CONCEPTUAL SUBVERSIONS

It seems that Kagel was postmodern almost from the start. The earliest works, such as the *Sexteto per cuerdas*, *Anagrama*, and *Transición II*, are still embedded in a modernist style and a modernist aesthetic, but one that is already being irreparably damaged. Then, by the time of its completion in 1960—astonishingly early compared to most European trends (and even fairly early compared to Cage's work and that of Fluxus)—the work *Sur scène* is already utterly postmodern, consisting only of fragments of the modern in a context that shows their emptiness. Kagel spent much of the ensuing decade mining the same conceptual vein—probably because, since so much of Western culture was still mouthing, if not practicing, the ethics of modernism, it must have seemed that these rebellions went unheard.

There is a book by Zarius on *Staatstheater* that is both descriptive and analytical. In search of a text that is less traditionally solid in format (in German a *Bleiwüste*, or desert of lead), he chose to scatter quotes from a lecture by Kagel, all of which distantly resemble political or aesthetic manifestoes, throughout his text:

> Decomposition is the composition of a decomposition. . . . Composition is the decomposition of an idea. . . . A record is the performance of a performance. . . . Composition is the performance of an inter-pretive process . . . . Interpretation is the performance of a record . . . Acoustic process is the performance of a process . . . Decomposition is the performance of a composition. . . . To compose is to change an acoustic past (Zarius 1977, 6, 9, 10, 64, 66, 71, 74, 76).[8]

Certainly, *Staatstheater* was seen as political, not only by its apologists, but also by many of the audience; Klüppelholz presents two letters responding to the performance, one of which, from the "Aktionsgemeinschaft junger Freunde deutscher Opernkunst" (Action Group of Young Friends of German Opera), is a sharply anti-Semitic and proto-Nazi statement of outrage that such a work could be allowed to be performed on a major operatic stage (Klüppelholz 1981, 42).

What makes such a work political? Each of these works involves a mocking attack on autonomy, both in its aesthetic and political forms. The question is presented: Who is behind all of this anyway? Who is the composer, what is the stage, the vocal ensemble, and what ideological business is being maintained by each of these structures and institutions? Answers are few, if there are any at all; Kagel excels at presenting paradoxical problems that create problems rather than answering them. But the shock of asking these questions and making simple answers—answers that are solid enough to attract allegiance and even adulation—is strong enough to awaken the attentive listener. Such an awakening, as it forces the splintering implosion of all ideologies, must be seen as anti-patriotic, as against many kinds of larger and (apparently) more important allegiances.

The main difficulty in theorizing about many works of Kagel's is that any interpretation seems relatively tautological: unlike works by Bussotti or Schnebel, it often seems that each work is definitely, definitively, and even perhaps merely a subversion of a clearly identified, chiefly modernist, ideology. The relation between the music work and the cultural theory it expresses is practically an identity in many of Kagel's works—the semiotic connection between the work of art and its implications is almost flat and without ambiguity. In this way, I would suggest that Kagel's originating ideological impulse is exceptionally focused, immediate, powerful and unquestionably subversive—but it is also, in a way that is difficult to concretely determine, more limited (reified, repetitive) than the work of other composers. Perhaps the illusion of transcendence in art is merely that; but in the absence of such illusion, the listener is less struck and surprised, and the probability of developing a new point of view is perhaps lessened. After all, the game is less exciting when all the cards are always on the table.

NOTES

An earlier version of this article appeared in my dissertation (Attinello 1997, 106–54). Translations are my own unless otherwise marked.

1. Although the German subtitle of *Transición II* translates as for "percussion," since there are no other instruments than the piano, it seems sensible to change it to "percussionist" as does Griffiths (1995, 137).

2. According to Fritz Muggler, ". . . although the work *Anagrama* ended up almost in oblivion for some time, and was first newly rehearsed [since the premiere] by the chorus for the Biennale in Venice in 1972 . . ." (Muggler 1973, 359). Thus, according to this reviewer, there were no performances between the premiere in 1960 and the Biennale performance in 1972, followed by the 1973 Zurich performance of which this was a review. It is worth noting that the Zurich evening involved two performances of this twenty-five-minute work with a lecture by the composer in between.

3. Kagel was born to a sophisticated, polyglot Jewish-Argentine family that brought him up with political opinions tending toward the far left. He himself carried this conceptual leftism even further; he has said that he was shatteringly disappointed in communism during the Spanish Civil War, when the communists chose to fight against the anarchists, making both easy prey for the ultimately victorious fas-

cists. Ever since, Kagel's sympathy has been with anarchists; thus his world view is associated with a band of the political spectrum which is as far to the left as possible, the one that most strongly resists reification into institutions or ideologies.

4. This is from Reger's scatological response to a critic: "I am sitting in the smallest room in my house. I have your review before me. In a moment it will be *behind* me."

5. Gottwald mentioned this in an interview (Stuttgart, March 16, 1994), and pointed out that the vocal lines in the "Ensemble" and "Début" sections of *Staatstheater* are similarly organized by references to bel canto vocalization.

6. Jahnke also mentions a recorded version wherein "the original is supplemented and newly illuminated through instrumental parts," which exists as a commercial LP (Deutsche Grammophon 643 544). I suspect that this is an earlier release of Deutsche Grammophon 137 010, or of another of the Schola Cantorum performances taped by various German radio stations in the 1970s. I believe that Jahnke is speaking of the panpipes played by the singers, an expansion of timbres which is included in the original score.

7. This is more plausible if one considers that German audiences accustomed to Brecht and to a more politicized and symbolic theater may indeed have perceived the actions on these terms.

8. Selected from Kagel, "Composition und Decomposition," unpublished work quoted by Zarius from (Schnebel 1970, 141–42).

WORKS CITED

Attinello, Paul. 1997. "The Interpretation of Chaos: a Critical Analysis of Meaning in European avant-garde Vocal Music, 1958–68." Ph.D. diss. University of California, Los Angeles.

Boehmer, Konrad. 1993. *Das böse Ohr: Texte zur Musik 1961–1991*. Cologne: DuMont.

Deutscher Musikrat. [n.d.]a. *Zeitgenössische Musik in der Bundesrepublik Deutschland,* vol. 4 (1950–60), DMR 1011. Sound recording; includes Kagel, *Anagrama*; program booklet by Werner Klüppelholz. n.p.: Deutscher Musikrat.

Deutscher Musikrat. [n.d.]b. *Zeitgenössische Musik in der Bundesrepublik Deutschland,* vol. 6 (1960–70), DMR 1016. Sound recording; includes Kagel, *Sur scène*; program booklet by Sigrid Wiesmann.[N.p.: Deutscher Musikrat.

Gottwald, Clytus. 1998. Hallelujah *und die Theorie des kommunikativen Handelns*. Stuttgart: Klett-Cotta.

Griffiths, Paul. 1995. *Modern Music and After: Directions since 1945*. Oxford: Oxford University Press.

Ingarden, Roman. 1986. *The Work of Music and the Problem of Its Identity.* Berkeley: University of California Press.

Jahnke, Sabine. 1977. "Vokale Vexierbilder in Kagels *Hallelujah*." *Musik und Bildung* 9 (November): 596–99.

Kagel, Mauricio. [1962] 1992. *Sexteto de cuerdas*. Reprint with May 1992 analytical introduction by the composer. London: Universal Edition.

———. 1963a. *Sur scène: kammermusikalisches Theaterstück in einem Akt*. Text without score. Frankfurt am Main: Henry Litolff/C. F. Peters.

———. 1963b. *Sur scène: kammermusikalisches Theaterstück (1959–1960)*. Score without text. Frankfurt am Main: Henry Litolff/C. F. Peters.

———. 1963c. *Transición II für Klavier, Schlagzeug und zwei Tonbänder (1958–59)*. London: Universal Edition.

———. 1965a. *Anagrama für vier Gesangsoli, Sprechchor und Kammerensemble (1957–58)*. London: Universal Edition.

———. 1965b. *Sur scène: chamber music theatre piece*. Text without score. Translated by Cornelius Cardew. Frankfurt am Main: Henry Litolff/C. F. Peters.

———. 1970a. *Hallelujah für sechzehn Stimmen a capella (1967)*. Manuscript version on rental. London: Universal Edition.

———. 1970b. *Hallelujah für Stimmen (1967)*. Printed version. London: Universal Edition.

———. 1971. *Staatstheater*. Sound recording with booklet by Ulrich Schreiber. Deutsche Grammophon Gesellschaft 2707 060.

———. 1972. *Staatstheater: szenische Komposition, 1967–70*. Vienna: Universal Edition.

Klüppelholz, Werner. 1981. *Mauricio Kagel, 1970–1980*. Cologne: DuMont.

Klüppelholz, Werner, ed. 1991a. *Kagel. . . . / 1991*. Cologne: DuMont.

———, ed. 1991b. *Kagel: Skizzen—Korrekturen—Partituren: Eine Austellung der Köln Musik und der Stadt Gütersloh*. Cologne: DuMont.

Knockaert, Yves. 1976. "An Analysis of Kagel's *Anagrama*." *Interface* 5: 173–88.

Ludlam, Charles. 1989. *Complete Plays*. New York: Harper & Row.

Metzger, Heinz-Klaus. n.d. Mauricio Kagel / *Hallelujah* / Dieter Schnebel / *für stimmen (. . . missa est)*. Sound recording. Deutsche Grammophon Gesellschaft 137 010.

Muggler, Fritz. 1973. "Zürich: Erstaufführung von Kagels *Anagrama*," *Schweizerische Musikzeitung/Revue musicale suisse* 113 (November/December): 359.

Schnebel, Dieter. 1970. *Mauricio Kagel: Musik—Theater—Film*. Cologne: DuMont.

Slonimsky, Nicolas. 1953. *Lexicon of Musical Invective*. Seattle: University of Washington Press.

Zarius, Karl-Heinz. 1977. Staatstheater *von Mauricio Kagel: Grenze und Übergang*. Vienna: Universal Edition.

CHAPTER 14

Collage vs. Compositional Control:
The Interdependency of Modernist and Postmodernist Approaches in the Work of Mauricio Kagel
Björn Heile

> Late Nietzsche needed a different music [compared to middle Nietzsche]: no more Schoenberg–Adorno, but [the music] of Cage or Kagel. He is not interested anymore in the critical character of form, but in the intense moment of the tone.
> —Jean-François Lyotard
> (1978b, 27; my translation)

> The conflict between modernism and postmodernism is based upon the illusion, that one could simply supersede the other, as if one would announce the decision that now irrationality is valid where rationality was valid before.
> —Mauricio Kagel

"Postmodernism" means many different things, and this multiplicity proves particularly confusing in the realm of music. Opinions about what postmodernist music is or could be and which composers or works may be so labeled differ widely. This is partly due to the equivocality of the term in general but also to the "check list approach" in which the perceived characteristics of a certain music are compared to a list of standard features of postmodernism and the music is segregated along the modernist/postmodernist divide (see the contributions to Marvin and Hermann 1995 and Kolleritsch 1993; the checklist approach is particularly evident in J. Kramer 1995 and Hartwell 1993). The problem with this approach is not that there are conflicting opinions but that the criteria for the application of postmodern theory to musical artworks are not always properly employed. Consequently, particular assessments often appear arbitrary.

I take a different approach in this paper, regarding postmodernism as something like the counter-image of modernism, embracing everything that modernism has excluded. Thus, while modernism emphasizes unity, postmodernism highlights heterogeneity; likewise modernism features closure and hermetic systems prominently, while postmodernism stresses openness. This list of divergences between the postmodern and the modern could be extended almost indefinitely into issues of hierarchy, order, pluralism, or intentionality (see L. Kramer 1995). "Divergent," though, does not mean "antithetical," and indeed I consider modernism/postmodernism as a dialogic relation in the Bakhtinian sense (see Bakhtin 1984, and idem 1986a): that is, as fundamentally intertwined and interacting, rather than opposing and mutually exclusive principles. There is no definite antagonism between modernism and postmodernism, nor is there a straightforward chronological distinction: postmodern and modern impulses occur simultaneously. If we take the distinctions discussed above as guidelines, it becomes obvious that few works of art lie exclusively on one side of the divide. It is hard to imagine a piece of music that is exclusively unified and functions as a completely self-contained, closed entity; equally difficult is the concept of a work of art without some degree of order and closure. It is more fruitful to recognize that both tendencies can and will be present within a single work and complement one another in the manner of a Bakhtinian dialogue.

Another Bakhtinian relation occurring in recent musical practices is closely related to the question of unity/heterogeneity: the dialogics of collage and compositional control. Collage, although in chronological terms a modernist innovation, can be regarded as a postmodernist principle entailing the abdication of authorship in favor of intertextual references and heterogeneity (see Watkins 1994). Compositional control can be understood as a modernist principle, ensuring the unity, the master trope of modernist aesthetics. As before, these principles do not necessarily negate one another. Although collage technique by definition implies a loosening of compositional authority on the most basic level, it cannot function without some regulatory framework, such a framework applying at various structuring levels. The conflicts and tensions between the two principles of collage and control, and more generally of heterogeneity and unity, run through the history of twentieth-century music. Indeed, it is these conflicts, not a work's ideological cohesion, that make twentieth-century music so fascinating.

This dialogics of modernist and postmodernist compositional principles will be exemplified in the work of the Argentine-German composer Mauricio Kagel. In his statements on the subject, Kagel takes a balanced, if not undecided, view of postmodernism, similar in many ways to the concepts I have developed above.[1] He emphasizes the presence of postmodernist elements from his early works of the 1960s on, referring to the need to communicate with the past. He also accuses some dogmatic advocates of multiple serialism, as the most radical exponents of modernist ideology, of "nearly proto-fascist aesthetics." Yet on the other hand, he feels uneasy with what he sees as the "settling of debts with the spirit of modernism" and connected to that, with "the wish that history were reversible." However, he spiritedly renounces any kind of eclecticism and, as a consequence, settles for some kind of reconciliation between modernism and postmodernism: "Modernism as a link in a logically sustainable development has, as the contemporary in itself, always been as necessary as the reasoning about the consequences and possible variants of everything new" (Kagel 1991a). These views stem from Kagel's thinking as a former member of the Darmstadt summer courses who, on one hand, sees the necessity of rethinking avant-garde positions, yet, on the other, recognizes the need to defend the achievements and principles of the avant-garde.

Kagel's work is generally characterized by a conglomeration of modernist and postmodernist tendencies similar to his comments on the matter.[2] His beginnings as a composer are quite typical of the post-war avant-garde, although his influence in this movement has not yet been fully recognized. After his first compositions, Kagel adopted serialism in his *Sexteto de cuerdas*, composed in 1953 (rev. 1957), while he was still living in Buenos Aires. And soon after this work, he concocted his peculiar blend of live electronics and aleatory technique in the revolutionary *Transición II* for piano, percussion, and two tape recorders, finished in 1959 after his move to Cologne, the "capital of multiple serialism" (see Schnebel 1970, 26–35). During this time he also experimented with vocal technique in *Anagrama* (1958), as were many of his contemporaries in the Darmstadt school (see Schnebel 1970, 15–26).[3] Yet, what is peculiar in Kagel's early works, which on the surface adhere closely to the avant-gardist aesthetics of the 1950s, is a certain critical distance, a skepticism toward the music produced and the role of compositional techniques involved. Kagel's techniques, such as the rotation techniques in *Transición II*, are far removed from the positivist pseudo-scientism of some multiple serialists and bear faint traces of irony, a trait distinct from the high seriousness and demonstrative self-confidence of many members of the post-war avant-garde. Kagel shares this ironic stance with his friend and fellow immigrant György Ligeti, who came to Cologne at nearly the same time as Kagel.

The ironic distance becomes more prominent in Kagel's work for mixed media, which occupies an important place in his output after 1960. In the service of works written and realized by Kagel for radio plays, films, and theater pieces, music obviously occupies a different place as compared with conventional composition. Thus these works tend to be *reflections on music* as much as simply *music*. Music becomes the object of discourse as well as its medium; in a Bakhtinian sense music assumes an objectified discourse — it presents itself as re-presented (see Bakhtin 1984, 198-200, and 1986b). Compositional technique, the obsession of the post-war avant-garde, and a criterion for musical progress in modernist criticism, features far less prominently in these works. All this can be seen most clearly in Kagel's most famous contribution to the history of new music, the "Instrumental Theatre" (Kagel generally capitalizes the term; see Kagel 1961).

The most important principle of the Instrumental Theatre is the insight that performing music is essentially an *action*, which has visual and dramatic qualities as well as sonic ones. Thus, sound-*producing* action and sound *produced* ideally form a whole. A good example is the first of these music-theatrical works, *Sur scène* (1961) (see Schnebel 1970, 50–60). *Sur scène* is scored for mute actor, speaker, baritone, and instrumentalists. In the performance, the actor is already on stage reading the program note, as the audience enters the hall. The piece proper consists of the speaker reading an absurd music-critical or musicological treatise, at times using an affected vocal inflection and at others speaking backwards. Simultaneously, the baritone sings fragments of text or strange vocal exercises, oblivious to what is going on around him. Meanwhile, the actor comments on the scene by aping one of the others, shaking his head disapprovingly, or through other actions. Throughout, the three musicians walk about the stage, sometimes playing a couple of notes here and there on keyboard instruments and percussion, at others taking a break.

This work is more a satirical commentary on contemporary musical culture than a piece of music as a unified, self-contained entity. Recalling certain recent developments in literature, the visual arts, or film, it fuses the inside and the outside of the work of art. The reception of the music is reflected in the piece itself—the actor obviously represents the audience in some way, and there is even a critic present commenting on the music in "real-time." And the juxtaposition of inside and outside components of the piece generate surreal connections. In addition to the focus on the "experience" of music, the *making of music* is also a subject *treated in the music*: the material played by the musicians and the way they wander about the stage is more reminiscent of practicing than actually performing the piece. This produces an aesthetic distance, which emphasizes the re-presented, theatrical aspect of the music: *Practicing* on stage will be seen as an at least latently dramatic *action*, a quality denied to the *performance* of music, where we are supposed to concentrate purely on the sounding result. Thus, in *Sur scène* as in other works of the Instrumental Theatre, it becomes virtually impossible to distinguish whether the musicians on stage actually perform a musical composition or whether they *act as if* they are playing music (like actors in a play or movie). Music happens on a meta-level, *re*-presented as much as presented. This ontological confusion concerning the essential quality of the music and the surrealism of the whole performance gives the piece its lasting impact.

Sur scène is a piece of music about playing, criticizing, and listening to music that resembles novels about writing novels or films about making films, which abound in recent decades. Yet, it is not the typically postmodern self-referentiality inherent in this meta-musical practice that has been crucial for theorists of postmodernity outside of music.[4] But within music, the postmodern debate has focused on references to tradition, which has been formulated through concepts of polystylism and collage (J. Kramer 1995; Watkins 1994; Kolleritsch 1993). This focus seems to derive from architectural discourse which also stresses these issues rather than literary discourse in which postmodernism is frequently conceived of as a continuation of the modernist avant-garde (see Hutcheon 1988). Thus the musical debate has frequently centered on neoconservatism and has resisted theorizing a postmodernist avant-garde in music.[5] It is therefore not surprising that discussions of postmodernist aesthetics in Kagel's work focus mostly on his music from the early '70s and after, which often alludes to tonal music and uses techniques of collage, and not to the meta-musical work of the Instrumental Theatre.

Ludwig van (1970) has been hailed as a specimen case of a postmodernist music in the neoconservative sense since it may be understood as exemplifying Roland Barthes's "Death of the Author" (Escal 1979 and 1984). Written for the bicentenary of Beethoven's birth, *Ludwig van* consists of fragments from his works, which can be played in any combination and order and with any combination and number of instruments (see Klüppelholz 1981, 11–21). The piece was originally part of Kagel's film of the same title, which mainly takes place in an imaginary "Beethoven house," whose rooms were designed by such celebrated visual artists as Joseph Beuys, Anselm Kiefer, and Ursula Burghardt. For the score of the chamber music version, which bears the subtitle *Homage by Beethoven*, Kagel has used still shots from the "music room" in the Beethoven house (designed by himself), where the walls and all objects are plastered all over with Beethoven's written music. Since the notation cannot always be deciphered correctly as a result of the camera shots and since key signatures or clefs are sometimes missing, the resulting music is a more or less distorted version of the original music.

The music is still, however, recognizably Beethovenian; it strikes one as somehow familiar, like an indistinct *déjà entendu*. It is no great surprise that this piece would be taken as typically postmodernist, consisting as it does of little more than a collage of pre-existing music from the canon. Yet, as in the case of the third movement of Berio's *Sinfonia*, which was also regarded as something like a postmodernist manifesto despite the composer's protestation and enmity toward postmodernism, it is quite an isolated case in Kagel's output (see Watkins 1994, 417; Budde 1993). Never again has he restricted compositional control and invention to such an extent as in *Ludwig van*, where all the musical material was composed by someone else.

Another work from around the same time and in the same spirit as *Ludwig van* is *Variationen ohne Fuge über 'Variationen und Fuge' über ein Thema von Händel für Klavier op. 24 von Johannes Brahms (1861/62)* from 1973.[6] In a Borgesian mood, Kagel writes a commentary on a commentary, thereby constructing a double refraction of the Handel piece. This work consists primarily of original material, quoting literally almost all of the Brahms variations. It is hardly recognizable as such, however, since the original is superimposed with various derivations. For instance, Kagel uses a technique of "*faux-faux-bourdon*": each note of the original serves as

root, third, or fifth of a new triad, resulting in up to three simultaneous triads in Kagel's "meta-variation." He also combines original melodies with
others having the same contour but varied intervals, that is, with their "het-
erophonic variants" in Kagel's terms.

Another technique is of particular relevance to issues of postmodern
aesthetics in Kagel's work. It entails the "non-linear" transposition of
chord sequences: each chord of the original is transposed by a different
interval resulting in a non-functional sequence of tonal chords (see
Klüppelholz 1981, 74–100). Kagel conceived the technique more generally
as "serial tonality" and has employed it in most compositions since the
early '70s (see Klüppelholz 1991a, 11–55; Reich 1995). Serial tonality
treats tonal material (i.e., triads) serially. Chords are assigned numbers, and
their sequence is governed by numerical rows. The intervals of the "non-
linear transpositions" in *Variationen ohne Fuge* are controlled by a numerical series. Serial tonality, then, fuses—or rather forces together—the
incompatible: it is systematically impure and intentionally unorganic. It
denies both the functionality of tonal chords and the systematic and unifying role of the series. The combination of historical tonal material with
recent serial manipulation effectively de-historicizes the music.[7]

Triadic sonorities have strong functional implications but they are
never fulfilled due to the serial ordering. Kagel's later music, relying on
"serial tonality," seems to come from a music-historical no-man's-land: a
Kagelian version of *post-histoire*.

Finally, discussion of a more recent composition provides further elaboration of the dialogics of collage and control in Kagel's work. *Osten*
("East") is the first of an eight-piece cycle called *Die Stücke der Windrose
für Salonorchester* (1988–94) ("Pieces of the Compass Card for Salon
Orchestra") in which Kagel paints imaginary musical portraits of the compass points and their associated world regions. The title of the composition
acts as a double reference: the geographic specification points outward,
away from the "self" toward a geographically, culturally, and musically
defined "other." But the specification of the geographical regions points to
a Western practice, that is, to a Western (pre-)conception of otherness, to
which the exotic associations with the salon orchestra contribute (see
Kogler 1994). Each piece of the cycle defracts a musical "other" through
the "turn-of-the-century, coffee house" orchestra, while each is transformed by the interventions of the composer.

Osten represents Eastern Europe without specifying any particular
locality (see Kagel, 15). The prominent clarinet melodies with modal inflec-
tions are faintly reminiscent of Eastern-European folk music, the characteristic augmented second adding some "oriental coloring." The stereotypical "oom-pah" accompaniment on minor chords for much of the piece
points to the presence of the salon orchestra.[8] Yet, the music as a whole
does not suggest either of these associations. The melodic line, as folk-

based as it may sound, is thoroughly atonal, and the root progression of the minor chords is at times serially based. This piece is not a "fantasy on folk tunes arranged for salon orchestra," but a playfully critical reflection on, or citation of, such a practice.

What sounds like a conglomeration of typical "Eastern" folk idioms and salon music practice has in actual fact a more specific background, as a study of the sketches reveals.[9] The melodic material for much of the piece is taken from a collection of Yiddish folk tunes (klezmer) recorded by Moshe Beregovsky in the Ukraine during the 1930s and recently re-edited by Mark Slobin (1982). A sketch sheet, with the heading "Mosche [*sic!*] Beregovsky Old Jewish Music," has specific references to the new collection and identifies the source of a melody and its development that occupies mm. 1–56 of the finished piece. The sketch differs little from the published work. Exactly why Kagel has not mentioned this pervasive and far-reaching borrowing of material in his program note or recognized it in the title of the piece poses an interesting question. Possibly he feels that it is against his honor as a composer to borrow material, or he thinks that the piece is better experienced if the audience is left to wonder about the origin of the folk material.

The presence of such "authentic" folk material in *Osten* will come as a surprise to listeners. The music sounds more like a Kagelian appropriation of a "folk-like" music—like a distant, indistinct memory. This effect is created by the combination of "original" material with newly composed music in the manner of a collage. Kagel neutralizes the harmonic implications of the tunes by providing a contrapuntal accompanimental with a high degree of chromaticism. This technique can be observed in Figure 14-1 (mm. 16–19) in which a Yiddish song, "Ay, du forst avek" (taken from Slobin 1982, 339), is accompanied by a chromatic succession of thirds in the same rhythm. There are no stark contrasts or juxtapositions of highly disparate material, as is typical from musical collages—on the contrary, *Osten*'s sonic surface is quite smooth. Kagel apparently used minor chords as a common ground between the diverse musical idioms of klezmer and salon music. Further, the minor chord—here represented as a minor third—fits well into three contexts: in addition to their occurrence in klezmer and salon music, the chords occur within the composer's own serial technique.

A passage at the beginning of the piece (mm. 1–16), of which the first four are cited in figure 14-2, nicely exemplifies this issue. This passage consists of four elements: a recurrent melodic figure in the clarinet; a rhythmically articulated "oom-pah" accompaniment on minor chords in the the lower strings; a freely-floating, improvisatory melodic line for the standing violinist; and a faster (relative to the "oom-pah") succession of minor chords in parallel motion in the piano, harmonium, and first violin. It is apparent at first hearing that these elements do not quite fit together in terms

Tpo II: Andantino (MM=72)

Figure 14-1. Kagel, *Osten*, mm. 16–19.

Figure 14-2. Kagel, *Osten*, mm. 1–6.

of harmony, rhythm, and phrase structure. The clarinet line is harmonically amorphous. Although it has a distinct modal feel, it runs through nearly all twelve steps of the chromatic scale in less than two bars and betrays no sense of a tonal center of any description. The accompanying "oompah" in the lower strings consists of minor chords with no harmonic functionality. And while the harmonic changes do sometimes coincide with the endings of phrases in the clarinet (e.g., m. 4), the phrase units of the two strands are typically unaligned. The two other—somewhat less prominent—textural layers retain their identities through register and speed: the violin plays well above the rest of the ensemble and the piano/harmonium layer projects a faster rhythmic pattern.

The straightforward melody assumes several accompanimental strands creating a multi-faceted texture of four layers which are seemingly independent of one another. The distinctions between the four strands with respect to the functions they perform may explain why the music seems at once so familiar and so strange. The result is a collage masquerading as conventionally structured music.

While collage techniques occupy an important place in Kagel's compositional procedures in this piece, they do not tell the whole story. We may understand *Osten* on the one hand as an un-hierarchic, pluralist mingling of foreign and native, of high and low, of old and new, very much in the spirit of postmodernism. Yet, on the other hand, it is apparent that Kagel retains control of his material in order to arrive at an if not *unified* at least *coherent* work of art of his own making. Even when quoting "foreign" material, he will not let it "speak for itself" as it were, but make it "his own" by integrating it with his newly composed music and conception of the piece as a whole. Such integration is itself possible by compositional choice: Kagel chooses material accessible to a number of different musical idioms.

This dialogics of collage technique and compositional control is observable in all of Kagel's works since the early '70s. The pieces considered here make use of borrowed material but also demonstrate the control of the composer. Borrowed material is always presented with some sort of alteration. In *Ludwig van*, the Beethovenian fragments are deformed by the performers in accordance to Kagel's visual estrangement of the original scores, more or less in the manner of aleatory technique. And in *Osten*, the integration of borrowed material nearly obliterates the identity of a "foreign" music. In each of these cases, compositional technique does not entail a simple presentation and juxtaposition but rather a transformation and integration. Musical interest resides in Kagel's transformation and elaboration of materials not in the original material as such.

Further, one may note that the meta-musical aspects of *Sur scène* in particular and of Instrumental Theatre in general still occur in *Osten*. The double refraction of the original klezmer material as represented by the salon orchestra and alienated by the composer makes manifest the objecti-fied nature of the musical quotations used. This feature of the music is heightened by its theatrical components: in the context of recent, concert music, it is possible to understand the musicians on the stage as enacting a salon orchestra from the heyday of imperialism (note the standing violin-ist!), whose members in turn imitate musicians identified with other parts of the world. Indeed one might understand *Osten* as if it is not Kagel him-self who borrows the Yiddish tunes but rather an imaginary—and rather dysfunctional—salon orchestra which plays a "Yiddish fantasy."

Within Kagel's music, postmodernist practices are inextricably linked to principles of modernist aesthetics. The dialogics of collage and compo-sitional control—of modernist and postmodernist principles—are so intri-cate that aligning Kagel's approach with either aesthetic pole appears com-pletely nonsensical. This dialogic relation proves instructive: it reveals the nature of postmodernist music and the interdependencies of modernism and postmodernism more than a partisan approach. Further, it is more rep-resentative of the conflicts facing most contemporary composers. Study limited to extreme test cases on either side of the modernist/postmodernist continuum will not penetrate to the heart of the matter. Musicological dis-cussion should not lose sight of this fact.

NOTES

1. At times, he also reverts to demonstrative indifference, as in a statement requested for a conference on postmodernism, in which he declared, "Who of today's composers are actually interested in [the postmodernism debate]? Certainly none of the important ones" (Kagel 1991b, 40–41).

2. For an introduction to Kagel's work see Schnebel 1970; Klüppelholz 1981, 1991a. There is also a long section on Kagel in *Musique en Jeu* 1973. There is as yet no general work on Kagel in English.

3. Exemplary works in this regard are Luigi Nono's *Il canto sospeso* (1956), Karlheinz Stockhausen's *Gesang der Jünglinge im Feuerofen* (1956), György Ligeti's *Aventures* (1962), and *Nouvelles Aventures* (1965), Luciano Berio's *Tema—Omaggio a Joyce* (1958), Bruno Maderna's *Invenzioni su una voce* (1960), and Herbert Eimert's *Epitaph für Aykichi Kuboyama* (1960).

4. I use the term "meta-musical" as an analogue to "metafictional."

5. As Danuser (1993) points out, such a postmodern avant-garde is theorized in the work of Jean-François Lyotard.

6. Both works were mentioned by Kagel as answering to postmodernist con-cerns (Kagel 1991a).

7. I have made a similar argument with respect to formal structure in Kagel's Third String Quartet (Heile 1998).

8. For accounts of the history and conventions of the salon orhestra, see Ballstaedt 1998; Widmaier 1989; Ballstaedt/Widmaier 1989; Kogler 1994. There is surprisingly little literature to be found on the salon orchestra; none of it is in

English—the absence largely due to the insignificant role of this ensemble in the Anglo-Saxon world.

9. The sketch materials and autographs to all of Kagel's finished compositions are kept in the Mauricio Kagel Collection of the Paul Sacher Foundation in Basel (Switzerland), which I have been able to study. Two sketch sheets for *Osten* are reproduced in Klüppelholz 1991b.

WORKS CITED

Abrams, Meyer Howard. 1988. *A Glossary of Literary Terms*. 5th ed. Fort Worth: Holt, Rinehart and Winston.

Bakhtin, Mikhail. 1984. *Problems of Dostoevsky's Poetics*. Translated and edited by Caryl Emerson. Manchester and New York: Manchester University Press.

———. 1986a. *The Dialogic Imagination. Four Essays*. Edited by Michael Holquist, translated by Caryl Emerson and Michael Holquist. Austin: University of Texas Press.

———. 1986b. "Discourse in the Novel" In Bakhtin 1986a: 259–422.

Ballstaedt, Andreas. 1998. Art. "Salonmusik." In *Die Musik in Geschichte und Gegenwart. Allgemeine Enzyklopädie der Musik*, vol. 8 Zweite, neubearbeitete Ausgabe, edited by Ludwig Finscher. Kassel and Stuttgart: Bärenreiter/ Metzler. 854–67.

Ballstaedt, Andreas, and Tobias Widmaier. 1989. *Salonmusik: Zur Geschichte und Funktion einer bürgerlichen Musikpraxis. Beihefte zum Archiv für Musikwissenschaft*, no. 28 .Wiesbaden.

Budde, Elmar. 1993. "Der Pluralismus der Moderne und/oder die Postmoderne." In Kolleritsch 1993. 50–62.

Danuser, Hermann. 1993. "Die Postmodernität des John Cage. Der experimentelle Künstler in der Sicht Jean-François Lyotards." In Kolleritsch 1993. 142–59.

Escal, Françoise. 1979. "Fonctionnement du text et/ou parodie dans la musique de Mauricio Kagel." *Cahiers du 20e siècle* 6: 111–38.

———. 1984. *Le Compositeur et ses modèles*. Paris: Presses Universitaires de France.

Hartwell, Robin. 1993. "Postmodernism and Art Music." In *The Last Post: Music after Modernism*, edited by Simon Miller. Manchester and New York: Manchester University Press. 27–51.

Heile, Björn. 1998. "Neutralising History: Mauricio Kagel's String Quartet No. 3." *British Postgraduate Musicology* 2: 16–23.

Hutcheon, Linda. 1988. *A Poetics of Postmodernism: History, Theory, Fiction*. New York and London: Routledge.

Kagel, Mauricio. 1961. "Über das Instrumentale Theater" (abridged). *Neue Musik. Kunst- und gesellschaftskritische Beiträge* 3: n.p. Reprints: *Nutida Musik* 5/3, (1960/61): n.p.; *Dansk Musiktidschrift* 37/7 (1962): n.p.; *Hefte des Ulmer Theaters* 63/7 (1963): n.p.; *Hefte der Kölner Bühnen* 4 (1963/64): n.p.; *La Musique et ses problèmes contemporaines. Cahiers Renauld-Barrault* 41 (1963): n.p.

———. 1991a. "Komponieren in der Postmoderne." Interview with Werner Klüppelholz, in *Worte über Musik*, by Mauricio Kagel. Munich: Piper. 99–107.

———. 1991b. "Post gleich Prä?" *Positionen* 9: 40–41.

———. n.d. "Compass Pieces for Salon Orchestra." Liner notes to compact disc *Mauricio Kagel 5. Stücke der Windrose: Osten, Süden, Nordosten, Nordwesten, Südosten. Fantasiestück.* Auvidis Montaigne. MO 782017: 13–17.

Klüppelholz, Werner. 1981. *Mauricio Kagel, 1970–1980*. Cologne: DuMont.

Klüppelholz, Werner, ed. 1991a. *Kagel. . . . / 1991*. Cologne: DuMont.

———.1991b. *Mauricio Kagel. Skizzen—Korrekturen—Partituren. Eine Ausstellung der Köln Musik und der Stadt Gütersloh.* Cologne: DuMont.

Kogler, Karl. 1994. "Das Salonorchester. Entstehung, Besetzung und Repertoire." In *Zur Situation der Musiker in Österreich: Referate der Musik-Symposien im Schloß Schloßhof (1989–92)*, edited by Paul v. Fürst. Schriftenreihe des Institutes für Wiener Klangstil an der Hochschule für Musik und darstellende Kunst in Wien, no. 2. Vienna: Institut für Wiener Klangstil. 393–96.

Kolleritsch, Otto, ed. 1993. *Wiederaneignung und Neubestimmung: Der Fall Postmoderne in der Musik.* Studien zur Wertungsforschung, no. 26. Vienna and Graz: Universal Edition.

Kramer, Jonathan D. 1995. "Beyond Unity: Toward an Understanding of Musical Postmodernism." In Marvin and Hermann 1995. 11–33.

Kramer, Lawrence. 1995. *Classical Music and Postmodern Knowledge.* Berkeley and Los Angeles: University of California Press.

Lyotard, Jean-François. 1973. *Des Dispositifs pulsionnels.* Paris: Union Générale d'Editions.

———. 1978a. *Intensitäten.* Berlin: Merve. Translation of excerpts from Lyotard 1973.

——— 1978b. "Bemerkungen über die Wiederkehr und das Kapital." In Lyotard 1978a. 15–34.

———. 1978c. "Adorno come diavolo." In Lyotard 1978a. 35–58.

———. 1985. "La philosopie et la peinture a l'ère de leur experimentation." In *L'Art des confins. Mélanges offerts à Maurice de Gaudillac*, edited by Annie Cazenade and Jean-François Lyotard. Paris: Presses Universitaires de France. 465–77. English translation as "Philosophy and Painting in the Age of their Experimentation," in *Camera Obscura* 12 (1984): 110–25.

Marvin, Elizabeth West, and Richard Hermann, eds. 1995. *Concert Music, Rock, and Jazz since 1945: Essays and Analytical Studies.* Rochester, N. Y.: University of Rochester Press.

Musique en Jeu. 1973. "Une Panique créateur." Special edition on Kagel. *Musique en jeu* 11: 39–63.

Reich, Wieland. 1994. "Der Hörer als Komponist. Über kompositionstechnische und didaktische Aspekte in neueren Werken Mauricio Kagels." In *Musikpädagogische Impulse*, edited by Reinhard Schneider and Lothar Schubert. Kassel: Bärenreiter (=*Musik im Diskurs*, no. 10): 24–33.

————. 1995. *Mauricio Kagel:* Sankt-Bach-Passion. *Kompositionstechnik und didaktische Perspektiven.* Saarbrücken: Pfau.

Schnebel, Dieter. 1970. *Mauricio Kagel. Musik—Theater—Film.* Cologne: DuMont.

Slobin, Mark, ed. 1982. *Old Jewish Folk Music: The Collections and Writings of Moshe Beregovski.* Philadelphia: University of Pennsylvania Press.

Stockhausen, Karlheinz. 1959. "... How Time Passes ..." *Die Reihe* 3: 10–41.

Watkins, Glenn. 1994. *Pyramids at the Louvre. Music, Culture, and Collage from Stravinsky to the Postmodernists.* Cambridge: Harvard University Press.

Widmaier, Tobias. 1989. "Salonmusik." In *Handwörterbuch der musikalischen Terminologie*, vol. 5, edited by Hans Heinrich Eggebrecht. 1–16.

Linking the Visual and Aural Domains

CHAPTER 15

Race and Reappropriation:
Spike Lee Meets Aaron Copland
Krin Gabbard

At the beginning of *He Got Game* (1998), written and directed by Spike Lee, the credit sequence contains an unusual juxtaposition. In two consecutive title cards the American composer Aaron Copland (1900–1990) is credited with "Music" and then the rap group *Public Enemy* is listed for "Songs." These credits combine a composer widely associated with the American heartland and an urban, highly political rap group. A correspondingly diverse set of images appears behind the credit sequence. Usually in slow motion, young Americans play basketball in a variety of locations, including pastoral landscapes in the Midwest and concrete playgrounds in the inner city. Behind the title card with Copland's name a young black man dribbles a ball along the Brooklyn Bridge, perhaps an acknowledgment that, although Copland and Spike Lee share very little else, they both grew up in Brooklyn. Throughout the credit sequence Copland's dissonant but compelling *John Henry* plays on the soundtrack. The music at this point has an appropriately auspicious quality, not unlike the beginnings of many big-budget American films. Copland was in fact familiar with the conventions of film music. He wrote soundtrack music for *Of Mice and Men* (1939), *Our Town* (1940), and *The Red Pony* (1949), as well as a few short films, and his score for *The Heiress* (1949) won an Academy Award. Portions of the soundtrack music for *Our Town* can even be heard in *He Got Game*.[1]

With its multicultural cast of basketball players, including young white women as well as African-American men, the opening sequence of *He Got Game* does not actually racialize the music of Copland, in spite of the fact that the legendary "steel-driver" John Henry was black. But about ten minutes into the film, after the principal characters have been introduced, Spike Lee is more provocative in mixing Copland's music with the images on the screen.[2] When a group of black youths arrive on a court at night and begin a vigorous game of full-court basketball, the soundtrack music is

303

"Hoe-Down," the final movement of Copland's 1942 ballet *Rodeo*. Spike Lee has made a powerful statement by combining images of young black men playing basketball with music written by the one composer in the classical tradition considered to be "the most American."[3] Writing in the *New York Times* in anticipation of the centennial of Copland's birth, Anthony Tommasini referred to the composer as "Mr. Musical Americana" (Tommasini 1999, 36). Copland's music, especially a composition as robust as "Hoe-Down," can signify the American spirit at its most positive. Wit, energy, spontaneity, romance, bravado, optimism, and grace all seem to emanate from the music, as if Copland's dancing cowboys transparently express the balletic soul of the American people. These kinds of associations have everything to do with the reception of Copland's music and nothing to do with anything intrinsic to it, but Spike Lee has made the most of the commonly accepted associations by linking "Hoe-Down" with vigorous young black men on a basketball court. Lee may be asserting that these African-American youths are as uniquely and thoroughly American as anything that Copland's ballet music might signify. As Lee himself has said, "When I listen to Aaron Copland's music, I hear America, and basketball is America" (Sterritt 1998).

THE INVISIBLE SIGNIFIER

In his choice of Aaron Copland, Spike Lee may also have sought to reverse the familiar Hollywood practice of using the invisible and "inaudible" sounds of black music to accompany the actions of white people (Gorbman 1987, 73). This convention is at its most benign when an unseen African-American singer provides a romantic atmosphere for white lovers. Clint Eastwood used this convention in *Play Misty for Me* (1971), when he appropriated the voice of Roberta Flack to enhance the love scenes between himself and Donna Mills, and then again twenty-four years later in *The Bridges of Madison County* (1995), when the songs of Johnny Hartman provided the precise degree of romance and masculinity that Eastwood's character might otherwise have lacked (Gabbard 2000). Similarly, in *Groundhog Day* (1997), when Bill Murray romances Andie McDowell (in a small-town location that includes virtually no black people), the soundtrack includes Ray Charles singing "You Don't Know Me" and Nat King Cole crooning "Almost Like Being in Love."

In a more sinister use of the voices of blacks to signify something other than black subjects, a film will make a menacing group of youths seem even more menacing by playing rap music on the soundtrack even if all the youths are white. Andrew Ross has pointed out that in *Batman* (1989) the Joker is played in whiteface by the white, middle-aged Jack Nicholson but that the character arouses white anxieties about black youths by speaking in rappish rhymes, prancing to the funk of Prince played on a boombox, and spray-painting graffiti on famous paintings in a museum (Ross 1990,

31). In all of these films, diegetic or extradiegetic music says what the film-makers are unwilling or afraid to say with images. While Eastwood and the makers of *Groundhog Day* engage in "permissible racism" (Meltzer 1993, 4) by associating African-American artists with intensified romance and sexuality, the singers are acknowledged only in the end credits, their black bodies kept offscreen in order to maintain the centrality of white characters. In *Batman*, director Tim Burton and his collaborators have avoided charges of overt racism by *not* showing black hooligans on the screen, but they have made the Joker more threatening by linking him to African-American musical performances that are despised by many white Americans.

In *He Got Game*, Spike Lee has essentially reversed these conventions. Instead of using black music as a supplement for white characters on the screen, Lee allows the music of a white composer to enhance the playfulness, grace, and masculinity of black youths on the basketball court. Lee may even have supposed that the early scene with "Hoe-Down" would be widely excerpted outside of its original context. We do not need to know the plot of the film or even the identity of the ballplayers to understand what the scene is saying. When I have presented the shorter, spoken version of this paper, I have made my case most forcefully by showing that scene. There are surely any number of academic presentations on Lee, Copland, and/or film music that have made or will make use of the same scene. By simply bleeping out the one use of the word "shit" on the soundtrack, the clip could even be a useful teaching tool in a grade-school music appreciation class. It would certainly bring the music of Copland home to a generation of American students more in touch with black urban culture than ever before. But even this scene must be understood in the larger context of *He Got Game*, of Spike Lee's other films, and of Aaron Copland's career. By combining the music of Copland with images that do not immediately appear apposite, Lee has suggested that viewers make a number of associations. In looking for even more associations, this paper is in effect continuing the work of the film.

CONSTRUCTING AMERICA

As the theorists of postmodernism have taught us, sounds and images do not adhere to grand narratives but circulate freely among systems of meaning that escape the conventional boundaries of academic disciplines. And as the New Musicology has taught us, musical meaning has as much to do with listening communities as it does with well-established attempts to "anchor" it in reassuring discourses.[4] Spike Lee has made several attempts to anchor the compositions of Copland to specific meanings at crucial moments in *He Got Game*, often lifting music out of its more familiar context so that it can signify in new ways. In the "Hoe-Down" sequence, however, Lee seems to follow traditional practice and casts Copland as an

Figure 15-1. While the audience hears Aaron Copland's *Orchestral Variations*, Jake Shuttlesworth (Denzel Washington) pleads for reconciliation with his son Jesus (Ray Allen) in *He Got Game* (1998). Jerry Ohlinger's Movie Material Store. © Touchstone Pictures. All rights reserved. Photo by David Lee.

"American" composer in the most positive and unproblematic sense. But Copland's identity as Mr. Musical Americana becomes highly problematic if we examine his own story.

Copland did in fact set out to compose music that was recognizably American, even in his earliest works. In an audacious rejection of the Eurocentric directions of most American classical music, Copland paid special attention to American folk melodies and quoted them in his compositions without irony or patronizing gestures. He also found tonalities that gave his music a spacious, uplifting quality that is today considered "American" even if the same chords that seem to symbolize the wide open plains of the American countryside can also be found in music that Palestrina wrote in sixteenth-century Italy (Tommasini 1999, 36). (Copland's Jewish roots have been connected to passages in his music, as when Pollack suggests that a central motive in the Piano Concerto of 1926 hint at "the calls of the shofar" [Pollack 1999, 522]).

But if Copland intended his music to represent the essence of America, he did so in a spirit that was by no means blandly jingoistic. Especially in the 1930s his politics were well left of center, leading him at one point to write what he called "my communist song," a setting for a Marxist lyric by Alfred Hayes (Pollack 1999, 276). In 1934 the song won the prize in a competition sponsored by the *New Masses*, a prominent magazine for "the proletarian avant-garde" (Denning 1997, 140). In writing this music, Copland succeeded by combining a musical style that might be called "revolutionary" with an appeal to mass taste (Pollack 1999, 276). Copland later disavowed the song, but its composition foreshadowed certain stylistic aspects of *Fanfare for the Common Man* (1942). Although the *Fanfare* was written to bolster the morale of Americans in the early stages of World War II, and although by the end of the millennium the piece was being used in television commercials for the U.S. Marine Corps, the music must also be regarded as a powerful statement of the composer's radical leftist sentiments. Pollack suggests that even Copland's invocations of Abraham Lincoln, Billy the Kid, and John Henry can be understood alongside Communist party leader Earl Browder's efforts to bring ultranationalist sentiments into the party's rhetoric (Pollack 1999, 279).[5]

Nor should Copland's homosexuality be overlooked in considering a music that has been characterized as "manly" as well as American. Keep in mind that the sounds of *Rodeo* and *Billy the Kid* that wash over the robustly masculine bodies in *He Got Game* were written for the ballet. Compared to the black athletes in Lee's film, the actual dancers who have performed these ballets may appear to resemble gay men in cowboy drag, especially to audiences used to seeing their cowboys in American movies. Indeed, as Susan McClary points out in an essay about the sexuality of male composers, "The straight boys claimed the moral high ground of modernism and fled to the universities, and the queers literally took center stage in concert halls and opera houses and ballet, all of which are musics that people are more likely to respond to" (McClary 1991, 79). As a gay man, Copland was surely fascinated by men who performed their masculinity in the dance, the cinema, and the opera, for all of which he wrote memorable music. And as Howard Pollack has written in his excellent biography of Copland, there were surely homosexual subtexts to much of this work:

> This would include the macabre eroticism of *Grohg*, the portrait of a rebel in *Billy the Kid*, the acceptance of difference in *The Second Hurricane*, and the male bonding in *Of Mice and Men* and *The Tender Land*. Moreover, *Rodeo*, *The Heiress*, *The Tender Land*, and *Something Wild*, all of which concern a young woman's sexual and emotional self-discovery, could be seen as "coming out" tales of one kind or another. (Pollack 1999, 526)

Of course, it is also possible to hear much of this same music as a "beard" to help Copland survive in a culture where Jews and homosexuals often have to pass for heterosexual gentiles. Regardless, in finding musical codes to express masculinity and heterosexual romance, Copland was demonstrating that he, like innumerable other gay composers, filmmakers, and performers, was highly sensitive to the performative nature of sexuality and gender.

Not every critic was comfortable associating a gay, Jewish socialist from Brooklyn with the most basic sounds of America. Pollack quotes a variety of writers who denounced Copland's attempts to create a uniquely American classical music. Many of these attacks were un-self-consciously anti-Semitic, such as the statement by one critic that Copland was guilty of "the usual clever Hebraic assimilation of the worst features of polytonalité" (Pollack 1999, 519). Perhaps the most vicious assault on Copland came from writer/composer Lazare Saminsky, who wrote in 1949 that Copland possessed "a small, cool creative gift, but an ego of much frenetic drive, a devious personality with a feline *savoir faire*, with his fine commercial acumen and acute sense of the direction of today's wind" (Pollack 1999, 520).

Half a century after these attacks, the music of Copland has won the admiration of a sufficient number of critics to overcome various slurs on his politics, ethnicity, and sexuality. More significantly, he influenced a significant number of younger composers who understood his ability to capture what could pass for the authentic American vernacular. If we think of Copland today as the most American of American composers, it is primarily because that was how his influence was felt by so many other composers. In fact, even the less positive aspects of Copland's compositions have been conceptualized as *echt* Americana. Wilfrid Mellers has said that Copland's "fragmentary, cubistlike forms and the static, nonmodulatory harmonies" represent "uprootedness and disintegration, reflective of American alienation" (Pollack 1999, 529). It may have been these aspects of Copland's music that inspired Spike Lee to use the opening, conflicted section of *Billy the Kid*, the ominous *Orchestral Variations*, and the less celebratory portions of *The Lincoln Portrait* for a story about the tensions between a father serving a long prison sentence and a son in constant danger of being used up and tossed aside by a culture that values him only as a commodity (Figure 15-1).

CORPORATE POPULISM OR REVOLUTIONARY ART?

Spike Lee's choice of Copland's music for a film about black basketball players might seem surprising in the light of perceptions about the director's politics. Lee is known as the director of *Malcolm X* (1992), a biopic of the black Muslim leader, and *Get on the Bus* (1996), a film about black men journeying to hear Louis Farrakhan at the Million Man March of 1995. Lee ends all his films with Malcolm X's phrase, "By any means necessary." *Do the Right Thing* (1989), which inspired some white commentators to charge Lee with inciting racial violence, is surely the most controversial film that Lee has made to date. That film paid close attention to the only surviving photograph of Malcolm X with Martin Luther King, Jr. In most discussions of identity politics, King is associated with the hope that black America can survive comfortably within the American mainstream while Malcolm X represents the nationalist view that African Americans must survive on their own apart from white America. At the end of *Do the Right Thing*, Lee ran two quotations, one from King and one from Malcolm X. King's eloquent endorsement of non-violence is *followed* by Malcolm's powerful defense of violence in self-defense, suggesting to some that Lee was endorsing Malcolm's statement. The facts that Lee ends his films with a quotation from Malcolm and that he made a film about Malcolm and not about King also suggest that Lee is more comfortable with the nationalist sentiments of Malcolm.

But many critics found Lee's *Malcolm X* (1992) to be a conventionally bland Hollywood biography. Amiri Baraka denounced Lee as the "quintessential buppie" who brought his own "petit bourgeois values" into the film (Baraka 1993, 146). Lee has even claimed that the juxtaposition of Martin and Malcolm that is so crucial to *Do the Right Thing* does not actually favor Malcolm (Carr 1997, 136). And it is surely significant that Smiley, the character in *Do the Right Thing* who constantly holds up the photograph of the two black leaders, can barely speak because of a severe stutter. The film's regular association of Smiley with the photograph may represent the inability of Lee or anyone else to articulate a satisfying synthesis of what the two extraordinary black men had to say.

The release of *Do the Right Thing* brought the additional charge that Spike Lee was a "corporate populist," more interested in selling the Nike Corporation's Air Jordan sneakers than in making politically responsible films (Christensen 1991). The same charge could be aimed at *He Got*

Game, especially when Jake Shuttlesworth expresses great delight as he purchases a pair of "the new Jordans" shortly after his release from prison. Spike Lee and Michael Jordan are surely the two public figures most associated with Nike sports shoes. Lee has directed television commercials for Nike that have featured Jordan, and Jordan himself appears in *He Got Game*. In fact Jordan can be seen in the film twice, once in a brief clip when he utters the three-word title of the film and again as the subject of a heroic statue in front of the United Center in Chicago that appears in the opening credit sequence. In the statue, Jordan strikes the same pose that appears as an icon on Nike products. Even the use of Copland's music in *He Got Game* can be interpreted as a corporate maneuver, since all of the recordings by Copland heard in the film have been issued on the CBS/Sony label. Most of this music can now be purchased on a CD with the title *He Got Game: Spike Lee Presents the Music of Aaron Copland* (Sony Classical SK 60593). Lee surely knows that CDs with music from a film can be as financially remunerative as the film itself. *Elvira Madigan* sold a Mozart piano concerto, *Ordinary People* sold Pachelbel's Canon, and *Platoon* sold Samuel Barber's "Adagio for Strings." Why shouldn't *He Got Game* sell *Rodeo* and *John Henry*?

But the charge that Lee is merely a shill for corporations such as Nike and Sony must be considered alongside the film industry's commitment to corporate advertising that virtually began with the birth of the American cinema (Hansen 1990). The possibility of an artist today surviving in *any* marketplace without some connection to corporate interests is scarcely possible. Todd Boyd compares Lee to Charles Barkley, who appeared in *He Got Game* prior to his retirement from professional basketball in 1999. Aggressive and voluble both on the court and off, Barkley was fond of making statements such as "I'm a '90s nigga. . . . I told you white boys you've never heard of a '90s nigga. We do what we want to" (Boyd 1997, 132). Boyd writes, "Lee's presence is quite like that of Barkley, a compromised image of Blackness for mass consumption in return for the financial power to challenge the racial status quo elsewhere" (Boyd 1997, 138). W. J. T. Mitchell has even suggested that *Do the Right Thing* can be read as a *critique* of corporate populism, which maintains a climate in which "no utopian public image or monument is available to symbolize collective aspirations" and in which purchasing a pair of sneakers is sadly among the few ways for dispossessed individuals to find a sense of personal identity (Mitchell 1997, 124).

In *He Got Game*, Jesus has no mother, does not trust his father, and is beset by predatory individuals who have little concern for him as a person. He can rely on no stable institution or, in Mitchell's words, "a monument" to make sense of his predicament. Instead he must contend with a cast of self-interested characters that includes his girlfriend, his uncle, his high school coach, a sleazy agent, college coaches, the media, and promiscuous white coeds, not to mention the governor of New York. Other than his cousin, the only character who does not seek a profit from Jesus and seems genuinely concerned about his welfare is "Big Time Willie," a local godfather who drives a red Mercedes sports car and claims to have put the word out on the street that Jesus must be left alone. Willie warns Jesus about drugs, alcohol, and the HIV-infected women who lie in wait for him and cautions the young man about the ballplayers who thought they could "make it out of Coney Island" but "didn't amount to shit." Jesus smiles when he corrects Willie by naming Stephon Marbury, even though he is the only athlete he can identify who provides a valid role model.

The mention of Marbury, the high-scoring point guard for the New Jersey Nets, is one entry in a virtual encyclopedia of basketball lore that runs through the film. The familiar faces of Dean Smith, Lute Olson, John Chaney, John Thompson, Nolan Richardson, Rick Pitino, Reggie Miller, Charles Barkley, Bill Walton, Shaquille O'Neal, and, of course, Michael Jordan all appear in *He Got Game*. Lee even stops the action of his film to let high school players speak nondiegetically about what the game means to them. There is a sense of pride and possibility in this early sequence when the five young men on the championship high school team talk about the game. Jesus, for example, says that for him "basketball is like poetry in motion." We later learn that Jesus Shuttlesworth was not named for the biblical character but for Earl Monroe, whose nickname was "Jesus" when he played in Philadelphia prior to becoming a star with the New York Knicks. When Jake tells Jesus about the origins of his name, he points out that the press referred to Monroe as "Black Jesus," but that the people in Philadelphia simply called him "Jesus." The discourses of big-time athletics can be meaningful to marginalized groups, and as Boyd powerfully argues, it can even provide a site of resistance to dominant culture. As is so often the case in his films, Lee has appropriated this discourse as part of his larger project of giving voice to disenfranchised groups such as young black males.

It is significant that Big Time Willie, who speaks so compellingly of the dangers that Jesus faces, is played by Roger Guenveur Smith, the same actor who played the stuttering Smiley in *Do the Right Thing* and who has appeared in almost all of Lee's films. A character who is basically incoherent in one film can be uniquely articulate in another. Hollywood films rarely dramatize the conflicts faced by a young black man, especially one like Jesus Shuttlesworth, who is portrayed as largely instinctual and unreflective. If we look for a political statement in a film such as *He Got Game*, we must find it within the complex web of achievement and cooptation that surrounds Lee's characters. Victoria A. Johnson has written,

> Lee's "politicized" voice is most conflicted . . . as his films grant expression to the voices that are typically marginalized in relation to the mainstream, only for those oppositions to be subsumed by larger commodification practices that recoup them for popular sale as black history and politics. Perhaps

in spite of themselves, however, Lee's films may represent a provocative, positive fusion of a prolific, chameleon-like visual-aural aesthetic—a fusion that incorporates diverse youth concerns (in terms of response rather than generational affiliation) and plays with spectator activity and popular knowledge in an unprecedented fashion. (Johnson 1997, 70)

He Got Game exposes the predicament of Jesus Shuttlesworth, who would seem to be among the most successful members of black youth culture. The film regularly contrasts Jesus's anxieties with the upbeat face placed on college athletics by the popular media, embodied most memorably in the manic figure of Dick Vitale, the sportscaster and former college coach who is even more over the top than usual in his brief appearance. A fictional character standing in apposition to Vitale is John Turturro's Billy Sunday, the coach at "Tech U" who tries to recruit Jesus with rhetoric more reminiscent of his namesake than of a basketball coach. Chick (Rick Fox), the college player who is escorting Jesus on his campus tour, smirks at Jesus during Turturro's speech. Like stuttering Smiley, Radio Raheem, and many other characters in Lee's films, the black athletes must rely upon alternative means to speak their minds.

Nevertheless, for all its celebration of the game and its flamboyant personalities, *He Got Game* does not hold out much hope for Jesus Shuttlesworth. As Big Time Willie persuasively argues, and as the film continually demonstrates, Jesus is entering a cutthroat world of agents, coaches, and hangers-on. Any number of mishaps can quickly end his career, even before he arrives in the NBA. As many have pointed out, an African-American male has a better chance of becoming a successful doctor or a lawyer than of playing in the NBA. The film is much more about the oedipal reconciliation between father and son than it is about a young man's rise to success in professional athletics.

INTERTEXTS, OEDIPAL AND OTHERWISE

I do not dispute every aspect of the claim that Spike Lee is out to reap the corporate benefits of his interventions. Like Victoria A. Johnson, however, I am convinced that the filmmaker is also committed to giving voice to the disempowered at the same time he relishes experimenting at the edge of the Hollywood style. The visual feel of *He Got Game* is in many ways as experimental as its soundtrack. Lee takes chances with flashes of light throughout the film, and he presents the opening moments of his film in staggered sequence, jumping back and forth between Jake's first conversation with the warden and the events leading to Jake's arrival at the motel on Coney Island. But there are other aspects to *He Got Game* that cannot be ignored once we acknowledge that the presence of Copland's music opens up a number of intertexts. I have already mentioned the montage of white and black ballplayers that the credit sequence links to Copland's *John Henry*.

Although the lyrics to the folksong reproduced in Copland's music tell the story of a black man, Lee seems to be associating the feats of the legendary steel-driver with an athletic discipline available to both blacks and whites. Later, in the scene in which Jesus hears the appeal of Coach Billy Sunday at Tech U, the young athlete is exposed to an elaborate video played over the gymnasium's huge monitors and public address system. Although it prominently features Copland's much-honored *Fanfare for the Common Man*, the video primarily reflects the histrionic religiosity of Coach Sunday. Playing with the connotations of the name Jesus, the video includes bits of footage from George Stevens's kitsch epic *The Greatest Story Ever Told* (1965). In the fast montage of images, we even see a mock cover of *Sports Illustrated* in which Jesus poses on a cross wearing his basketball uniform and a crown of thorns. Lee has made Copland's music part of a postmodern pastiche, deflating the auspicious sounds associated nowadays with individuals and institutions more well-healed than your average "common man."[6] The transformation of *Fanfare for the Common Man* by the popular media has become an intertext that Lee acknowledges in a film that otherwise tends to treat Copland's music without irony.

But Lee may not have intended to unleash all the intertexts in a film with so much of Copland's music. For example, by using "Hoe-Down" to ennoble a spirited game of playground basketball, Lee and his collaborators inevitably suggest comparison with Agnes de Mille's scenario for *Rodeo*. The "Hoe-Down" section of the ballet was clearly intended as a dance of sexual aggression in which the cross-dressing, adventuresome Cowgirl reveals her femininity, only to be subdued in a vigorous dance by the overbearing Buck. In *He Got Game* Copland's music for *Rodeo* has been joined to an action that has nothing to do with women but everything to do with phallic aggressivity and male display. That Copland was writing as a gay man fascinated by staged masculinity undermines the black athletes' seemingly natural display of their gender. At the same time the music looks forward to the subordination of women that is an all too significant element in *He Got Game*.

The film's final music before the end credits is from *Billy the Kid*, the ballet that Copland wrote in 1938 to a scenario by Eugene Loring. Like Jesus Shuttlesworth, the Billy of Loring's scenario witnesses the accidental death of his mother when he is still a child. In a rage, the twelve-year-old Billy publicly kills the man who shot his mother as she passed by during a gunfight. Billy is protected from the crowd by Pat Garrett, who functions in the early stages of the ballet as a father surrogate for the boy. Garrett rides with Billy for a period, but then becomes disillusioned, takes a job as a lawman, and ultimately fires the shot that kills Billy. This narrative is framed by a solemn procession of people headed westward, some of whom fall by the wayside or succumb to madness. The music of this processional plays throughout the final scene after Jesus seems to have definitively rejected his father. We first hear it on the soundtrack when Jake, back in prison for we know not how long, writes a letter to his son. We then see Jake reading the letter, clearly moved by his father's words. The music continues as Jake risks being shot by a guard when he walks into the off-limits area of the prison basketball court and hurls a ball over the wall. The basketball magically arrives at the gymnasium at Big State where Jesus practices alone. He picks up the ball, examines it, and smiles. He may even be crying, but it is difficult to identify tears among the rivulets of perspiration on his face. The diegesis of the film ends here along with Copland's music.

In its original incarnation as music for a ballet, the processional from *Billy the Kid* depicted the epic movement of settlers across the American continent. Copland surely wrote it in the spirit of the radical populism of the 1930s, dramatizing the struggles of ordinary men and women who built America before capital turned their descendants into wage slaves. There is of course an irony in Lee's reappropriation of this music to accompany the imprisonment of a black man whose ancestors may have helped settle the West, in some cases as slaves. There is also an irony in the use of music associated with a narrative of oedipal aggressivity to add emotional depth to the reconciliation between father and son at the end of *He Got Game*. I have no idea if Spike Lee or Alex Steyermark, who is credited with supervising the film's music, were aware of the oedipal struggle between Billy the Kid and Pat Garrett that is central to the ballet's narrative. For that matter, I don't know if Copland's politics, sexuality, or ethnicity were under consideration as Lee and Steyermark picked out the music for *He Got Game*. Nevertheless, by combining Copland's music with the incidents in the film, Lee and his collaborators have activated a host of intertextual possibilities.

He Got Game is not the only film written or directed by Spike Lee that contains powerful oedipal elements. *He Got Game* might be regarded as the third installment of Spike Lee's autobiography. The director has long regarded his own father with a great deal of ambivalence. Bill Lee, who has been an important bass-player in the New York jazz community for several decades, refused to play electric bass or accommodate himself to more popular musics in the 1960s (Lee and Jones 1990, 163). As a result, the Lee family could not live on his income, and Spike Lee's mother Jacquelyn went to work as a schoolteacher to support Spike and his siblings. Jacquelyn Lee died of cancer when Spike Lee was nineteen, and a few years later Bill Lee began living with a Jewish woman, much to the chagrin of his son, who resented what he perceived as an insult to his mother's memory as much as he resented the color of his father's new companion. Even a largely hagiographic biography observes that Spike Lee and his father could barely speak without arguing, including the time when Bill Lee was writing memorable music for his son's early films (Haskins 1997, 35).

As I have argued elsewhere, *Mo' Better Blues* (1990) can be regarded as a wish-fulfillment fantasy in which Spike Lee rewrites his own story

(Gabbard 1996, 155–56). Bleek Gilliam, the jazz musician protagonist of the film, grows up in a house in which the father and the son are dominated by the mother, played with great authority by Abbey Lincoln. Unlike Spike Lee's father, however, Bleek Gilliam abandons jazz and grows up to become a strong father who gently gives orders to his wife in a final scene that precisely reproduces all but the matriarchal dominance depicted in the film's opening. In Spike Lee's *Crooklyn*, an even more overtly autobiographical film from 1994, the father is an underemployed jazz pianist who greatly disappoints his oldest son by insisting that he attend a recital on a night when the son would much rather be watching the New York Knicks play in the NBA finals. Alfre Woodard plays the mother as a loving but overwhelmed and often angry woman who struggles mightily to keep a large family afloat. Although Woodard's character is not entirely sympathetic at first, her death is played for pathos toward the end. Significantly, the father in *Crooklyn* is played by Delroy Lindo, a talented but sinister-looking actor who would later play a murderous drug-dealer in Lee's *Clockers* (1995). If *Crooklyn* can be read as the story of Spike Lee as a child, *He Got Game* might be regarded as a narrative of Spike Lee in late adolescence. The later film dramatizes the crises of a talented young black man from Brooklyn who must overcome the many predatory individuals hoping to profit from his fame. The young hero is at odds with his father, who at one point has sexual relations with a white woman.

The mother in *He Got Game* is even more idealized than the mothers in Lee's previous films. Seen briefly in flashbacks, Martha Shuttlesworth sends her son loving letters while he is away at camp. In the film she is played by Lonette McKee, who looks much younger than the Abbey Lincoln of *Mo' Better Blues* and is perhaps more strikingly beautiful than the Alfre Woodard of *Crooklyn*. Although the father in *He Got Game* has actually killed the mother, the film is told from his point of view. Jake endures much when he is temporarily set free from prison, and yet he resourcefully makes the most of it. In the flashback that precedes the mother's death, Copland's Orchestral Variations plays on the soundtrack as Jake drives Jesus mercilessly on the basketball court, calling him "a little bitch" and at one point throwing a ball directly into his face. But we also see that the end result is almost entirely positive: Jesus is the nation's most sought-after high school player. The audience's sympathy is drawn immediately to Jake if only because he is played by Denzel Washington, surely the most eminent African-American leading man in American film today. He certainly possesses more charisma than Jesus, played by Ray Allen, a real-life NBA basketball player and not a professional actor. The intense dislike that Jesus expresses for his father alongside the extremely sympathetic treatment given to Jake by the film suggest that Spike Lee is as ambivalent as ever about his own father.

Perhaps as a result of the powerful oedipal content in *He Got Game*, the women of the film do not fare well. Like Freud's male child, Jesus must renounce the oceanic feeling associated with the mother—and her surrogates—and embrace the values of his father in order to achieve manhood. Jesus is given many reasons to move beyond the stage of dependence upon a woman. During the scene when Big Time Willie lectures Jesus about the dangers of women, he asks, "How you spell pussy? H.I.V." Jesus's girlfriend Lala openly cavorts in a swimming pool with D'Andre (Leonard Roberts), whom she identifies as her brother, while Jesus looks on. Presumably looking after the best interests of his son, Jake later breaks D'Andre's nose and then reminds Jesus of the story of Samson and Delilah. Jesus subsequently understands the extent to which Lala cares only for herself and sends her away with the phrase "Good riddance." In addition to sexual experiences with the duplicitous Lala, Jesus has sex with two large-breasted coeds at Tech U who are obviously interested primarily in recruiting him to their college. Jake has sex with a prostitute who professes her love for a vicious pimp with a pock-marked face. These sexually degraded women stand in stark contrast to the idealized Martha, whose photograph Jesus kisses shortly after he has seen Lala in the pool with D'Andre.[7] When Jake visits Martha's grave and embraces the headstone, we hear Copland's "Grover's Corners" on the soundtrack, perhaps the most lyrical music in the film. But Martha is dead, the victim of the film's brutal oedipal struggles. She is the only positive female character in the film perhaps because she is safely out of the picture during the action of the film.

ANNOTATING WHITE MUSIC

As well-trained deconstructionists, we could follow many other chains of signifiers at each of the links between Spike Lee and Aaron Copland. I conclude this exercise by identifying another set of associations that follows from the work of this paper but that may be more consistent with the intentions of the filmmakers. Although they do not take up as much time on the soundtrack as do the compositions of Copland, the songs of Public Enemy drive home many of the film's ideas. As with much of rap music, the lyrics of the songs are highly didactic. Consider Chuck D's lyric:

> People use, even murder's excused . . .
> Still a thousand and one way to lose with the shoes. . . .

Indeed, the world painted by Public Enemy holds almost as little promise for Jesus Shuttlesworth as it does for his imprisoned father. But within the film, the songs provide a microcosm of the interracial connections resulting from the juxtaposition of Copland and black basketball. Public Enemy comments on white music, especially a tradition of popular music in the white mainstream that tends to hide its debt to African-American traditions. This commentary provides a relevant and perhaps even oppositional comment on the use of Copland.

Public Enemy is surely Spike Lee's favorite rap group. Their version of "Fight the Power" was the anthem for *Do the Right Thing* even if that film was dominated musically by the symphonic jazz of Bill Lee that strongly suggests the influence of Aaron Copland.[8] The musicians who make up Public Enemy have taken their role seriously as spokesmen for marginalized and exploited people, often denouncing record companies that prevent artists from interacting more directly with their audiences. At the end of the 1990s, the group was fighting with Def Jam Records, which refused to release some of the group's music. Group member Chuck D received some public attention when he took the music to the Internet and made it available in high quality audio format to anyone with a computer, a sound card, and a modem. Def Jam subsequently released the withheld music.

For *He Got Game*, Public Enemy composed a number of songs in which they articulate values of revolutionary youth and present themselves as candid commentators on urban life. Their song "He Got Game" is especially significant for its title as well as for its prominence in the end credits. In fact the song begins immediately after the last strains of Copland's *Billy The Kid* fade from the soundtrack along with the image of Jesus holding the basketball mystically delivered to him by his father. Public Enemy's "He Got Game" is the last music audiences hear as they leave the theater. The opening sounds of the song are a sampling of the 1967 recording of "For What It's Worth" by the folk-rock group Buffalo Springfield. Actually, Public Enemy does more than just sample the recording. The entirety of "He Got Game" is layered over the earlier record. The chime-like whole-notes alternating between an E and B in portions of "For What It's Worth" can be heard throughout Public Enemy's record. Chuck D convinced Stephen Stills to join the group in the studio so that he could re-record his thirty-one-year-old lyrics to "For What It's Worth" (Brunner 1998, 61). Even so, Public Enemy's Flava Flav plays the trickster, engaging in call and response with Stills. When the aging rocker sings, "There's a man with a gun over there," Flava responds with a knowing "Yeah, that's right. Hah hah."

The rapper's intrusions into the mild protest rock of the 1960s become especially plangent when the female voices of the Shabach Community Choir of Long Island are heard late in the recording. Although they sing the same lyrics as Stephen Stills, the choir was added to the mix in 1998 by Public Enemy. The female singers embody the African-American gospel traditions that have found their way into white popular music, usually as a means of validating the authenticity of the white singer. Innumerable white vocalists have performed in front of a group that consists primarily or exclusively of black singers and dancers, including the Rolling Stones, Laura Nyro, Carole King, The Talking Heads, Madonna, and most recently, Vonda Shepherd, a ubiquitous presence in the weekly television program *Ally McBeal*. Although Shepherd is a white woman with blonde hair, she sings very much in the style of black soul singers and is always accompanied by a trio of African-American female vocalists.

By essentially holding up Buffalo Springfield's music to the scrutiny of black artists, the appropriation of African-American voices by white artists becomes especially obvious, not at all like the invisibility of black singers in Hollywood's *The Bridges of Madison County* and *Groundhog Day*. Similarly, Public Enemy's annotations of "For What It's Worth" allude to the role of the civil rights movement in the rhetoric of the student protest movement of the 1960s. When Stephen Stills sings about the ominous presence of men with guns, he is poaching on the much greater fears that African Americans felt as they faced down police in the civil rights struggles of the 1950s and '60s. (Do Public Enemy and Spike Lee also ask that we compare the brutality directed at blacks during the civil rights movement with what white labor organizers experienced in the 1930s when Copland sympathized with their struggles?) The knowing responses of Flava Flav to the lyrics of "For What It's Worth" register the gap between the anxieties of white hippies like Stills and the daily exposure to racism experienced by black Americans.

But then Public Enemy has also done its share of poaching by appropriating the white musicians of Buffalo Springfield for their performance. By employing Public Enemy, Spike Lee has again called attention to the common but invisible practice of mixing black music into performances by white artists. In a sense Lee and Public Enemy have called attention to the inseparability of "white" popular music and African-American traditions, a synthesis so profound that to separate the two would be, in the words of Ralph Ellison, an attempt at "a delicate brain surgery with a switch-blade" (Ellison 1964, 246). I am quoting Ellison's review of *Blues People*, the 1963 book by Amiri Baraka (LeRoi Jones) that first made a powerful case for the centrality of the black experience in jazz and blues. Ellison was charging Baraka with overlooking the extent to which African-American culture has become an inseparable part of the American mainstream. Aaron Copland did after all look to jazz in his early years to find an American vernacular. He later looked to folk traditions which had effectively absorbed Negro influences long before Copland got to them. By the time he was writing his great ballets and film music, it had become impossible to identify which elements in Copland's music were indisputably "white" and which were the undiluted products of black culture. Because Ralph Ellison was writing as a high modernist in his critique of Baraka, he was less interested in the identity politics and institutional boundaries that Baraka was developing, ultimately with great success. But I am convinced that Ellison, as a modernist and an integrationist, would have been very pleased with Spike Lee's appropriation of Aaron Copland.

NOTES

1. Copland's music has also been highly influential in the history of music for films. In the same year as the release of *He Got Game*, the music for Steven Spielberg's *Saving Private Ryan* (1998) was also Coplandesque.

2. *He Got Game* takes place during the few days when Jesus Shuttlesworth (Ray Allen) must decide where he will attend college. The most sought-after high school basketball player in the nation, Jesus is recruited by a large group of college coaches, many of whom appear as themselves in the film. Even his girlfriend Lala (Rosario Dawson) is involved with an agent who wants to profit from Jesus's decision. Jesus's father, Jake Shuttlesworth (Denzel Washington), is in a state penitentiary serving a long prison sentence for killing his wife in an incident of domestic violence when Jesus and his sister Mary (Zelda Harris) were children. The warden (Ned Beatty) tells Jake that the governor, who is a graduate of "Big State," wants Jesus to attend his alma mater and that Jake may have his sentence reduced if he can convince Jesus to attend Big State. Carefully watched over by prison guards in plainclothes, Jake is taken to a sleazy motel on Coney Island where he must overcome the enduring bitterness of a son who still blames him for the death of a beloved mother. At the motel Jake becomes involved with a prostitute (Milla Jovovich), who returns to her home in the Midwest after she makes love to Jake. At the climax of the film, Jake challenges Jesus to a game of one-on-one, telling Jesus that if the father loses, he will permanently stay out of Jesus's life. If Jake wins, the son must sign the letter of intent for Big State that Jake carries with him. Jake loses the game and is taken back to prison, but the next day Jesus announces at a press conference that he will attend Big State. The warden, however, tells Jake that since he did not actually get Jesus's signature on the letter of intent, the governor may not honor his promise to reduce Jake's sentence.

3. For the purposes of this essay, I have separated America's concert traditions from what has become known as "popular" music. While one might understand jazz as "America's classical music" and Duke Ellington as America's greatest composer, I will respect the separation of traditions because it seems to be respected in the film.

4. Roland Barthes has argued that the polysemy of a photograph in a magazine can be stripped of a wide range of possible meanings and anchored to a specific few by means of the caption below the picture (Barthes 1977, 39). Claudia Gorbman has employed this concept in her discussion of how soundtrack music can anchor the images in a film to a selected range of meaning (1987, 32).

5. But Michael Denning argues that invocations of Lincoln were more typical of "the official Americanisms of the Depression." Members of the Popular Front and other radical groups were more likely to associate themselves with the abolitionist John Brown (Denning 1997, 131).

6. As Pollack has pointed out, *Fanfare for the Common Man* has been recruited for bombastic purposes by the Rolling Stones, Woody Herman's New Thundering Herd, Emerson, Lake, and Palmer, and numerous producers of television news programs.

7. The sexual politics of the film are further complicated by the racial dynamics at Tech U, where Jesus is surrounded by white coeds who are, in the words of Chick, "freaks." When Chick and Jesus walk across the campus with two white girls, they encounter a group of black coeds, one of whom says, "That's not right, Chick." While Jesus speaks with one of the white girls, Chick attempts to mollify the black girls by saying that he will see them at church on Sunday. Later, Chick explains in detail why he prefers white girls, who will wash his "dirty drawers," as opposed to black girls who "make you work too hard."

8. Writing at least a year before the release of *He Got Game*, Johnson referred to Bill Lee's score for *Do the Right Thing* as "Coplandesque" (Johnson 1997, 55).

WORKS CITED

Baraka, Amiri (as LeRoi Jones). 1963. *Blues People: Negro Music in White America.* New York: Morrow.

———. 1993. "Spike Lee at the Movies." *Black American Cinema*, edited by Manthia Diawara. New York: Routledge. 145–53.

Barthes, Roland. 1977. "Rhetoric of the Image." *Image—Music—Text.* Translated by Stephen Heath. New York: Hill and Wang. 32–51.

Boyd, Todd. 1997. "The Day the Niggaz Took Over: Basketball, Commodity Culture, and Black Masculinity." In *Out of Bounds: Sports, Media, and the Politics of Identity*, edited by Aaron Baker and Todd Boyd. Bloomington: Indiana University Press. 122–42.

Brunner, Rob. 1998. "Game Boys." *Entertainment Weekly* (May 1): 61.

Carr, Jay. 1997. "Spike Lee Spotlights Race Relations." In *Spike Lee's "Do the Right Thing,"* edited by Mark A. Reid. Cambridge Film Handbooks. Cambridge: Cambridge University Press. 134–37.

Christensen, Jerome. 1991. "Spike Lee, Corporate Populist." *Critical Inquiry* 17: 582–95.

Denning, Michael. 1997. *The Cultural Front: The Laboring of American Culture in the Twentieth Century.* London and New York: Verso.

Ellison, Ralph. 1964. *Shadow and Act.* New York: Random House.

Gabbard, Krin. 1996. *Jammin' at the Margins: Jazz and the American Cinema.* Chicago: University of Chicago Press.

———. 2002. "Borrowing Black Masculinity: The Role of Johnny Hartman in *The Bridges of Madison County*." In *Soundtrack Available: Essays on Film and Popular Music*, edited by Arthur Knight and Pamela Robertson. Durham: Duke University Press. Forthcoming.

Gates, Henry Louis, Jr. 1988. *The Signifying Monkey: A Theory of Afro-American Literary Criticism.* New York: Oxford University Press.

Gorbman, Claudia. 1987. *Unheard Melodies: Narrative Film Music.* Bloomington: Indiana University Press.

Hansen, Miriam. 1990. "Adventures of Goldilocks: Spectatorship, Consumerism, and Public Life." *Camera Obscura* 22: 51–71.

Haskins, Jim. 1997. *Spike Lee: By Any Means Necessary*. New York: Walker.

Johnson, Victoria A. 1997. "Polyphony and Cultural Expression: Interpreting Musical Traditions in *Do the Right Thing*." In *Spike Lee's "Do the Right Thing*," edited by Mark A. Reid. Cambridge Film Handbooks. Cambridge: Cambridge University Press. 50–72.

Kalinak, Kathryn. 1992. *Settling the Score: Music and the Classical Hollywood Cinema*. Madison: University of Wisconsin Press.

Lee, Spike, with Lisa Jones. 1990. *Mo' Better Blues: The Companion Volume to the Universal Pictures Film*. New York: Fireside.

McClary, Susan. 1991. *Feminine Endings: Music, Gender, and Sexuality*. Minneapolis: University of Minnesota Press.

Meltzer, David. 1993. *Reading Jazz*. San Francisco: Mercury House.

Mitchell, W. J. T. 1997. "The Violence of Public Art." In *Spike Lee's "Do the Right Thing*," edited by Mark A. Reid. Cambridge Film Handbooks. Cambridge: Cambridge University Press. 107–28.

Oja, Carol. 1994. "Gershwin and American Modernists of the 1920s." *Musical Quarterly* 78: 646–68.

Pollack, Howard. 1999. *Aaron Copland: The Life and Work of an Uncommon Man*. New York: Henry Holt.

Ross, Andrew. 1990. "Bullets, Ballots, or Batmen: Can Cultural Studies Do the Right Thing?" *Screen* 31/1: 27–43.

Shohat, Ella. 1991. "Ethnicities-in-Relation: Toward a Multicultural Reading of American Cinema." In *Unspeakable Images: Ethnicity and the American Cinema*, edited by Lester Friedman. Urbana: University of Illinois Press.

Sterritt, David. 1998. "Spike Lee Chooses Copland Classics For Soundtrack." *Christian Science Monitor* (May 8).

Tommasini, Anthony. 1999. "Aaron Copland, Champion of the American Sound." *New York Times*, Arts and Leisure section (November 21): 1, 36.

CHAPTER 16

The Politics of Feminism, Postmodernism, and Rock:

Revisited, with Reference to Parmar's
Righteous Babes
E. Ann Kaplan

Pratibha Parmar's 1999 documentary, *Righteous Babes*, is an ideal site within which to revisit late 1980s debates about feminism, postmodernism, and rock music. In current academic scholarship, those debates tend to be subsumed into new concerns—for example, multiculturalism, postcolonial studies, queer studies—as postmodernism becomes an assumed part of the intellectual landscape. And yet for the new generations of young women (in this case, fans, rock stars, journalists) growing up in the millennium and not necessarily linked to academic scholarship or networks, there are still real questions about what feminism can mean in a postmodern, "millennial" context. Not that the women would necessarily frame their questions in these terms: but through a close reading of Parmar's film, I will show first that some questions in academic feminists' 1980s debates underlie the women's statements and frame their struggles; and second, that 1990s artists build on their 1980s fore-sisters. I will use the film not only to chart the generational differences that separate women, but to highlight as well how popular culture—and in particular the rock music that the film focuses on—becomes a site that brings women of all ages together. An overall focus will be to compare and contrast the different discursive modes of theoretical feminist discourse and a documentary film as they both engage the topic of feminism, postmodernism, and rock music.

I'll begin with the theoretical feminist discourse as it evolved in relation to 1980s feminism/postmodernism debates since it is these that bear on Parmar's film—both in terms of its content and its cinematic techniques. In the 1980s, there were two main women's studies positions vis-à-vis postmodern debates about the subject and aesthetics: one position argued that feminists and minorities had already implicitly (and of necessity) been living and practicing postmodern modes[1] that became academically influential only once articulated by male scholars, like Jean-François Lyotard, Michel Foucault, Deleuze/Guattari, Fredric Jameson, or Jean Baudrillard. (This is

not to deny the influence of these and other male theorists on subsequent—
especially North American—feminist research. But it *is* to note the blindness of white male scholars to incipient postmodern concerns of much feminist and minority discourse, despite the absence of articles explicitly titled
"Feminism and Postmodernism" before 1987.)[2] The second position, in its
most extreme form anyway, simply viewed postmodernism as the death-
knell of feminism.

Briefly, the first set of scholars, influenced by French feminists such as
Helene Cixous and Julia Kristeva, includes scholars like Alice Jardine,
Meaghan Morris, and Gayatri Spivak, who saw value for women in postmodern destabilizing of established social and academic categories and
boundaries—that is, its decentering of patriarchal, heterosexual positions;
its challenge to foundational paradigms like psychoanalysis or Marxism; its
problematizing of history as an orderly, chronological process. Minority
women, meanwhile, out of their oppressive positioning in mainstream culture celebrated hybrid subjectivities. For instance, from her 1981 coedited
volume *This Bridge Called My Back* to her 1993 piece, "La Conciencia de
la Mestiza," Gloria Anzaldua evoked in a compelling and poetic manner
the decentered, hybrid female subject in-between Mexico and the United
States, in-between cultures, languages, bodily ways of being.[3]

The second set of scholars, including Seyla Benhabib and Nancy Fraser
(in their 1995 *Feminist Contentions*) and Linda Nicholson in her work
with Nancy Fraser, argued for the resisting modernist tradition as the one
which best served women's agendas. Benhabib, for example, argued that
"the postmodernist position(s) thought through to their conclusions may
eliminate not only the specificity of feminist theory but place in question
the very emancipatory ideals of the women's movements altogether"
(Benhabib 1995, 20). Benhabib concludes by doubting that, "as feminists
we can adopt postmodernism as a theoretical ally. Social criticism without
philosophy is not possible, and without social criticism the project of feminist theory, which is at once committed to knowledge and to the emancipatory interests of women is inconceivable" (25).

Implicit here, however, is tension between the desire for women to
become fully "human" subjects, in the sense of the Enlightenment insistence
on white male sovereignty—the right of civil liberties vis-à-vis the state and
the nation—and awareness of the specifically *white male* assumption vis-à-
vis this "subject." As literary scholar Mary Poovey put it, "Gender functions
as the bedrock of the humanist juridical subject . . . because an orderly system of gender differences seems to be the basis of our cultural systems of
meaning and, therefore, of the very notions of coherence and continuity"
(Poovey 1988, 47). But insisting on bringing women into this humanist subject position in one sense (that is, making changes vis-à-vis voting rights and
other civil liberties) does not undo the dependence of the humanist subject
category and the laws that uphold it, "upon a binary and differential organ-

ization of gender (and within gender, upon such differential determinants as race) . . ." (48). Women are still, if differently, excluded from the humanist subject position "and (as a group) made the guardians of the entire cultural order" (48).

The 1980s debates within women's studies, then, arose from two sources: first, from some women appreciating new kinds of subjectivities (either understanding their hybrid identities as inevitable, or, along with French theorists, interested in destabilizing the subject); and second, from concern with women's giving up of the humanist subject as a stable site from which to launch political and social struggles. Meanwhile, some cultural studies feminists like myself took a third path: influenced by French feminisms as well as by Fredric Jameson's initiatives, and sensitive to both positions being taken up in women's studies, I focused on the politics of postmodernism through attention to its aesthetics. I began to introduce women's studies courses aimed at distinguishing modernist from postmodern aesthetic strategies. I suggested two kinds of postmodern aesthetics that differed from modernist ones.[4] The first was a set of techniques I called a feminist "utopian" postmodernism because of the visionary quality of the discourse: the discourse moved beyond existing repressive social forms and institutions, and beyond class and race as categories that divide women and may prevent them from even imagining a liberated world. The second I called a commercial, co-opted, and capitalist postmodernism (Kaplan 1988, 4–5) because of its being circulated by commercial entrepreneurs.[5]

I decided to explore links between postmodern aesthetic strategies and feminism in a form with obvious postmodern characteristics—namely, Music Television. I viewed MTV as increasingly an instance of the "co-opted" or "commercial" postmodernism in which parody, satire, and repetition predominated, and which rendered critical feminist positions of the modernist kind all but impossible. While parody or pastiche and repetition could be utilized for progressive ends (compare Judith Butler's notion of performativity, as practiced, perhaps, in vogue dancing), it more often was used commercially to exclude critique. Postmodernism, I argued, cut both ways: it had the potential for subversion and transgression of dominant norms, *and* for co-optation back into those norms. However, I saw a need to explore the commercial postmodernism evident in much popular culture, especially in Music Television, in order to discover what spaces for critique of prevailing ideas and stereotypes MTV might provide. I did find, in videos by various female rock stars, some elements that may be liberating for women: stars such as Tina Turner, Pat Benatar, Donna Summer, Cyndi Lauper, Janet Jackson, Annie Lennox, and Aretha Franklin were already addressing women's sexual exploitation, wife battering, racism, tragedies of rape, the politics of abortion and divorce, and so on. I made particular study of Madonna's videos in those years from 1981 to 1987, when she produced brilliant, daring commentaries on a whole series of topics pertinent to young women. But I also found in male videos a continuing exploitation of women's bodies and sexuality, especially in the style of heavy metal that was then still confined to male rock groups. I concluded that women should be invested in moving culture beyond dysfunctional gender polarities, but a superficial, easy collapsing of prior rigid gender constructs (often only as far as female videos could go) was not enough. Women needed to exploit MTV's possibilities for a dialogic interchange between male/female categories and enjoy the opportunity for mixing of forms in the manner postmodernism had opened up.

Parmar's film usefully returns to the story I had left in 1987 and as it has been continued in scholarship on Music Television since then (see, for example, Lewis 1992). But what is she able to communicate using an entirely different form from that of academic scholars studying popular culture and having different aims? Setting her documentary form against feminist theoretical discourse may reveal interesting advantages and limitations of *both* forms.

In *Righteous Babes,* Parmar interviews a wide range of women rock stars of the 1990s, several critics and journalists, and some rock fans and students. Given this, Parmar's film is well-suited for exploring, first, the conjuncture outlined above between modernist and postmodern concepts of feminism (relayed through the critics and scholars previously mentioned), second, feminist artistic practices (demonstrated through specific artists' work and their comments about their work), and, finally, ideas of public intellectuals and fans. I want to show how the varied discussions of feminism and rock music in this film, interlaced with performances of various artists, at once echoes *and* challenges the categories that I set up some years ago as noted above.

One of the main premises of the film—noted by critics, performers, and fans alike throughout the work—is that feminism has cracked open the mainstream, or in the final words of the voice-over commentary, "Women in rock have brought '90s feminism to mainstream culture where it belongs." But the question that sentences like this beg (and as Sinéad O'Connor at one point notes) is precisely what is meant by "feminism" in this context? The speakers rarely specify what they mean, leaving the viewer to gather what is meant by the accumulation of references. Largely, it seems that the term has come to mean women resisting the normative "feminine"—that is, women as quiet, submissive, subordinates to males, sexually inert, in the background. What the critics and artists alike celebrate is how female 1990s rock stars are challenging and overthrowing prior concepts of the feminine: as the voice-over puts it early on in the film, "Female rock stars have turned the male world of rock music inside out: Bold, sexy, ballsy, and loud, their sexuality is their strength . . . transforming what it means to be female in the 1990s." Rock women trash the idea that women are meant to be sweet and kept on the back shelf, and they show that feminism can be a vibrant force. The voice-over also notes that women in rock feel they are carrying the torch, pushing the frontiers of what it means to do things for themselves on their own terms.

This message is underscored by Camille Paglia, an older, second-wave feminist. Paglia claims that while early feminism was text-based, theoretical, and polemical, now it has moved into popular entertainment. She asserts that rock music is the only means by which women now can get the feminist message, and that it was Madonna who first breached the gap between feminism and popular culture. Gloria Steinem, the well-known first-wave feminist, also notes that feminism has freed the talents of women, who, entering into popular culture, allow feminism to have a far greater reach.

Some of the artists, too, confirm this concept of feminism as resistance to a mainstream desire to keep women's issues silenced—feminism as a kind of "speaking out"—thus communicating to young women what culture refuses to "know." Ani DiFranco, for example, states that she has not consciously tried to be feminist, but that as a woman she brings what she sees to her songs—she is "by nature" a feminist. Saffron from Republica picks up the theme of women refusing to conform to someone else's idea, and praises Courtney Love for screaming down the microphone as a "card-carrying feminist." Fans interviewed seem to agree: they see rock music as at the forefront of feminism; one fan notes that before girls were supposed to sleep with the band, not *be* the band, but that things have now changed. Fans reveal their identification with stars like Madonna because of her open sexuality; for similar reasons they like the Spice Girls.

Various artists testify to the impact that their songs about "the darker side of women's lives" have had on their fans. We are shown Tori Amos singing her haunting song about surviving rape, and then in a moving interview Amos describes how she became a focal point for thousands of women who finally found their experience voiced. Shots of Amos performing are inter-cut with ads for pornography so as to highlight the cultural endorsement of sexual exploitation of women. This, in turn, prepares for statements by another second-wave, 1970s feminist, Andrea Dworkin, whose anti-pornography work is well known.

In another interesting moment, Sinéad O'Connor reflects back on her earlier performances and moment of great personal anger about child abuse. We are given powerful images of O'Connor's famous performances where, as she puts it, she screamed her rage out, like "an open wound running around the world." Like Tori Amos, O'Connor notes that she now understands the power of music to make points without the screaming.

Later on, *Righteous Babes* shows how some female rock stars have pushed the envelope in regard to challenging mainstream ideas of the "feminine." Interviews with, and performances featuring, Skin Skunk Anansie provide an example of female groups no longer leaving punk and heavy metal to males, as in the 1980s. Skin sees herself as continuing the early 1990s "girl power" concept exemplified by the Riotgrrrl trend. She coined the provocative term "clit rock" to describe the group's very confrontational performances. A critic comments on the difficulty of Skunk's image—its being disturbing and hard to take—something Skin understands but believes nevertheless she must continue. She celebrates the fact that more young women are appreciating heavy metal music and coming to her gigs.

But aren't these artists and critics ignoring the many earlier female musicians who developed some of the qualities attributed to the "new" 1990s feminist rock? Skin is one of the few to even refer to the Riotgrrrl movement. It was in the post-punk underground music scenes in the 1980s that the idea of "girl power" was born, and gaining power through screaming celebrated.[6] *Righteous Babes* follows for the most part women musicians who are commercially successful and/or mainstream artists. Why didn't Parmar explore further and interview less popular women musicians?

Here is where we need to address differences between documentary filmmakers like Parmar and academic scholars in terms of the concept of audience. Academics seek to further theoretical positions—to build out from or work against positions other scholars have taken. An academic rock critic would be interested in questions of mainstream versus underground, and also in the history of female rock music. This is because the audience for theoretical work is largely scholars, teachers, and students studying in the same field. Parmar's audience (and thus her overall aim) was quite different. Indeed, as Parmar noted in an interview with me in 1999, *Righteous Babes* was "deliberately limited to looking at popular culture and feminism—at where the young women today are getting their so-called feminist role models" (Kaplan n.d.). She goes on to note that "they certainly aren't getting them from the likes of us." Parmar saw herself as "making an intervention in mainstream television, so that a film like this could go out and be watched by a million people. To use the word "feminist" and make an argument for feminism, showing that feminism is very much alive in this accessible way was important to me." This makes clear, I think, why Parmar focused on mainstream female musicians: it is these artists that most young people watch. It is these artists from whom Parmar hopes some sort of "feminist" message—even in the limited forms noted earlier—is getting to young women growing up in the postmodern, postsocialist era.

But I was still worried about an aspect of the film that Parmar, as director, did not find a way to comment upon. This was the problem that for some interviewees, "feminism" seemed to mean "getting it all," whereas for me, it had always implied concern about improving the lives of disadvantaged women as well. In the interview already alluded to, I asked Parmar why she had not pushed her interviewees on this question. Once again, Parmar point-ed to the limited aims of the project, namely to reach women who were not getting any feminist ideas from books or consciousness-raising groups. Indeed, it seems that Parmar specifically wanted to educate young women about the older generation of female rock stars who had been outspoken about their feminist positions. I believe she deliberately wanted to bring back those posi-tions as a way of introducing them to young women at the turn of the new century.

If the predominant theme seems, therefore, quite deliberately to be feminism as personal resistance to prevailing and continuing concepts of the stereotypical "feminine," from the start the theme of marketing has sur-faced. At times, marketing is seen positively as enabling what so many applaud—namely, enabling female rock with strong anti-patriarchal state-ments to reach masses of young women who would otherwise not hear such views. Such is the statement by the voice-over early on that "through commodification, feminism has cracked open the mainstream." Picking up this theme much later on, the voice-over notes, with barely a suggestion of criticism: "In [a] world of media hype, women's self-assertion has been good marketing." Entrepreneurs have cashed in on the slogan of female empowerment, we are told. The example given is that of the Spice Girls being constructed solely for commercial ends. In an interesting manner (which I wish had been used more often) differing viewpoints are given on the Spice Girls. A student notes that for young girls to be interested in fem-inism it has to be about lovely things. But Sinéad O'Connor complains bit-terly that the Spice Girls have "sucked the life out of feminism," and that they are more about marketing than liberation. She even worries about the term "girl" linked to spice (recalling the folk saying that "girls are made of spice and all things nice") having pedophilic aspects. Ani DiFranco is equally concerned about the Spice Girls, while admitting that at least girls are seeing female images. The issue of resisting patriarchal oppressions is brought up again in connection with female exploitation by managers and agents marketing them. Sinéad O'Connor describes some such experiences, and Gerri Hershey, a journalist, notes how now many stars own their own record companies to avoid exploitation.

The following section hints at interesting issues that I wish the film could have pursued—namely, the idea of a backlash against even the min-imal concept of feminism that is developed in *Righteous Babes*; and that of the negative baggage that the term "feminism" still carries. The voice over notes that as feminism has become popular, the idea of postfeminism has arisen and asks why, if feminism is no longer needed, there are still retro ads for dieting etc. *Bridget Jones's Diary*—evidently a lesson in how not to be left on the shelf—opened up a kind of 1990s backlash to feminism, sim-ilar to what Ally McBeal is also said to manifest in the United States. The postfeminist idea—that women can flirt with men and still be strong—vies with the negative baggage that the word "feminism" now carries for young women. Associations of dowdy bra-burners still cling to the word, we are told, and the slippage between lesbian and feminist remains. Someone notes that for feminism to work it must transcend the category. Rock stars claim that they are the living definition of feminism because they have moved beyond words to performing. "Feminism is a good word with a bad press, and it's time for it to be used again." One interviewee asserts that for her, feminism is "the right to be angry—the right to live as I really want."

This returns me to the problem regarding how far this 1990s rock movement really can be said to show, in the words of my colleague mentioned earlier, "feminism as a vibrant force" sufficient to bring about social change. The question is whether or not, by the 1990s, this very type of feminism that Parmar wanted to "introduce" (retrospectively) to young women has or has not become a stereotype, easily marketable to 1990s audiences. In provoking this question, the film raises, but does not go on to address, a really important issue about which debates are currently circulating. My colleague mentions a Mountain Dew ad, featuring a group of attractive Generation-X young women, whose screaming is inter-cut with shots of rugged 1990s sports activities. The last frame of the commercial pans to a group of young slacker males basically appraising the scenario as they exclaim, "I think I'm in love." Isn't this, my colleague asks, similar to young males' response to some bikini-clad models? In addition, he adds, "Are the female fans who identify with these women artists taking up feminist causes, or are they simply listening to the music because it is 'cool'?" These are good questions: in relation to the first, I would argue that there *is* a difference between males looking at bikini-clad women or women engaged in rugged sports. The women playing rugged sports at least are active, rather than passive; they probably are fully aware of the position of the young males looking on, rather than being unconscious or passive objects of the gaze, as in modernism. In relation to the second question, only empirical data could tell us if the women listening to female musicians take in the "feminist" message. In regard to Parmar's film itself, it would be hard to watch it without getting its point, I think.

For me, this whole discussion, as also the formulation of feminism having "cracked open" the mainstream through commodification, is very intriguing in light of my rather negative 1980s definition about the commercial postmodern noted earlier as part of the feminist theoretical discourse I began with. In 1987, it was difficult to see the virtues of commodification. Or, rather, it was hard to accept commodification as achieving positive things at all, as at times it is accepted as achieving in *Righteous Babes*. Perhaps in 1987 I still retained some modernist and purist possibility for serious art, not tainted by the market, to somehow circulate widely. What Parmar's film demonstrates beautifully is that postmodernism, simply put, is here, *is* necessary, and is not necessarily all bad.

I flirted with this position in *Rocking around the Clock*, when I talked about postmodernism as having potential for both subversion and co-optation, although I largely stayed on the fence about this. Looking from the point of view of speakers in the film, it seems true that the market—commodification—is enabling a certain kind of feminist message to reach masses of women who, without such music, would be completely untouched by any counter-hegemonic message.

But what kind of feminist message is this? I can imagine what my second set of feminist scholars above might have said about the kind of feminism the film presents: surely, for them this would be no more than "bourgeois" feminism, or personal liberation. Postmodern media like MTV enable superficial identification with images that in reality are beyond the reach of minorities and the working classes. Some of the women's statements would confirm academic 1980s feminists' notion that postmodernism, in propagating the idea of subjectivity as something fluid, fragmented and thus malleable, is the death knell of feminism in ignoring the real political struggles at stake.

But such a view is too monolithic: certain rock stars are fully aware of the larger issues at stake, as the critiques of the Spice Girls showed. Sinéad O'Connor went further to claim that for her feminism is about equality, not about a female world—something that the second set of scholars would surely agree with. And as I noted above, since postmodern, global capitalism has arrived, it makes much more sense for feminists to work with, rather than against, it.

I think what most impresses me regarding the two discourses I have juxtaposed—the feminist theorist and the voices of artists and critics in a documentary film—is the different things each can accomplish. The feminist theorist discourse has the ability to categorize, to make taxonomies, to self-consciously historicize: it can mark large shifts in consciousness, place what's going on today in a larger political perspective, and engage social questions about different definitions of feminism, and about what we can expect or not regarding the realities of women's lives. The second kind of discourse—the documentary film—has the ability to present the immediacy of the personal in all its intensity, credibility, reality *to a million or more young people*. Parmar can interview artists, fans, and journalists in a way that is difficult for most scholars. She could obtain clips of performances that bring so much vitality and clarity to points made through ordinary language. The issues come alive as expressed in unique ways by each speaker and each performer. Interviewing fans as well as stars allows the young women Parmar hopes to reach to experience the impact of messages in the songs and to engage a level of reality that feminist theoretical discourse is not designed for. Yet there is some overlap in terms of positions vis-à-vis feminism, postmodernism, and rock. Some speakers raise similar questions to the feminist theorists, but the context of the documentary film is not such as to permit in-depth development of ideas.

Finally, what I value also about the film is its bringing together different generations of women over the project of rock music. Young women performers address the meanings of their music vis-à-vis female issues; and this music has attracted the interest of older feminist scholars and critics. These older feminists—once reached by women's rock music—are challenged to engage issues that confront the younger women. In a sense, the film projects three generations of women: the second-wave feminist critics and scholars; the 1980s–'90s generation of women musicians; and the turn-of-the-century young teenagers (we hope) watching Parmar's film.

But what about the form of the film, the techniques Parmar uses? Is the film itself "postmodern"? In some senses, perhaps, yes: as noted, we have a collage of voices, crossing feminist generations in both the critics and the artists interviewed. The film combines conventional documentary with voice-over, and cinéma vérité techniques in which subjects speak for themselves without the ordering of the voice-over. In a way, then, this voice-over is itself problematized as it seeks from time to time to "order" the material—which it cannot do. Very varied positions are expressed, but there is no attempt to situate these voices. The film leaves it up to the viewers to absorb what they've seen and heard, and interpret for themselves.

I hope I have both conveyed a sense of what's missing in the film and the strategic reasons Parmar had for such omissions. Most of the speakers address issues in terms of their personal struggles, the reflection of these in their art, and their easing this way the personal burdens of other women. Only rarely is the stance of the broader political level addressed. But if the deeper level of politics—in the sense of changing society in order to prevent some of the darker aspects of women's lives from continuing—is omitted, it is in the service of conveying a simpler message to a broad spectrum of young women about personal power, with which, after all, any larger change has to begin.

Let me then conclude with what I think the 1980s academic discourse was about. My own feminist discourse about postmodernism, I would now argue, reveals the modernist intellectual's desire to make order out of rapid changes in artistic practices, as creative women responded to the new conditions of post-'60s Europe and the United States. Artists *respond* to new situations expressively, while intellectuals attempt to *understand and explain* them. Especially left-leaning intellectuals worried about challenges to their categories—carefully constructed in an attempt to control the always threatening disorder—including especially the disordering of class categories on which ideas about change for justice depended. But events would not stay put: and as we struggled to understand the shape of things now challenging modernist categories, we coined the term "postmodernism" and tried to describe differences between modernism (which we thought we understood) and the new state of things (which we did not). So postmodernism got addressed in terms of how it was *not* modernism.

Something similar happened to other feminist categories: the first- and second-wave feminists forged their theories and practices out of modernist (Marxist, Freudian, post-structuralist) categories. But artists broke through those categories, again creating disorder for the modernist intellectual, who now struggled to fit modernist (socialist-feminism, radical feminism) onto what was going on. Parmar's film, through its differing modality, refuses in the end to "control" its voices, to leave a monolithic stamp on the film. In this sense, it beautifully images a 1990s cultural moment.

NOTES

1. For instance, in their 1981 volume, *This Bridge Called My Back: Writings By Radical Women of Color*, Gloria Anzaldua and Cherri Moraga gathered essays by minority women as "subjects in between." In 1987, in her *Borderlands/La Frontera: The New Mestiza*, Anzaldua formulated the concept of "borderlands," and in 1988, in her *The Pirate's Fiancee*, Meaghan Morris noted an apparent "continued, repeated, basic *exclusion* of women's work from a highly invested field of intellectual and political endeavour" (Morris 1988, 12). In her 1990 study, *Yearning: Race, Gender, and Cultural Politics*, bell hooks argued both that lived experience for blacks was already "postmodern" in being decentered, marginalized, excluded from the totalizing narratives, *and* that postmodern theory's critique of essentialism could empower African Americans "to recognize multiple experiences of black identity that are the lived conditions which make diverse cultural productions possible"(hooks 1990, 29). Jane Flax has important arguments about the relationship of postmodernism to feminism in her 1991 *Thinking Fragments*.

2. See Meaghan Morris, "Introduction," in *The Pirate's Fiancee* (Morris 1988, 12). Morris's book was in press in 1987 as I was indeed linking feminism and postmodernism, first in my book *Rocking around the Clock: Music Television, Postmodernism, and Consumer Culture* (Kaplan 1987); and then in my edited collection *Postmodernism and Its Discontents: Theories and Practices* (Kaplan 1988).

3. But see as well important work on hybridity by many other women scholars and artists, such as Trinh T. Minh-ha, Inderpal Grewal and Caren Kaplan, and many others.

4. See my "Introduction" and "Feminism/Postmodernism: MTV and the Avant-garde" in Kaplan 1988.

5. I did not see much use in the apocalyptic, dystopic theories of some postmodernists for feminists because all categories such as gender, class, and race were evacuated by the projection of drastic transformation of life on earth as we know it to a world of nothing but simulation and ecstatic communication. It seemed that white males were the ones who found these ideas exciting.

6. I want to thank my Stony Brook colleague Theo Cateforis for urging me to include this point. See my references to more of Cateforis's questions when I discuss "my colleague" below.

WORKS CITED

Anzaldua, Gloria. 1987. *Borderlands/La Frontera: The New Mestiza*. San Francisco: Aunt Lute.

———. 1993. "La Conciencia de la Mestiza: Towards a New Consciousness." In *American Feminist Thought at the Century's End*, edited by Linda S. Kauffman. Cambridge: Blackwell.

Anzaldua, Gloria, and Cherri Moraga, eds. 1981. *This Bridge Called My Back:Writings by Radical Women of Color*. Watertown, Mass.: Persephone Press.

Benhabib, Seyla, Judith Butler, Drucilla Cornell, and Nancy Fraser, eds. 1995. *Feminist Contentions*. New York and London: Routledge.

Bordo, Susan. 1993. "'Material Girl': The Effacements of Postmodern Culture." In *Unbearable Weight: Feminism, Western Culture and the Body*. Berkeley: University of California Press. 245–76.

Fraser, Nancy, and Linda Nicholson. 1990. "Social Criticism with Philosophy: An Encounter Between Feminism and Postmodernism." In *Feminism/Postmodernism*, edited by Linda Nicholson. New York: Routledge.

Flax, Jane. 1991. *Thinking Fragments: Psychoanalysis, Feminism, and Postmodernism in the Contemporary West*. Berkeley: University of California Press.

hooks, bell. 1990. "Postmodern Blackness." In *Yearning: Race, Gender, and Cultural Politics*. Boston: South End Press. 23–31.

———. 1992. *Black Looks: Race and Representation*. Boston: South End Press.

Kaplan, E. Ann. 1986. "Feminist Film Criticism: Current Issues and Future Directions" *Studies in the Literary Imagination* 19/1 (Spring): 7–20. Reprinted in *The Cinematic Text: Contemporary Methods and Practice*, edited by Robert Palmer. 1988. Atlanta: Georgia State University Press. 155–71.

———. 1987. *Rocking around the Clock: Music Television, Postmodernism, and Consumer Culture*. New York: Routledge.

———. 1988. "Introduction," and "Feminism/Oedipus/Postmodernism: The Case of MTV." In *Postmodernism and Its Discontents: Theories, Practices*, edited by E. Ann Kaplan. London: Verso. 1–9 and 30–43.

———. 1993. "Feminism(s)/Postmodernism(s): MTV and Alternate Women's Videos." Special Feature, *Women and Performance* 6/2 (Summer): 55–76.

———. 1993. "Madonna Politics: Masks And/Or Mastery?" In *The Madonna Connection: Representational Politics, Subcultural Identities and Cultural Theory*, edited by Cathy Schwichtenberg. Boulder: Westview Press: 149–64.

———. n.d. "An Interview with Pratibha Parmar." Forthcoming.

Lewis, Lisa. 1992. *Gender Politics and MTV: Voicing the Difference*. Philadelphia: Temple University Press.

Morris, Meaghan. 1988. *The Pirate's Fiancee*. New York and London: Routledge.

Poovey, Mary. 1988. *Uneven Developments: The Ideological Work of Gender in Mid-Victorian England*. Chicago: University of Chicago Press.

CHAPTER 17

Natural Born Killers:
Music and Image in Postmodern Film
Jason Hanley

Oliver Stone is a name that often elicits strong opinions from the American public, a response which should come as no surprise to those acquainted with his films. In August of 1994 Regency Pictures released a film directed by Stone entitled *Natural Born Killers*. The screenplay, written by Oliver Stone, Richard Rutowski, and David Veloz, is based on a story by Hollywood hotshot Quentin Tarantino. While initially receiving many positive acknowledgments from movie critics, audiences had a hard time following the fast-paced editing, which some suggested was like watching two hours of MTV. Reports and misgivings regarding the extreme and unashamed violence of the film soon overpowered the positive reviews. While obliged to acknowledge the visual depictions of violence present in the film, we must also ask what Stone intended through the filmic medium beyond the basic story written by Quentin Tarantino.

I argue here that Oliver Stone's film, *Natural Born Killers,* embodies a "postmodern narrative discourse," in which linear narrative time is fragmented and narrative events are interpreted from various points of view. This decentered, multi-perspective narrative is realized not only by the visual images but also by the music in the film. The soundtrack, conceived and produced by Oliver Stone, and edited by Stone, Brian Berdan, Hank Corwin, Alex Gibson, and Carl Kaller, uses existing musical material from such musicians as Bob Dylan, Peter Gabriel, Leonard Cohen, Alban Berg, Diamanda Galas, Modest Moussorgsky, L7, and Nine Inch Nails.[1] Visual and musical techniques such as montage, collage, and other editing strategies help to create the postmodern narrative discourse in the film.[2]

THE POSTMODERN NARRATIVE DISCOURSE

The story of *Natural Born Killers* revolves around the lives of Mickey and Mallory Knox (played by Woody Harrelson and Juliette Lewis), two young lovers who engage in a killing spree across the American Southwest.[3] They are chased by two individuals: Detective Jack Scagnetti (Tom Sizemore), who is motivated more by media fame than justice; and tabloid television reporter Wayne Gale (Robert Downey, Jr.), who is looking for the exclusive first interview. Mickey and Mallory eventually end up lost in the desert where they meet an American Indian who tries to help them work through their memories and personal demons. This soul-searching leads Mickey into a psychotic rage, in which he accidentally kills the Indian (who symbolizes Mickey's possible chance for redemption). Mickey and Mallory are finally captured in a drug store shoot-out with Detective Scagnetti. The second half of the film deals with their lives in prison, the revival of their celebrity status by Wayne Gale, and their eventual jailbreak.

The *story* of the film is clear but the *plot*, defined here as the artistic ordering of events that make up the story, is much more complex. The linear narrative of the story is reordered and developed in the plot using a postmodern narrative discourse, which consists of two major features, which I will discuss in relation to the film: 1) a sense of "fractured time" and 2) constantly shifting "points of view."

Fractured time is closely related to what Fredric Jameson designates as the second basic feature of postmodernism: schizophrenia (a term he himself borrows from Lacan). Jameson's term relates to the breakdown of the signifying chain leading to what he calls a "rubble of distinct and unrelated signifiers" (Jameson [1991] 1993, 324). Temporal signifiers that ordinarily establish a clear sense of linear progression cease to connect among themselves and one can no longer "unify the past, present and future" (324). The world becomes a series of unrelated and perpetual presents. In film, this "schizophrenic" time occurs as a loss of sequential connection from one scene to the next and results in the audience's subsequent inability to develop a sense of linear, "narrative" time. Events are not merely reorganized within a stable background continuity that the audience constructs, but the narrative sequence is itself deconstructed on the phenomenological level.

The second basic feature of the postmodern narrative discourse is the continual alternation in points of view. While Stone frequently makes use of changes in the camera's point of view, something more complex happens in *Natural Born Killers* which questions the emplotment of history in the twentieth century and examines the multiple stories that can be told pertaining to any single event. Hayden White discusses what he sees as the problems facing current historians, problems relating to the dissolution of the "event" as a basic building-block of history. "It [appears] impossible to tell any single authoritative story about what really happened—which [means] that one [can] tell any number of possible stories about it" (White 1996, 24.) For White, an event occurring in the late twentieth century can no longer be historically understood simply by stating the "facts." What constitutes a fact of an event is open to interpretation and multiple representations.

From the very opening moments of the film, Stone and Robert Richardson (the director of photography) make use of filmic techniques that consistently alter our point of view. Shots are filmed in either black and white, full color, or tinted in post-production, which casts a uniform hue of any chosen color over the image. There are also changes in film format, jumping between high-quality 35-millimeter film to 16mm, 8mm, and video. The visual plane engages in off-angle shots in which the camera tilts from side to side or up and down. These techniques result in a kaleidoscope of color, grain, focus, line, and scope which draws the audience's attention to the self-reflexive nature of the film and makes it very difficult to ever engage a single point of view. Stone confirms this self-reflexivity in a statement made in a 1996 documentary about the film: "You are aware [that you are] watching a movie, the techniques enforce that, or reinforce that, so you are constantly aware of the shifting points of view" (Stone 1996).

The following analysis focuses on four particular scenes that demonstrate how music contributes to the movie's postmodern narrative discourse. These scenes are diagrammed in Figures 17-1 through 17-4, which show timing reference points, the narrative location of the scene, the number of visual cuts made during a specific time frame, any striking visual or postmodern aspects (connected to the material I will be discussing), and the musical elements. The time references in the examples are listed as minutes and seconds (m:s) with 0:00 representing the start of the film.[4] There is not a 1:1 ratio between time and graphic space in the examples (allowing for more detail and text when needed), and all time references made within the following text refer both to the film and the examples.

THE DINER SCENE

The film opens to the song "Waiting for the Miracle" by Leonard Cohen. The visual plane is then filled with a series of shots in alternating film formats that show either desert scenery or the inside of a diner. Thirty seconds into the film the camera comes to rest inside the diner and a dialogue begins between Mickey and a waitress as the music fades into the background. Something as simple as this first musical cue, indicated in Figure 17-1 at the 30" mark, leads an audience to make certain assumptions about the use of music in the film. For instance, when "Waiting for the Miracle" fades into the background to allow the dialogue to take center stage, the audience is sure that the music is nondiegetic, that is, music that does not form, or attempt to form, a part of the "universe of objects and object-events that the characters we see are supposed to be able to see, touch, smell, feel, and/or hear" (Brown 1994, 22). Diegetic music, on the other hand, is an object or object-event in the universe of the film, such as music coming from a radio that is turned on by one of the characters.

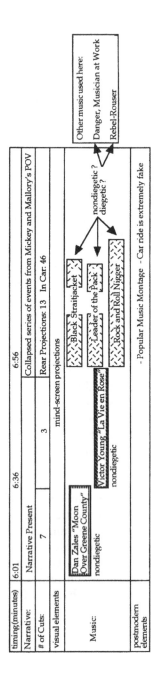

Figure 17-1. *Natural Born Killers*, "Diner" scene.

When Mickey finishes his conversation with the waitress, the Leonard Cohen song begins its second verse and the volume rises to the original level from the opening of the film reinforcing the music's non-diegetic nature. Mallory then walks over to a jukebox, places a quarter in the slot and picks out a song. The visual image cuts to the inside of the jukebox as a record is placed down and starts to spin. What we hear is not a new song but a continuation of "Waiting for the Miracle," as the song enters the chorus. When the camera cuts back to Mallory, at 1'30" in Figure 17-1, she appears to be dancing to the rhythm of the song. When we see a synchronization between music and visual images, especially after a strong visual cue like the jukebox, we assume that the music is diegetic. Cohen's song jumps from the nondiegetic to the diegetic.

Many films make use of this technique but Stone develops it a step further. The music continues to play as the visual image cuts to a shot of a scorpion being run over by a tire. The camera pulls back to follow a truck into the parking lot of the diner. Three men exit the truck and as two of them open the door to walk inside the Leonard Cohen tune fades out and the song "Now" by Chris McGregor takes its place. Next we see the inside of the diner as Mallory dances to the McGregor tune much as she was to the Cohen tune. This event suggests that "Waiting for the Miracle" was nondiegetic the entire time and that Mallory was actually dancing to the diegetic McGregor song, which the characters could hear but we could not. In Figure 17-1, a dotted line moves back in time from the 2' mark to show how our perception of the Cohen song has changed, and that it appears to have been nondiegetic the entire time.

In this scene, the music upsets the relationship between the diegesis and the audience. This upset characterizes a postmodern filmic narrative strategy, breaking down, as Royal Brown suggests in his *Overtones and Undertones*, "the classic distinction between music as nondiegetic affect and music as diegetic action" (Brown 1994, 247). Stone manipulates this relationship so that the audience is never quite sure who the music is intended for, the viewers or the characters within the diegesis.

The music of *Natural Born Killers* continues to alternate and confuse us. When Mallory enters into a fight with one of the men from the truck, the camera cuts back to the inside of the jukebox and a new record is placed down. This time the song "Shitlist" by L7 comes on and Mallory begins to kick the "living daylights" out of the man from the truck. While this tune appears to be diegetic, it does not sit comfortably in relation to the story. While both the Cohen and McGregor songs are possible choices for a jukebox in a southwestern roadside diner, "Shitlist" by L7 is an unlikely selection since the track is an aggressive punk-rock song, with vulgar lyrics, performed by an all-female band. The L7 song is out of place because of its musical style (one would expect something closer to country music), its language (this is a roadside diner and not a bar), and the gender of the performers. While the typical clientele of the diner (represented by its current patrons) may be able to handle a performance by Patsy Cline, they would almost certainly never be able to stomach an aggressive female punk band like L7.[5] The peculiarity of the music makes it difficult to decide if this song is really playing on the jukebox or if it is nondiegetic music expressing the mood of the scene. As the fight continues, Mallory begins to sing the lyrics of the song. Is the music in her mind or on the jukebox? The fact that we don't know raises questions about narrative agency. If the music is nondiegetic and is being used for its affect, to represent Mallory's rage, then it should not be audible to the characters within the diegesis. If the music is diegetic, then how do we justify the fact that the music starts at the exact moment of the fight and consists of a punk-rock song like "Shitlist" in a country diner? The fight scene is further complicated by the frequent changes in film format, the shifting of visual images in and out of synchronization with the dialogue, and the repetition of several events from slightly different camera angles. It is difficult to say if Mallory, another character, a cinematic narrator, or even Oliver Stone himself has control over the point of view. The visual and audio cues that typically allow an audience to determine if events are diegetic or nondiegetic generate ambiguity. The process of signification is disrupted and we are no longer sure how the audiovisual signifiers relate to the narrative signifieds.

While it becomes increasingly difficult for the audience to locate the narrative source of the music, this in no way diminishes the importance of the music to the scene. One of the significant aspects of this film is the way the music and the visuals often depend on one another to create meaning, as the remainder of the diner fight scene demonstrates. The L7 song and the fight scene action are interrupted several times by other pieces of music and distinct visuals. Soon after Mickey enters the fight he pulls out a gun and shoots the short-order cook. The visual image changes to black and white as the camera follows the bullet on its course to its victim. At the same time there is an abrupt cut in the audio track as the L7 tune is replaced with the music from the murder scene from Alban Berg's *Wozzeck*—the music taken from the exact moment that Wozzeck stabs Marie and she screams "Hilfe!" Once the bullet finds its target the visual image returns to the fight in the diner and the music returns to "Shitlist." A similar interruption happens when Mickey throws his knife at another victim except that the music changes to a scene from Puccini's *Madame Butterfly* (Love Duet, Act I). Both times the weapon's point of view is represented not only with opera but opera dealing with a love affair that goes tragically wrong. Whether or not audiences connect this music to its exact source, these operatic interruptions resonate with late-twentieth-century readings of opera as melodramatic tragedy, especially for general film audiences.

The kinds of musical interruptions in this scene are uncommon when a soundtrack consists of previously composed music and even rarer when the soundtrack uses popular music. As Jeff Smith suggests, "The compilation score . . . generally resists the fragmentation and variation that are the hallmarks of the classical score's leitmotivic or thematic structure" (Smith 1995, 332). In *Natural Born Killers*, however, the music is subjected to the same kind of cut-up restructuring that is evident in the visual realm of the film.

These musical interruptions are not *simulacra*,[6] entirely disconnected from the context of their source; instead they function as social commentary through juxtaposition and combination. The soundtrack, as a whole, assumes general associations with musical styles to create meaning, while the specific musical pieces allow for "deeper" resonance. The film, consequently, works on several levels. The specific audience member's ability to recognize and associate the cultural references contained within the film, whether they are musical or visual quotations, allows him/her to piece together Stone's critique of late-twentieth-century life in the United States. Much of this critique is developed through the way visual elements are pieced together and how they are combined with specific pieces of music. In the introduction to the director's cut, Stone stated that the social criticism enacted through the film's visual/musical interruptions was lost in the 1994 release which, through the elimination of many shots crucial to this critical strategy, lost much of its original satirical attitude.

> I especially fought for this movie [the director's cut] because it was censored when it first came out by the Motion Picture Association, and they cut or trimmed about 150 things in this movie. . . . The opening diner scene is restored to give a sense of the madness and surreality of the violence. . . . The irony is that in cutting these three minutes much of the black humor in the film was lost. A shot of a knife going through a window, a bullet going through a hand and creating a hole in it, take the edge off it and make the film in a way more comfortable and easier to watch because you realize it is ridiculous. I think that by cutting some of that stuff, it makes it grimmer and allows certain people to not completely grasp the attitude of the movie. (Stone [1994] 1996)

The operatic music combined with the unrealistic "Weapon's Point of View" (in which we are viewing the action the way the knife or the bullet sees it) may make audience members more "comfortable" since they serve to remind viewers that they are watching a film. The visual shots and the audio soundtrack are over-dramatic, calling attention to the artifice of the film medium. It is the earlier, more realistic shots of Mallory beating up the diner patron that are the most disturbing.

At the end of the mostly black-and-white fight scene, the film returns to full color. As Mickey and Mallory move into an embrace, the lighting in the diner goes dark, obscuring the aftermath of the previous fight. At the 6'36" mark in Figure 17-1 they begin to dance to the tune "La Vie en Rose" played by Victor Young and his Singing Strings, as the walls of the diner light up with film projections of a city and fireworks. At this point one might remember Humphrey Bogart and Audrey Hepburn dancing to the same tune as they fall in love in the 1954 Paramount film *Sabrina*. This "romantic" encounter may seem at odds with the previous "killing" scene, but for Mickey and Mallory this is a new moment—they are alone and in love—and it is not connected to the previous mayhem. "La Vie en Rose" is not being played in the diner and the city images not presented on its walls; rather, these aural and visual images project Mickey and Mallory's thoughts and feelings creating a visual "mind-screen." Both the music and the visuals support their fantasy world, and the narrative agency clearly revolves around them now and throughout the following main credits.

The film credits and the underlying "mind-screen" montage of visual images, including a fake car ride and shots reminiscent of the opening credits of a James Bond film, are accompanied by a musical montage consisting of the songs "Leader of the Pack" by the Shangri-las, "Rock 'n Roll Nigger" by Patti Smith, "Black Straitjacket" by Elmer Bernstein (from the United Artists film *The Caretakers*), "Danger Musician at Work" by Syd Dale, and "Rebel-Rouser" by Duane Eddy. This credits scene is a compilation of sights and sounds from across the American cultural landscape. The visual cuts and the musical quotations require an active role on the part of the viewer-listener in order to construct meaning. Each listener will bring a different cultural-memory to the film and hence make distinct connections between the various signifiers.

THE "I LOVE MALLORY" AND "AMERICAN MANIACS" SCENES

After the opening credits the diegesis enters into one of two real flashbacks in the film, that is, into one of those flashbacks in which the plot is working from the narrative present back to the past. Mallory's flashback occurs in a now visually typical manner: wavy lines and an out-of-focus shot. Untypically, the plot does not return to the "narrative" present after the flashback. The temporal point of reference defined by the opening diner scene is not regained by the diegetic sequence.

The flashback transition focuses on the living room of a house as Mallory leaps down the center staircase and post-production lettering appears on the screen spelling out "I Love Mallory" in an exact replica of the old "I Love Lucy" logo. Within this scene (represented in Figure 17-2) Mallory attempts to recreate her past within the framework of a situation comedy and while it is painfully obvious to us that her life differs greatly from that of the *Brady Bunch* or *I Love Lucy*, she needs to believe that her life fits within these television-defined norms. The music in this scene, which consists of the short orchestral cues used in television situation

timing (minutes)	9:51 14:13
Narrative:	Narrative Past
# of Cuts:	51 (roughly equivalent to "I Love Lucy" average of 10 per minute)
visual elements	Sitcom set design
Music:	Sitcom Theme music / Orchestral Cues nondiegetic laugh track and applause Atonal Chords
postmodern elements	- Memory of past projected onto "I Love Lucy"

Figure 17-2. *Natural Born Killers,* "I Love Mallory" scene.

comedies, helps to create a juxtaposition between Mallory's actual memories and the example offered to us by prime-time television. Most of these cues were provided by Associated Production Music (APM) and include: "Domestic Fun" by E. Tomlinson, "Happy Families" and "Pizzicato Playtime" by Sam Fonteyn, "Sentimental Song" by David Farnon, and "Funny Little Man" by E. Henry. The titles of these orchestral cues themselves indicate the intended musical effect—the way Mallory wants to feel. But they are directly opposed to the visual representations of family life Stone shows us on screen—an abusive father, a mother in denial, and rebellious children. During part of the scene, we hear a bouncy tune that is reminiscent of "Leave it to Beaver," but as Mallory's father makes sexual advances toward her, the dark atonal synthesizer chords of Robert Cornford's "Shocking" begin to break through the texture. They are quickly submerged again as Mallory tries her hardest to continue with the façade of a happy family memory. Stone further undermines the film's narrative point of view when at the end of the scene he inserts scrolling credits for the false "I Love Mallory" show. These credits and the orchestral cue music reinforce the film's self-reflexivity and Stone's authorial critique.

After the sit-com credits, the flashback continues through a number of scenes, including Mickey's time in jail for car theft, the murder of Mallory's parents, and Mickey and Mallory's feigned wedding on a bridge. During all of these scenes the temporal signifiers allows the audience to construct a causal linear narrative. The transitions between scenes, however, which consist of short television commercials or cartoons, work against our perception of these images as realistic representations. They are an obvious comment on the way American television viewers might "flip" through people's lives as they change the television channel from one "real-life situation show" to the other—between such shows as *Cops, Rescue 911,* or *America's Most*

Wanted. Just like the previous "I Love Mallory" credits, these commercial transitions also continually provoke us to question the narrative perspective of the film. Exactly who is doing the channel flipping here?

Mallory's flashbacks are interrupted by a mock television show called *American Maniacs* which upsets every notion we have had so far about the narrative discourse (see Figure 17-3). It first appears that the television show has brought us back into the narrative present of the diner scene. The host of the show, Wayne Gale, treats us to an *America's Most Wanted*–style history of Mickey and Mallory's murderous exploits. The music in this scene, aside from the opening theme song played over the show's introduction, consists of Brian Berdan's quiet synthesizer drone entitled "bb tone."[7] It is barely audible under Wayne Gale's narration, and it helps to create the feeling of a documentary or tabloid news show. Within the television show, actors other than Woody Harrelson and Juliette Lewis play Mickey and Mallory. This medium within a medium distorts the narrative and visual signifiers and draws attention to the constructedness of such visual representations of past events both within the film and in contemporary society generally.

timing(minutes)	23:25		23:55		25:41	
Narrative:	Narrative Present?				Narrative Present? Future	
# of Cuts:			51		9	
visual elements	T.V. show animation			Tape stop transition		
Music:	American Maniacs Theme Song diegetic		Berdan "bb tone" nondiegetic		NO MUSIC	
postmodern elements			- Mickey and Mallory actors		Real World	

Figure 17-3. *Natural Born Killers*, "American Maniacs" scene.

The scene changes, at 25'41" into the film, to a television station editing room. There, Wayne Gale and his assistants are preparing the second episode of *American Maniacs* to feature Mickey and Mallory. This is one of the few scenes in *Natural Born Killers* that contains no music whatsoever, as if to suggest the silent "reality" of Wayne Gale's world. Close inspection of the television monitors in the editing room reveals the depiction of several events that have not yet occurred with respect to the plot constructed so far. During the course of his conversation with his assistant, Wayne makes references to the prison interview he is about to have with Mickey, an event that could only occur if Mickey were already caught, which has not yet happened in the film's narrative.[8] At one point during the scene, the camera focuses on another editing screen which shows Wayne

Gale interviewing a crowd of people as the Remmy Ongala tune "Kipenda Roho" plays in the soundtrack (not shown in Figure 17-3). This music is not from Wayne's "real" world but from his television world, as a soundtrack to one of his interviews. While the interviewees respond with excitement and delight as they profess their love for Mickey and Mallory, magazine covers showing pictures from various stages of the killing spree fill the screen. What we do not know at this point in the story is that these interviews take place during the trial of Mickey and Mallory, and like the other scenes shown on Wayne's editing screens these are events that have not occurred yet within the film's plot. The narrative thread of the film has been deconstructed and replaced with a collection of memories and temporally ill-defined scenes. While it is possible to locate events in the past or the future, when using a reference point such as the opening diner scene, the exact chronological order of these events is impossible to determine precisely.

THE AMERICAN INDIAN SCENE

The last section of the film considered here is the American Indian scene that occurs approximately 38' into the film and is the apex of its first half. At this point, the film has returned to the narrative present and the couple's road trip across the American southwest. When their car runs out of gas in the desert, Mickey and Mallory are forced to head out on foot in search of a town, presumably to find gasoline. They soon begin to blame each other for their current problems and as the argument escalates Mallory begins to question their murderous actions during the past three weeks. The delicate piano melody of the Nine Inch Nails song "Something I Can Never Have" plays quietly in the background. This song takes on a special, almost leitmotivic function within the film, for it appears both here, during the crucial Indian scene, and again at the end of the film, when Mickey and Mallory kill Wayne Gale. Both of these scenes focus on Mickey and Mallory's brief awareness of their past actions; times when they are able to step back from the immediacy of events in order to assess the repercussions of their actions and ask themselves where they are going (physically, mentally, and spiritually).

They soon come upon a small shack in the desert surrounded by sheep. When Mickey knocks on the door each impact resounds with an unrealistic boom and the Nine Inch Nails tune slowly fades out (see 39'14" in figure 17-4). Inside the shack they find an American Indian shaman, who lives alone with his adolescent grandson. The Indian, through some form of psychic or mystic ability, is able to see into the minds of Mickey and Mallory, and his revelations are represented to the film's audience as words that appear projected on their subject. For example, when the Indian looks at Mickey the word "demon" appears in white letters across Mickey's chest. Stone chooses not to place these words into the scene during

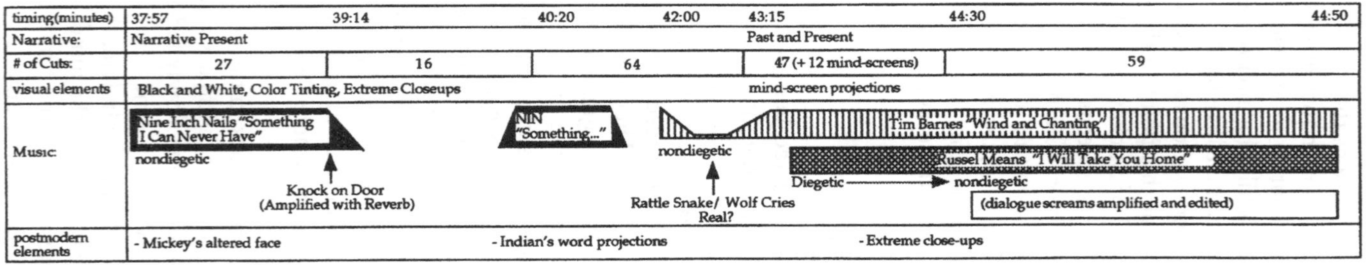

timing(minutes)	37:57	39:14	40:20	42:00	43:15	44:30	44:50
Narrative:	Narrative Present				Past and Present		
# of Cuts:	27	16		64	47 (+ 12 mind-screens)	59	
visual elements	Black and White, Color Tinting, Extreme Closeups				mind-screen projections		
Music	Nine Inch Nails "Something I Can Never Have" nondiegetic — Knock on Door (Amplified with Reverb)		NIN "Something..." nondiegetic — Rattle Snake/ Wolf Cries Real?		Tim Barnes "Wind and Chanting"; Russel Means "I Will Take You Home" — Diegetic ——→ nondiegetic (dialogue screams amplified and edited)		
postmodern elements	- Mickey's altered face		- Indian's word projections		- Extreme close-ups		

Figure 17-4. *Natural Born Killers*, "American Indian" scene.

post-production but instead employs actual stenciled light projections during the filming. These words signify the Indian's mystic vision but also continue to remind us of the film's self-reflexive nature.

The appearance of the Indian's word-visions prompts the return of the Nine Inch Nails song, this time within the chorus, the words of which are reproduced below:

Nine Inch Nails, "Something I Can Never Have"
Lyric excerpt used in *Natural Born Killers*

I still recall the taste of your tears,
echoing your voice just like the ringing in my ears.
My favorite dreams of you still wash ashore,
Scraping through my head 'till I don't want to sleep anymore.

You make this all go away, You make this all go away,
I'm down to just one thing and I'm starting to scare myself.
You make this all go away, You make this all go away,
I just want something, I just want something I can never have.

The vocals to the song are audible during the pauses in the characters' dialogue and we hear Reznor sing the last two lines of the chorus. The phrase, "You make this all go away," seems to echo Mickey and Mallory's current desire to escape their situation and suggests the Indian's ability to help them on their journey. However, when Reznor sings, "I just want something I can never have," the Indian is telling Mallory that his wife has died, and the lyrics appear to foreshadow Mickey and Mallory's inability to work through their personal demons despite the Indian's help. After the last words of the chorus the song dies away once again.

When the Indian begins to tell a story about a woman and a poisonous snake, the soundtrack is filled with the nondiegetic sounds of Tim Barnes's new age track, entitled simply, "Wind and Chanting." The piece features American Indian chanting and amplified wind sounds over a low-pitched synthesizer drone. The chant and wind sounds quickly fade into the background but the drone remains as the Indian continues his tale. As he speaks, sound effects of a rattlesnake and a wolf cry are brought to the foreground of the audio mix. Tim Barnes's music returns to full volume when the Indian begins to dance around the central campfire of the hut. During his dance the Indian, played by American Indian activist Russell Means, begins to vocalize his own chant, entitled "I Will Take You Home," over the Tim Barnes track. The two chants have been combined into a single audio montage that occupies both the realistic diegetic world and the abstract nondiegetic domain (see 43'15" in Figure 17-4). At the same time the visual field is organized into a collage of images related to Mickey's memories, including shots of an abusive father, an uncaring mother and a beaten child. These shots are not only presented to us as full-frame images, but also as rear screen projections behind the characters within the scene, much like the car ride during the opening credits. The scene intensifies as the Indian physically enters into Mickey's memories. Not a part of the original memory, the Indian intervenes in Mickey's past and by doing so brings the memories into the present. The memories are no longer showing us the real past-events of Mickey's life, but are instead showing us Mickey's current battle with his demons, mediated by the Indian. Fractured time has done more than simply allow the audience to experience Mickey's past, it has made that past a physical object in the present, one with which Mickey and the Indian can interact. As Linda Hutcheon suggests, this kind of postmodern action is ". . . a re-evaluation of, and a dialogue with, the past in the light of the present" (Hutcheon [1987] 1993, 261). The framing of the individual shots reinforces the "dialogue" nature of the scene. Almost every character that participates in the vision speaks directly to the camera and is filmed in a tight close-up. Not only are these memories in dialogue with Mickey and the Indian, they are also speaking directly to the film's viewers.

The energy level of the vision builds and the visual collage increases in tempo to an almost unrecognizable pace. These visual transformations are matched by alternations of the spoken dialogue of the scene. Russell Means's chanting is subjected to alterations in pitch and duration as well as audio effects such as reverberation and delay, which cause it to move out of synch with the visual images. The characters' screams, Russell Means laughter, and Mickey's grunts are all amplified until near distortion, and then abruptly cut off, creating "unnatural" sounds. Just after 44'30" into the film, the audio collage consists of three separate layers suspended somewhere between the diegetic and nondiegetic. Fredric Jameson's account of "schizophrenic" behavior and its relation to postmodern time is apt here:

> . . . as temporal continuities break down, the experience of the present becomes powerfully, overwhelmingly vivid and "material": the world comes before the schizophrenic with heightened intensity, bearing a mysterious and oppressive charge of affect, glowing with hallucinatory energy. (Jameson 1983, 120)

The sights and sounds of this scene take on an almost psychotic charge of energy which blends the past, present, and future together into one overwhelming and single present. The charge quickly becomes so powerful that Mickey can endure it no longer. He grabs his gun and begins to shoot the Indian who now personifies all of Mickey's demons. The flashback has become part of the present and will not be relegated to some distant "past." The Indian's attempt to grant Mickey a moment of clarity, to bring all of the elements of his life together proves too much for Mickey to handle and the Indian, along with the clarity he represents, is destroyed.

CONSTRUCTING THE TIME LINE FROM MULTIPLE POINTS OF VIEW

The film's point of view shifts continually between several characters, each of whom has a different relationship to the narrative thread. Events that occur within the film are subject to interpretation by each of these characters, leaving the audience with several representations of each event. These multiple points of view and their relationship to "linear narrative time" are presented as a graph in Figure 17-5. Since *Natural Born Killers* never actually resolves the question of when, or in what order, the events of the film occur, it is almost impossible to accurately reconstruct the time line. There is an apparent tendency of movie audiences, however, to create a linear story that comprehends all narrative events.[9] Figure 17-5 depicts such a viewer-constructed time line. If we consider the opening "Diner" scene as our reference point $[X_0]$ then it is possible to place events before or after that, within a certain limit $[X_{-1}, X_{-2}, X_{+1},$ or X_{+2} (the film's end)].

Mickey and Mallory, and the events in which they are depicted, characterize the postmodern sense of fractured time taken to an extreme. Much like Jameson's diagnoses of schizophrenia for the mental state of the postmodern mind, this extreme sense of fractured time can be viewed as the representation of the psychotic mind,[10] Stone makes this explicit: the movie is "a startling glimpse inside the mind of a mass murderer, rampant with horror and confusion, [and] it is simply too much for most people" (Riordan 1995, 517). Stone places Mickey and Mallory outside of linear time and we see every moment of their lives, be it past, present or future as if it were the here and now. Causality of events is suggested but is not depicted as action in the film. Since Mickey and Mallory are not compelled to organize events into a linear progression or to accept a single portrayal of those events, the audience can not make a clear chronological connection between them either. Mickey describes his point of view in a letter to Mallory when they are separated from each other in jail. He has located himself at the moment of his and Mallory's first kiss, that is his narrative present: "I lie in my bed and go over every day, every minute of our happiness. Take it all as it comes, and I live that day again. And babe, when I get to our first kiss, they are not just memories, and I feel that joy again" (Stone [1994] 1996).[11]

Wayne Gale's point of view is focused on the moment just before his television interview with Mickey and while he wants to move forward he can't help dwelling on the past. He attempts, unsuccessfully, to understand and piece together the events that have occurred in the three-week killing

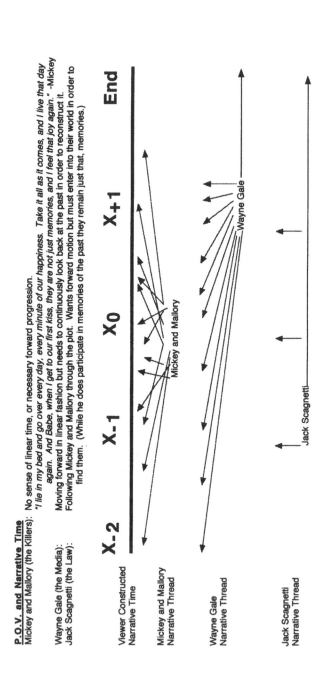

P.O.V. and Narrative Time

Mickey and Mallory (the Killers): No sense of linear time, or necessary forward progression.
"I lie in my bed and go over every day, every minute of our happiness. Take it all as it comes, and I live that day again. And Babe, when I get to our first kiss, they are not just memories, and I feel that joy again." -Mickey

Wayne Gale (the Media): Moving forward in linear fashion but needs to continuously look back at the past in order to reconstruct it.

Jack Scagnetti (the Law): Following Mickey and Mallory through the plot. Wants forward motion but must enter into their world in order to find them. (While he does participate in memories of the past they remain just that, memories.)

X-2   X-1   X0   X+1   End

Viewer Constructed Narrative Time

Mickey and Mallory Narrative Thread

Mickey and Mallory

Wayne Gale Narrative Thread

Wayne Gale

Jack Scagnetti Narrative Thread

Jack Scagnetti

Figure 17-5. *Natural Born Killers*, Point-of-View and Narrative

spree. But like a jigsaw puzzle without enough pieces, all Wayne can do is arrange and rearrange the events in a different order hoping that some answer will come to him. He talks to psychiatrists, fans, victims, and police, but in the end all he has is a collection of events—disconnected signifiers— which resist narrative closure. There is nothing left to do but constantly recount events in an attempt to tell the story.

Jack Scagnetti is the one character in the film who is always moving forward in time. When he tells stories about his past, mostly relating to his bestselling book, *Scagnetti on Scagnetti*, his memories have no visual or aural presence in the film depiction, as if to suggest that they remain in the past as memories. His life moves forward off camera and he only intersects with the film's narrative at the moments when he has to deal with Mickey and Mallory and enter into their world. Only in the second half of the film, when Scagnetti's point of view combines with Gale's does time settle into a linear, narrative progression, but the film always keeps alive the possibility that Mickey and Mallory may disrupt this future progress.

Natural Born Killers is a film in which the soundtrack is as essential as the images in the creation of a postmodern narrative discourse. Oliver Stone has created a narrative disruption in the film, one that causes the audience to question the representation of events on the screen. The force behind this disruption is the amalgamation of sensory domains. Just as the past, present, and future have become loosened from their chronological homes for Mickey, Mallory, and Wayne Gale, the audience has experienced the same through the loosening of the visual images and the audio soundtrack. The images and sounds do not serve their respective "functions" and we are not always sure which one to believe. The music can either help us to understand the visuals, as in the Indian scene, or it can confuse us— causing the breakdown of the signifying chain—as in the opening diner scene. As Stone suggests in the 1996 documentary about the film: "When people march to these different extremes, the law, the media, and the killers, the center will no longer hold" (Stone 1996). The postmodern narrative discourse of the film allows Stone and his production team to tell a "postmodern" tale, one that moves beyond the original "shoot-'em-up action film with a twist" story written by Quentin Tarantino. The film comments on the breakdown of the "event" in our society, and looks at a world where every possible point of view is accessible and one can replay each moment over and over again.

APPENDIX
MUSICAL CREDITS FROM THE FILM

"NATURAL BORN KILLERS" Main and End Credits/FINAL DRAFT July 8, 1994

Reprinted with permission from Bud Carr, Oliver Stone, and Warner Brothers
[This list does not include the names of several short compositions licensed from Associated Production Music, and Capitol/Ole Georg Music; such as the orchestral cues used in the "I Love Mallory" scene.]

"WAITING FOR THE MIRACLE"
Written by Leonard Cohen & Sharon Robinson
Performed by LEONARD COHEN
Courtesy of Columbia Records
by arrangement with Sony Music Licensing

"NOW"
Written and Performed by CHRIS McGREGOR
Courtesy of Gallo Records
by arrangement with Windswept Pacific Entertainment

"THE WAY I WALK"
Written by Jack Scott
Performed by ROBERT GORDON
Courtesy of RCA Records label of BMG Music

"NOAH HUTTON BUG SPRAY"
Written and Produced by Otis Conner
Courtesy of Axcess Broadcast Services

"SHITLIST"
Written by Donita Sparks
Performed by L7
Courtesy of Slash Records

Excerpts from "WOZZECK"
Written by Alban Berg
Performed by PARIS NATIONAL OPERA ORCHESTRA & CHORUS, PIERRE BOULEZ

Vocal Solos by WALTER BERRY & ISABEL STRAUSS
Courtesy of Sony Classical
by arrangement with Sony Music Licensing

"MADAME BUTTERFLY"
Written by Giacomo Puccini
Performed by THE SOFIA NATIONAL OPERA CHORUS & ORCHESTRA
Courtesy of Delta Music, Inc.

"CONTROL ROOM"
"SNAKE FIELD"
"LOVE TO HANK"
"SHOWER"
"WILD DRONE"
"MALLORY CELLO"
"INTERVIEW"
Written and Performed by tomandandy
Courtesy of tomandandy MUSIC

"MOON OVER GREENE COUNTY"
Written and Performed by DAN ZANES

"LA VIE EN ROSE"
Written by Mack David, Edith Piaf & Louiguy
Performed by VICTOR YOUNG & HIS SINGING STRINGS
Courtesy of MCA Records

"BLACK STRAIT JACKET"
from the United Artists motion picture
The Caretakers
Composed and Conducted by ELMER
BERNSTEIN
Courtesy of Metro-Goldwyn-Mayer
Inc.

"LEADER OF THE PACK"
Written by George Morton, Jeff Barry
& Ellie Greenwich
Performed by THE SHANGRI-LAS
Courtesy of Sun Entertainment Corp.
by arrangement with Celebrity
Licensing, Inc.

"REBEL-ROUSER"
Written by Duane Eddy & Lee
Hazlewood
Performed by DUANE EDDY
Courtesy of Jamie Record Co.

"ROCK & ROLL NIGGER"
Written by Patti Smith & Lenny Kaye
Performed by PATTI SMITH
Courtesy of Arista Records, Inc.

"ME AND HER OUTSIDE"
Poetry written by Steven Jesse
Bernstein
under license from Steven J. Bernstein
Archives
Performed by STEVEN JESSE BERN-
STEIN
Courtesy of Sub Pop Records, Ltd.

"SWEET JANE"
Written by Lou Reed
Performed by COWBOY JUNKIES
Courtesy of BMG Music Canada, Inc.

Various Selections
Courtesy of Associated Production
Music

"WILD PLATE RUBS"
Written and Performed by SCOTT
GRUSIN

Various Selections
Written and Performed by BRIAN
BERDAN

"YOU BELONG TO ME"
Written by Pee Wee King, Redd
Stewart & Chilton Price
Performed by BOB DYLAN
Production Supervised by Debbie Gold
Courtesy of Columbia Records
by arrangement with Sony Music
Licensing

"THE TREMBLER"
Written by Duane Eddy & Ravi
Shankar
Performed by DUANE EDDY
Courtesy of Capitol Records
under license from CEMA Special
Markets

"CARTOONICIDE" and "B SWELL"
Written and Conducted by RICHARD
GIBBS
"SHAZAM!"
Written by Duane Eddy & Lee
Hazlewood
Performed by DUANE EDDY
Courtesy of Jamie Record Co.

"IF YOU WERE THE WOMAN AND
I WAS THE MAN"
Written by Michael Timmins
Performed by COWBOY JUNKIES
Courtesy of BMG Music Canada, Inc.

"KIPENDA ROHO"
Written by Remmy Ongala
Performed by REMMY ONGALA &
ORCHESTRE SUPER MATIMILA

Courtesy of Real World Records
Ltd./Virgin Records Ltd.

"BACK IN BABY'S ARMS"
Written by Bob Montgomery
Performed by PATSY CLINE
Courtesy of MCA Records

"TABOO"
Written and Performed by PETER
GABRIEL & NUSRAT FATEH ALI
KHAN
Courtesy of Real World Records
Ltd./Geffen Records
and Virgin Records Ltd.

"TED JUST ADMIT IT"
Written and Performed by JANE'S
ADDICTION
Courtesy of Warner Bros. Records Inc.
by arrangement with Warner Special
Products

"I PUT A SPELL ON YOU"
Written by Jay Hawkins
Performed by DIAMANDA GALAS
Courtesy of Mute Records
by arrangement with Warner Special
Products

"HISTORY (REPEATS ITSELF)"
Written by T. Wilbrandt, K. Buhlert &
F. Lovsky
Performed by A.O.S.
Courtesy of Thamos Productions

"SOMETHING I CAN NEVER
HAVE"
Written by Trent Reznor
Performed by NINE INCH NAILS
Courtesy of TVT Records

"I WILL TAKE YOU HOME"
Written and Performed by RUSSELL
MEANS

"DRUMS A-GO-GO"
Written by Paul Buff
Performed by THE HOLLYWOOD
PERSUADERS
Courtesy of Original Sound Record
Co., Inc.

"ON THE WRONG SIDE OF
RELAXATION"
Written and Performed by BARRY
ADAMSON
Courtesy of Mute Records
by arrangement with Warner Special
Products

"UNDER WRAPS"
Written and Performed by BARRY
ADAMSON
Courtesy of Mute Records
by arrangement with Warner Special
Products

"THE HEAT"
"IN DOUBT"
Written and Performed by PETER
GABRIEL
Courtesy of Peter Gabriel Ltd./Geffen
Records
and Virgin Records Ltd.

"REED MY LIPS"
Written by Brent Lewis
Performed by BRENT LEWIS &
RICHARD HARDY
Courtesy of Ikauma Records

"EARTH"
Written and Performed by PETER
KATER & R. CARLOS NAKAI
Courtesy of Silver Wave Records

Excerpts from CARMINA BURANA
Written by Carl Orff
Performed by PRAGUE FESTIVAL

ORCHESTRA & CHORUS
Courtesy of Delta Music Inc.

"THESE BOOTS ARE MADE FOR
WALKIN"
Written by Lee Hazlewood
Performed by JULIETTE LEWIS

"CHECKPOINT CHARLIE"
Written and Performed by BARRY
ADAMSON
Courtesy of Mute Records
by arrangement with Warner Special
Products

"JUDGEMENT DAY"
"VENA CAVA"
Written and Performed by DIAMAN-
DA GALAS
Courtesy of Mute Records
by arrangement with Warner Special
Products

"THE VIOLATION OF EXPECTA-
TION"
Written and Performed by BARRY
ADAMSON
Courtesy of Mute Records
by arrangement with Warner Special
Products

"THE DAY THE NIGGAZ TOOK
OVER"
Written by Dr. Dre, Snoop, Daz, Toni
C. & RBX
Performed by DR. DRE
Courtesy of Interscope Records
by arrangement with Warner Special
Products
and Jive Records

"GHOST TOWN"
Written by J. Dammers
Performed by THE SPECIALS
Courtesy of Chrysalis Records, Inc.

under license from CEMA Special
Markets

"THE HAY WAIN"
Composed and Performed by SERGIO
CERVETTI
Courtesy of Periodic Music/Ron
Goldberg and Sergio Cervetti

"BORN BAD"
Written by Cissie Cobb
Performed by JULIETTE LEWIS

"THE IN CROWD"
Written by Billy Page
Performed by THE RAMSEY LEWIS
TRIO
Courtesy of MCA Records

"DOOM TAC A DOOM"
Written and Performed by BRENT
LEWIS
Courtesy of Ikauma Records

"THE LORD IS MY SHEPHERD"
Arranged and Performed by DIAMAN-
DA GALAS
Courtesy of Mute Records
by arrangement with Warner Special
Products

"SPREAD EAGLE BEAGLE"
Written by Roger Osbourne
Performed by MELVINS
Courtesy of Atlantic Recording Corp.
by arrangement with Warner Special
Products

"CYCLOPS"
Written and Performed by MARILYN
MANSON
Courtesy of Nothing/Interscope
Records

"FORKBOY"
Written by Jello Biafra, Paul Barker, A1
Jourgensen, Jeff Ward & Bill Rieflin
Performed by LARD
Courtesy of Alternative Tentacles
Records

"BOMBTRACK"
"TAKE THE POWER BACK"
Lyrics by Zack de la Rocha
Written, Arranged and Performed by
RAGE AGAINST THE MACHINE
Courtesy of Epic Associated
by arrangement with Sony Music
Licensing

"FUN"
Written by Mona Elliott, Marc
Orleans, Ayal Noar, Christian Negrete
Performed by SPORE
Courtesy of Taang! Records

"A NIGHT ON THE BARE MOUN-
TAIN"
Written by Modest Mussorgsky
Performed by BUDAPEST PHILHAR-
MONIC ORCHESTRA, J. SANDOR
Courtesy of Delta Music Inc.

"A WARM PLACE"
Written by Trent Reznor
Performed by NINE INCH NAILS
Courtesy of Interscope Records
by arrangement with Warner Special
Products and TVT Records

"ALLAH, MOHAMMED, CHAR,
YAAR"
Written by Nusrat Fateh Ali Khan
Performed by NUSRAT FATEH ALI
KHAN QAWWAL & PARTY
Courtesy of Real World Records
Ltd./Virgin Records Ltd.

"NUSRAT 1083/NUSRAT"
Written and Performed by NUSRAT
FATEH ALI KHAN
Courtesy of Real World Records
Ltd./Virgin Records Ltd.

"OVERLAY"
Written by David Bridie, John Phillips,
Rowan McKinnon, Russel Bradley,
James Southall and Tim Cole
Performed by NOT DROWNING,
WAVING
Courtesy of Reprise Records
by arrangement with Warner Special

"ANTHEM"
Written and Performed by LEONARD
COHEN
Courtesy of Columbia Records
by arrangement with Sony Music
Licensing

Selections by Capitol/Ole Georg Music

"SOBAMA MOON"
Written by Leonard Eto
Performed by Kodô
Courtesy of Sony Music Entertainment
(Japan) Inc.
by arrangement with Sony Music
Licensing

"THE FUTURE"
Written and Performed by LEONARD
COHEN
Courtesy of Columbia Records
by arrangement with Sony Music
Licensing

SOUNDTRACK ALBUM ON
NOTHING/INTERSCOPE
RECORDS
Filmed with PANAVISION- Cameras
and Lenses
DOLBY STEREO (SRD) In Selected
Theatres
Approved #33047 (emblem) (IATSE
LABEL)

Motion Picture Association of
America, Inc.
©1994 Warner Bros. Productions Ltd.,
Monarchy Enterprises C.V.

NOTES

Portions of this essay were previously presented at the Society for Ethnomusicology—Mid-Atlantic Chapter (MACSEM), and the American Musicological Society—Greater New York Chapter. I would like to thank: Judy Lochhead for her time and patience; Sergio Cervetti for helping me contact the right people; Bud Carr's office for helping me get the right information; Ross Rosen, Jeff Slippen, Trent Reznor, and TVT for use of the lyrics; and Oliver Stone.

1. The history of the musical soundtrack for the film is complex, and at least ten people have claimed to have worked on it at some time during the production of the film. Bud Carr (executive music producer for the film), in a phone conversation with the author on September 17, 1999, spoke about the development of the film's music. Mr. Carr called this soundtrack "one of the most complex movie business transactions ever done," explaining that prior to filming, Stone decided to use many styles of previously existing music and not to have the film scored by a single composer. Mr. Carr was responsible for organizing the music and assembling the legal permission (at least sixty pieces of music were cleared for use before even filming). The film editors were Hank Corwin and Brian Berdan (who contributed his "bb tone" to the Indian scene discussed later), both of whom were involved in the musical aspect as they pieced the various shots of the film together. The musical editors on the film were Alex Gibson and Carlton Kaller. Other contributors to the musical selection phase (when new music was still being added to the soundtrack) were Jane Hamsher (one of the film's producers) and Trent Reznor (from the industrial rock band Nine Inch Nails and the music editor for the *Natural Born Killers* soundtrack compact disc).

2. The term collage, originally from the art world, is often used in electronic music to describe a musical work in which bits and pieces of source material are spliced together, one after the other, but do not overlap. The term montage is used when various musical ideas are layered to create a composite. Hence, juxtaposition (collage) versus superimposition (montage).

3. I will be referring to the director's cut of the film, released on video in May 1996, which restored several minutes of footage cut from the original release in order to receive an "R" rating instead of "NC-17." By reintegrating the deleted scenes the director's cut recaptures Stone's original artistic vision for the film.

4. I highly recommend watching the film, so that the way the images and music appear and function together in the film becomes clear. Originally the scene graphs in Figures 17–1 through 17–4 were to contain stills from the film (to be used as reference points); however, Warner Bros. film division was unwilling to allow these pictures to be reprinted here. In order to synchronize the timings in Figures 17–1 through 17–4 with the timing on your VCR you must reset the counter clock. I have set the 0:00 mark (the start of the film) for when the Regency logo is on the screen and the Leonard Cohen tune begins to fade in.

5. L7 has often been called a feminist-grunge-punk-rock band. Their explosive sound and vulgar but poignant lyrics have made them one of the hottest underground rock bands. *Rolling Stone* magazine reported that "in 1992 L7 seemed to challenge the masculine clichés of rock quite literally when [the lead singer] Sparks pulled a tampon from her vagina and threw it onto the crowd at England's mammoth Reading Festival" (http://www.rollingstone.tunes.com/sections/artists/text). The song "Shitlist" describes how the singer is making out a list of people that "won't be missed." Their website contains a literal list of people the band would like to see disappear while the song itself seems to remain figurative.

6. The term *simulacrum* is from Baudrillard.

7. Brian Berdan contributed several short compositions to the film's soundtrack, each of which is prefixed with "bb" in the playlist which is reproduced here in the appendix.

8. In fact, some of the scenes shown on the editing screens may be placed in the story's loosely constructed chronology as occurring just before Mickey and Mallory's arrest in the drug store. Also, the entire scene of Wayne and his assistants arguing in the editing room is also used later in the film (during the second half), just before Wayne's "in jail" interview with Mickey. The second time the scene is shown it is shot using different camera angles and focuses on different story elements.

9. This fact is most obvious when one looks at the many "fan" websites for the film. Many people have attempted to organize the scenes into an exact time line by looking for "hidden" clues in the film such as the dates and headlines on newspapers the characters are reading.

10. Jameson's use of the term "schizophrenia" can often be problematic since it projects a negative spin onto the concept of postmodernism, and it is for this reason I have chosen to use the term "fractured time." When looking into the minds of Mickey and Mallory, however, the implications of schizophrenia do seem to apply. Mickey and Mallory are disconnected from linear time and are almost unable to organize events in a linear fashion (as illustrated in the Indian scene).

11. The sentence also has obvious sexual reference.

WORKS CITED

Brown, Royal S. 1994. *Overtones and Undertones: Reading Film Music.* Berkeley: University of California Press.

Carr, Bud. 1999. Private telephone conversation with the author.

Hutcheon, Linda. [1987] 1993. "Beginning to Theorize Postmodernism." In *A Postmodern Reader*, edited by Joseph Natoli and Linda Hutcheon. New York: State University of New York Press. 243–72.

Jameson, Fredric. 1983. "Postmodernism and Consumer Society." In *The Anti-Aesthetic.* Port Townsend, Wash.: Bay Press.

———. [1991] 1993. "The Cultural Logic of Late Capitalism." In *A Postmodern Reader*, edited by Joseph Natoli and Linda Hutcheon. New York: State University of New York Press: 312–32.

Riordan, James. 1995. *Stone: The Controversies, Excesses, and Exploits of a Radical Filmmaker.* New York: Hyperion.

Smith, Jeff. 1995 "The Sounds of Commerce: Popular Film Music From 1960–1973." Ph.D. diss., University of Wisconsin-Madison.

Stone, Oliver. [1994] 1996. *Natural Born Killers—The Director's Cut.* Letterbox edition. Produced and directed by Oliver Stone. Regency Pictures (distributed by Warner Brothers). Videocassette–Vidmark Entertainment.

———. 1996. *Chaos Rising: The Storm Around Natural Born Killers.* Documentary film produced and directed by Charles Kiselyak. Videocassette–Vidmark Entertainment.

White, Hayden. 1996. "The Modernist Event." In *The Persistence of History: Cinema, Television, and the Modern Event*, edited by Vivian Sobchack. New York: Routledge. 17–38.

Contributors

Paul Attinello is an assistant professor of music at the University of Hong Kong. His 1997 dissertation analyzed anti-serial aspects of European vocal music from the 1960s. He has published in the *Journal of Musicological Research, Musik-Konzepte*, and *Musica/Realta*, among others. He created the Newsletter of the Gay & Lesbian Study Group of the American Musicological Society, editing its first three volumes, and contributed to *Queering the Pitch: The New Lesbian and Gay Musicology*.

Joseph Auner, associate professor of music, State University of New York at Stony Brook, is currently editing *A Schoenberg Reader* for Yale University Press, and in the spring of 2001 he became editor of *The Journal of the American Musicological Society*. Articles and reviews have appeared in the *Journal of the American Musicological Society, Music Theory Spectrum,* and other journals. He is the recipient of fellowships from the Alexander von Humboldt Stiftung, the National Endowment for the Humanities, and J. Paul Getty Center.

Mark Berry is a doctoral candidate in music history and theory at State University of New York at Stony Brook whose research focuses on the relationship between American culture and music in the 1960s and 1970s.

David Brackett teaches in the Music Department at the State University of New York, Binghamton. His publications about the analysis and aesthetics of twentieth-century music include the book *Interpreting Popular Music*. He is currently editing a *Rock and Roll Reader* for Oxford University Press and writing a history of the phenomenon of "crossover" in popular music of the twentieth century. Brackett is also active as a composer, and has received many performances of his works in North America and Europe.

Jane Piper Clendinning is an associate professor of music theory at Florida State University. Her current research interests include intersections between music and visual arts and architecture, theories and analysis of twentieth-century music, music theory pedagogy, and topics in the history of music theory.

Renée T. Coulombe is a composer, improviser and scholar. Her written work is primarily concerned with intersections of race, class, gender, sexuality, and power in modern musical identities. She is assistant professor of music theory and composition at the University of California, Riverside. She has recently joined *Perspectives of New Music* for a three year term as an associate editor.

Ross Feller received his D.M.A and M.M. degrees in theory and composition from the University of Illinois at Urbana-Champaign. Currently he is an Assistant Professor of Music at Georgia College and State University. He has also taught at Minnesota State University, Moorhead, Butler University, Indianapolis, and at the University of Illinois. He has published articles on the music of Brian Ferneyhough in the following books: *Settling New Scores, 21st Century Perspectives on 20th Century Sketches* (Cambridge, the *Proceedings of the Einstein Meets Magritte Conference*, the *Proceedings of the ICMS7 Conference*, and in journals such as the *Mitteilungen der Paul Sacher Stiftung, ex tempore*, and *Open Space*. His interview with the composer is published in *Brian Ferneyhough: Collected Writings*.

Krin Gabbard is professor and chair, Department of Comparative Literature, State University of New York at Stony Brook. He is author of *Jammin' at the Margins: Jazz and the American Cinema* (1996) and editor of *Jazz among the Discourses* and *Representing Jazz* (1995). He is currently completing a book, tentatively titled *Music, Movies, and Men*.

Jason Hanley is currently a Ph.D. student in musicology and composition at the State University of New York at Stony Brook. He has delivered papers on the topics of popular music and film music at several North American universities and conferences. In addition to composing music for several theater productions, and cocomposing the music for the Academy Award–winning student film *Memories of Mathews Place*, directed by Daniel Bova, he has also performed on, composed, and produced several popular music records. He is an adjunct faculty member at Hofstra University and a faculty member in the Stony Brook Precollege Music Program.

Björn Heile was born in Berlin and studied musicology as well as English and American literature at the Technical University Berlin and in Exeter (England) as an ERASMUS exchange student. He is currently working on a Ph.D. thesis on Mauricio Kagel's *Die Stücke der Windrose für Salonorchester* at the University of Southampton (England).

Luke Howard completed undergraduate studies in piano and music education at the Sydney Conservatorium of Music in his native Australia. After graduate work at Brigham Young University, he received the Ph.D. in musicology from the University of Michigan in 1997 with a dissertation on Górecki's Third Symphony. He has served on the music faculty at Minnesota State University Moorhead and is currently Assistant Professor of Music History in the Conservatory at the University of Missouri, Kansas City. His primary research interests center on appropriations of classical music in popular culture.

E. Ann Kaplan, is Professor of English and Comparative Literature at SUNY Stony Brook, where she also founded and directs The Humanities Institute. Kaplan has written many books and articles on topics in cultural studies, media and women's studies, from diverse theoretical perspectives, including psychoanalysis, feminism, and postmodernism. A companion volume to her 1983 *Women and Film: Both Sides of the Camera*, titled *Looking For the Other: Feminism, Film And The Imperial Gaze*, appeared in 1997, along with her co-edited *Generations: Academic Women In Dialogue*. Recent edited volumes include a revised expanded version of *Women In Film Noir* and *Playing Dolly: Technocultural Formations, Fantasies and Fictions of Assisted Reproduction* (with Susan Squier). Her anthology, *Feminism and Film*, appeared in 2000. She is currently working on a book-length project, *Performing Age: Trauma, Cinema, The Body*, as well as on two more co-edited volumes on related themes.

Jonathan D. Kramer, composer and theorist, is professor of music at Columbia University. He is also program annotator for the Cincinnati Symphony Orchestra, for which he served as Composer-in-Residence, 1984–92. He is author of *The Time of Music* and *Listen to the Music*, and he edited *Time in Contemporary Musical Thought*, an issue of *Contemporary Music Review*. He is currently writing a book on postmodernism and music, and is composing a work for the Cincinnati Symphony.

Anne LeBaron, a composer, harpist, and musician, teaches composition at the University of Pittsburgh. She completed her doctorate at Columbia University, where her composition teachers included Mario Davidovsky and Chou Wen-chung; as a Fulbright scholar she studied with György Ligeti. She has received numerous awards for her widely performed works, including a Guggenheim Foundation Fellowship, a Fromm Foundation commission, and a McKim commission from the Library of Congress; in 1996 she was the recipient of the CalArts/Alpert Award in the Arts.

Judy Lochhead is professor and chair of music at the State University of New York at Stony Brook where she teaches history and theory courses relevant to music of the twentieth and twenty-first centuries. She published articles on Berg's *Lulu*, the music of Roger Sessions, performance practice in the indeterminate works of John Cage, and phenomenological approaches to music analysis of recent music in the

Western concert tradition. Recent work focuses on issues of embodiment with respect to music analysis and the relation of music in the 1960s to chaos theory.

Martin Scherzinger is an assistant professor of music at the Eastman School of Music, Rochester, New York. His published work has appeared in diverse venues and reflects an interest in music history, music theory, ethnomusicology, as well as cultural studies and philosophy.

Timothy D. Taylor is a musicologist who teaches in the Department of Music at Columbia University. His publications include *Global Pop: World Music, World Markets* (Routledge, 1997) and numerous articles on various popular and classical musics. He is currently completing a book about music and technology in the post-war era.

Joakim Tillman (né Andersson) studied musicology and philosophy at Stockholm University, where he presented his doctoral dissertation "Ingvar Lidholm and the Twelve-Tone Technique: Analytical and Historical Perspectives on Ingvar Lidholm's Music from the 1950s" in 1995. He presently teaches courses in musical analysis and music history at Stockholm University, and has recently finished a study about the reaction against modernism in Swedish art music from the 1960s to the early '90s.

Index

Aalto, Alvar, 121
abstract expressionism, 123
Adamowicz, Elsa, 28
Adams, John, 13, 109, 130
Adorno, Theodor, 110, 141, 216, 251, 280
Aktionsgemeinschaft junger Freunde deutscher Opernkunst (Action Group of Young Friends of German Opera), 282
aleatoricism, 249, 253, 264
Alberman, David, 252, 257
Allen, Ray, 315
Ally McBeal, 329
allusions, 134
America's Most Wanted, 343–44
Amos, Tori, 327
Anderson, Hans Christian, 257
Anderson, Laurie, 94, 225
Antheil, George, 31
antimodernist, 13
anxiety of influence, 128
Anzaldua, Gloria, 324, 333
Aragon, Louis, 61
Armstrong, Craig, 201–2, 205
Arnason, 125–6
ars combinatoria, 235
Art Deco, 126
Ashley, Robert, 46

Asian Dub Federation, 191
Association for the Advancement of Creative Musicians, 215
Atherton, David, 204
atonality, 132
authenticity, 84–85, 183, 218, 225
authorship, 210
automatism, 27
autonomy, 282
avant-garde, 77, 81
Ayres, Ben, 179–80, 185–6, 190
Babbitt, Milton, 130, 137
baby boomers, 101
Bach, Johann Sebastian, 130, 254
Backstreet Boys, 223, 226
Bailey, Derek, 40
Bakhtin, Mikhail, 288
Bang on a Can, (BOAC) 212–213, 216, 219
Baraka, Amiri, 309, 315
Barber, Samuel, 198, 310
Barkley, Charles, 310
Barnes, Tim, 347
Barlow, Andy, 199–200
Barham, Meriel, 199
Barr, Alfred, 121, 128–129, 136
Barthes, Roland, 7, 319
Bartok, Bela, 129, 133–134, 243

Baudrillard, Jean, 99, 120, 207, 211, 216, 323
Bauhaus, 122
Beatles, The, 186, 217, 220
Beaumarchais, Pierre Augustin Caron de, 131–133
Beck, 218, 222–223
Beckett, Samuel, 130
Beethoven, Ludwig van, 202–204, 243, 291
Benatar, Pat, 325
Benedictine Monks of Santo Domingo de Silos, 225
Benhabib, Seyla, 324
Berdan, Brian, 344
Berg, Alban, 129, 263, 340
Berio, Luciano, 14, 79, 130, 270, 274
Berman, Marshall, 93
Bernstein, Elmer, 342
Bernstein, Leonard, 205
Beuys, Joseph, 291
Björk, 201, 219–220, 222–223
Blier, Bertrand, 196
Bloom, Allan, 110
Bloom, Harold, 128
blues, 218
Boehmer, Konrad, 276
Bolcolm, William, 15
Boretz, Benjamin, 141
borrowings, see quotation
Bosle, Asha, 188
bossa nova, 218
Boulez, Pierre, 33, 36, 129–130, 196, 257, 265–266
Bourdieu, Pierre, 143
Brahms, Johannes, 291
Braxton, Anthony, 39
Brecht, Bertold, 284
Breton, André, 27
bricolage, 94, 99
Brooker, Peter, 120
Brutalist, 137
Buffalo Springfield, 317
Bürger, Peter, 87, 211
Burghardt, Ursula, 291
Burkholder, J. Peter, 59
Burman, R. D., 222
Burton, Tim, 305

Bussotti, Sylvano, 283
Butler, Judith, 166, 325
Butthole Surfers, 202
Cage, John, 35, 77, 129, 215, 249, 281–282
camp, 211
Cardew, Cornelius, 271
cartoon music, 214
Caskel, Christoph, 265
Castells, Manuel, 103, 112
Cateforis, Theo, 333
Chadbourne, Eugene, 57
Charles, Ray, 304
Chénieux-Gendron, Jacqueline, 34
Chester, Andrew, 212
Chopin, Frederic, 202–204
Cixous, Helene, 324
class, 332–333
clit rock, 328
Cocteau, Jean, 31
Cohen, Leonard, 337
Cole, Nat King, 304
Coleman, Anthony, 214
collage, 27–28, 79, 134, 197, 219, 288, 290
Coltrane, John, 40
commedia dell'arte, 133
complexity, 109, 135
consumer society, 203
Copland, Aaron, 303
Cops, 343
Corigliano, John, 14, 131–134, 137–138, 216
Cornershop, 179–192
Cornford, Robert, 343
country, 186, 208, 214
country rock, 218
Cowell, Henry, 259
Cream, 217
crossover, 225
Crumb, George, 83
cultural dominant, 98
Cutler, Chris, 50
Da Ponte, Lorenzo, 138
Dale, Syd, 342
Danuser, Hermann, 76 ff.
Darmstadt, 289
Das Neue Bauen, 124

Daugherty, Michael, 109, 210–212, 215–219
Davis, Anthony, 41
Dean, Roger, 38
Death in Venice (Visconti), 246
de Chirico, Giorgio, 29, 59
deconstruction, 263, 281
Deep Forest, 177–178, 223
de la Motte-Haber, Helga, 75
de Mille, Agnes, 313
Deleuze, Gilles, 141, 323
Deleuze/Guattari, 323
depthlessness, 217
Derrida, Jacques, 6, 253–255
Des'ree, 202
DiFranco, Ani, 327, 329
disco, 218, 221
discontinuities, 15, 181
Disney, 216
disunity, 127, 135, 138
double coding, 209, 217
Dresher, Paul, 109
Dworkin, Andrea, 327
Dylan, Bob, 218
Eastwood, Clint, 304
eclecticism, 21, 128, 130, 132, 181, 197, 207, 209–219
Eco, Umberto, 14
Eddy, Duane, 342
Ehrenreich, Barbara and John, 101
Eisner, Michael, 216
electronic, 264
elitism and anti-elitism, 13, 24, 106
Ellison, Ralph, 318
Elvira Madigan, 310
Enigma, 191
Enlightenment, 120
epistemology, non-foundational, 6

Ernst, Max, 50
exoticism, 179, 184, 225–226
expressionism, 123
expressivity, problems of, 85
Exquisite Corpse, 29, 46
Farnon, David, 343
Farrakhan, Louis, 309
Faust, 197–198, 202
Feld, Steven, 191

Feldman, Morton, 54
feminism, 323–333
Ferneyhough, Brian, 249, 251–253, 257, 259, 261
Field, Margaret, 204
film music, 214
Flack, Roberta, 304
Flax, Jane, 333
Fluxus, 282
folk, 217–218, 222
folk rock, 219
Fonteyn, Sam, 343
Fordism, 98
form, 109
Foss, Lukas, 40
Foster, Hal, 5, 209, 236, 250–251
Foucault, Michel, 7, 323
fractured time, 336
Franklin, Aretha, 325
Fraser, Nancy, 324
free improvisation, 37
Freedman, Hal, 57
Freudian, 333
Frith, Fred, 46
funk, 187, 189, 214, 218–219, 221–222
Gann, Kyle, 108–9, 212
Garbage, 200, 202
gender and sexuality, 208, 220, 250, 324, 326, 333
Gergen, Kenneth J., 19
Gilroy, Paul, 220–222, 226
Ginsberg, Allen, 183–185
Gipsy Kings, 196
glam rock, 218
Glass, Philip, 94, 130, 132, 213, 215
global flows of information, 210
global village, 239
Goehr, Lydia, 159
Goldie, 201–202
Goodwin, Andrew, 223
Gorbman, Claudia, 319
Gorecki, Henryk, 13, 195–205, 225
Gottwald, Clytus, 272, 274–275, 284
Gratzer, Wolfgang, 84
Graves, Michael, 124–126
The Greatest Story Ever Told, 313
Greenberg, Clement, 209, 250

Greene String Quartet, 104
Griffiths, Paul, 265
Gropius, Walter, 121
Grossberg, Lawrence, 209
Guattari, Felix, 141, 323
Guck, Marion, 161
Habermas, Jürgen, 1, 75, 275
Hall, Pete, 179
Hamburg National Opera, 275–276
Hanslick, Eduard, 148
Haraway, Donna, 225
Harriot, Joe, 39
Harrison, George, 186
Harrison, Lou, 48
Hartman, Johnny, 304
Harvey, David, 97–8
Harvey, Jonathan, 252
Hassan, Ihab, 94–5
Hayes, Alfred, 307
heavy metal, 327–328
Hebdige, Dick, 93, 103
Hegel, G. W. F., 141
Heilbroner, Robert L., 240
Henry, Pierre, 106
Hershey, Gerri, 329
high and low art, 94, 123, 126,
    195–196, 202–203, 207–208,
    210–211, 217, 220, 250
Hildegard of Bingen, 191
Hindi film music, 222
hip-hop, 186–187, 189, 218–219,
    220–221, 226, 250
Hirsch, Shelley, 55ff.
history 123, 128, 133, 138, 203, 208,
    211, 215, 240, 254
Hitchcock, Henry-Russell, 136
Hockings, Elke, 251
Hoffman, William M., 138
hooks, bell, 333
Hooreman, Paul and Souris, André, 47
Horowitz, Joseph, 210
Horkheimer, 110
Huber, Klaus, 252
Huyssen, Andreas, 94
Hutcheon, Linda, 120
hybridity, 179, 183, 190
hyperreality, 223
Hyman, 121, 125, 127–128, 137

I Love Lucy, 342
identity, 182–183, 190, 220
Ildfrost, 197, 202
image, 99
impressionism, 136
indeterminacy, 249, 263
industrial, 220
informationalism, 103
Internationale Ferienkurse für Neue
    Music, 249, 265
International Style, 120–128, 136, 137
interpretation, 7
intertextuality, 94, 133
irony, 127, 135, 181–182, 185, 189,
    211, 218, 265–266, 270–271,
    273, 289
Ives, Charles, 211, 225
Jackson, Janet, 104, 325
Jackson, Michael, 51
Jameson, Fredric, 98, 120, 195–196,
    202–203, 209, 211, 323, 325,
    336, 348
Jardine, Alice, 324
Jarvinen, Arthur, 108
jazz, 214–215
Jazz Composers Orchestra Association,
    215
jazz fusion, 214
Jefferson Airplane, 217
Jencks, Charles, 95, 209, 216
Johnson, Philip, 122, 124, 126, 133,
    136–137
Jones, LeRoi, 318
Jordan, Michael, 310
Joy Division, 196
Kagel, Mauricio, 263–283, 288
Karkoschka, Erhard, 265
Keane, Shake, 39
Kernis, Aaron Jay, 215–216, 219
Kiefer, Anselm, 291
King, Anthony D., 222
Koostra, Taco, 259
Kramer, Jonathan D., 102, 137–138,
    181, 236, 257
Krauze, Zygmunt, 13
Kristeva, Julia, 324
Kronos Quartet, 104
Kupkovic, Ladislav, 76, 78

L7, 339
Labi, Gyimah, 60
Lacan, Jacques, 99, 141, 203
Lachenmann, Helmut, 249, 251–256,
    261
Lamb, 199, 200, 202, 204
Lang, David, 212
Language Poets, 251
Lash, Scott, 100, 103
Lauper, Cyndi, 325
Lawrence, Robert, 138
Le Corbusier, 121–122
Lee, Bill, 314
Lee, Spike, 303
Lennox, Annie, 325
Lieberman, Lowell, 13
Ligetti, Gyorgy, 78, 131, 133–134,
    138, 215, 270, 275, 281
Lipsitz, George, 221
Longman, Evelyn, 125
lounge, 222
Love, Courtney, 327
Luaka Bop, 192
Luhrman, Baz, 201
Lukacs, Georg, 141
Lutoslawski, Witold, 214–215
Lyotard, Jean Francois, 6, 14, 99, 120,
    250, 261, 323
Lysloff, René T., 223
Mâche, Francois-Bernard, 32
machine-style, 121
Madonna, 195, 197, 201, 325, 327
Mahler, Gustav, 130, 211, 216, 225,
    243
Malcolm X, 309
Marbury, Stephon, 311
marginality, 182
marketing, 93, 104
Martland, Steve, 197
Marxism, 324, 333
Massive Attack, 200–201
Maus, Fred, 143
maximal minimalism, 130
McClary, Susan, 307
McGregor, Chris, 339
McLuhan, Marshall, 239
Means, Russell, 347
media culture, 210

Mellers, Wilfrid, 308
merveilleux, 56
meta-narratives, 6, incredulity towards
    99, 120, 210, 222–223
Metzger, 273
Meyer, Leonard, 241
micropolyphony, 134
minimalism, 129, 130, 136, 212–213
Mitchell, W. J. T., 310
mixed media, 123, 135, 197
mobiles, 272
modality, 132
moment form, 264
Monroe, Earl, 311
monumentalism, 133
Moraga Cherri, 333
Morgan, Robert, 21
Morris, Lawrence D. "Butch," 46
Morris, Meaghan, 324, 333
Mozart, Wolfgang Amadeus, 138,
    144–146
MTV, 218, 325–326, 331
Muggler, Fritz, 283
multiple meanings, 127
Musica Elettronica Viva, 40
musique concrÈte, 35, 254–255
Nakamura, Dan "The Automator,"
    186, 191
narrative, 120, 181, 271
Neill, Ben, 108
neo-conservative, 235–236, 291
neo-Romanticism, 215
Neue Vocalsolisten Stuttgart, 274
New Age, 223
new bourgeoisie, 101
New Kids on the Block, 226
New Music Ensemble, 40
New Musicology, 2, 141, 305
New Simplicity, 251
Nicholson, Linda, 324
Nicholson, Vanessa-Mae, 106
Nine Inch Nails, 345ff.
Nono, Luigi, 251–253, 270, 273
nostalgia, 59, 235
Nougé, Paul, 32
Nutt, Craig, 41
O'Connor, Sinéad, 326–327, 329, 331
Oldfield, Mike, 197

Oliveros, Pauline, 36, 40
Ongala, Remmy, 345
opera, 132–133
Orbit, William, 198, 202
Ordinary People, 310
organicism (and unity) 14, 79, 123,
   129, 135, 211–212, 236
organized/disorganized capitalism, 100
Oriental, 106
Ortner, Sherry B., 102
Osmond Brothers, 226
Oswald, John, 49ff., 223
Pachelbel, Johann, 310
Paglia, Camille, 327
Pale Saints, 199, 200, 202
Pareles, Jon, 183, 191, 218
Parker, Evan, 39
Parmar, Pratibha, 323, 326–332
parody, 56, 202, 211–212, 218–219,
   265, 270–271, 325
Pärt, Arvo, 83, 198
Pasler, Jann, 236
pastiche, 94, 99, 138, 202, 209,
   211–212, 217, 222, 250, 313,
   325
pataphysics, 41
Paz, Octavio, 61
Penderecki, Krzysztof, 76, 131, 214,
   270
performativity, 325
Pfeil, Fred, 101
philosophy of inclusiveness, 47
Platoon, 310 .
playfulness, 127
plunderphonics, 49ff., 223
pluralism, 223, 261
politics, 180, 189, 192, 197, 203, 252,
   269, 275, 278, 282, 284, 325,
   331–332
Pollack, Howard, 307
polystylism, 290
pop, 208
Pop Art, 126
Portishead, 200
post-colonial, 178–190, 220–221, 323
postfeminism, 329
postminimalism, 212
postmodern narrative discourse, 335

post-punk, 218, 328
post-structuralism, 180–181, 333
Potter, Russell, 99, 226
practices, 103
Presley, Elvis, 52
production, 104
professional managerial class, 101
progress, 130
Puccini, 340
psychedelia, 41, 218–219, 222
Public Enemy, 303, 316ff.
Public Image Ltd., 196
punk, 214, 225, 327
quotation, 15, 56, 60, 79, 82, 125,
   127, 181, 195, 198–199, 203,
   214–215, 218, 242
R & B, 208, 221
race, 333
racism, 220
Rand, Bernard, 14
Rappoport-Gelfand, Lidia, 205
reception, 203
recording technology, 15
Reger, Max, 284
Reich, Steve, 14, 106, 130, 213
Reise, Jay, 245
REM, 195, 197
representation, 7, 93, 104
Rescue 911, 343
resistance, 250, 253
Rhodes, Louise, 199
Rihm, Wolfgang, 82
Riley, Terry, 213
Riot Grrrl, 220, 328
Rochberg, George, 13, 76, 78, 84
rock'n'roll, 212, 215, 217, 323,
   327–331
Rorty, Richard, 6
Rose, Tricia, 220–221
Ross, Andrew, 304
Rossini, Gioacchino, 138
Rouse, Mikel, 108ff.
Rudolph, Paul, 124, 137
Rusbridger, Alan, 196
Ruzicka, Peter, 85
Said, Edward, 182, 190
Saarinen, Eero, 121
Sabri Brothers, 191

Saffery, Anthony, 179
Saffron, 327
Salerno-Sonnenberg, Nadia, 104
sampling, 183–185, 197–198,
    200–201, 204, 218, 222
Satie, Erik, 30, 198
Saul, John Ralston, 110
Schafer, Thomas, 85
Schaffner, Ingrid, 49
Schick, Steven, 259
schizophonic, 190
schizophrenia, 99, 336
schizophrenia, temporal, 202–203
Schlovsky, Viktor, 254
Schlüter, Wilhelm, 265
Schnabel, Julian, 196
Schnebel, Dieter, 264, 267, 269, 283
Schnittke, Alfred, 13, 80, 83
Schoenberg, Arnold, 129, 243
Schola Cantorum Stuttgart, 274, 276
Scriabin, Alexander, 266
Searle, John, 87
Second Viennese School, 129
Segerman, Steven, 201
serialism, 129, 133–134, 215, 249,
    251–253, 263–268, 270, 273,
    276, 292
sexuality, see gender and sexuality
Shabach Community Choir of Long
    Island, 315
Shakespeare, William, 205
Shangri-las, 342
shifting points of view, 336
Silliman, Ron, 261
Simms, Nick, 179
Simon, Paul, 191
simulacrum, 99
Singh, Talvin, 191
Singh, Tjinder, 179–191
situated knowledge, 6
Skin Skunk Anansie, 327–328
Slonimsky, Nicolas, 34
Smashing Pumpkins, 198
Smith, LaDonna, 38, 41–46
Smith, Patti, 342
Smith, Roger Guenveur, 311
soul, 218–219, 221–222
Souther, Richard 191

Spears, Britney, 223
speed metal, 250
Spice Girls, 223, 327, 329, 331
Spivak, Gayatri, 324
St. Augustine, 5
Steinem, Gloria, 327
Sterbini, Cesare, 138
Stern, Robert A. M., 125, 127, 137
Steyermark, Alex, 314
St. John, Lara, 104
stochastic, 264
Stockhausen, Karlheinz, 35, 79, 129,
    214, 251, 265–266, 276
Stone, Oliver, 335, 341
strategic essentialism, 221
Strauss, Joseph, 128
Stravinsky, Igor, 129, 133, 211, 243
subject, 324–325
subjectivity, 84, 331
Summer, Donna, 325
Sun Ra, 40
surrealism, 28, 211, 270
Swingle Singers, 274
Talking Heads, 218
Tarrantino, Quentin, 335
Tavener, John, 204
Taylor, Charles, 160
Taylor, Timothy, 191
techno dance, 220, 223
technology, 210, 219–222, 254
teeny pop, 223
Teitelbaum, Richard, 40
teleology, 6, 17–18, 238
Tenney, James, 52
Test Department, 197–198, 202
Theater of the Absurd, 272
Theater of the Ridiculous, 272
Thomas, Adrian, 200
Thomas, Michael Tilson, 104
Tommasini, Anthony, 304
tonality, 132, 134
Toop, Richard, 251
Torke, Michael, 13, 216
totalism, 107, 212
Tricky, 200–202
Tudor, David, 215,
Turner, Tina, 325
Turtle Island, 104

U2, 201
unity, see organicism
Upshaw, Dawn, 205
Urry, Jonathan, 100, 103
Van Alen, William, 125
van der Rohe, Mies, 121
Varèse, Edgar, 129, 137, 257
Venturi, Robert, 120, 122, 124, 130,
    133, 135
Victor Young and his Singing Strings,
    342
Visconti, Luchino, 246
Vitale, Dick, 312
Warfield, Justin, 186
Warhol, Andy, 251
Washington, Denzel, 315
Weber, Horst, 84
Webern, Anton, 129, 253, 267, 268
Wellmer, Albrecht, 155
Welsch, Wolfgang, 76, 87
West, Cornel, 112

Weir, Peter, 196
White, Barry, 196
White, Hayden, 336
Wiederhorn, Jon, 191
Williams, Davey, 38, 41–46
world music, 132, 134, 177, 183, 209,
    215, 223
Wright, Frank Lloyd, 121–122, 137
Wu Tang Clan, 221–223
Xenakis, Iannis, 264
Yamasaki, Minoru, 122, 137
Young, Iris Marion, 7
Zappa, Frank ,217
Zimmerman, 79
Zola, Emile, 165
Zorn, John, 15, 46, 48, 138, 185,
    213–216, 219, 225, 236

Lightning Source UK Ltd.
Milton Keynes UK
UKOW06f1002131115

262509UK00019B/242/P